VOICES FROM THE
CHINESE CENTURY

VOICES FROM THE CHINESE CENTURY

Public Intellectual Debate from Contemporary China

Edited by Timothy Cheek, David Ownby, and Joshua A. Fogel

Columbia University Press
New York

Columbia University Press
Publishers Since 1893
New York   Chichester, West Sussex
cup.columbia.edu

Library of Congress Cataloging-in-Publication Data
Names: Cheek, Timothy, 1955– editor. | Ownby, David, 1958– editor. |
    Fogel, Joshua A., 1950– editor.
Title: Voices from the Chinese century : public intellectual debate from
    contemporary China / edited by Timothy Cheek, David Ownby, and
    Joshua A. Fogel.
Description: New York : Columbia University Press, [2019] | Includes
    bibliographical references and index. | In English, translated from
    original Chinese.
Identifiers: LCCN 2019011884 (print) | LCCN 2019015450 (ebook) |
    ISBN 9780231551250 (electronic) | ISBN 9780231195225 (cloth : alk. paper) |
    ISBN 9780231195232 (pbk.) | ISBN 9780231551250 (ebk.)
Subjects: LCSH: China—Politics and government—2002– | China—Social
    conditions—2000– | China Intellectual life—21st century.
Classification: LCC DS779.46 (ebook) | LCC DS779.46 .V65 2019 (print)
LC record available at https://lccn.loc.gov/2019011884

Columbia University Press books are printed on permanent and durable
acid-free paper.
Printed in the United States of America

Cover design: Noah Arlow

CONTENTS

VOICES FROM THE CHINESE CENTURY

INTRODUCTION

Thinking China in the Age of Xi Jinping

TIMOTHY CHEEK, DAVID OWNBY, AND JOSHUA A. FOGEL

The greatest challenge of the twenty-first century is the need to come to a new understanding of China and moreover to be able to come to a true understanding of our China in comparative context.

—Gan Yang, *Unifying the Three Traditions* (2005)

The future of China lies in rebuilding a China rich in thought, in restoring the unity of theory and practice, and in the development of values that accord with human justice.

—Rong Jian, "A China Bereft of Thought" (2013)

Gan Yang and Rong Jian, hardly intellectual comrades-in-arms, reflect the challenges facing China and China's intellectuals in the twenty-first century. After some forty years of post-Mao reforms, Gan Yang, an inveterate reformer who was seen as liberal in the 1990s and as some combination of leftist and Confucian in the new century, has identified the question of the day: How are China's history and role in the world to be understood? Meanwhile, Rong Jian, an outspoken businessman intellectual (and therefore independent of the strictures of Chinese universities) challenges fellow intellectuals to provide serious moral thought for Chinese political life.

Gan Yang calls on his readers to "unify the three traditions" of modern China (Confucian, Maoist, and Dengist liberal reform); Rong Jian taunts them for being "bereft of thought" and challenges them to contribute to a "thinking China." With fifteen examples of thinking China, this volume shows that Gan Yang's and Rong Jian's hopes have not been in vain. These essays are from some of the best minds in China today thinking about China—Where has it come from? What is it today? What should it be in the future?

Chinese scholars, having benefitted from China's openness to the world and the relative relaxation of political pressure in China (until recently), have much to say about China and the world that merits our attention. They disagree with each other, and their debates throw light not only on these key questions for understanding China itself but also on its role in the world. The disagreements as well as the underlying shared assumptions of these thoughtful and fractious public intellectuals provide a rich and complex understanding of China today and its role in our future. We have selected writings that we, the editors, in conjunction with our Chinese colleagues, feel capture the diversity of intelligent opinion about just what is or should be the "China Dream."

The selection of texts translated in this volume reflects our commitment to Chinese voices over our North American concerns or preferences. Over the course of a five-year project, we engaged with our Chinese colleagues to find out which writers and texts they feel are important.[1] Scholars and writers in Shanghai and Beijing, of course, hardly constitute the full range of Chinese opinion, but they do include thoughtful and open-minded intellectuals, some of them well known in the public sphere. They responded with diligence and grace—as well as with arguments among themselves and with the non-Chinese members of our project—to the challenge of representing as wide a range of intellectual perspectives as could be achieved, especially including standpoints with which they personally disagreed. The first result of the project was a series of five collaboratively drafted mappings of the intellectual public sphere in China today published in *China Information* in 2018.[2] This book and other translations from our project are the next result of this collaboration.

These translations are voices from the Chinese century and offer the careful reader an opportunity to enter the world of intellectual debate inside China today on fundamental questions of politics and society. For Western readers, the selections from Liberal voices will likely be most familiar, though for those with progressive commitments some of the leftist voices will resonate. However, several of these texts may surprise readers, at least at first inspection. How, for example, is a eulogy for a disillusioned Communist Party intellectual (Xu Jilin's essay on Wang Yuanhua) a worthwhile contribution to public debate? Or Qian Liqun's very personal "introduction" to a course (and now a two-volume book) on the Mao period? Do people really read the dense prose of Sun Ge's postcolonial theorizing? Aside from our assurance that our Chinese colleagues made the case for each of these authors, these diverse texts reflect the variety of literary forms adopted by Chinese intellectuals writing under Party supervision in the early twenty-first century. Xu Jilin's contemporary literati elegy is one style of expression used by China's public intellectuals—here to evoke the historical experience of the older intellectuals active in these debates. Similarly, the personal style of Qian Liqun's lecture encodes a stinging analysis of the Mao period and a call to arms to face the historical tragedies of "Mao culture" within the form of "a letter to my father and introduction to a generation who don't know this history." Several of the essays included in this volume look more academic, their authors displaying different sorts of "expertise"—Liu Qing gives a nuanced philosophical reading heavy with citations to philosophers such as Charles Taylor; Wang Shaoguang offers a careful political-economy analysis with charts and tables; Chen Lai peppers his history with arcane characters and terms from Confucianism's long history; Cai Xia provides a robust defense of constitutional democracy entirely on the basis of the Marxist-Leninist cannon; and Sun Ge reflects the engagement of some in the Sinophone Left with international postcolonial theory that has an audience as much in Japan, Korea, and Taiwan as inside China. We also include notable public lectures reposted on Internet fora (Rong Jian), thoughtful posts on Weibo and Weixin (Guo Yuhua and Cai Xia), and focused conversations between like-minded intellectuals, also made widely available over the Internet (Chen Ming and his fellow debaters).

The vast majority of public intellectuals in China—in particular public intellectuals who publish in high-profile venues—are men. We may deplore this limitation, but at present it appears to be a sociological fact, even if the reasons for the imbalance are not immediately clear. Two of us met with the outspoken sociologist Guo Yuhua at Tsinghua University in early December 2018, and when we asked her to explain the male domination of China's public intellectual world, she replied with a wry smile that "systems are gendered, too." As we have consulted more widely, other voices have quickly emerged, and we include the commentaries by Guo Yuhua and Cai Xia of the Central Party School as well as by Sun Ge to reflect more of women's contributions to thinking China.

Individual introductions to each text provide specific information on each Chinese author and the context and key points of that text and address any salient issues of translation or terminology. This general introduction to the volume as a whole introduces the three main "voices" that Chinese intellectuals themselves recognize—Liberal, Left, and New Confucian—and offers a survey of the historical context, political system, and intellectual worlds that have shaped these intellectuals and their analysis of contemporary China. We explore the key themes and issues we see emerging from these debates and their significance for understanding China, China's role in the world, and what China's intellectuals might have to offer from a newly powerful China in a time of profound challenges to the liberal global order.

Mapping the Intellectual Public Sphere

Our volume begins with Gan Yang's lecture at Tsinghua University in 2005. He appears as "the challenge" because we feel his characterization of contemporary China as shaped by three traditions from the twentieth century—Confucianism, Maoism, and liberal reform under Deng Xiaoping (1904–1997)—has been broadly embraced by most intellectuals who currently debate China's political reforms in the People's Republic of China (PRC) today. In addition, Gan's challenge aptly identifies the questions and reflects the categories that animate all the thinkers and writers we have surveyed: how to identify and integrate the best of China's traditional, socialist, and liberal heritages and their focus on thought, culture, and moral discourse.

To present the range of answers to the challenge Gan Yang articulates, we adopt the widely accepted Chinese division of the world of public intellectuals into three "streams of thought" (*sichao*): the Liberals, the New Left, and the New Confucians.[3] The Liberals are in many ways the most familiar to Western observers. Liu Xiaobo (b. 1955), who died in the summer of 2017 and was a prisoner of conscience and a Nobel Peace Prize winner in 2010, represents the world of Chinese dissidents who continue to struggle for the causes of democracy and human rights in China and who are willing to confront Chinese Communist Party (CCP) authority directly. However, many public intellectuals in China are liberal in a less confrontational fashion and labor in their books and on their websites to achieve liberal goals in less revolutionary ways by working within the system, by exploring forgotten liberal traditions in China, by criticizing illiberal practices in contemporary Chinese society, and by engaging New Left and New Confucian authors in debate. These Chinese Liberals seek to make China truly "modern" in the face of repressive traditions (both traditional Chinese and revolutionary) by salvaging the heritage of Western liberalism—individual freedoms, rule of law—even as they struggle with the postmodern readings of China's rise.

The five Liberals included in part II of this volume offer five ways these issues are addressed in public in China today: as careful scholarly analyses applied to burning problems, as public lectures, as snappy and direct blog posts, as analyses cast in orthodox Party language, and as heartfelt literary examples to inspire. In chapter 2, Liu Qing, a professor of political science in Shanghai, speaks from within the academy but to a broader audience in 2004 through the well-known intellectual journal *Kaifang Shidai* (Open times) published in

Guangzhou. Liu Qing gives a rigorously theoretical account of the issues confronting China and defends liberalism, drawing particularly from the communitarian liberalism of the Canadian philosopher Charles Taylor. Liu's goal is to identify and apply useful categories of analysis to construct his liberal vision of China's problems and solutions. He also invokes the "three traditions" of China's twentieth century, signaling that he has joined the conversation launched by Gan Yang. Yet Liu searches for historical continuity in different ways, arguing that whatever one might think of liberalism in an abstract sense, the liberal mindset has become part of Chinese culture over the course of the past century.

Chapter 3, a lecture Rong Jian delivered in Beijing in 2013, is a trenchant critique of Party rule and ideology as it applies to critical thought. It is the most politically direct and penetrating of all of the essays included in the volume (no doubt reflecting Rong's independent status as a "businessman intellectual"). He gives a Liberal's "history" of China's developments and considerable detail on the conditions of intellectual public life. Rong ends with a call for a "marketplace for ideas" in China, which, in miniature, this volume reflects. The two offerings by Guo Yuhua begin in chapter 4 with a short (and now deleted) blog post chiding the government in the wake of a crude expulsion of " low-quality people " from Beijing in 2017. In chapter 5, Guo uses a modified question-and-answer format to provide a ferocious critique of "communist civilization" by basically undercutting all the shibboleths of Maoist and post-Mao leftist writers in a Chinese version of Hans Christian Andersen's story "The Emperor's New Clothes"—she takes few prisoners. In chapter 6, Cai Xia offers as strong a defense of democratic politics as Liu Qing and as harsh an assessment of Communist rule as Guo Yuhua but does so entirely on the basis of the Marxist-Leninist canon in the rhetoric of what Geremie Barmé calls "Party New-Speak." In the final essay in part II, Xu Jilin, among the most noted of Liberal voices in China,[4] is represented with a moving eulogy to one establishment intellectual: Wang Yuanhua (1920–2008). Xu offers a concrete, historical, and personal account of the emergence of Chinese liberal thought in the 1990s through the example of Wang, a disillusioned Party intellectual whose life reflects the experiences that have shaped the elder generation arguing in this volume (and parallels Qian Liqun's reminiscences of his life under Mao Zedong in chapter 8).

We have chosen thematic rather than chronological order in our presentation of these texts, but it is worth noting the chronology here: liberal thought was relatively ascendant in the early 2000s but has been eclipsed since 2012 and especially since the rise of Xi Jinping. Rong Jian's critique from 2013 is among the last forceful expressions of Chinese liberal thought that we have seen, bar Cai Xia's remarkable liberal defense in orthodox Party language. Guo's more recent blog post was, as noted, quickly taken down.

The New Left includes figures that avow socialist goals of egalitarianism and social justice. Many New Left intellectuals are more accepting of China's revolutionary and Maoist heritage than are the Liberals and engage in both political and scholarly activism as a means to address the inequalities and corruption that have been by-products of China's rapid economic growth. They are universally critical of the Euro-American "neoliberal" economic order, and some criticize the Chinese government for not being leftist enough. At the same time, these intellectuals embrace the current Party-state in ways Liberals do not. Some of these figures were attracted to the "Chongqing model" (which endures despite the purge and sentencing of Bo Xilai, the model's advocate, in 2012).[5] That model seeks to combine state economic intervention, police crackdown on criminality and corruption, and nostalgic Maoist populism to better the lives of Chinese workers and peasants, many of whom have not benefitted from China's "market socialism." One way or another, the New Left intellectuals seek to make China a truly revolutionary alternative to a neoliberal world.

The New Left voices in part III include five diverse intellectuals. We begin in chapter 8 with Qian Liqun, a respected elder academic and intellectual activist. He offers a profound assessment of Mao, Maoism, and intellectuals' involvement with Mao and the consequences of this history for himself, for intellectuals, and for China. Qian identifies himself, as did Mao, with the people or, in today's lingo, as *minjian* (among the people, grassroots). A professor of literature at Peking University, Qian embodies, in the tension between his elite status and populist identity, the challenge that confronts most of the New Left intellectuals in China today. Qian faces this challenge and the tormented history of socialism squarely, in particular Mao's abuses of power and intellectuals' complicity in his rule. His answers are not simple, but they are compelling. He concludes with the call for a "thorough clearing up" (*qingli*) of Mao Zedong Thought and culture before China can truly absorb and digest its twentieth-century history and move forward. Xiao Gongqin, a professor at Shanghai Normal University, published his short essay in the Shanghai newspaper *Dongfang Zaobao* (Oriental morning post) in 2012. In chapter 9, Xiao, considered a leftist but also a representative of neoauthoritarian thought, offers another, more orthodox reading of history that justifies the reformist Leninism of Deng Xiaoping. Xiao addresses the question of democracy—a topic that runs through most of our texts—and comes down squarely on the authoritarian populist model known, since the days of Sun Yat-sen (1866–1925), as "political tutelage." That is, the authoritarian state will teach the people of China the civic values necessary for a future constitutional system. Where Qian invokes the self-critical tradition in Chinese leftism, Xiao shows just what is worth keeping from China's century of socialism but really offers an instrumentalist defense of authoritarianism as the best road to civil society and democracy.

Gan Yang returns in chapter 10 with a global political history of democracy that makes the case for what Wang Shaoguang in chapter 11 calls "representational democracy." Both intellectuals offer a spirited critique of liberal democracy as practiced in Western nations today. This is not the stuff of partisan name-calling, but thoughtful and challenging historical and political science analyses of the foibles of electoral democracy. This essay by Gan Yang was published in 1999, and Liu Qing's liberal text from 2004 (chapter 2) may be seen as a rejoinder. Gan's theme is the inherent elitism of liberal thought and its irrelevance to the practical needs of ordinary Chinese. In making his case, Gan reflects a deep understanding of Western political theory (his academic specialty), from Edmund Burke to Rousseau to Tocqueville to Benjamin Constant and Isaiah Berlin.

In contrast, Wang Shaoguang, professor emeritus at the Chinese University of Hong Kong and currently a Schwarzman Scholar at Tsinghua University in Beijing, deploys the tools of academic political science—tables, charts, surveys—to make his case for "representational" (or "responsive") democracy as better than Western representative democracy. His goal in this essay from 2014, also published in *Open Times*, is to make the case why China under Xi Jinping should not be called "authoritarian" but is in fact more truly democratic than America. Finally in part III, Sun Ge's essay from 2017 in chapter 12 offers a postmodern critical reading of Okinawan history as a window into the challenges for leftist thought in China today. Sun is a specialist on Japan and a professor of literature at the Academy of Social Sciences in Beijing. She is actively engaged with the Inter-Asia Cultural Studies group of East Asian intellectuals who seek to draw from subaltern theory to build an independent (non-Western) Asian theory. Although a minority voice (as a woman) in Chinese intellectual circles today, Sun also shows that New Left thought need not be limited to domestic concerns.

New Confucians are convinced that China's and ultimately the world's future lies in the revival (or reinvention) of China's Confucian past. These figures argue that China's twentieth-century pursuit of Western knowledge was wrong-headed because neither liberalism nor Marxism will ever be sufficiently *Chinese*. Grounding themselves in notions of cultural exceptionalism ("China is different"), these intellectuals are convinced that the Confucian tradition of "benevolent rule" can be updated to provide a new and much-needed legitimacy to China's authoritarian polity. They imagine a moral meritocracy that will function as a genuinely benevolent dictatorship and thereby will outperform liberal democratic regimes, corrupted by lobbying and private interests. Moreover, such a stance grows organically out of China's glorious past and restores the traditional personal relations—China's Confucian hierarchy—destroyed by a century of Western-inspired revolution. These intellectuals seek to make China truly Chinese in a modern world dominated by Western culture.

In part IV, New Confucian voices are represented by three texts: a round-table discussion published in a movement-oriented journal but more broadly accessed over the Internet, a historical survey in a university journal, and an interview published online. Indeed, the predominance of Internet material among China's New Confucians reflects their popular orientation and ambivalent relationship with standard scholarship (and academic intellectuals such as Xu Jilin and Ge Zhaoguang are very critical of the scholarly bona fides of these advocates).[6] In chapter 13, Chen Ming heads up a spirited debate among New Confucians in June 2014 that gives a vivid sense of the intellectual energy, even humor, of this community. The discussion also presents a startling narrative that simply sidelines Chinese socialism and the CCP, essentially framing the Party as a twentieth-century artifact that has fulfilled its historical mission and now needs to get out of the way of China's true revival—Confucian civilization. The shared focus in this debate is the figure Kang Youwei (1858–1927), the radical Confucian reformer. In chapter 14, Chen Lai, a noted professor of philosophy at Tsinghua University in Beijing, offers his version of China's modern history, focusing, understandably, on the role and fate of Confucian thought. Readers can contrast the liberal version of this history given by Rong Jian and the leftist histories offered by Qian Liqun and Xiao Gongqin. Chen Lai answers Gan Yang's challenge to integrate China's past and present by placing Confucian thought and social practice (Chen speaks in terms of the "subconscious" aspect of Confucianism in society) at the center of his narrative. Our final text, an interview with Jiang Qing, the noted Confucian activist and advocate for a Confucian constitution and state religion,[7] returns to a major theme of China's modern history: the May Fourth Movement. Although the title of this interview in 2015 (available on the Chinese Internet) addresses the place of modern women in society, in fact Jiang Qing does not do that topic justice but focuses on the failure of this signature movement in China's modern and socialist history. If our volume begins with a predictable critique of Party rule by Liberals on behalf of modern values, it ends with a somewhat surprising conservative criticism of the Party by Confucians against both.

The Diverse Worlds of Thinking China

It is well to keep in mind our speakers' social place or position. All of them address the same challenges facing China today, but they do so from different social spaces and with varying identities and organizational homes. They are representatives of thinking China but cannot represent all Chinese. In this volume, we see a range of public intellectuals—academic and independent. The voices represented here draw from humanist intellectuals who speak from their university perches but to a public intellectual audience—such as Xu Jilin, Liu

Qing, and Xiao Gongqin in Shanghai and Sun Ge, Qian Liqun, Cai Xia, Guo Yuhua, Wang Shaoguang, and Chen Lai in Beijing. They give a sense of this vibrant world dominated by intellectual stand-offs between the New Left and Liberal camps and of the New Confucians' rising confidence. Cai Xia is fully in the establishment due to her long work in the Central Party School. Gan Yang, Rong Jian, and Jiang Qing—each broadly associated with one of the three notable *sichao*—are our entryway into the world of independent public intellectuals where commerce, religious and local associations, including a range of New Confucian organizations, and the Internet intersect. Between and beyond these roles for public intellectuals live the lonely souls who choose open dissent, from Nobel laureate Liu Xiaobo and Ai Weiwei, the performance-art enfant terrible of the establishment, to a host of less well-known activists, lawyers, and muckrakers.[8] These voices are not included here but are increasingly available in recent studies and translations.[9]

Although we use modern China's "three traditions" to organize the voices in this volume, these identities are not hard and fast. These clusters define *ideal types*; not all intellectuals identify as Liberal or New Left or New Confucian. For example, among intellectuals translated in this volume, Liu Qing identifies as a Left Liberal; Gan Yang has moved from a liberal position to a Left Confucian stand; and although many New Left intellectuals have come in recent years to embrace the Chinese state, Sun Ge seeks to find a critical community of interests in the Sinophone Left inside and outside the PRC. Initial consultations with Chinese colleagues have emphasized two other trends of thought: *neoauthoritarianism* (or new conservatism), as in Xiao Gongqin, who appears in this volume, and Wang Huning (b. 1955), who is the ghost writer for the CCP leadership, and *democratic socialism*, as in Xie Tao (1922–2010).[10] In all, the three thought streams are handy for an initial orientation to China's diverse and dynamic intellectual world, but we should be wary of singling out of any one intellectual as embodying this or that stream.

It may be more helpful to think in terms of an intellectual's orientation and approach, or what we are calling "voices." Intellectuals identifying as New Confucian are looking for *Chinese* solutions and drawing from indigenous Chinese thinkers. Chinese Liberals are looking for ways China can embrace and develop *universal* or global norms and draw from Western liberal thinkers. And many New Left intellectuals are looking for *Asian* solutions as well as socialist traditions that engage but are not limited to either Chinese or Western or universal norms; they often draw from Asian thinkers in the Global South. These distinctly different concerns contribute to a certain amount of "talking past each other" among intellectuals identified with one or none of the three *sichao*. Moreover, many of the ideas defended by various public intellectuals are paired with larger political, social, and intellectual projects: New Confucians build academies and launch nongovernmental organizations; New Left intellectuals serve in the brain trusts of politicians whose ideas they respect; Liberals seek out partnerships with Western universities and academics to use that cultural capital for influence and protection in China's still fragile civil society.

Our speakers are *academic public intellectuals*—scholars who have chosen to use their specialized knowledge and status to engage with the public conversation on China's challenges. Most are currently employed in Chinese universities, but the independent intellectuals, such as Rong Jian, also adopt scholarly personae. The historians among them are reexamining China's past to uncover themes, practices, forgotten traditions, and missed opportunities that might fill the void at the core of China's current political/cultural identity and help forge China's future. The sociologists, political scientists, and philosophers seek to find models and mine traditions to offer solutions to current problems. These debates are subtle, varied, and wide ranging, and they suggest a breadth and sophistication rarely hinted at in media discussions of China's intellectual world. These qualities have impelled us to translate these texts in full so that English readers can engage with the details of these Chinese public intellectuals' arguments and analyses. We think they have important things to say.

Of course, academic public intellectuals, as significant as their work is to Chinese political contention, hardly describe the entire population of China's lively, if not free, public sphere. There are important actors and issues not included in this corner of China's intellectual public sphere, which is a subset of the raucous and generally commercial broader public sphere. For example, the use of China's vibrant social media is taken up mostly with shopping, gossiping, and the equivalent of watching cat videos; a scant 10 percent of Chinese social media are used for political or social discussion.[11] China's intellectual public sphere includes journalists, business leaders speaking on social and political issues, some artists, local nongovernmental organizations, lawyers, and other social activists. All are important and covered, at least in part, in recent studies, but these actors generally focus on specific issues, particular communities, and individual cases. These public intellectuals address issues of feminism, leisure, futurism, and animal rights, along with a host of other important social and local political issues.[12] Academic public intellectuals address their attention to the discursive sinews of power in the CCP's China—ideology and "China's story."

New studies highlight the importance of these ideological and cultural concerns. Kerry Brown's new study of Xi Jinping's revival of Party ideology forcefully argues that the key power issue confronting the CCP today is neither military nor economic but cultural.[13] Brown sees Xi's reforms and pronouncements, including his brutal anticorruption campaign, as efforts to re-create a moral narrative for the CCP, to make the Party legitimate in the hearts of China's citizens. Christian Sorace's political ethnography has documented this moral politics in practice at the local level in the case of the Party's response to the Sichuan earthquake in 2008.[14] This battle for legitimacy is now being fought precisely on the level of the ideas and norms that China's New Confucians, Liberals, and New Left intellectuals have been debating over the past two decades. It is no wonder that the Party is now coming down hard not just on Chinese Liberals but also on New Confucians and New Left intellectuals who impugn the Party's dignity, idealism, or ethical legitimacy.

At the same time, neither the Party apparatus nor the intellectual elite fully represent the efforts of China's resilient intellectuals across society. Sebastian Veg provides the most up-to-date and comprehensive study of China's fearless *minjian*, or "grassroots," intellectuals.[15] They are educated people, lawyers, activists, and documentary filmmakers who eschew high theory to address concrete social problems and engage with local communities. Like Foucault's "specific intellectuals," these *minjian* intellectuals act out their politics. In China, this has meant a dangerous dance with the Party, both the central security forces and the often corrupt local governments. Perhaps the most important message from Veg's book is how these grassroots intellectuals are collectively changing the society that the Party and China's fractious academic intellectuals seek to improve.

Xi Jinping has emphasized the need to "tell China's story well" since his directive given at the National Propaganda and Ideology Work Conference in August 2013, and he has been promoting his "China Dream" as the main narrative of that story. However, recent research has shown that public opinion, at least among China's educated urban netizens, is still far more diverse than official propaganda would suggest.[16] Academic public intellectuals are key voices in this struggle to define and tell "China's story." These theoretical, sometimes obscure, and often philosophical debates are a major forum in which Chinese public policy—at the strategic level—is contested within China's directed public sphere. New Confucians assert that the Chinese must think with indigenous concepts such as *dao* (the Way), *li* (rites), and *ren* (benevolence), for otherwise they are in the thrall of foreign powers. For Chinese Liberals, the reasoning and logic of liberalism will save the Chinese from stultifying traditionalism and radical despotism. New Left intellectuals find that only neo-Marxism and postcolonial theory can open the Chinese population's eyes to the ills of neoliberalism and lead them to the pathway toward social equity. If we doubt the importance of these debates, simply recall that the two major outlets in which these sorts of debates have appeared within China—the journal *Yanhuang Chunqiu* (China through the ages) and the website Gongshi Wang (Consensus Net) were shut down by the end of 2016. The Party does not censor what it does not think is significant.

It is not the case that political and social theorizing is necessarily the preferred voice for China's academic intellectuals—who also pen lively topical commentaries on daily life and local issues. Rather, the convoluted language of some of these intellectual debates is doubly political in contemporary China. The carrot is the promise of political influence. The Party, especially under Xi Jinping, continues to champion the "guiding role" of thought, and so intellectuals who hope to influence public policy perforce must cast their proposals in ideological language congenial to state actors.[17] Most of the Chinese writings translated in this volume seek to identify "correct thought," the right way to think about big issues—be it liberal political theory, neo-Marxism, or some version or other of Confucian thought. Disagreement is rife, and political retribution a constant danger, but all sides appear to accept the primary importance of getting the thought right, even Liberals, who embrace tolerance as a necessity lacking in current Chinese thought worlds.[18] The second political attribute of these theoretical discussions reflects the stick: the need under China's repressive political system, as Gloria Davies has shown, to "speak obliquely" to avoid political repression. Academic jargon serves as a screen against political criticism, an indirect avenue of criticism, and a public "hidden transcript" in which the educated reader is expected to connect the dots between Max Weber or John Rawls and current politics in China.[19] In the process, we discover a great range of opinions can be expressed without openly transgressing Party orthodoxy.

Same History, Different Dreams

The essays translated in this volume give three clearly different narratives of the same China over recent decades. These contending narratives buttress their divergent solutions for China's new century. For the New Confucians, the failures of socialism and the depredations of Western "hollowing out of Chinese culture" in the twentieth century cry out for a traditional Chinese solution—Confucianism. There are, of course, different Confucian solutions on offer, from Jiang Qing's political institutions to Kang Xiaoguang's state religion to Chen Ming's or Bai Tongdong's search for a sort of civil religion. According to Deng Jun and Craig Smith, these propositions offer various forms of a Chinese and de-secularized solution that reunites religion and politics for China today.[20]

The same world according to Chinese Liberals is a history of socialist failure and market-reform success now challenged by the lack of political reform. These challenges cry out for the best political solutions human civilizations have produced, and liberalism, they argue, has the best track record for producing stable, just, and prosperous societies in modern history. Rational and fair-minded, Chinese Liberals acknowledge the limitations of Western liberalism in practice (especially since the global financial crisis of 2008 and the populist revolts in the United Kingdom and the United States in recent years). They see modern Chinese history as a local variant of universal human history and thus focus on the challenges of balancing liberty and equality, addressing challenges to civil society and how to reinvigorate the tradition of Chinese constitutional government. Thoughtful assessments and suggestions are offered by Rong Jian, Xu Jilin, Guo Yuhua, Cai Xia, and Liu Qing in our translations. Among other liberal intellectuals, Qin Hui draws critically on Russian, Soviet, and post-Soviet history; Sun Liping diagnoses a "fractured society"; and Yu Jianrong focuses on how to address social conflict. All these propositions are offered in the context of debates with Left and Confucian intellectuals, and Chinese liberalism has been under considerable attack in recent years.[21]

Recent history, according to New Left intellectuals, shows the need for a revival of the best of state socialism as a defense against global neoliberalism. For mainland New Left intellectuals, only the Chinese state, as a reformed socialist entity, ultimately has the wherewithal to withstand the depredations of neoliberal globalization.[22] Wang Hui (b. 1959) is most widely known in the West for making this case.[23] In our translations, Wang Shaoguang offers a thorough critique of Western politics and economics while making the case for Chinese-style "representational" democracy that, he feels, can succeed where Western representative democracy is now failing. As mainland Chinese New Left intellectuals engage their fellow leftist intellectuals in Taiwan and Hong Kong, they confront the disturbing challenge that *they* as PRC citizens are part of a new colonial power. Left intellectuals in these three areas have discovered that the same ideas (anti-imperialism, anticolonialism) have different meanings in each place and that the failure to appreciate the different historical experiences in each bedevils their search for a new, emancipatory "Asian perspective."[24] Chen Kuan-hsing in Taiwan, Sun Ge in mainland China, and Johnson Chang in Hong Kong represent promising efforts to engage these different experiences and build that common Asian perspective. In our translations, Sun Ge takes the example of Japan and Okinawa as a metaphor for the challenges also facing China and the solutions that a critical theory approach can offer.

We also can see some *shared assumptions* in this Sinophone thought among PRC academic public intellectuals as they debate and criticize each other. First, the West looms large for all sides, particularly since China's rise has made the race between China and the West all the more exciting. For the New Confucians, Western influence, both power and culture, has been pernicious. It has hollowed out Chinese culture and left a spiritual vacuum. The "West" for New Confucians, however, includes both socialism and liberalism as invasive foreign species in China's garden. The New Confucians frequently compare their solutions to foreign solutions, reflecting a certain lack of self-confidence. Chinese Liberals, of course, look to the best of the West while critically engaging the limitations and failures of liberal democratic practice and attending to the areas where current international liberal norms do not fit China's situation or require adaptation (as in the avoidance among these academic intellectuals of any substantive discussion on electoral democracy at this stage). They pragmatically focus on the liberal side of liberal democracy—looking for sound ways to implement constraints on the use of power. For New Left intellectuals, the West is both the source of emancipatory theory (though critical theory has also been greatly enriched by voices from the Global South) and the great enemy and home of neoliberalism. In all, we cannot understand contemporary Chinese intellectual life absent its profound engagement with the West—ideas from the West, political examples from the West, and examples from Western history that populate nearly every Chinese essay covered by our mapping. All efforts to create a Chinese identity among these elites inevitably come from a critical engagement with the global order that Western nations have shaped and up to now have dominated.

Second, as noted, the voices in this volume accept that it is important to get one's thinking, one's ideology or *sixiang*, right. The philosophical idealism (as opposed to materialism) of most of these essays also connects contemporary Chinese thought with a long tradition of twentieth-century Chinese political thought. Finally, there is a "shared civility" among these academic public intellectuals for all but a few extremists. Despite their vociferous contention over solutions, so far none of these intellectuals is denouncing any others as "counterrevolutionaries" or for "hurting the feelings of the Chinese people." Sadly, the increasing limitations put on public debate in China in the past few years under Xi Jinping and the increased demand that intellectuals conform to the ideology of "the leader" challenge this period of a hundred schools contending in early-twenty-first-century China.

Thinking China in Today's World

The current ideological moment in China—the question of the day and the remembered recent history of the past decades that shape the world of intellectuals translated in this volume—is part of the global ideological moment, albeit an importantly distinct part. The question all the voices in this volume are addressing in one way or another is: *How can China become a truly great power as well as a just society and a positive leader in the world?*[25] Thus, although we emphasize the local conditions, domestic concerns, and parochial arguments among these intellectuals, we also see powerful resonances with our own societies in Europe, North America, and Australasia and the challenges we face today, particularly in the rising populist anger in America, the United Kingdom, and around the world. From this global perspective, China's "new era" of the CCP's increasingly autocratic regime under its "supreme leader," Xi Jinping, not only is a stage and phase in the history of modern China but also partakes of the global populist reaction to the failings of a neoliberal order that has produced obscene wealth for the few, left many in poverty and insecurity, and gutted the middle classes around the world.[26] We no more see Xi Jinping as "the solution" than we do Donald Trump or Brexit. The point is that the Chinese intellectuals translated in this volume are consciously engaged in the assessment of these global developments. Their essays are impressively well informed on international conditions (and modern European history) and address problems we all face: the failures of political representation, the rise of social intolerance, the perdurance of economic inequality, and looming environmental crises. Thus, the translations in this volume offer insight to conditions and issues of China today as well as specifically Chinese solutions to the shared problems of governance we all face.[27]

Naturally enough, China's intellectuals cast their response to these global challenges not only in terms of local ideas and experiences but also in terms of the impact of these changes on their world—their work, their lives, their society. We suggest that China's rise and the West's simultaneous decline from unchallenged global supremacy has had an effect on the Chinese intellectual world equivalent to that of the May Fourth period a century ago. May Fourth marked the moment when much of the intellectual elite in China decided that Confucian civilization was at best no longer functional and at worst an obstacle to China's progress. Lu Xun's (1881–1936) dark humor and despair reflected the gravity of that recognition, the sense of free fall. Others were less somber and set about the grim tasks of reform or revolution with appropriate energy, but with a few notable exceptions most of China's intellectual elite at the time believed that China's future lay in some version of modernity, be it liberal democratic or socialist.[28] "With Chinese characteristics" was always there as an asterisk—Deng Xiaoping did not invent the idea—but by 1925 Chinese civilization had become a dinosaur: something fascinating, maybe worthy of study, but also something extinct. Mao may have Sinified Marxism, compared himself to Qin Shihuang, the founding emperor of the Qin dynasty in 221 BCE, and wrote classical-style poetry, but even when he soured on socialism, his goal was to remake the revolution, not to revive "feudal China." The dictates of nationalism required modernity, and there was no obvious link between Chinese tradition and modernity. Maoism and state socialism blended the two at midcentury, but by the 1980s most Chinese felt the combination was no longer working.

China's rise in the twenty-first century has meant, first and foremost, that China has achieved modernity in the form of wealth and power. The global crisis of capitalism beginning in 2008, followed by the election of Donald Trump in 2016 and the many signs of malaise afflicting the liberal democratic world, have only boosted China's self-confidence. Calls such as Wei Jingsheng's (b. 1950) for a "fifth modernization" (i.e., democracy) in 1979, which may well have nagged at the conscience (or perhaps confidence) of many a reformer of the Deng era (and after), now fall flat. China's governance today offers what the world seems to want: wealth, stability, mobility, promise—to most citizens who keep their noses clean and their mouths shut. The Chinese state has replaced the United States as the world's model of efficiency and competence. Whether we like their chosen direction or not, China's leaders appear to know where China is going and how to get there. We have entered the Chinese century.

The effects of this new era on China's intellectuals have been astounding. Reading these texts gives the impression that they inhabit a brave new world where conceptually and intellectually anything is possible; the sky's the limit. This is a reversal of May Fourth's antitraditionalism because "China's back, baby, and she's better than ever." Lu Xun went into free fall, while a century later Chen Ming and his New Confucian colleagues soar, unmoored. Of course, this characterization does not match the lived experience of intellectuals in today's China. As our Liberal friends and colleagues constantly remind us, what Xi Jinping hopes to achieve may well mark the beginning of the end of this period of experimentation. But many texts, in particular those of the mainland New Confucians and the New Left, seem to reflect the notion that China not only requires but is also on the verge of capturing an entirely new *sixiang*, a new story, a new ideology, which, by the way, will be of world-historical significance—as Chinese thought once was in the past.

This is what is behind much of the work of Gan Yang and of the epigraph from him at the start of this introduction. Gan insists that China needs a new epistemology, a new historiography, that will bring together the experiences of Confucianism, socialism, and reform-era capitalism with Chinese characteristics *and* make sense of all of these things in a global, comparative context. Although at first glance the idea of "putting the twentieth century behind us," particularly the political history of the twentieth century, reads like a mindless slogan, it seems to be enormously popular among Chinese intellectuals, who appear to be convinced that conventional historiography, conventional narratives, no longer apply. Like the image of Chinese tradition during the May Fourth era, for these intellectuals the notion of "China's twentieth century" seems to stand in the way of China's twenty-first century.

Much of this iconoclasm is, of course, explained by a general rejection of the narrative of the Enlightenment, a rejection shared by many members of the New Left and the mainland New Confucians. For the mainland New Confucians, this rejection is straightforward and near total.[29] Jiang Qing's piece on women in this volume hammers this point repeatedly; in fact, the piece spends more time condemning the May Fourth movement than it does talking about women. May Fourth was, to the mainland New Confucians, a disaster from which China is only now beginning to recover, as was Maoism. These and other New Confucian critiques indict China's liberal tradition—the notion that China's modernization will inevitably lead to Western-style democracy—as well as its socialist heritage, in particular its internationalist aspects, and Mao Zedong's Cultural Revolution. The "transcendence" of China's liberal and socialist traditions will be based on the "Chinese people/nation" (*Zhonghua minzu*)—the two are conflated both linguistically and discursively—and their/its concrete needs rather than on abstract ideas based on Enlightenment discourse. This is a Confucian co-optation of the Maoist notion of "practice." By "uniting the three traditions," Gan Yang demands the construction of a new historical narrative that will reunite the experiences of the Qing Empire, the Republic of China, and the PRC, despite the ruptures that the current historical records have emphasized. This demand reflects a goal shared by Chen Ming and others—and demonstrated in the roundtable discussion with Chen and Gan in this volume: to *create a new cultural continuity* based on *sixiang*, to replace the manifest *political discontinuity* that has marked China's experience since the Opium War.

The New Left has made similar discursive moves. Their rejection of the Enlightenment is less obvious and less complete than the mainland New Confucians' rejection, but Wang Shaoguang, who has spent his career trying to help China build "state capacity," has turned his sights in recent years to a criticism of Western democracy. To Wang, "electoral democracy" is more "electoral" than "democratic," and he proposes the Chinese model of "representational democracy" and "good governance" in which results rather than process or political form are what count. In addition, after years of positioning themselves as "critical intellectuals," citing postmodern theory to criticize what they saw as the neoliberal character of China's reforms during the 1980s and 1990s, members of the New Left have moved in recent years to embrace the state. Their intellectual inspiration is likely to be Carl Schmitt or Leo Strauss rather than Roberto Unger or Slavoj Žižek, and they fetishize state power instead of defending the interests of the little people. This shift may not be a rejection of the Enlightenment, but it is surely a subversion of it. The New Left, like the mainland New Confucians, are also engaged in reimagining China's modern history. This, of course, is part of Wang Hui's major, multivolume work on the history of Chinese thought, which he started long before China's definitive rise, but Wang Shaoguang also proposes a periodization based on the rise and achievement of state power and capacity rather than on regime change.[30] Perhaps due to the sensitivity of the subject, the CCP is rarely mentioned as an important actor in the drama of China's modern and contemporary history, even by members of the New Left—or at least it wasn't until Xi Jinping came to town.

These shifts have left China's Liberals on the defensive. Xu Jilin has devoted much of his writing over the past ten years not only to a denunciation of the cult of state power but also, more importantly, to an analysis of its intellectual underpinnings: the ideas of statism and historicism. Whatever historicism may have meant elsewhere, in the contemporary Chinese context it is the idea that universal values do not exist; meaning and identity are the pure products of local history and culture, embodied in the state. Hence, notions of historicism and statism are mutually supportive and fuel the cultural pride of the main-land New Confucians, for whom traditional Chinese civilization is unique and glorious, as well as the nationalist pride of those touting the "China model," including New Left intellectuals such as Wang Shaoguang. Xu has also attempted to fashion a liberal compromise with Chinese tradition, discussing the possi-bility of Confucianism's serving as China's "civil religion" and attempting to craft a new, more cosmopolitan Chinese foreign policy by proposing "*tianxia-zhuyi* (Chinese universalism) 2.0."[31] Likewise, we have seen Liu Qing's robust defense of liberalism's ability to address the realities of China's "social imagi-nary" today.

As of 2018, these debates were inconclusive in China's intellectual and polit-ical circles. Whatever the intellectual merits of these voices, these three "streams of thought," there has been no conclusive signal that one has gained popular traction at the expense of the others. As Liu Qing and others have noted, China today and therefore thinking among various Chinese are plural. Pluralism is not a widely embraced norm, but a plural public sphere in China is a social fact. However, changes in 2018—in particular the reconfirmation of Xi Jinping's leadership, the removal of the previous expectation that he would serve at most two terms as national leader, and the increased propaganda on Marxist ideology in general and Xi Thought in particular—all suggest that this period of a hundred flowers blooming is about to pass.[32] This shift is captured on the one hand by the shutting down of the journal *Yanhuang Chunqiu* and the website Gongshi Wang, along with continued repression of human rights lawyers and non-Han populations in Xinjiang, and on the other hand by a con-certed effort to install Xi Thought. In January 2018, Jiang Shigong's stunning essay "Philosophy and History: Interpreting the 'Xi Jinping Era' Through Xi's Report at the Nineteenth National Congress of the CCP" made an ambitious attempt at a new synthesis that, if successful, might create the new *sixiang* for which all our authors are searching and thus impose a new orthodoxy.[33] His version of Gan Yang's "unifying the three traditions" is China's "standing up, getting rich, and getting strong," and the chief actor in this historical drama is not the CCP, but the Chinese people/nation, which are *led* of course by the CCP and its remarkable and brilliant leader Xi Jinping. This unification represents a new synthesis of Soviet socialism and Western capitalism, a dialectical tran-scendence that will allow China to resume its position as world leader and move humanity forward. Xi Thought, which presumably will function as the new state orthodoxy as well, provides an official answer to Gan Yang's questions and would shut out most of the voices in this volume. It remains to be seen if the age of new orthodoxy has arrived or not.

The Challenges of Listening: Scholarly Literature on China's Intellectuals

These translations and the collaborative project that produced many of them have been undertaken with the belief that it is worth hearing these Chinese voices. It is a worthwhile goal, but the task, we have discovered, has been neither simple nor straightforward. The first challenge we had to face is our own assumptions, presumptions, and habits. The second challenge was finding a way to convey what the Chinese texts say in readable, engaging, and sensible English. It turns out that *listening* takes considerable work.

China's intellectuals have been on the minds of Western academics and general readers at least since the start of the PRC. As exemplified by the influential works of Merle Goldman, Chinese intellectuals have often been seen as dissidents, or "Russian refuseniks with Chinese characteristics."[34] The intellectuals who have most spoken to Western readers were cast as Chinese versions of Solzhenitsyn or Sakharov. This characterization may have made sense during the Cold War, but today the "two camps" no longer exist, contact between people inside and outside of China is much greater, and shared experiences of globalized commerce and media have changed the relationship between China and "the West." Indeed, with so much Chinese emigration and Chinese presence in most societies around the world, the dichotomy no longer makes simple sense. Nonetheless, intellectual habits endure well beyond the advent of social change, and the reader is well advised to be prepared for these Chinese intellectuals not to fit what he or she might expect. The texts included here are not dissent in the classical sense, nor are they Party propaganda. They are sincere intellectual interventions shaped by the strictures of China's directed public sphere, the expectations of Sinophone discourse, and the social experience of the writers themselves.

As academics, we cannot but be influenced by the work of our colleagues in the Western academy who have written extensively on Chinese intellectuals and Chinese public discourse. Since at least the 1950s, the scholarly focus has been on the relationship between intellectuals and the state.[35] Scholarship of the 1980s and 1990s focused on the participation of intellectuals in the CCP as establishment intellectuals and their efforts to reform, rather than replace, Maoism by working from within the system.[36] More recent studies have focused on the post-1992 period, emphasizing the modification of this establishment role as a result of the increasing impact of a commercial (yet controlled) media and the emergence of formal academic identities and professional responsibilities outside the state bureaucracy.[37] Of course, the power and influence of the Party's propaganda and censorship system remain defining characteristics of Chinese intellectual life. That said, recent research has shown that most intellectuals in today's China are politically "disestablished" from the Party-state and are finding unprecedented opportunities as academics and professionals, enjoying study abroad, contact with foreign scholars and diaspora Chinese, better academic pay, and—for the lucky few—considerable earning potential in China's flourishing book and media markets.[38] Scholars engaged in cultural studies have also addressed these issues from a broader cultural and academic Marxist perspective, not least Dai Jinhua and Jing Wang.[39] From our perspective, what is most remarkable about today's public intellectuals in China is that they have found their own voice, which means that their writing is increasingly important for its own sake and on its own terms, as discourse.[40] In other words, intellectuals are no longer simply stalking horses for factions within the Party-state, although the political dimension of their work remains significant.

The fact that Chinese intellectuals are finding their own public voices opens up new comparative possibilities. New work on knowledge production in Republican China (up to 1950) led by Robert Culp, Eddy U, and Wen-hsin Yeh provides one useful baseline in that intellectuals in the 1920s, 1930s, and 1940s were similarly engaged and independent.[41] We embrace this historical-comparative perspective. In addition, a project led by Leigh Jenco looks at Chinese thought for what it can contribute to general social theory and provides a vocabulary for comparing Chinese knowledge production with Western examples, particularly in the context of political philosophy.[42] This approach highlights the role of Chinese thought beyond China itself.

Two new books offer useful surveys of public intellectual debates, one for the benefit of Chinese readers (even though it has recently been partially translated into English) and one for English readers. In early 2012, the Chinese journalist Ma Licheng produced a popular account of eight trends of social thought in contemporary China.[43] Ma's focus is on streams of thought, from "socialism with Chinese characteristics" in the 1980s and the "old leftism" of Maoist thought during the Cultural Revolution to the New Left, democratic socialism, liberalism, nationalism, populism, and New Confucianism. His scope is wider than our focus on academic public intellectuals and by necessity more schematic in such a broad survey.[44] In 2015, He Li, a political scientist teaching in the United States, published a valuable survey of political intellectual discourse in China. He, too, surveys the basic three *sichao*, which he translates as "schools of thought"—Liberal, New Left, and New Confucian—as well as two others: neoauthoritarianism and democratic socialism.[45] Finally, some dozen scholars in our research project Reading and Writing the Chinese Dream dig into key issues and notable writers in some detail to see how their arguments build and engage others.[46]

The voices offered in this volume join a notable collection of fine translations (and some reportage) of Chinese intellectuals and citizens as well as studies focused on their thinking, including Wm. Theodore de Bary and Richard Lufrano, *Sources of Chinese Tradition* (2000); Gloria Davies, *Voicing Concerns*

(2001); Wang Chaohua, *One China, Many Paths* (2003); Sang Ye, *China Candid* (2006);[47] Judy Polumbaum, *China Ink* (2008) (profiles of Chinese journalists); and Angilee Shah and Jeffrey Wasserstrom, *Chinese Characters* (2012).[48] They also join insightful analyses of contemporary Chinese thinking about public affairs, such as Davies, *Worrying About China* (2007); Mark Leonard, *What Does China Think?* (2008); Yu Hua, *China in Ten Words* (2010); and William Callahan, *China Dreams* (2013).[49] Our volume of translations offers a more recent collection of China's influential thinkers and writers on China's dream.

Collaborative Translation and the Coproduction of Knowledge

The translations in this volume have been produced in part through a process of collaborative translation and a commitment to the coproduction of knowledge. Our approach builds upon previous research by giving priority to Chinese voices over Western frameworks and by working with Chinese scholars in collaborative translations and interpretations of these vital contemporary debates over the Chinese dream. We take as our inspiration the "New Sinology," an approach articulated by Geremie Barmé, late of the Australian National University, which combines both theory and method.[50] New Sinology is grounded in respect for Sinophone discourse and insists that research on contemporary China be based on a deep knowledge of Chinese sources, both the literary and the vernacular lects. Classical Sinology focused largely on the formative texts of China's traditional civilization, whereas the New Sinology extends its focus to modern and contemporary Chinese discourses and their political and social contexts. This theoretical/methodological perspective in no way excludes mainstream historical and social science approaches but requires that scholarship on China be grounded in Chinese-language sources and that today's New Sinologists work "with Chinese" rather than simply "on China." What this means is that we are engaged in collaborative research with Chinese colleagues, not deciphering the messages hidden in their work, an approach that characterized much earlier scholarship on post-1949 China.

Our core method in this project—*collaborative translation*—is essentially new to the treatment of works by China's contemporary academic public intellectuals. Our inspiration comes from Gloria Davies's book *Voicing Concerns*, which problematized the process of translation by transforming it into a collaborative endeavor involving Chinese and foreign scholars in conversation. For example, Davies engaged with the Beijing scholar Liu Dong (b. 1951) on clarifications and emendations to his notable essay criticizing intellectual debate in the 1990s as "pidgin scholarship."[51] We also take inspiration from Gail Hershatter's collaboration with a Chinese colleague to produce separate books on women's work in post-1949 China.[52] Thus, this introduction is the work of three

Western scholars coming out of the collaborations in this project, while Chinese colleagues are doing likewise and presenting their versions in Chinese. Five of the translations in this volume are direct products of this collaborative process, as noted by the dual translators (one Anglophone, one Sinophone) for specific texts. However, from the orientation to selection of texts and the individual translations, all the work in this volume is shaped by this cooperative and collaborative approach in the international project from which it comes, Reading and Writing the Chinese Dream.

This approach is fueled by a particular kind of *fieldwork*, constructed on the basis of personal and professional relationships between specific Canadian/ Western and Chinese scholars. It is consciously designed to be a sensitive reflection of the production of knowledge in contemporary Chinese intellectual circles to address the challenge of "translating" this production of knowledge in terms understandable by a Canadian/Western audience eager to understand "what China is thinking." We rely in particular on the project collaborators to strengthen this work. By involving our students (from both Chinese and international universities) in our personal and professional networks, we project the process forward to a new generation, consolidate the linkages between Canadian/Western and Chinese scholars and intellectuals, and seek to produce information of use to scholars, policy makers, and the broader public.

Notes

1. The project "Reading and Writing the Chinese Dream" was funded by the Canadian Social Sciences and Humanities Research Council (Grant 435-2014-0584). See "Reading and Writing the Chinese Dream: Introducing a Project," The China Story: Thinking China, January 26, 2016, https://www.thechinastory.org/cot/reading-and-writing -the-chinese-dream-introducing-a-project/, and the project's webpage, Reading the China Dream, https://www.readingthechinadream.com/about.html.
2. See "Mapping the Intellectual Public Sphere in China Today," special section, *China Information* 32, no. 1, and 32, no. 2 (2018).
3. Gan Yang, *Tong san tong* (Unifying the three traditions) (Beijing: Sanlian Shudian, 2007), reprinting his lecture of May 12, 2005. See also the special section of *China Information* in 2018, "Mapping the Intellectual Public Sphere in China Today." Whereas Liberals and New Confucians generally embrace this nomenclature,Left intellectuals generally bristle at the name "New Left." We have maintained the name because it is in current usage and no popular alternative has yet emerged.
4. See Xu Jilin, *Rethinking China's Rise: A Liberal Critique*, ed. and trans. David Ownby (Cambridge: Cambridge University Press, 2018).
5. Bo Xilai (b. 1949) is still in jail. Andreas Mulvad, "Competing Hegemonic Projects Within China's Variegated Capitalism: 'Liberal' Guangdong vs. 'Statist' Chongqing," *New Political Economy* 20, no. 2 (2014): 199–227.
6. See Xu Jilin, "What Body for Confucianism's Lonely Soul?" in *Rethinking China's Rise*, 113–26, also at https://www.readingthechinadream.com/xu-jilin-what-body-for

-confucianism.html; Ge Zhaoguang, "The Political Demands of Mainland New Confucians in Recent Years" (2017), in *China Dream Chasers*, ed. David Ownby (Cambridge: Cambridge University Press, forthcoming), also at https://www.reading thechinadream.com/ge-zhaoguang-if-horses-had-wings.html. As of August 2018, we have had difficulty accessing some New Confucian websites, but we have yet to see official notification of closings.

7. Jiang Qing, *A Confucian Constitutional Order: How China's Ancient Past Can Shape Its Political Future*, ed. Daniel A. Bell and Ruiping Fan, trans. Edmund Ryden (Princeton, NJ: Princeton University Press, 2012).

8. These intellectual worlds and their histories are sketched in Timothy Cheek, *The Intellectual in Modern Chinese History* (Cambridge: Cambridge University Press, 2015).

9. See, for example, Liu Xiaobo, *No Enemies, No Hatred: Selected Essays and Poems*, ed. Perry Link, Tienchi Martin-Liao, and Liu Xia (Cambridge, MA: Harvard University Press, 2012); William A. Callahan, "Citizen Ai: Warrior, Jester, and Middleman," *Journal of Asian Studies* 73, no. 4 (November 2014): 899–920; Sebastian Veg, *Among the Silent Majority: The Rise of China's Grassroots Intellectuals* (New York: Columbia University Press, 2019).

10. See Ma Licheng, *Dangdai Zhongguo bazhong shehui sichao / Eight Social Thoughts in Contemporary China* (English title on the cover of the Chinese edition) (Beijing: Shehui Kexue Wenyi, 2012). The first half of this book has been published in English as Licheng Ma, *Leading Schools of Thought in Contemporary China* (Singapore: World Scientific, 2013).

11. Lotus Yang Ruan and Timothy Cheek, "Social Media in China: What Canadians Need to Know," *Canada-Asia Agenda*, 2016, https://www.asiapacific.ca/canada-asia-agenda /social-media-china-what-canadians-need-know.

12. Guobin Yang, *The Power of the Internet in China: Citizen Activism Online* (New York: Columbia University Press, 2009).

13. Kerry Brown, *China's Dream: The Culture of Chinese Communism and the Secret Source of Its Power* (London: Polity, 2018).

14. Christian P. Sorace, *Shaken Authority: China's Communist Party and the 2008 Sichuan Earthquake* (Ithaca, NY: Cornell University Press, 2017).

15. Veg, *Among the Silent Majority*.

16. See Ya-wen Lei, *The Contentious Public Sphere: Law, Media, and Authoritarian Rule in China* (Princeton, NJ: Princeton University Press, 2018); Kristin Shi-Kupfer, Mareike Ohlberg, Simon Lang, and Bertram Lang, "Ideas and Ideologies Competing for China's Political Future: How Online Pluralism Challenges Official Orthodoxy," *MERICS Papers on China* 5 (October 2017), https://www.merics.org/en/papers-on-china/ideas -and-ideologies-competing-chinas-political-future.

17. See Joseph Fewsmith, "Where Do Correct Ideas Come From?—The Party School, Key Think Tanks, and the Intellectuals," in *China's Leadership in the 21st Century: The Rise of the Fourth Generation*, ed. David M. Finkelstein and Maryanne Kivlehan (Armonk, NY: M. E. Sharpe, 2003), 154. This is the general thesis of Kalpana Misra's fine study *From Post-Maoism to Post-Marxism: The Erosion of Official Ideology in Deng's China* (London: Routledge, 1998).

18. Timothy Cheek, "Xu Jilin and the Thought Work of China's Public Intellectuals," *China Quarterly* 186 (2006): 404–5.

19. Gloria Davies, *Voicing Concerns: Contemporary Chinese Critical Inquiry* (Boulder, CO: Rowman and Littlefield, 2001).

20. Jun Deng and Craig A. Smith, "The Rise of New Confucianism and the Return of Spirituality to Politics in Mainland China," *China Information* 33, no. 2 (2018): 294–314.

21. See Tang Xiaobing and Mark McConaghy, "Liberalism in Contemporary China: Questions, Strategies, Directions," *China Information* 32, no. 1 (2018): 121–38; Lu Hua and Matthew Galway, "Freedom and Its Limitations: The Contemporary Mainland China Debate Over Liberalism," *China Information* 32, no. 2 (2018): 315–35.

22. Shi Anshu, François Lachapelle, and Matthew Galway, "The Recasting of Chinese Socialism: The Chinese New Left Since 2000," *China Information* 32, no. 1 (2018): 139–59.

23. See Wang Hui, *The End of the Revolution: China and the Limits of Modernity* (London: Verso, 2009), and Wang Hui, *The Politics of Imagining Asia*, trans. Theodore Huters (Cambridge, MA: Harvard University Press, 2011).

24. Li Zhiyu and Morgan Rocks, "The Sinosphere Left Looks at Rising China: Missed Dialogues and the Search for an 'Asian Perspective,'" *China Information* 32, no. 2 (2018): 336–57.

25. Cheek, *The Intellectual in Modern Chinese History*, 266.

26. John B. Judis, *The Populist Explosion: How the Great Recession Transformed American and European Politics* (New York: Columbia Global Reports, 2016).

27. Leigh Jenco and her colleagues explore efforts to address these global issues through Chinese concepts in Leigh Jenco, ed., *Chinese Thought as Global Theory: Diversifying Knowledge Production in the Social Sciences and Humanities* (Albany: State University of New York Press, 2016); see also Leigh Jenco, *Changing Referents: Learning Across Space and Time in China and the West* (Oxford: Oxford University Press, 2015).

28. This history is engagingly retold in Jonathan Spence, *The Search for Modern China* (New York: Norton, 2001). A rich selection of translations from Lu Xun and others from the May Fourth period and after are included in Wm. Theodore de Bary and Richard Lufrano, eds., *Sources of Chinese Tradition: From 1600 Through the Twentieth Century*, 2nd ed. (New York: Columbia University Press, 2001), and in Eileen J. Cheng and Kirk Denton, eds., *Jottings Under Lamplight: Lu Xun* (Cambridge, MA: Harvard University Press, 2017).

29. Ge Zhaoguang makes this clear in his devastating criticism of recent trends in Confucian thought in the PRC. See Ge Zhaoguang's essay "The Political Demands of Mainland New Confucians in Recent Years," cited in note 6.

30. A detailed introduction to Wang Hui's four-volume Chinese study is given in Zhang Yongle, "The Future of the Past: On Wang Hui's *Rise of Modern Chinese Thought*," *New Left Review* 62 (2010): 47–85.

31. Xu Jilin, *Rethinking China's Rise. Tianxiazhuyi* is a difficult term to translate—roughly meaning "universalism," but one in which the center of the universe is in China.

32. Timothy Cheek and David Ownby, "Make China Marxist Again," *Dissent* 65, no. 4 (2018): 71–77.

33. Jiang Shigong, "Zhexue yu lishi—cong dang de shijiu da baogao jiedu 'Xi Jinping shidai,'" *Kaifang Shidai* (Open times); translated in full by David Ownby as Jiang Shigong, "Philosophy and History: Interpreting the 'Xi Jinping Era' through Xi's Report to the Nineteenth National Congress of the CCP," Reading the China Dream, 2018, https://www.readingthechinadream.com/jiang-shigong-philosophy-and-history.html.

34. Cheek, *The Intellectual in Modern Chinese History*, 21.

35. See, for instance, Merle Goldman, *Literary Opposition in Communist China* (Cambridge, MA: Harvard University Press, 1967), and *China's Intellectuals: Advise and Dissent* (Cambridge, MA: Harvard University Press, 1981); John King Fairbank, *The United States and China*, 4th ed. (Cambridge, MA: Harvard University Press, 1983);

and Maurice Meisner, *Mao's China and After: A History of the People's Republic* (New York: Free Press, 1999).

36. See Bonnie S. McDougall, ed., *Popular Chinese Literature and the Performing Arts in the People's Republic of China, 1949–1976* (Berkeley: University of California Press, 1984); Carol Lee Hamrin and Timothy Cheek, eds., *China's Establishment Intellectuals* (Armonk, NY: M. E. Sharpe, 1986); Joshua A. Fogel, *Ai Ssu-ch'i's Contribution to the Development of Chinese Marxism*, Contemporary China series (Cambridge, MA: Harvard University, 1987); Bill Brugger and David Kelly, *Chinese Marxism in the Post-Mao Era* (Stanford, CA: Stanford University Press, 1990); Timothy Cheek, "From Priests to Professionals: Intellectuals and the State Under the CCP," in *Popular Protest and Political Culture in China*, ed. Jeffery Wasserstrom and Elizabeth Perry (Boulder, CO: Westview Press, 1992), 124–45; Lyman Miller, *Science and Dissent in Post-Mao China: The Politics of Knowledge* (Seattle: University of Washington Press, 1986); Timothy Cheek, *Propaganda and Culture in Mao's China: Deng Tuo and the Intelligentsia* (Oxford: Oxford University Press, 1997); and James H. Williams, "Fang Lizhi's Big Bang: A Physicist and the State in China," *Historical Studies in the Physical and Biological Sciences* 30, no. 1 (1999): 49–87.

37. Misra, *From Post-Maoism to Post-Marxism*; Min Lin and Maria Galikowski, *The Search for Modernity: Chinese Intellectuals and Cultural Discourse in the Post-Mao Era* (New York: St. Martin's Press, 1999); Geremie Barmé, "The Revolution of Resistance," in *Chinese Society: Change, Conflict, and Resistance*, ed. Elizabeth J. Perry and Mark Selden (London: Routledge, 2000), 198–220; Davies, *Voicing Concerns*; Joseph Fewsmith, *China Since Tiananmen: The Politics of Transition* (New York: Cambridge University Press, 2008); Zhang, Xudong, ed., *Whither China? Intellectual Politics in Contemporary China* (Durham, NC: Duke University Press, 2001); Zhidong Hao, *Intellectuals at a Crossroads: The Changing Politics of China's Knowledge Workers* (Albany: State University of New York Press, 2003); Chaohua Wang, ed., *One China: Many Paths* (New York: Verso, 2003); David A. Kelly, "Citizen Movements and China's Public Intellectuals in the Hu-Wen Era," *Pacific Affairs* 79, no. 2 (2006): 183–204; Gloria Davies, *Worrying About China: The Language of Chinese Critical Enquiry* (Cambridge, MA: Harvard University Press, 2007).

38. See Miller, *Science and Dissent in Post-Mao China*; Misra, *From Post-Maoism to Post-Marxism*; Wang, *One China*; Erika E. S. Evasdottir, *Obedient Autonomy: Chinese Intellectuals and the Achievement of Orderly Life* (Vancouver: University of British Columbia Press, 2004); Zhao Yuezhi, *Communication in China: Political Economy, Power, and Conflict* (Boulder, CO: Rowman and Littlefield, 2008); and William A. Callahan, *China Dreams: 20 Visions of the Future* (Oxford: Oxford University Press, 2013).

39. Tani E. Barlow, ed., *New Asian Marxisms* (Durham, NC: Duke University Press, 2002).

40. Davies, *Worrying About China*; David Ownby, "Kang Xiaoguang: Social Science, Civil Society, and Confucian Religion," *China Perspectives* 4 (2009): 101–11; Callahan, *China Dreams*; Cheek, *The Intellectual in Modern Chinese History*.

41. Robert Culp, Eddy U, and Wen-hsin Yeh, eds., *Knowledge Acts in Modern China: Ideas, Institutions, and Identities* (Berkeley: Institute of East Asian Studies, University of California, 2016).

42. See Jenco, *Changing Referents*, and Michaelle L. Browers, *Democracy and Civil Society in Arab Political Thought: Transcultural Possibilities* (Syracuse, NY: Syracuse University Press, 2006).

43. Ma Licheng, *Dangdai Zhongguo*; Licheng Ma, *Leading Schools of Thought*.

44. The Chinese edition of Ma Licheng's book *Dangdai Zhongguo*, but not the English version, also includes a section of scholarly reflections on these eight strains of social thought and a selection of five essays by noted academic public intellectuals Ge Zhaoguang, Xiao Gongqin, Xu Youyu, Wang Di, and Zhao Fusan.

45. He Li, *Political Thought and China's Transformation: Ideas Shaping Reform in Post-Mao China* (New York: Palgrave, 2015).

46. See the essays in "Mapping the Intellectual Public Sphere in China Today," the special section of *China Information* cited in note 2.

47. Sang Ye, *China Candid: The People on the People's Republic*, ed. Geremie Barmé, with Miriam Lang (Berkeley: University of California Press, 2006).

48. Judy Polumbaum, with Xiong Lei, *China Ink: The Changing Face of Chinese Journalism* (Lanham, MD: Rowman and Littlefield, 2008); Angilee Shah and Jeffrey Wasserstrom, eds., *Chinese Characters: Profiles of Fast-Changing Lives in a Fast-Changing Land* (Berkeley: University of California Press, 2012).

49. Mark Leonard, *What Does China Think?* (New York: PublicAffairs, 2008); Yu Hua, *China in Ten Words*, trans. Allan H. Barr (New York: Pantheon Books, 2011).

50. See Geremie Barmé, "New Sinology," *Chinese Studies Association of Australia Newsletter* 31 (May 2005), http://ciw.anu.edu.au/new_sinology/index.php; Geremie Barmé, "Worrying China and New Sinology," *China Heritage Quarterly* 14 (2008), http://www.chinaheritagequarterly.org/articles.php?searchterm=014_worryingChina.inc&issue=014.

51. Davies, *Voicing Concerns*, 87–108.

52. Gail Hershatter, *The Gender of Memory: Rural Women and China's Collective Past* (Berkeley: University of California Press, 2011).

PART I

THE CHALLENGE

CHAPTER 1

"UNIFYING THE THREE TRADITIONS" IN THE NEW ERA[1]

GAN YANG

TRANSLATION BY DAVID OWNBY

Translator's Introduction

Although Gan Yang (b. 1952) has published sparingly compared to figures such as Wang Hui (b. 1959) and Xu Jilin (b. 1957), he is a major figure in the thought world of contemporary China, known both for the ideas he has espoused and for his efforts at institution building. He first came to prominence during the "culture fever" (*wenhua re*) of the 1980s as the chief editor of the influential book series Wenhua: Zhongguo yu shijie (Culture: China in the World), which made available hundreds of volumes of translations of Western thought and philosophy to Chinese readers.[2] Gan himself studied Western philosophy, first at Peking University and subsequently at the University of Chicago. He is currently dean of the Boya Institute at Zhongshan University in Guangzhou and holds concurrent positions at Tsinghua University and other institutions.

Gan's intellectual orientation has evolved over the years. His engagement with the China in the World series gives the impression that he was a westernizing Liberal in the 1980s, but as he explains in the text translated here, he sees the West not as a model to be followed or imported, but as a body of historical experiences and institutional experiments that China should learn from but only selectively copy, if at all. Gan also identifies with many of the stances of China's New Left, as illustrated by William Sima and Tang Xiaobing's translation of his essay "Liberalism: For the Aristocrats or for the People?" in chapter 10, in which Gan's preference for mass democracy is clear. Gan also embraces a certain cultural conservatism, as illustrated by his discussion of "unifying the three traditions" in the text translated here, which on occasion positions him close to China's New Confucians. In the preface to the volume from which this translation is drawn, Gan includes a long discussion of Kang Youwei (1858–1927) and Kang's efforts to imagine a future world where Confucian civilization would be part of a new universal modernity. Studies of Kang have subsequently become a staple of the mainland New Confucian repertoire, insisting that Kang, rather than Sun Yat-sen or Mao Zedong, should be seen as the architect of modern China.[3]

Compared with the bombastic tone of many authors touting the "China model" today, the tone of Gan's text recalls an era when Chinese were more modest about their accomplishments and their heritage. Yet despite its simplicity and its lack of scholarly flourish, this text on "unifying the three traditions" has had an immense impact on the evolution of much of the Chinese thought world in the period since China's rise. Gan argues that the task before China is to effect the merging of the "three traditions" that undergird China's modern experience: the Confucian tradition (elitism, affective personal and local relationships), the Maoist tradition (equality and justice), and the Dengist tradition (markets and competition). Gan's argument is essentially conservative in the sense that he believes that China needs to find a new equilibrium after a century of revolution. Appropriately, his idea of merging the three traditions draws on Confucian discourse concerning the evolution of China's classical civilization: the "unification" of the varied historical experiences of the Xia, Shang, and Zhou dynasties over the course of the three millennia before China's first political unification under Qin Shihuang (259–210 BCE). The argument, first advanced by the Confucian scholar Dong Zhongshu (179–104 BCE) in the Western Han period, is that despite important differences in terms of culture and institutions and in spite of the violence that marked dynastic transitions, rulers of the successive dynasties sought out continuities linking one regime to another, which the Zhou kings crystallized into an institutional and ritual order that laid the framework for centuries of enduring, stable Confucian rule.

One may question the accuracy of this origin myth. After all, China did not become thoroughly Confucian until the Song dynasty, more than a thousand years after the end of the Zhou period, and thinkers such as Qin Hui (b. 1953) have argued that the basic institutional wiring of China's classical political order was more Legalist than Confucian.[4] But Gan's argument speaks to a powerful yearning within contemporary Chinese culture to find peace with itself and with its past. He argues, in essence, that Chinese do not have to choose between market efficiency and social justice or between being modern and being Chinese. All they need is the creativity and imagination to rethink China's recent historical experience in the light of China's imminent return to great-power status.

It seems obvious that "unifying the three traditions" cannot occur without ignoring the manifest discontinuities that make up modern Chinese history, but Gan's proposal electrified the Chinese thought world, and Liberals, New Confucians, and New Leftists began to experiment with the basic periodization of modern and contemporary Chinese history in search of a new formulation that would restore continuity to China's modern experience. In the process, scholars added and subtracted "traditions" as they sought to fill in the details of Gan's original template and build their arguments for the kind of state and society they would like China to become. The most audacious among them, such as the mainland New Confucian Chen Ming (b. 1962), basically ignored China's socialist tradition in their pursuit of a "Confucian interpretation of the China dream."[5] The liberal constitutional scholar Gao Quanxi (b. 1962) built his argument around key "constitutional moments" in modern and contemporary Chinese history that are leading to the establishment of a postrevolutionary order.[6] Scholarly enthusiasm for recasting the foundational myths of modern and contemporary China over the past decade has ultimately produced a backlash, however. Gan Yang himself has scolded mainland New Confucians for their overly ardent embrace of Kang Youwei,[7] and the legal scholar Jiang Shigong (b. 1967), in what looks to be an authoritative essay issued in 2018 and linked to Xi Jinping's efforts to reimpose ideological uniformity on China's thought world, brings the three traditions back onto orthodox ground, identifying them as Mao Zedong's tradition, in which China stood up; Deng Xiaoping's tradition, in which China got rich; and Xi Jinping's tradition, in which China is becoming powerful.[8]

It is too early to tell if Xi Jinping's attempts to control China's narrative will succeed or if the efforts by Chinese intellectuals to rethink China's recent past and future will continue. (One might note that Xi himself has on varying occasions embraced Gan's three traditions.) In any event, Gan Yang's essay on "unifying the three traditions" stands as one of the most influential texts shaping intellectual currents in the age of rising China.

"Unifying the Three Traditions" in the New Era: The Merging of Three Chinese Traditions

(Lecture presented at Tsinghua University on May 12, 2005)

The Coexistence of Three Traditions in Contemporary China

At present, we can identify three traditions in China. One is the tradition that has taken shape after twenty-five years of reform. Although this is not a lengthy tradition, many ideas and terms that have grown out of reform and opening are already deeply impressed on the people's minds and have entered into the daily language of the Chinese people, basically becoming a kind of tradition. This tradition has, for the most part, grown out of the "market" and includes many concepts with which we all are familiar today, such as freedom and rights. Another tradition began with the establishment of the People's Republic and took form during the Mao Zedong era. This is a tradition characterized particularly by its emphasis on equality and justice. It is clear today that from the mid- to late-1990s the Maoist tradition of equality has been quite powerful, and beginning in the mid-1990s there has been a great deal of discussion of the Mao era. Ten years earlier, this would have seemed impossible, but the Maoist tradition of equality has become a powerful tradition in contemporary China. Finally, of course, there is also the tradition of Chinese civilization, forged over thousands of years. This is what we often call "traditional Chinese culture" or "Confucian culture." It is often difficult to describe traditional Chinese culture, but in the everyday life of the Chinese people it is basically expressed, to put it simply, in terms of interpersonal relationships and ties of locality. This can be seen very clearly in many current television dramas in today's China, especially those focusing on the family or on marriage and divorce.

The coexistence of these three traditions is a unique feature of Chinese society, particularly on the Chinese mainland. If we make a comparison with Hong Kong society, we note that it has the first tradition (the tradition of markets and freedom) as well as the third tradition (highly developed sensitivity to interpersonal relations and ties of locality), but it lacks the second tradition, a tradition with a strong emphasis on "equality." For this reason, even if Hong Kong is a highly unequal society, and even if many people are working to relieve this inequality, the problem of inequality has never provoked an intense ideological conflict. From another perspective, if we make a comparison with the United States, it has the first two traditions, with a strong emphasis on both freedom and equality—in fact, we might say that the tension between these two traditions constitutes the basic national character of the United States—but America does not have the third tradition and thus pays less attention to interpersonal relationships and locality ties and especially lacks the cultural traditions and cultural psychology that lie behind China's third tradition.

Yet we often observe in discussions in contemporary China that these three traditions seem to be placed in a position of mutual opposition. Some people will particularly emphasize one tradition while rejecting the others. Everyone has surely felt that Chinese society since the 1990s has been full of debate and that these debates have come to influence even people's individual lives. Good friends whose relationships go back for decades suddenly have opposing viewpoints, and when the divergences become important, the friendship is threatened, which leaves everyone hurt. This is because in some of these larger debates, in particular those concerning the Mao era, differences of opinion are significant, and the debates easily become emotional.

The topic of today's lecture, "the uniting of the three traditions and the revival of Chinese civilization," is based on an interview published at the end of 2004 in *Ershiyi Shiji Jingji Baodao* (Economic reporting on the twenty-first century). In that interview, I talked in premature and simplistic terms about my view that today we need a new understanding of the linkages and continuity between the success of reform and opening and the Mao era as well as a new understanding of the foundational role that traditional Chinese history and civilization have played in modern China. The main point of my talk today is to emphasize that the Confucian tradition, the Mao Zedong tradition, and the Deng Xiaoping tradition all belong to a unified continuity in China's history and civilization. To use the terms of the *Gongyang* tradition,[9] we need to "unify the three traditions" of the new age.

What Is "the Problem of Chinese Culture?"

It seems that most people today can readily accept a positive vision of China's traditional culture or that even if there are differences of opinion, these differences don't necessarily lead to fights that hurt people's feelings. But this is something that has evolved only over the past two or three years, and in the past discussions of traditional Chinese culture often led to violent disagreements.

The reason for this is that behind the problem of Chinese culture in fact lies the problem of the opposition of Chinese and Western culture. What you say about Chinese culture reveals what you think about Western culture and often contains a hidden comparison of China and the West, which speaks to the debate between Chinese and Western culture that has raged incessantly across the entire twentieth century. In the 1980s, Chinese intellectuals were most worked up about the so-called culture fever (*wenhua re*), which in fact was nothing more than yet another "debate about Chinese and Western culture." The good thing about the debate in the 1980s was that it led contemporary Chinese intellectuals back to the problem of Chinese tradition that had agonized Chinese intellectuals from late-Qing times onward. This problem reflected "changes unprecedented in three thousand years,"[10] the fact that beginning in the late Qing all of Chinese civilization disintegrated, completely fell apart, including not only the political system and the economic system but also the cultural and educational institutions, which meant that beginning in the twentieth century Chinese intellectuals, whether studying China or the West, consistently invoked the West as their authority. They might mention Confucius but would never cite him as an authority. This seems to have started to change over the past few years, and at the end of 2004 *Nanfang Zhoumo* (Southern weekend) and other mainland periodicals asserted that 2004 was the year of the return of traditional culture.

This year marks the centenary of the abolition of the Confucian examination system. People today have a hard time imagining what the abolition of the exams meant, what kind of attack the abolition was on Chinese intellectuals of the period. By way of comparison, imagine today's Tsinghua students, who tested into middle school from primary school, from middle school to high school, and from high school into university. What if when you graduated, there was an announcement saying that everything you had studied to that point was useless, that your studies were not going to help you find a job? What would you think? You would surely go crazy, and some would surely think about jumping off a building. The shock would be that great. Can you imagine this sort of attack? The disintegration of Chinese society at the time was thorough and comprehensive.

What was the examination system? Today's Chinese are used to thinking about the examination system dismissively. But at the simplest level, the examination system was a basic mechanism for the reproduction of the elite system of Chinese society as a whole. In traditional China, in theory all students could take the exams. Of course, not many would make the top (*jinshi*) level, but all students would think about taking the exams, and at a subconscious level they would identify with the thought and the lifestyle of the Chinese traditional elites. So even if you did not become a *jinshi*, you were still part of China's elite. And you could keep trying year after year; in the traditional Chinese exam system there was no age limit, so you could keep trying until you were in your seventies or eighties. Sometimes, even if you still failed, the emperor would be impressed by your age and would grant you a *jinshi*. Why? So that China's latent elite would always have hope; it functioned to maintain the reproduction of the elite system. From its beginnings in the Sui-Tang period, the examination system endured for at least thirteen hundred years and was traditional China's most basic political-cultural mechanism.

The abolition of the examination system in the late Qing simply meant the thorough collapse and disintegration of the entirety of the traditional Chinese political-cultural mechanism. With its collapse, China faced the vast mission of reorganizing its society. For a society like this to establish a new set of mechanisms is no easy task. In the West, the transition from tradition to modernity required several centuries, while in China only a century or so has transpired since the Qing collapsed. We today are still living this transition, and we must see the entire process, from the late-Qing collapse through the Chinese revolution and reform, as a continuous process whose goal is the search for a new continuity on which to base modern China.

Familiarity Is Not True Knowledge

The American Joshua Ramo [b. 1968, vice chairman and co-chief executive of Kissinger Associates] recently coined the concept of the "Beijing Consensus" and argued that it had already displaced the "Washington Consensus."[11] The concrete details of his argument are debatable, but the point of his initiative is to remind us that understanding China is extremely difficult and requires going beyond popular clichés. From the Western perspective, the biggest problem of the twenty-first century is China. China is a problem for the West because the West has already ruled the world for several centuries, and the Western-dominated world has created a certain number of norms and procedures. Today's China is like someone who just crashed the party, which has led the entire system to waver. What is to be done? What will China be like in the future? No one knows. Two or three months ago, the *Boston Globe* published an editorial criticizing the American secretary of defense, who in an interview made the following very interesting remark about China: "We pray that China will enter the civilized world in a well-behaved manner." The editorial in the *Boston Globe* took exception and at the outset of the piece noted that China has three thousand years of history as a civilized nation, whereas America has been established for only a little more than two hundred years. The civilization you are talking about has been around for more than three thousand years, and yet you treat China like a country from beyond the bounds of civilization and hope that it will enter the civilized world in a well-behaved manner? The editorial advised Americans to study Chinese history and noted that China is reviving the glory and greatness that characterized her in the past. I, of course, consider that the *Boston Globe* editorial had a lot of insight.

But the problem is that many people in China look at China in the same way as the American defense secretary. Opinions have circulated in China in recent years with which I do not agree. For example, many in the media say that "China must enter the mainstream of international civilized society," by which they mean that Chinese people should see themselves as barbarians and that they need to completely remake themselves to "enter mainstream civilized society." For this reason, since the 1990s there has been a kind of attitude that believes that the basis of legitimacy in China should not come from China herself, but rather from Western acknowledgment. It used to be that the United States was the United States and China was China, but sometimes Chinese take the side of the Americans and argue until they are blue in the face. What has brought this about? I think it is because a fair number of Chinese think that China should stand with the United States on everything, that if America attacks Iraq, China should naturally follow along, or, to put it more generally, their overall goal in all things is to make the West happy—and especially to avoid upsetting the United States. But I think there have been positive developments on this front in recent years. In other words, more and more Chinese people have begun to understand that there are many instances in which China has no way to satisfy the West, no way to always make it happy—unless we want to surrender completely. For example, all of a sudden all the Western countries are talking about the problem of the Chinese currency, the Renminbi (RMB). I don't know whether the RMB should be devalued, but this should be something that Chinese people decide for themselves, something that Chinese people will decide based on their own interests. Another example is that everyone talks about the World Trade Organization (WTO) and free trade, but at the same time the United States and Europe use their own laws to limit imports of Chinese fabrics. Compare this to China. China followed the rules, and after entering the WTO China engaged in domestic propaganda telling Chinese companies that they had to be ready to face the competition. But other countries use their own laws to impose quotas on Chinese fabrics. We seemed to think that once we were in the WTO, these questions would be regulated by the WTO and that it was completely out of our hands. Only China was naive enough to believe that international organizations were bigger than the Chinese government, while all Americans know that their government is bigger than any international organization. When did the United States ever pay attention to international law or international organizations?

There are two kinds of people in the West. One is fond of China and admits that if Chinese economic growth has reached a certain level by 2020, then by 2030 it might be second only to the United States. The other sees China as always on the verge of collapse, citing any number of Western theories and any number of Chinese problems—for example, the notion that China's GINI coefficient [a common statistical measure of inequality] has been in dangerous territory for some time now or maybe the current crisis in raw materials. Yet I never care that much if Westerners are well meaning or not; all that matters is the basis of their judgment. The complexity of things at the present time resides in the fact that almost anything you can say about China has some basis in fact. We should not think that because we are Chinese, we have a better understanding of China. I don't think that we do, or at least I really don't. Part of this has to do with my academic specialty, which is to study the West. When I was at Peking University, I studied Western philosophy, and when I was in the United States, I spent most of my time studying the West. While I was there, I was always afraid that someone would ask me about China because I really didn't understand China. This isn't false modesty because I feel that I understand certain things, but not China. Looking at China from the Western perspective, it is truly hard to understand China. I urge everyone to be a bit more modest and not to think that you understand China just because you are Chinese. Of course, we know a lot of things about China, but it's like what Hegel said: "What is 'familiarly known' is not properly known, precisely for the reason that it is familiar."[12] Why? Because you think you know the matter well, you don't look further into the "why" of the matter, which means that you really don't understand.

Regarding China, I could ask a lot of questions that those in the audience would not necessarily be able to answer. For example, in the course of twenty-five years of reform and opening, Chinese results have been quite extraordinary, but I have yet to find an entirely satisfactory explanation for this. In fact, from the early 1980s through the early 1990s, no one in the Western academy approved of China's economic reform. The reason is simple. They quite naturally felt that if the economic reforms in the Soviet Union and eastern Europe did not succeed, then why would they succeed in China? Especially inasmuch as the Soviet Union was ahead of China in terms of industrialization, modernization, and education, her agricultural population was also less than China's, and overall living standards were higher than China's. For example, Western scholars discovered that in 1978 the average educational level of China's factory heads or managers was a ninth- to eleventh-grade level. Ninth grade is middle school. Eleventh grade is still high school level because twelve years are required to graduate. And in the Soviet Union at the time, the managers were uniformly college graduates. And comparisons of living standards between China and the Soviet Union and eastern Europe were even less flattering to China. When I first arrived in the United States, I had a friend from Yugoslavia. At the time, all the various regions of Yugoslavia had proclaimed their independence, and war was everywhere. My friend was from Sarajevo, and after visiting China for three or four months, he told me that China was rising and Yugoslavia falling, but that China still had a long way to go to catch up with Yugoslavia. It's easy to imagine their sense of superiority and pride. In the 1980s, most Chinese homes had no telephones, to say nothing of cars. Yet in the Soviet Union and eastern Europe, electrical appliances and cars had long since been part of daily life. From a commonsense standpoint, all Western countries reasoned that since they all were centrally planned economies, then why would China's reforms work when those of the Soviet Union and eastern Europe did not? This is a very natural way to think. In the West, everyone thought that if the economic reforms in the Soviet Union and eastern Europe had succeeded as they did in China, then the subsequent collapse would not have occurred. It was because the reforms did not work that the collapse was so comprehensive.

We all know that China's reforms started in 1978, yet throughout the entire decade of the 1980s economic reforms were not the chief subject of concern from China's intellectuals, who were instead focused on thought and culture, including what was called the "culture fever" of the 1980s. We know now that the Chinese economy grew at an annual rate of 10 percent during the 1980s, but those of us living in China at the time did not notice it, didn't know it, weren't aware of it. I don't think it was just me, but rather that no intellectual who lived through the 1980s noticed that the economy had taken off. It was the West that started talking about a Chinese take-off, which was reported for the first time in 1992, probably on the front page of the *New York Times* in September of that year based on a report by the World Bank and accompanied by a big picture. We all were surprised when we saw it because prior to that point all discussions about China were about when it would fall apart. Western scholars also said that China's economy not only had grown by 10 percent a year during the 1980s but also had maintained a high rate of growth from 1949 through the beginning of the Cultural Revolution, although during that period most of the gains were reinvested in the economy instead of being distributed to the people. Everyone who heard this for the first time was stunned because it seemed as if those living in China didn't understand China as well as the Westerners did.

Conclusion

The questions I have tried to raise today suggest that we need to reenvision China. Perhaps our understanding of China is only at the beginning. We must understand it anew. This includes why these twenty-five years of reform have achieved such great results. We need to understand it all anew. We need a new understanding of the connections and continuities between the achievements of reform and the Mao era and of the foundational role that traditional Chinese history and civilization have played in modern China. Today we must emphasize that the tradition of Confucius, the tradition of Mao Zedong, and the tradition of Deng Xiaoping are part of the continuous whole of Chinese history and civilization. To borrow the language of China's old *Gongyang* school, we should "unify the three traditions" (*tong san tong*) for the new era.

In sum, the greatest challenge of the twenty-first century is the need to come to a new understanding of China, an understanding that can be based only on comparison with other countries. There is one point on which I hope I won't be misunderstood. I do not agree with those who argue that now we can completely ignore the West and simply study China from a Chinese perspective. I have long emphasized that to deeply study China one must first study the West. This is because in reality we live today in a Western-dominated globalized world. The West's influence is everywhere. So, a very important part of studying China is studying the West. Only when we deeply study the West can we develop the ability to be discriminating.

First of all, we must understand that in reality over the past century we all have used Western perspectives to look at China. Marxism is also Western. Since the early twentieth century, Chinese judgments of China are in fact implicit judgments of the West. These comparisons have dominated all twentieth-century discussions about China. There is nothing inherently wrong with comparison. The problem is that many people who think they understand things base themselves on unreliable premises. People who blather on at length about the West often know little about it. After we achieve a deep understanding of the West, we will be able to see that so much of what Chinese say about the West reflects that they do not know what they are talking about. The West is not so superficial. It's easy to spout sloganistic Western ideological discourse, like people who champion democracy. This requires no particular intelligence. But to deeply understand the West is no simple or easy matter. Even Westerners themselves do not necessarily understand the West, in the same way that I have argued today that Chinese do not necessarily understand China. To understand the West or to understand China requires the expenditure of a great deal of effort.

In fact, not many Chinese really understand the West, and plenty manage to make a hash of it. But the truth is that today everybody takes the West as a reference, which is as it should be. The problem is how precisely to go about it. For example, today it is 2005. Should our reference point be the West in 2005? Should the reform of Peking University in 2003 be based on the newest and most recent methods of Harvard University? This sort of sloppy so-called following of international practices is suspect. It can easily become an ignorant and mindless reference point that ignores Western history. My personal opinion is that the Western reference point most worthy of consideration for today's China is either England of around 1800 or America around 1900. These two periods more resemble the China of around 2000. At the turn of the nineteenth century, England's Industrial Revolution had produced a huge transformation of English social structure. From 1780, there was huge economic growth on the one hand and on the other a large divergence of rich and poor along with sharpening social contradictions. We need to understand how England, at this turning point of its own modern transformation, resolved the sharp social differentiation and conflicts that accompany modern economic development. In addition, there is America at the turn of the twentieth century. Strictly speaking, after the Civil War, from around 1870 to 1930, America had its own modern transformation. Both its economy and society underwent huge changes, likewise experiencing high-speed economic growth as well as huge social differentiation and conflicts. All of these conditions greatly resemble ours at the present day, including various social movements that violently criticized America's New Rich. The social contradictions and conflicts of this transformation continued down to the 1930s, when Roosevelt's "New Deal" created a new social and political order. The "New Deal" was something most people from various parts of society could accept, a product of compromise, and even if some people remained unsatisfied, the New Deal established a basic social consensus. Many of the practices employed by England and America at the turning point of their own modern transformation are worthy reference points for us. Only when our understanding of and reference to the West proceed from our own questions can we know which aspects are profitable for us. For this reason, we should not set up the study of China and the study of the West in opposition to each other. Rather, we should more deeply and more broadly study the West. We should study the West on a large scale and deeply study the entire history of the West because in any event the West influences us in many areas, influences our thinking. Only when we have trained a great number of people who truly understand the West deeply will we be able to get past the false understanding of many so-called experts. This is why it is so important for the study of China to deeply study the West.

Translator's Notes

1. Gan Yang, "Xin shidai de 'tong san tong': Zhongguo sanzhong chuantong de rong-hui" ("Unifying the three traditions" in the new era: The merging of three Chinese traditions), in *Tong san tong* (Unifying the three traditions) (Beijing: Sanlian Shudian, 2007), 1–13, 45–49. This extract includes the first two sections and the conclusion of the book's long first chapter and focuses on Gan's influential thesis of the "three traditions" in modern China.

2. On the "culture fever," see Xudong Zhang, "On Some Motifs in the 'Cultural Fever' of the Late 1980s: Social Change, Ideology, and Theory," *Social Text* 39 (Summer 1994): 129–56; and Chen Fong-ching and Jin Guantao, *Youthful Manuscripts to River Elegy: The Chinese Popular Cultural Movement and Political Transformation, 1979–1989* (Hong Kong: Chinese University Press, 1997).

3. Among many studies of Kang Youwei, see Zeng Yi, "Cong Kang Youwei dao Deng Xiaoping" (From Kang Youwei to Deng Xiaoping), *Tianfu xinlun* 6 (2016), https://sns.91ddcc.com/b/45992, available in translation at Reading the China Dream, https://www.readingthechinadream.com/kang-xiaowei-to-deng-xiaoping.html; and Gan Yang, Qiu Feng, Chen Ming, Chen Bisheng, Liu Xiaofeng, et al., "Kang Youwei yu zhiduhua Ruxue" (Kang Youwei and institutionalized Confucianism), transcription of a round-table discussion, Ai Sixiang Wang, November 2014, http://www.aisixiang.com/data/79543.html, available in translation at Reading the China Dream, https://www.readingthechinadream.com/kang-youwei-and-institutional-confucianism.html.

4. Qin Hui, "Zhongguo wenhua zuida de wenti shi biao-Ru li-Fa" (China's greatest cultural problem is that it is outwardly Confucian but inwardly Legalist), January 2010, http://finance.sina.com.cn/hy/20100116/18207257091.shtml.

5. See Chen Ming, "Transcend Left and Right, Unite the Three Traditions, Renew the Party-State: A Confucian Interpretation of the China Dream," Reading the China Dream, 2015, https://www.readingthechinadream.com/chen-ming-transcend-left-and-right.html.

6. See Gao Quanxi, Zhang Wei, and Tian Feilong, *The Road to the Rule of Law in Modern China* (Berlin: Springer, 2015); Gao Quanxi, "The Political Maturity of Chinese Liberalism," Reading the China Dream, 2012, https://www.readingthechinadream.com/gao-quanxi-political-maturity.html.

7. See Gan's opening comments in Gan Yang et al., "Kang Youwei yu zhiduhua Ruxue."

8. See Jiang Shigong, "Philosophy and History: Interpreting the 'Xi Jinping Era' through Xi's Report to the Nineteenth National Congress of the CCP," Reading the China Dream, 2018, https://www.readingthechinadream.com/jiang-shigong-philosophy-and -history.html.

9. The *Gongyang*, or *Gongyang zhuan*, is a commentary on the *Spring and Autumn Annals*, a work classically attributed to Confucius, in which Confucius appears to be a visionary reformer. The commentary belongs to what are known as "New Texts" in the history of Confucianism, texts that were recompiled (and hence "new") by early Han-period scholars who survived the Qin dynasty and the burning of the original Confucian classics. The New Texts fell out of favor with the fall of the Han dynasty but were revived by Confucian scholars of the Ming and Qing eras as part of a movement against the perceived sterility of Song-period Neo-Confucianism. See Benjamin A. Elman, *Classicism, Politics, and Kingship: The Chang-chou School of New Text Confucianism in Late Imperial China* (Berkeley: University of California Press, 1990). In China's modern period, the *Gongyang* has been used by Confucians, such as Kang Youwei and the contemporary mainland New Confucian Jiang Qing, who are dedicated to profound political change.

10. A remark attributed to the nineteenth-century Chinese statesman Li Hongzhang (1823–1901), which is often cited to suggest the magnitude of the changes China faced in the modern era.

11. On Joshua Ramo and the Beijing Consensus, see Shaun Breslin, "The 'China Model and the Global Crisis': From Friedrich List to a Chinese Mode of Governance," *International Affairs* 87, no. 6 (2011): 1323–43, http://www.chinaelections.org/uploadfile /200909/20090918021638239.pdf.

12. G. W. F. Hegel, preface to *Phenomenology of Mind* (1807), https://www.marxists.org /reference/archive/hegel/works/ph/phprefac.htm.

PART II

LIBERAL VOICES

CHAPTER 2

LIBERALISM IN THE CHINESE CONTEXT[1]

LIU QING

TRANSLATION BY MATTHEW GALWAY AND LU HUA

Translators' Introduction

L
iu Qing (b. 1963) is professor of political science at East China
Normal University and a leading liberal public intellectual in
China. Born in Shanghai, Liu spent much of his youth in Xinjiang
and returned to Shanghai for university, where he earned degrees in chemical
engineering before turning to the social sciences. In the 1990s, he studied Western political thought in the United States, obtaining an MA from Marquette
University and a PhD from the University of Minnesota. Before joining the faculty of East China Normal University in 2003, Liu was a research associate in
the Institute of Chinese Studies at the Chinese University of Hong Kong as well
as coeditor of the well-known Hong Kong magazine *Ershiyi Shiji* (Twenty-first
century).

The defense of liberalism Liu offers in the text translated here is part of a
broader liberal response to the challenges posed by the success of "China's rise."
Most post-Mao Chinese Liberals imagined the ultimate conclusion of "reform
and opening" to be some form of democracy, which would complement the
market economy. The shock of the collapse of the Soviet Union in 1991 and Russia's subsequent struggles to implant either democracy or free markets sparked
fierce debates between Chinese Liberals and the New Left and sapped the
Liberals of their original confidence in China's democratic future. China's
rise—and the West's apparent decline—in the early twenty-first century moved
the terms of the debate even further. Easy assumptions about the inevitability

of democratic politics or the relevance of "universal values" gave way to a chest-thumping pride in the "China model" and "Chinese solutions," wherein democracy was either condemned (as corrupt) or redefined (as "responsive-ness") by mainland New Confucians and China's New Left. China's Liberals now had trouble arguing that history was on their side.

Chinese Liberals have addressed this problem in various ways. Xu Jilin (b. 1957) offers frank and penetrating criticisms of the statist and historicist arguments that have accompanied China's rise but also attempts a liberal reappropriation of Confucianism as part of a reimagined Chinese "civil reli-gion" and a new Chinese world order.[2] Gao Quanxi (b. 1962) argues that China has little or no liberal tradition beyond knee-jerk calls for Isaiah Berlin's "neg-ative freedom" and implores like-thinking colleagues to devote themselves anew to liberal state creation (or nation building), the historical narrative of liberalism (or storytelling), and the construction of liberal agency (or engaged liberal citizenship).[3]

Liu Qing's argument is both theoretically sophisticated and refreshingly direct. Taking aim at cultural nationalists such as the mainland New Confu-cians, he notes that Western thought and institutions, despite their "foreign" origins, have become part and parcel of Chinese life since the mid–nineteenth century, to the point that any notion of "returning" to a state of "pure Chinese-ness" is at best fanciful. This means, of course, that China's sociopolitical order is neither "Western" nor "liberal," but instead pluralistic, a pluralism that has grown exponentially over the course of the reform-and-opening period. Liu's argument is not that China must necessarily become a liberal democracy, but that of all the choices facing China today, only liberalism can protect the plu-ral social order that is now the norm.

At the same time, Liu also acknowledges liberalism's limitations: its "thin engagement" with cultural and ethical issues, its somewhat naive faith in human rationality. He uses the example of the massive cultural activities that accom-pany the Chinese New Year to probe the notion that all societies possess cul-tural values that go beyond the procedural norms of liberalism and that deserve to be preserved and defended as a part of the history of any civilization. Thus, compared to the "liberal" thinkers of the May Fourth era, who condemned superstition and backwardness, Liu Qing has in a sense come full circle. Liber-alism, he insists, is a necessary protection against any kind of modernity gone astray.

Liberalism in the Chinese Context: Potential and Predicaments

We live in a time of great changes and face many complex theoretical problems: How do we understand the problems of present-day Chinese society? How might we find a path for China's future development? Chinese intellectual circles have formulated many competing perspectives on these questions that draw from different intellectual traditions. At present, three schools of thought (in the broad sense) are most influential: socialism, liberalism, and Confucian theory. In the debates over China's future, each of these schools should marshal its reasons to demonstrate why their particular tradition of thought and its aims are both desirable and feasible for China's future development.

This article explores the potential of liberalism in the Chinese context and some of the dilemmas that it has encountered, offering both an argument in its defense and a critical reflection on it. In contrast to contemporary liberal discourse, the starting point of this paper neither assumes the universality of human nature or civilization nor presumes that liberalism is superior because it better accords with basic human nature and universal civilization. At the level of theory, a universalist discourse involves complex metaphysical arguments (on which this article does not take a position). In practice, however, liberalism is often the product of the hegemony of Western knowledge and ideology over China. This article defends a particular form of liberalism by arguing that the desirability and feasibility of liberalism do not originate from an "end of history" teleology or from external pressures (the so-called Western model). Rather, the desirability and feasibility of liberalism derive from China's contemporary social and cultural context and its own historical experience. At the same time, this article reflects on the challenges that liberalism faces in the Chinese context. Instead of examining the specific theoretical principles and propositions of Chinese liberalism (although related), we seek to uncover the relationship between liberalism and contemporary China's cultural context and to explore the feasibility of and potential challenges to Chinese liberalism. Our ultimate goal is to propose some preliminary thoughts on the possibility of liberalism's future development in China.

Chinese Tradition Under Critical Contextualism

Liberalism has often been viewed [in China] as an extrinsic "Western thought," and its relevance to Chinese tradition and realities is not self-evident. Accordingly, we examine first the relationship between external thought and the Chinese context. We agree with the broad sense of contextualist claims and seek to maintain a high degree of sensitivity toward the interrelation between intellectual discourse and its social context. In China studies, scholars are also generally inclined to accept the argument that "outside ideas and concepts should be examined in the context of Chinese culture." This is correct in a general sense in that it displays sensitivity to Chinese historical tradition and culture. But many popular contextualist studies are subject to a theoretical blind spot in that they posit a fixed, clearly defined boundary between "foreign thought" and "Chinese context." Scholars often use the metaphor of a "transplant," whereby they compare the influence of foreign ideas on Chinese culture to the cultivation of foreign plants outside their native country (the plant's survival depending entirely on whether it can adapt to local soil conditions). However, contextualist interpretations only grasp one part of the truth about cultural practice. The other, overlooked part is that the line between "external thought" and "Chinese context" is not fixed, clear, or self-evident. This is because foreign ideas may flow into a local culture such as China's and later change its cultural setting, ultimately becoming part of the setting itself. If we borrow the "transplant" metaphor, then we can say that plants from foreign lands, whether they struggle or flourish, are likely to change the local soil conditions. This also means that the success or failure of the previous "transplant" does not determine the fate of future "transplants."

For this reason, we argue that understanding cultural practice requires a more reflexive contextualist perspective, which we call "critical contextualism."[4] In this view, cultural traditions do not have an eternal nature because any culture contains within it a series of internal tensions between "core and periphery," "unity and diversity," "internal and external," and "continuity and rupture," among others. Such tensions may be the impetus for the development of cultural change, but they may also cause a cultural tradition to fall into crises under particular conditions. In terms of contemporary China studies, critical contextualism opposes all reductionist theses that, in defining the distinctive nature of the indigenous Chinese context, would reduce Chinese culture to traditional culture, traditional culture to Confucian culture, and Confucian culture to the Confucian classics. Such understandings of cultural backgrounds may represent a form of "contextualism," but they lack genuine sensitivity to the Chinese context and often fall into the "traditional/modern" and "China/ West" binaries or subscribe to the essentialist "myth of Chineseness." For this reason, such arguments cannot grasp dialectically the inherent tensions and complexities of cultural practice and fail to handle appropriately the mutually structured relationship between indigenous context and foreign ideas.

In this sense, an emphasis on the uniqueness of Chinese traditional culture cannot translate into an appropriate understanding of the contemporary Chinese cultural context. What the late Qing scholar-official Li Hongzhang [1823–1901] called "great changes unprecedented in three thousand years" suggested that China was then experiencing a transcivilizational, historical transformation. In the following century, at least two types of ideological discourse that originated from outside China—Marxism (socialism) and liberalism—had transformative effects on traditional Chinese culture. The former, Marxism, became the official state ideology after the establishment of the People's Republic of China (PRC) in 1949, and the latter laid the groundwork for changes in the economic, social, and political life of the (post-Mao) era of reform and open-ing. It is difficult to imagine that socialist practice built the planned economy, created the *danwei* (work unit) system, and went through the "Cultural Revo-lution" without changing China's cultural setting. It is also hard to imagine that today's Chinese, who have been learning Western science and technology since childhood, have invested much more time and energy in learning foreign lan-guages than in studying classical Chinese writings and culture, and have grown up immersed in Western popular culture (fiction, film, and music), can avoid the profound influence of Western culture. If a century ago we could distin-guish more easily the differences between "internal" and "external"—the dif-ferences among Chinese traditions, local practices, and foreign concepts—then today's "cross-civilizational" encounter has already created a cultural pattern wherein "inner and outer are interwoven and blended together."

Today, China's political ideology, cultural values, social system, economic production, public media and communication, and daily life are at all levels inextricable from the so-called Western world. Thus, we can only theoretically identify non-Chinese and Chinese elements within contemporary Chinese cul-ture (through the study of the evolution of Chinese cultural history), whereas in cultural practice so-called Western elements are already inherent to China. Indeed, present-day China is a product of a complex historical process: cultural factors from ancient and modern China and a variety of ideas from the so-called West" have "synchronically" constructed the horizons of our cultural practice and form a "constitutive" aspect of Chinese people's self-understanding.[5] But we must stress that this does not mean that traditional culture has nothing to do with contemporary China or that traditional culture has no sustained impact (often hidden and important). The key point of critical contextualism is to emphasize that a rigid concept of "China" measured against "the West" in a dualistic framework has lost its explanatory power and fails to capture real experiences. To explore the particularity and complexity of the contemporary Chinese cultural context, we must deal sensitively and appropriately with the dialectical relationship between "internal" and "external," "continuity" and "rupture," "theory" and "practice." For this reason, it is necessary to adopt a suitable interpretive framework.

Here, we introduce the concept of "the social imaginary," which helps us to form an effective interpretive framework for grasping cultural practices and their changes. According to Charles Taylor [b. 1931], the social imaginary "incor-porates a common sense of expectations that we have of one another, a com-mon understanding that allows us to carry out the collective practice that has created our social life. This incorporates a sense of how we fit together in real-izing common practice. This understanding is both factual and 'normative,' that is, we have a sense of how things happen, but this is intertwined with an idea of how things should happen, of what mistakes would invalidate the practice."[6]

Therefore, the social imaginary is "how people think about their social existence, how they live in harmony with others . . . and hidden behind these expectations is a deeper level of normative ideas and views." Taylor explains further that there are three important differences between a social imaginary and a thinker's theory: (1) a social imaginary is not theoretical and is generated by images, stories, and myths that are ordinary features of everyday life; (2) theory is often in the possession of a small minority, whereas what is interesting in the social imaginary is that it is shared by large groups of people, if not the whole of society; and (3) a social imaginary is a kind of common understanding that makes possible common practices and a widely shared sense of legitimacy. However, a specific theory and social imaginary have an important connection. "Often the theories that are held by the minority come to infiltrate the social imaginary, perhaps first of elites, and then of society as a whole."[7]

The conceptual framework of a social imaginary inspires us to attach importance to the interaction between ideas and social practice. The efficacy of a particular idea on cultural practice is not necessarily equivalent to its theoretical validity. In other words, if not all philosophically defensible ideas can be shared broadly, then a specific idea will be subject to the conditions of social practices if it is to penetrate and spread among the public. Whether a specific idea can compete with other new ideas and constitute a social imaginary depends not only on the theoretical value and logical consistency of the idea itself but also on whether it can provide an effective way of understanding and a guide to meaning for people to use in their daily lives. Moreover, it depends on whether it can enable the people to more fully make sense of themselves and their condition and help them to find meaning in their lifeworld. For instance, throughout human history there have been two different concepts of time: cyclical time and linear developmental time. Intellectually speaking, neither is superior in a philosophical sense. However, during the development of modernity linear time came to replace cyclical time in the social imaginary of people (including the Chinese). This is so since the former can deal more effectively with the structure and conditions of "modern" society, help people to understand and explain the social practices of modern conditions, and better embed people's conventional expectations within this practice.

Using the conceptual framework of the social imaginary to investigate the influence of foreign thought on modern China's transformation might afford us a new perspective, which, in turn, could enable us to establish a set of critical principles concerning various competing concepts. These could then be used to judge the practicality and desirability of these concepts in terms of cultural practice. First, only when the original Chinese social imaginary was in crisis could foreign thought have a far-reaching impact, for otherwise it could only be a theoretical doctrine of interest to a small part of the intellectual elite. Second, even in times of crisis, cultural traditions can reestablish a social imaginary through powerful self-adjustment, such as in the reshaping of the relationship between core and periphery in such traditions, or through the partial absorption and integration of foreign ideas. Yet it may not lead to an outcome in which local (indigenous) tradition is transformed substantially by foreign ideas (the development of Song–Ming Neo-Confucianism after the introduction of Buddhism is perhaps one such example). Third, even in the case of cultural traditions that find self-adjustment difficult, the result is not necessarily that foreign ideas will replace indigenous thought. Various ideas, whether new, old, foreign, or indigenous, often exist in a kind of synchronic competitive relationship, and the result of ideological competition is likely to produce a collision and confluence of ideas, making the dominant idea in a new social imaginary unable to maintain all of its original features. Fourth, in the transformation of the social imaginary, the relative superiority of a particular theory in practice depends on whether it can solve the crisis affecting the original social imaginary. Also important is whether it can provide new alternatives for people to use in their daily lives (a more effective way of understanding and a guide to meaning that the original dominant thought could not provide). This is both a criterion of feasibility and an evaluation of desirability.[8]

Critical contextualism goes beyond the extremes of cultural essentialism and radical constructivism. It views Chinese cultural traditions as the practical development of and dialectical interaction between various tensions—core/periphery, unity/diversity, internal/external, continuity/rupture. The modern transformation of the Chinese social imaginary is precisely the embodiment of this practical development, in which liberalism underwent a process of evolution that moved from external to internal, from periphery to core, and from elite thought to popular ideology.

The Potential and Superiority of Liberalism as a Program for Chinese Modernity

By the first half of the twentieth century, China had already produced a clearly outlined and self-conscious liberal discourse, embodied in the thought of intellectuals such as Yan Fu [1854–1921] and Hu Shi [1891–1962]. The major concern of such liberal intellectuals was the predicament of China's modern development, and their understanding and expression of liberalism were in many ways influenced, whether consciously or not, by traditional Chinese thought. However, liberalism was still generally regarded at that time as "a foreign idea" in contravention to Chinese tradition, and its influence was confined largely to a closed group of elite intellectuals and, thus, was unable to reach the level of a social imaginary. Throughout the first thirty years of the PRC, *liberalism* was a derogatory term, and was suppressed and purged. After the Cultural Revolution, society had a moment of political freedom and the expression of democracy, but this was soon reversed. Only in the past twenty-plus years has liberalism gradually penetrated and suffused the social imaginary, entering the stage of indigenization.[9] This is because a reform-and-opening environment created new social practices and reshaped people's self-understanding, thus making the core concepts and basic principles of liberalism overflow the theoretical discourse of elite intellectuals, enter the public sphere, penetrate and spread to a societal level, and gradually become a constituent part of the Chinese social imaginary.

In this process, we can identify three main factors that favor the localization of liberalism: (1) the appeal of egalitarian values; (2) individuation of self-understanding; and (3) pluralization of life ideals and personal beliefs. These are the three prominent and nearly irreversible trends in the development of China's modernity, and liberal theory has at the same time been able to fit these three tendencies, creating an effective and productive interaction between ideas and practice that has provided people in the midst of personal change with a cognitive framework and resources for belief. Therefore, dialectically speaking, liberalism not only promotes the modern transformation of a social imaginary but is also the result of this transformation. The new social imaginary constitutes the local foundation of Chinese liberalism, and it is the reason for its appeal.

First, the egalitarian ideal manifested itself in all major historical developments in twentieth-century China, from the Republican Revolution of 1911 and the New Culture Movement to the Communist Revolution and socialist construction to the past thirty years of reform. It has penetrated the deep cultural background and become an undisputed and natural core value of the social imaginary. Egalitarianism is the conviction that human beings have no inborn distinctions of superior or inferior, that each person's life is of equal value and moral status, and each should have equal opportunities for development (including education, health, employment, and political participation). People should not be targets for discrimination based on distinctions of ethnicity, birthplace, gender, or family status. Egalitarianism is compatible with China's Confucian tradition in some respects and in conflict with it in others. In any case, inasmuch as egalitarianism presented itself through the form of modern universalism and has already been widely accepted in China, it has become a core value for modern Chinese. Politically, it rejects the legitimacy of politics of traditional theocracy or kingship and demands that "popular sovereignty" serve as the basic principle of political legitimacy, although it allows several options for the specific form of democratic government. Egalitarianism does not lead to liberalism directly, but it does have an intrinsic affinity with modern political liberalism.

Second, the concept of "self" has shifted gradually, moving from being centered on the group to being centered on the individual. China's modernization process has also set in motion tremendous changes to its social structure, which have been accompanied by a modern transformation of self-understanding. In traditional society, the individual "embeds" itself in organic communities, and the community-based identity is the core of its self-understanding. Large-scale industrialization, urbanization, and commercialization that are common features of the process of modernization around the world have led a large portion of the population to "disembed" from the traditional organic community and "reembed" themselves increasingly in a modern institutionalized structure. This process has shaped a new, modern, individual-based self-understanding.[10] In comparison to Western countries, China's "disembedding/reembedding" process has its own characteristics. In the first three decades of the PRC, the state-led project of modernization based on industrialization undermined the previously existing form of civil society. The urban population was reembedded in accordance with the collective *danwei* system. Meanwhile, the vast rural population did not migrate on a large scale, and so original clan members were transferred in their home areas into the people's commune system.[11] This was a process of implicit "individualization" whereby a new collectivist identity overrode the traditional community-based clan identity instead of generating an individual-based self-understanding. China's reform and opening over the past three decades has led to large-scale urbanization and commercialization, resulting in enormous flows of population crossing both geospatial boundaries and social stratifications. At the same time, the expansion of the market-economy model promoted the marketization of labor, the privatization of property and means of production, and the contractualization of interpersonal relations. Individuals have thus become bearers of rights and responsibilities within contractual relationships. These changes have largely undermined communal and collective identity and have cultivated an individualistically oriented self-understanding.[12] The concept of individualism is becoming an increasingly important part in the social imaginary of contemporary China. The emergence of new social terminology over the past three decades—for taxpayers, corporations, shareholders, proprietors, vehicle owners, privacy, and property rights, among others—vividly reveals the shift to an individualistic perspective of society that has been reshaping people's framework of social cognition and changing the ways in which one relates (practically and normatively) to state and society. Individualism as both a cognitive idea about what the social reality is and a normative idea about how one should act in a given social context is ultimately an important prerequisite of liberal principles.

Third, the commercialization of the mass media since the reform era has prompted the public sphere to emerge and express an increasingly high degree of cultural diversity. This not only reinforces the tendencies of egalitarianism and individualism but also provides increasingly more diversified possibilities and resources for personal choices of ways of life and values that underline those choices. Especially in our Internet Age, the information environment to which those with a basic educational background are exposed is no longer local, but global. For better or worse, Chinese people today vary significantly, with diverse ideals of life, beliefs, and political ideologies. Pluralism has thus become a matter of fact in Chinese society and constitutes a shared social knowledge among ordinary Chinese. The fact of pluralism is different from the notion of valuing pluralism. To understand that pluralism exists is to tolerate differences and not to judge "alien ideas" as inconceivable or unreasonable, but this understanding does not necessarily refer to the identification or agreement with value pluralism.[13] Whether endorsed or not, pluralism has become a shared social understanding and has been absorbed into the social imaginary of contemporary Chinese. No longer would a Chinese be surprised to run into those who embrace different lifestyles and ideals of life or ideologies—whether Buddhist, Confucian, Christian, Maoist, Communist, liberal, patriotic, or believers in the inherent superiority of Chinese civilization, fervent anti-Chinese critics, pro- or anti-Western commentators, environmentalists, feminists, LGBTQ persons, celibates, vegetarians, and so on. Most importantly, the emergence of pluralism means that the social homogeneity in which people called each other "comrade" in the years before reform is fading away, as the title *comrade* has almost disappeared or lost its original meaning. In the place of homogeneity, Chinese society is becoming a widely diversified and heterogeneous community. Naturally, Chinese people still live under the influence of their cultural traditions, but the tradition that shaped us is not unified, but diverse. Indeed, it comprises at least four traditions: (1) millennia-old traditional Chinese culture (especially the Confucian tradition); (2) May Fourth/New Culture; (3) the socialist tradition of the PRC; and (4) the culture of reform and opening up of the past three decades. These four traditions have shaped values and beliefs of contemporary Chinese, but their influences are not shared equally among all groups of people or among individuals. Some may weigh more heavily than others, thereby creating a diversity of beliefs and ideologies in accompanying the emergence of differences and disagreements. Although pluralism certainly presents a serious challenge to moral and political life in contemporary China, dealing with the problems of pluralized society is precisely the strength of modern liberalism.

In sum, egalitarianism, individualism, and pluralism are basic characteristics of contemporary Chinese society. The ability to interpret and deal effectively with these three important social trends becomes the test for judging the comparative advantages of various ideological arguments for planning China's modernity. In the existing mainstream discourse on modernity, traditional socialist planning can, in principle, meet the demands of egalitarianism, but unless it is liberalized, it cannot cope with the irreversible tendencies of individualization and pluralism. Contemporary Confucianism's revival is an ongoing process. Indeed, the development of the school of Confucianism, which focuses on *xin* (mind/heart) and *xing* (human nature), has been quite successful over the past century. Yet the emphasis on being an inner saint rather than a real-world king became its weak point, and thus it cannot provide the basic principles of politics for modern society. The recent rise of "political Confucianism," meanwhile, has several different orientations. Revivalist political Confucianism still insists on regarding the characteristics of modernity as foreign elements external to Chinese tradition and holds that they can be undone, which neglects partially or wholly the profound changes in and the powerful condition of the Chinese social imaginary.[14] The concepts of "Confucian socialism" and traditional socialism face an equally difficult challenge in confronting individualism and pluralism. The program of "Confucian liberalism" may be a promising option, but it must deal with tensions between Confucian and liberal core principles. If Confucianism compromises or "reconciles" too much with modernity, then it may lose its ethical essence. By contrast, if it persists in the overall preservation of Confucian culture, then it may be difficult to compete with, transform, or absorb the modern demands of egalitarianism, individualism, and pluralism. Thus, the fundamental problem of Confucianism's modern revival is that China's modern transformation is a "cross-civilizational" transition that has led to a change in the basic "paradigm" (including cosmology—the conception of nature, time, civilization, humanity, etc.). Such a change has ultimately made contemporary Chinese experience a mixed rather than a simple horizon wherein reverting to an original "paradigm" is neither convincing nor attractive.

In terms of the basic principles of social politics, liberalism is more likely than other ideologies to satisfy the demands and restrictions of egalitarianism, individualism, and pluralism as well as to facilitate a normative discussion of the desirability and feasibility of Chinese modernity. Liberalism is a "family resemblance" thought tradition, with a variety of representative versions.[15] The English political philosopher John Gray [b. 1948] identifies four basic features that are shared widely across liberal thought traditions: individualism, egalitarianism, universalism, and social meliorism.[16] Liberalism's decisive advantage is its ability to establish a just moral and political order in a pluralistic situation. In the face of the real challenge of pluralism, liberalism does not attempt to eliminate but instead coexists with diversity to maximize the recognition of "reasonable differences" between people's life ideals and beliefs, and on this basis it establishes and maintains the basic order of the political community.[17] Ronald Dworkin [1931–2013] argues that "equal concern and respect" are the core principles of liberalism, which is consistent with the concept of "equal freedom" advocated by John Rawls [1921–2002] and developed further by Charles

Larmore [b. 1950], whose "equal respect" concept is quite similar. Liberalism's particularity thus lies in attaching more importance to personal freedom (than in traditional socialism) and in its stress on equality over cultural conservatism, and thus it can respond most effectively to the challenges of pluralism and maximize the equal treatment of all kinds of life ideals and religious beliefs. This is often mistakenly referred to as the "neutrality principle" of political liberalism, which is a perplexing term that makes it easy to call into question liberalism's paradoxes or contradictions: on the one hand, it asserts a particular value (equal freedom), and, on the other, it declares value neutrality. But this term, in fact, misunderstands completely the exact meaning of the so-called neutrality principle. Neutrality as a political principle is by no means value free, and it is, at root, a value assertion that affirms the value of "equal respect" and thus forms a clear normative idea that differs or competes with other political moralities. The so-called neutrality refers to the fact that this political morality does not depend on the concept of a specific good and maintains the highest level of concern and respect for all kinds of life ethics. Thus, it is the lowest (thinnest) principle in the universally justified sense of "equal treatment" of life ideals in all reasonable disputes. Yet its recourse as a guiding political principle is to the moral requirements of the highest (strongest) principle, which are those ideals or beliefs that conflict with the principle of "equal respect" that must force themselves to obey its moral teaching in the political sphere.

In the modern social imaginary consisting of egalitarianism, individualism, and pluralism, although each particular group or individual may not necessarily regard "equal respect" as its highest moral principle, in the field of social politics only "equal respect" can serve as the most basic universal moral principle. On this basis, the fundamental norms of the political community can be established. In addition to other social and political programs, there will be conflicts with the core values of a social imaginary and a lack of desirability or feasibility. This is why left-wing liberalism, or "egalitarian liberalism," has an unparalleled superiority as a sociopolitical plan. This judgment is not based on a so-called universal standard that is divorced from the Chinese context or external to China, but it instead stems from the basic understanding of contemporary "Chinese characteristics" and the value demands of the Chinese people.

Traditional Spiritual Remnants and the Predicament of Chinese Liberalism

In contemporary China's historical transformation, liberalism is capable of responding effectively to changes in the important conditions of social practice. As a program of modernity, liberalism can provide desirable and feasible normative principles for the basic structure of society and politics and has obvious or potential advantages over other competing ideologies. The process of localizing the fundamental ideas and principles of liberalism, from something external to Chinese culture to something intrinsic to it, from the periphery to the core, has made it an important constitutive part of the Chinese social imaginary. From the standpoint of cultural conservatism, it is virtually a process of "cultural colonization." From the perspective of critical contextualism, however, changes in human culture have always involved the reconstruction of internal and external boundaries. At the same time, liberalism's localization in China is still unfinished and has its shortcomings, and there may be some deformation or deterioration. Liberalism indeed faces many serious challenges in the contemporary Chinese context.

First are the social and political challenges. Market-oriented reforms have brought significant economic growth but have created serious social problems, such as greater polarization between rich and poor, corruption, and environmental pollution. Although liberalism presents a theoretical guideline on which China's economic reforms are based, the negative effects of the reforms have created some resistance to liberalism and negative repercussions. However, this problem is not caused by liberal theory itself, but by its distorted form in China's particular political situation. In the absence of a sensible rule of law and democratic supervision of its conditions, the state-led market-economy reforms lead inevitably to the evil consequences of "oligarchy." Although crony capitalism resorts to liberal theory to justify itself, a highly selective strategy of utilization is what separates so-called economic liberalism from the general idea of liberalism.[18]

Ronald Dworkin has argued emphatically that the "principle of equality of freedom" is the "constitutive principle" of liberal sociopolitical programs (valued for their own sake). The capitalist market economy, however, is only liberalism's "derivative principle"—only a means of realizing its constitutive principles, valued only as a strategy. Liberalism will, in some cases, support a market-economy program not out of the "principle of efficiency" (because the market can create high returns), but out of the "principle of equality" because the market economy can deal with a wide range of life choices more equitably than a planned economy can. If the "market" threatens equality, liberalism advocates imposing restrictions on the market and can even support a mixed economy or "market-socialist" economy.[19] Liberal sociopolitical principles oppose a simple developmentalist mindset, the unrestricted private ownership of the means of production, and laissez-faire capitalism and its indifference to social fairness and justice.[20] Because of this, China's current reform is not a complete manifestation of the liberal modernity program; rather, it runs counter to the basic proposition of modern liberalism on the important principles of political democracy, constitutionalism, rule of law, freedom of speech, the supervision of government power, social welfare, and equitable redistribution.

In short, the negative repercussions of China's reform and opening up are not problems inherent in liberal theory. On the contrary, the comprehensive implementation of liberal sociopolitical principles can minimize and overcome the drawbacks that have emerged with reform. Thus, the challenges that Chinese liberalism faces from a sociopolitical standpoint are strategic issues that can be dealt with (and only need to be dealt with) tactically. Although not a problem in theory, it is a difficult problem in practice, with effective coping strategies bound to produce "Chinese characteristics."

The true challenge facing liberalism in China is on the spiritual level, which does touch on flaws inherent in liberal theory. Enlightenment rationalism is a dominant feature of modern liberalism, with obvious secularized characteristics. Modern society is understood as a completely "disenchanted" world in which modern people exist as rational subjects who have cast off traditional principles of enchantment. There is little substantive or positive discussion of the ethical significance of life and society, emotional attachment to community, the sanctity of national politics, faith, and ultimate concerns over the transcendent, except for advocacy of procedural principles such as rational reflection and independent choices. This is because, in the vision of secular liberalism, any experience or desire that cannot be explained through rational thought—whether it be emotional experiences that are difficult to describe or spiritual needs that transcend real interests—are globally branded as "premodern" (traditional) spiritual residue that should be removed from the public realm and dealt with by the individual. Otherwise, the public spirit may descend into superstition and fanaticism, and politics may go dangerously astray. This feature is largely related to the historical background of liberalism (the traumatic experience of religious conflicts in Europe) and to liberalism's specific theoretical approach to dealing with differences in modern societies (discarding comprehensive doctrines to deal with the conflicts of pluralist ideals). In other words, liberalism's theoretical advantage in terms of basic principles of society and politics comes at the expense of discussions of the spiritual world. Thus, modern liberal theory leaves little room for transcendent emotional and spiritual meaning.

As Clifford Geertz once stated, however, "Man is an animal suspended in webs of significance he himself has spun."[21] Human life is not merely about satisfying interests that can be rationally calculated, nor about the legitimate institutional arrangements facilitating the satisfaction of these interests. Mankind's social life inevitably seeks emotional and spiritual meaning, in the past as in the present, which is an anthropological or existential truth. Modern people are still tempted by and attracted to spiritual charisma, even though their world has become disenchanted. To understand modernity as a totally rational world led by reason is a simplistic misunderstanding of liberalism. Max Weber's [1864–1920] "disenchantment of the world" refers to "those ultimate and noble values that have retreated from public life," but this does not mean that these values have since become irrelevant or that modern people have decided to give up the pursuit of such values; rather, such transcendental values "enter into the transcendent realm of mystic life or into the friendship of direct and personal human relations."[22] Noble values have not wholly disappeared but instead have been dispelled from the public domain and welcomed into the private. However, the remnants of various religious beliefs are likely to reenter the public domain. Weber even suggested the possibility of sublime values reentering the public sphere; otherwise, there is no need to mention a "war among the gods."[23] This war among different gods—that is, competing ultimate values—remains an important issue in public affairs.

Similarly, Taylor has clearly pointed out that equating modern civilization with the end of religion is a misunderstanding because the relationship between modern secularism and religion is much more complicated than the notion that "God is dead." Indeed, religion is no longer a shared worldview, nor is religious language a common language of society; but religion remains one guide to life and of crucial importance to many. Thus, the so-called secular era reveals a high degree of faith pluralism: different spiritual traditions and ethical principles overlap. Orthodox religions represent one extreme, and radical materialist atheism another. Because of this "schizophrenic tendency of the secular era," modern people often feel "cross-pressures" from different values.[24] As Taylor notes, there are various levels of belief on the spectrum, with firm spiritual beliefs on one end and atheism on the other. In our personal and interpersonal relationships as well as in our social lives more generally, then, we encounter various levels and forms of conflicts about personal beliefs in daily and social lives.

Because the transcendent demands of human life and politics are classified as "premodern charisma," liberal theory has lost its comprehensive and profound grasp of modernity and cannot confront "premodern spiritual remnants." Over the past three decades, significant academic research on the theme of "reenchanting" and "de-secularization" has provided useful critical reflections on the secularization of modernity.[25] The modern social imaginary still contains a variety of emotional and spiritual dimensions—namely, the uniqueness of cultural identity, the sense of belonging to a community, the sanctity of the state, and the value of human life. In these dimensions, liberalism is constantly challenged and criticized in Western societies, and these issues present particular challenges to liberalism in the contemporary Chinese context.

The secular orientation of Chinese culture may not possess "religion" in the Western sense, but as an "axial civilization" China contains a distinct spirit of transcendence. Some examples include the following: Feng Youlan's [1895–1990] concept of the "existence of consciousness of the universe in which human beings both live within and beyond this world (the realms of heaven and earth transcend the moral realm in which human beings reside and go beyond secular life at the same time)"; Tu Wei-ming's [b. 1940] concept of "immanent transcendence"; and the notion of "inward transcendence" as formulated by Yu Ying-shih [b. 1930].[26] This transcendence and its pursuit of meaning have been subjected to the challenges of secularization in the process of China's modernization, but have not disappeared completely.[27]

The unique phenomenon of the "Spring Festival travel peak" in China is a good example of this. During the roughly forty days of the Spring Festival, more than two hundred million people travel (migrant workers living away from home make up the majority of these travelers), which causes a serious and extraordinary traffic burden. Many people line up overnight to buy train tickets and endure overcrowded stations and other hardships to "go home for the New Year (*guonian*)." An analysis of this phenomenon in terms of pure rationality would find nothing more than a series of activities to satisfy identifiable interests: reunions with families, meetings with friends, and food and entertainment. These benefits would surely not be sufficient to offset the huge costs of participating in the Spring Festival. Clearly, family reunions could occur at other times of the year, thus avoiding the travel peak of the Spring Festival, and food and entertainment could be found in local venues, thereby satisfying those interests at a lower cost. Thus, viewed through "disenchanted" eyes, the Spring Festival phenomenon appears completely inconceivable and exemplifies an "irrational custom." But culturally symbolic activities such as "spending the New Year with family" cannot be evaluated purely from a cost–benefit analysis; rather, it is an activity that possesses cultural symbolic significance. At this specific moment, the Spring Festival, activities such as reunions with family members, staying up all night on New Year's Eve, New Year's greetings, and other activities acquire a noncalculative ethical significance. It is the expression of filial piety and respect, gratitude, and a rekindling of family kinship as well as strengthening family bonds, etc. In such customary rituals, people experience identity, deep care, and connectivity, and from this experience of human relations they develop a feeling of harmony with all things in the world. This is not a narrow pursuit of "interest," but a Chinese pursuit of "being a human being," which highlights Chinese tradition's distinct humanity.

The Spring Festival phenomenon also shows that the Chinese people's social imaginary is in a changing state of internal "cross pressure." On the one hand, it is impossible that the Spring Festival phenomenon would have occurred without large numbers of migrants leaving the villages to work in the big cities. This shows that the interests understood by modern rationality have a strong driving force and are disintegrating the traditional concept of "not straying far from home while one's parents are still alive." On the other hand, the custom of "spending the New Year (*guonian*) with family" continues to this day, which shows that humanist demands in Chinese tradition have not vanished completely because of modernization.

How can liberalism handle such demands? In theory, liberalism respects the affiliations and emotions in human relations and humanistic appeals in Chinese tradition, but such respect often manifests itself as indifferent neutrality. In practice, however, liberalism sets the standard of fairness and justice based on the individual-centered social unit, and the socioeconomic institutional arrangements that it promotes tend to be individualistic and not conducive to family-based and community-based lifestyles, which threatens traditional moral feelings and humanistic spirit. Although (as noted earlier) the individualization of self-understanding has entered the social imaginary of contemporary Chinese, at the same time relational self-understanding, humanistic appeals, and spiritual aspirations persist in the social imaginary. Liberalism's neutrality principle cannot deal with this complex situation of old intertwined with new in a balanced way because it does not propose an effective way to absorb and integrate traditional demands and often exacerbates the rupture and conflict of self-understanding. Although many Chinese who hold traditional feelings support the liberal principles of fairness and justice rationally, they feel a profound sense of emotional loss because for them certain important and distinctive ethical values have not been preserved. Thus, how to cherish traditional ethical values and how to deal with emotional estrangement and the resistance of traditional attitudes to modernity are the challenges that liberalism encounters on the spiritual level.

Equally important, the pursuit of transcendence is not limited to the private lives of individuals and families but is reflected in public political life and often expressed as the sacred expectations of state politics. Liberal theory has inherent shortcomings with regard to the state because it lacks a complete and dynamic (positive) state theory. In the tradition of liberal ideology (theories of the state of nature, contract, and consent), the individual is the foundation of human existence, whereas the state represents an artificial creature, derivative and instrumental; the state itself has no intrinsic or transcendental values, only instrumental ones. Liberalism therefore especially opposes statism (for example, according to Hegel, "the state is the realization of ethical ideas; the state is the realization of concrete freedom; the state is the highest embodiment of the Divine Idea on earth"). Therefore, the theory of liberalism is often not a theory "about the state,"[28] but one "against the state," treating it as a "necessary evil" and advocating the need for a "night watchman" of "the smallest state." Of course, between libertarianism and left-wing liberalism there are important differences in principles and controversies over understandings of state politics. Even in the left-wing liberal theory of the welfare state, the state can play a more active role in intervention, but the significance of such intervention remains largely instrumental.

In a larger perspective, however, the sacredness of politics is a more universal and enduring phenomenon. Religion and transcendental beliefs have always had and will continue to have profound implications for politics. Naturally, modern transformations occur, and one outstanding manifestation in the West is "the separation of church and state." Mark Lilla's [b. 1956] research reveals, however, that the separation of church and state is far from a universal and inevitable outcome of historical development but is in fact a special, fragile, and therefore unstable modern Western outcome. As he notes, "We Westerners have decided that it is strange and inconceivable that theological ideas are still burning in the hearts and minds of people, arousing passions that leave societies in ruin or salvation. We had assumed that this is no longer possible and that mankind has learned to separate religious issues from political ones and that political theology had been dead since sixteenth century Europe. But we were wrong. We are that kind of fragile exception."[29] From a historical perspective, "political theology is the original form of political thought." Political philosophy has never tampered with political theology completely (nor can it). Thus, a "big separation" of church and state is not only exceptional to the West but also exceptional to all human history. Political theology has an eternal strength to inspire and attract. In fact, even in modern Western politics of separation of church from state, the discourse of sacredness, as in sacrificing for the country, has not disappeared entirely. In a recent study, Paul W. Kahn [b. 1952] notes that countries (meaning liberal nations) can resort to political violence—whether appearing in the form of domestic revolutionary or foreign violence. Thus, political experience certainly contains "elements rooted in conviction and sacrifice." "We disregard this type of lofty political rhetoric of sacrifice as dangerous because it is irrational, but only according to liberal theory must the state be a 'rational' enterprise." Therefore, "if we view politics only by way of contemporary liberal theory, then we misunderstand the nature of political experience and the significance that citizens realize in and through their political identity."[30] The state is thus a rational institutional arrangement that serves people's well-being and has the transcendental symbolism to satisfy people's sense of belonging to a community. This [arrangement] allows one to transcend the "insignificant selfish individual" and reach the "exalted human being" who is associated with a noble and eternal cause and may understand the meaning of existence through this transcendence.

Liberalism has a negative attitude and indifference toward the transcendence of politics—less a substantive positive discussion and more the prevention of negative discussion—because the liberal tradition lacks the proper vocabulary to describe the complex relationship between politics and religion; thus, it is even harder to deal with the complicated relationship between faith and politics in the non-Western world. Although traditional Chinese religion is different from Western religion, it does not lack the transcendental significance of politics. The traditional concepts of "heaven, earth, emperor, parents, and teachers" and "monarch–subject, father–son" are not only institutional, but also a type of structure of meaning in which the "*tianxia*-state" has transcendental sanctity. The sacredness of the world and state is also at the heart of the Chinese traditional spirit of transcendence. On the surface, this sacred investment of hope has vanished from China's centuries-old history ever since the Revolution of 1911, but it has not disintegrated completely. It has instead manifested itself in various modern forms of ideals: first was Kang Youwei's [1858–1927] "*datong shijie*" (world of great harmony); then the Communist new man and the appeal of leading the world revolution; and now various imaginative versions of nationalism and patriotism. "The Rise of Great Powers," "the Great Rejuvenation of the Chinese Nation," "the Chinese Century," and so on—the ideal to which they appeal is much more than the wealth and happiness of modern secular significance, but rather the sacred belief in state and politics and the spiritual significance of an individual's sublimation in politics.

Chinese liberals have made efforts to distinguish *tianxia*, "all under heaven," from "state" and "state" from "government," but ideological and intellectual efforts are often ineffective, and it is hard to contain the "fanatical political enthusiasm" of nationalism and patriotism. Because the aspiration for political sanctity persists in contemporary China, this appeal must base itself upon something; without the "government" as the entity on which to rely, both the state and *tianxia* become vague and unworkable symbols. The liberal-democratic state as envisioned by liberals contains "bureaucrats employed by taxpayers," "public-goods providers," and "managers of the redistribution of social resources." The state's instrumental and functional nature faces difficulty in accommodating and realizing the sacred value of politics: an individual's solidarity with, loyalty to, and sacrifice for the state. Xu Jilin has noted the rise of statism in China in recent years, criticizing and analyzing its dangerous tendencies.[31] Not unlike a criticism of fanatical nationalism, a warning of the dangers of statism may still be ineffective. If Chinese liberals attribute the "irrational political appeal" entirely to the confusing and misleading nature of political propaganda, deluded and induced by the Party-state, and fail to understand fully the meaning of politics, to explain the influence of transcendent spirit in modern political life, and to understand the sacred value of finding a positive and effective alternative, then the "spiritual remnants of premodern politics" will act like an irrepressible "ghost" that, having lost its physical body, will continue to seek mortal reincarnation in other forms. The danger is that ideologies such as extreme nationalism, xenophobia, statism, and fascism may be the form that this ghost will inhabit.

In sum, traditional ethical sentiments and their transcendent spirit have not vanished in present-day China but instead exist either overtly or implicitly and manifest powerful influences. The main challenges for Chinese liberalism are how to understand fully the sustained influence of Chinese tradition under conditions of modernity and how to confront and handle effectively dissatisfaction, disappointment, and conflicts that underlay traditional demands for planning a liberal modernity.

Conclusion: Liberalism and Beyond

The modern Western social imaginary took form after nearly five hundred years of history. China's social imaginary, however, is still in the midst of a modern transformation and may not necessarily follow the same path as that taken in the West. Antonio Gramsci [1891–1937] noted that "the starting point of critical elaboration is to be consciously aware of who one is, which requires 'knowing yourself' as a product of the historical processes to date, which has accumulated countless traces on you without leaving an inventory; compiling this inventory is the priority from the very beginning."[32] Contemporary China's social imaginary has accumulated intricate "traces of history," and the process of differentiation and integration of various values is still under way.

We have noted that the ideal of egalitarianism, the liberty of the individual with its individual sense of self and its needs, and the reality of pluralism with its demands for respect, tolerance, and the spirit of rational dialogue constitute the three prominent and virtually irreversible value claims of modernity. As a fundamental principle of social politics, liberalism has a strong ideological potential to respond to these claims and therefore has obvious advantages. In today's Chinese social imaginary, meanwhile, some "premodern" sentiments and spiritual values have not altogether disappeared and appear constantly in the form of various modern variations that seek expression and satisfaction. Moreover, liberalism has not provided enough theoretical space and effective ways to respond to these transcendental spiritual needs. This is the challenge for Chinese liberalism, and indeed for liberalism throughout the world, where the liberal management of modernity has often proven equally unsatisfactory. Modern people's sense of loneliness and emptiness, estrangement and alienation from social relations, unfair political and social lives, malignant inflation and cyclical crises of capitalism, dictatorial and hegemonic international relations—all make for doubts and conflicts in the practice of liberalism in China.

In this context, both the notion of an "alternative modernity" (whether a moderate and reparative program or a completely alternative modernity) and the proposition of Chinese cultural particularization are emotionally appealing. Socialist advocates uphold the socialist revolution's legitimacy and practice in China and attempt to satisfy the demands of freedom and equality in modern politics with different forms of democratic ideas. Their response to pluralistic trends is either with institutional innovations or the adoption of a revised version of the "new socialist man" to create a new cultural, political, and spiritual world.[33] The contemporary revival of Confucianism has taken on a variety of forms, but all such forms take as their basis the particularity of Chinese civilization. Previous understandings of cultural particularity can, in principle, be placed in the framework of cultural pluralism. At present, however, the theory of cultural particularity as advocated by either socialism or Confucianism does not endorse the particularity of localism, but a more superior universality: China's particularity is not desirable because of its particularity but, rather, depends on its universal sense of desirability. According to criticisms of the plight of Western modernity, advocates of both socialism and Confucianism believe that it is possible for China to develop a superior universal civilization from its own particular cultural tradition. This civilization will not only respond to the requirements of equality and fairness in sociopolitical arrangements but also meet the requirements of the spiritual world and realize more fully the transcendental meanings of life ideals, ethical feelings, social solidarity, political loyalty, moral order, and spiritual transcendence.[34]

Many efforts to develop these ideas are ongoing processes whose potential has not yet been fully realized. Their shared feature is a backlash against past radical and antitraditional ideological trends. Since the May Fourth Movement, the New Cultural tradition in China has sought to establish new value standards—progressive, revolutionary, healthy, and scientific—to oppose those characteristics of ancient Chinese tradition (backward, reactionary, decadent, and ignorant). One may question whether this radical antitraditional movement understands traditions correctly and fairly and whether the value standard established is itself credible. Yet in criticizing the May Fourth and New Culture Movements, we encounter many difficulties in trying to resort to the ideological particularities of Chinese culture.

First, Confucianism and socialism must provide more convincing historical explanations for traditional Chinese political culture's decline and the plight of Mao Zedong–era socialist practice, respectively. If China's distinct culture contains a sense of civilizational superiority, how can we explain its historical crises? China's recent rise has been interpreted by many as a unique "China model" and as a backdrop to the rise of cultural particularism.[35] Many empirical analyses of socioeconomic studies, however, reveal that there is a closer relation between China's rise and that of liberal modernity than between China's rise and its particular cultural tradition.[36] If this is the case, then as China's rise continues, her social imaginary will grow ever more distant from an idealistic vision of cultural particularism.

Second, how to realize the values of equality and individual liberty under the conditions of pluralism remains a huge challenge to Confucianism and socialism. Today, China has lost its homogenous collective identity because a unified standard of "the Chinese people" with a firm, definite, and clear definition no longer exists. Who are we? How should we go about our lives? What direction should China pursue? The definitive answers to these fundamental questions no longer exist. This is a fundamentally important fact, even as it is a fundamentally important problem. Future Chinese imaginaries and solutions cannot but face this difficult problem. Both contemporary Confucianism and traditional socialism have to face an important choice: Are "reasonable disagreements" between different life ideals and beliefs to be accepted as factual premises and starting points for discussion—as they are in liberalism—or is disagreement an unacceptable "disorder of modernity" that must be eliminated?

In contemporary mainland China, for some socialists and Confucians, having the state assume the functions of moral cultivation, promoting the cause of "ideological unification," establishing a homogeneous community by eliminating heterodoxy, and achieving the ideal of egalitarianism through an institutional planning that is different from that of liberalism is still a possible and desirable choice. In their view, although this undertaking is daunting, it is a worthy endeavor. It is a particularly attractive proposition, especially in times of chaos and moral crisis. However, even if we put aside the value judgment, how to eliminate "heterodoxy" is a serious problem in terms of feasibility. Are persuasion, education, and transformation sufficient? Will expulsion, suppression, and prohibition lead to conflict? Is use of violence necessary? What are the justifications for and limits of violence? At any cost? In the end, it is hard to say who is heterodox. To regard oneself as orthodox and demand the eradication of heterodoxy is to run the risk of ultimately becoming heterodox oneself and a target for elimination—such bloody ironies are not unusual throughout history.

There is a pattern of coexistence between liberal choice and pluralist difference. History teaches us that one of the important reasons why liberalism emerged in Europe was as a response to the disasters of sixteenth-century religious wars. Liberalism's rise in mainland China after the 1980s was also related closely to a historical reflection on the violent struggle of the Cultural Revolution. These grim historical experiences show that orthodoxy will certainly have its heterodoxy, and if orthodoxy is founded on an arbitrary and unified belief as the basic principle of society and politics, then it will often result in enormous human costs. Thus, to treat heterodoxy in a tolerant manner rather than excluding or abolishing it and to coexist peacefully with heterodoxy is the most desirable social and political solution. But in moral philosophy, liberals uphold a belief in "equal freedom" and hold that "individuals are the ends rather than means." Liberals thus refuse to impose a project of "ideological remodeling" based on altruistic beliefs in a mandatory way because ideological coercion implies a deviation from the important liberal principle of equal freedoms and uses others as a means rather than an end. Nevertheless, liberals are more willing and confident to live peacefully with those who hold different beliefs (even hostile ones) and have practical institutional precedents on which to rely.

Yet liberals' claims may not succeed in convincing their intellectual opponents. In the latter's view, efforts to boycott and overcome pluralism are justified, and the regarding of certain efforts as "irrational" or "dictatorial and autocratic" is dismissed as liberal prejudice. It is unacceptable to separate the public political world from the world of human life and ethics, which runs counter to the integrity of cultural values. The reason that liberals resort to "peaceful coexistence" may not be valid, either, because it must first assume that "peace" or "fear of conflict and death" have a higher priority in the ranking of values. In the nonliberal viewpoint, "pluralism" is an unverified and controversial value concept in which value pluralism itself is allegedly "arbitrary." This article does not provide a full assessment of disputes between liberals and critics but instead seeks to show that in today's world it is extremely difficult to bridge the differences between different ideas.

However, the demand for consensus building for China's future development has become increasingly urgent in recent years. We have to say that all, whether contemporary Confucian, socialist, or liberal, agree that there are serious problems with China's current development, and all hope to find solutions with basic common ground. Indeed, there is consensus that China must exist as a complete community; its citizens must coexist with each other's differences. As a result, an endless stream of reconciled ideas of "harmony without uniformity" and "inclusiveness" has emerged, with some commentators arguing that future development ought to integrate many traditions, combining socialism, conservatism, and liberalism.[37]

Can liberalism's core principle of "equal freedom" serve as the basis of a common understanding? As far as possibilities are concerned, each tradition—Confucianism, socialism, and modern liberalism—has specific value bases to support norms of equal respect. Confucian tradition contains rich and complex moral ideas. These ideas include doctrines of equality, respect, and tolerance, such as *renyi* (benevolence and righteousness) and *shudao* (the way of reciprocity) as well as hierarchical rules (namely, the tiered structure of "monarch–subjects, father–sons"), which contain principles of neutrality (harmony without uniformity). Many scholars devote themselves to exploring the potential elements within Confucianism that are compatible with ideas of modern liberal equality and freedom and entertain the possibility that Confucian traditions may achieve "creative transformation" under modern conditions.[38]

Socialist ideology likewise contains a strong egalitarian orientation at its core, but traditional socialist egalitarianism fails to emphasize "equal respect" and seeks mainly to "eliminate class differences." In the thirty years following the founding of the PRC, socialism's commitment to equality revealed "differ-entiation internally and externally"—advocating for equality, solidarity, and fraternity within the proletariat and adopting the principles of reform/trans-formation and struggle toward other classes. But socialist ideology and prac-tice have made tremendous contributions to the promotion and deepening of "equality" as a value, notably in having a positive impact on breaking down tra-ditional notions of hierarchy (such as discrimination against women). Espe-cially in the post-Mao era, when the discourse of "class struggle" was muted, the principle of equality applied in theory to all citizens. At the same time, the state transformed the nature of its authority, shrinking ideological areas of con-trol so that members of society could have "individual lives" in which they had some space to choose, objectively tending toward a greater respect for the diverse freedom of individual lifestyles.

Although equal respect is the core feature of modern liberalism, it needs to transcend its limitations of secularization and rationalism and open up to dif-ferent intellectual traditions at the emotional and spiritual levels. The perfec-tionist liberal tradition shares in common the national moral cultivation of Confucianism.[39] Constitutional patriotism as advocated by Jürgen Habermas [b. 1929] can also transform its overly rational connotation and be compatible with people's particular attachments and transcendental appeals to their civi-lizational traditions and political communities.[40] For liberals, it is important to recognize that neither social nor personal life can be purely "liberal" (liber-alism by itself is not enough). And for other schools of thought that compete with liberalism, it is necessary to recognize that social and political arrange-ments that lack the spirit of liberalism are dangerous and fragile unless funda-mental modifications are made to the conditions of modernity. Because such "universal values" as "egalitarianism," "individual liberty," and "pluralistic tol-erance and respect" have become values that the Chinese themselves acknowl-edge, they are being engraved on modern China's cultural background and con-stitute the horizon of our lives.

Notes

1. Liu Qing, "Zhongguo yu jingxia de ziyouzhuyi: Qianli yu kunjing" (Liberalism in con-temporary China, potential and predicaments), *Kaifang Shidai* 4 (2013): 106–23.
2. See the following essays by Xu Jilin in *Rethinking China's Rise: A Liberal Critique*, ed. and trans. David Ownby (Cambridge: Cambridge University Press, 2018): "The Spec-ter of Leviathan: A Critique of Chinese Statism Since 2000," 20–60; "Universal Civi-lization, or Chinese Values? A Critique of Historicist Thought Since 2000," 61–94; "What Body of Confucianism's Lonely Soul?" 113–26; "The New *Tianxia*: Rebuilding China's Internal and External Order," 127–54, also available at Reading the China Dream, https://www.readingthechinadream.com/xu-jilin-the-new-tianxia.html.

3. See Gao Quanxi, "The Political Maturity of Chinese Liberalism," Reading the China Dream, 2012, https://www.readingthechinadream.com/gao-quanxi-political-maturity .html.

4. In recent years, scholars from many disciplines, including philosophy, cognitive science, anthropology, psychology, and pedagogy, have used the concept of "critical contextualism" with different meanings. In the study of the history of political thought, critical contextualism is a reflection of the traditional methodology of contextualism and its normativeness. See Stephanie Lawson, "Political Studies and the Contextual Turn: A Methodological/Normative Critique," *Political Studies* 56 (2008): 584–603.

5. *Translators' note*: Liu Qing is drawing from H. G. Gadamer's conception of "horizon" as the "standpoint" that shapes one's vision. See H. G. Gadamer, *Truth and Method* (New York: Continuum, 1997), 302.

6. Charles Taylor, *A Secular Age* (Cambridge, MA: Harvard University Press, 2007), 172. *Translators' note*: We have translated back into English Liu Qing's Chinese translation of the passage from Taylor, so the wording of this quote is slightly different from Taylor's original. We aim to give the reader what the Chinese reader gets, and we quote the original only when there is a meaningful difference.

7. Charles Taylor, *Modern Social Imaginaries* (Durham, NC: Duke University Press, 2003), 2, 23–24.

8. That "conformity" between ideological concepts and social imaginary should be used as a criterion of desirability is controversial. For a fuller discussion, see Liu Qing, "Guojia zhongli xing yuanze de daode weidu" (The ethical dimension of the national neutrality principle), *Huadong Shifan Daxue Xuebao* (*Zhexue Shehui Kexue*) 2 (2009): n.p.

9. *Translators' note*: Liu Qing uses *bentuhua* here, which we translate as "localization" or "indigenization" depending on context.

10. Ulrich Beck and Elisabeth Beck-Gernsheim, *Individualization: Institutionalized Individualism and Its Social and Political Consequences* (London: Sage, 2002).

11. See Cao Jinqing, "Song yilai xiangcun zuzhi chongjian, lishi shijiaoxia de xin nongcun jianshe" (Reconstruction of rural organizations since the Song dynasty, building a new countryside in historical perspective), in *Ruhe yanjiu Zhongguo* (How to research China), ed. Cao Jinqing (Shanghai: Shanghai Renmin, 2010), n.p.

12. Yunxiang Yan, *The Individualization of Chinese Society* (Oxford: Berg, 2009), and "The Chinese Path to Individualization," *British Journal of Sociology* 61, no. 3 (2010): 489–512.

13. *Translators' note*: For differences between "the fact of pluralism" and "value pluralism," see Charles Larmore, "Political Liberalism," in *Morals of Modernity* (Cambridge: Cambridge University Press, 1996), chap. 6.

14. See Jiang Qing, *Zhengzhi Ruxue, dangdai Ruxue de zhuanxiang, tezhi yu fazhan* (Political Confucianism: The turn of contemporary Confucianism, its characteristics, and its development) (Beijing: Sanlian Shudian, 2003).

15. *Translators' note*: "Family resemblance" is a philosophical idea made popular by Ludwig Wittgenstein (1889–1951). He argues that things that can be thought to be connected by one essential common feature may in fact be connected by a series of overlapping similarities, where no one feature is common to all of the things.

16. John Gray, introduction to *Ziyouzhuyi* (Liberalism), trans. Cao Haijun and Liu Xun (Changchun: Jilin Renmin, 2005), n.p.

17. Ronald Dworkin, "Liberalism," in *A Matter of Principle* (Cambridge, MA: Harvard University Press, 1985), chap. 8; Larmore, "Political Liberalism." See also John Rawls, *Political Liberalism* (New York: Columbia University Press, 1993).

18. See Yao Zhongqiu, "Zhongguo ziyouzhuyi ershinian de tuishi" (The twenty-year decline of Chinese liberalism), *Ershiyi Shiji* (August 2011): 15–28.

19. Dworkin, "Liberalism."

20. See Zhou Baosong, *Ziyou ren de pingdeng zhengzhi* (Equal politics of free people) (Beijing: Sanlian Shudian, 2010), chaps. 1 and 2.

21. Clifford Geertz, *Wenhua de jieshi* (The interpretation of cultures), trans. Han Li (Nanjing: Fanlin, 1995), 5.

22. Max Weber, "Science as a Vocation" (1917), in *Essays in Sociology*, trans. H. H. Gerth and C. W. Mills (New York: Oxford University Press, 1958), 155.

23. *Translators' note*: "War among the gods" was Max Weber's image of the irresolvable conflict between different ultimate values that cannot be reconciled and cannot supplant all the others.

24. Taylor, *A Secular Age*, 390–91.

25. For instance, see Morris Berman, *The Re-enchantment of the World* (Ithaca, NY: Cornell University Press, 1981); Peter L. Berger, ed., *The De-secularization of the World: Resurgent Religion and World Politics* (Washington, DC: Ethics and Public Policy Centre and Eerdmans, 1999); James Elkins and David Morgan, eds., *Re-enchantment* (New York: Routledge, 2008).

26. *Translators' note*: Whereas Chinese philosopher Feng Youlan contends that "immanence is one world and transcendence is two worlds," New Confucian scholar Tu Weiming, professor of humanities at Peking University, describes "immanent transcendence" as a wisdom or truth that logical analysis cannot understand because it is accessible only via private access—an intuition crafted through hard work and moral practice. Fellow New Confucian and former Harvard, Yale, and Princeton professor Yu Ying-shih, however, does not regard realms of the transcendent and worldly as separate; rather, transcendence is a force beyond, the foundation and pinnacle of our existence, and the fundamental basis of our morality. See Yonghua Ge, "Transcendence, Immanence, and Creation: A Comparative Study of Christian and Daoist Thoughts with Special Reference to Robert Neville," in *Transcendence, Immanence, and Intercultural Philosophy*, ed. Nahum Brown and William Frankeeds (Dordrecht, Netherlands: Springer, 2016), 97; Karl-Heinz Pohl, "'Immanent Transcendence' in the Chinese Tradition: Remarks on a Chinese (and Sinological) Controversy," in *Transcendence, Immanence, and Intercultural Philosophy*, ed. Brown and Frankeeds, 111–12.

27. Tong Shijun, *Zhong-Xi duihua zhong de xiandaixing wenti* (Modernity in dialogue between China and the West) (Shanghai: Xuelin, 2010), chap. 8: "Shehui shisuhua tiaojian xia dangdai Zhongguo ren de jingshen shenghuo" (The spiritual life of contemporary Chinese under the condition of social secularization).

28. See Wilhelm von Humboldt, *Lun guojia de zuoyong* (On the function of the state), trans. Lin Rongyuan and Feng Xingyuan (Beijing: Zhongguo Shehui Kexue, 1998). This is a translation of Humbolt's book *The Sphere and Duties of Government (The Limits of State Action)*, originally published in 1792.

29. Mark Lilla, introduction to *Yaozhe de shangdi—zongjiao, zhengzhi yu xiandai Xifang* (The stillborn God: Religion, politics, and the modern West), trans. Xiao Yi (Beijing: Xinxing, 2010), n.p.

30. Paul W. Kahn, *Political Theology: Four New Chapters on the Concept of Sovereignty* (New York: Columbia University Press, 2011), 25.

31. Xu Jilin, "Zhongguo xuyao liweitan?—Jinshinian lai Zhongguo guojiazhuyi sichao zhi pipan," *Sixiang* 18 (2011): n.p. *Translators' note*: This article is translated as "The Specter of Leviathan: A Critique of Chinese Statism since 2000," in Xu Jilin, *Rethinking*

China's Rise: A Liberal Critique, ed. David Ownby (Cambridge: Cambridge University Press, 2018), 20–60.

32. Antonio Gramsci, *Selections from the Prison Notebooks*, trans. and ed. Quintin Hoare and Geoffrey N. Smith (New York: International, 1971), 323.

33. See Wang Shaoguang, *Anbang zhi dao: Guojia zhuanxing de mubiao yu tujing* (Anbang Road, the goal and approach of national transformation) (Beijing: Sanlian Shudian, 2007); Zhang Xudong, *Quanqiuhua shidai de wenhua rentong: Xifang pubianzhuyi huayu de lishi pipan* (Cultural identity in the era of globalization: Historical criticism of Western universalist discourse) (Beijing: Beijing Daxue, 2005); Liu Xiaofeng et al.,"Zuowei xueshu shijiao de shehuizhuyi xin chuantong" (New socialist tradition as an academic perspective), *Kaifang Shidai* 1 (2007): n.p.

34. Chen Ming, *Ruzhe zhi wei* (The Confucian dimension) (Beijing: Beijing Daxue, 2004); Sheng Hong, *Wei wanshi kai taiping: Yige jingji xuejia dui wenming wenti de sikao* (To open the world for all: One economist's thinking on issues of civilization) (Beijing: Beijing Fazhan, 2010); Chen Yun, "Tianxia sixiang yu xiandaixing de Zhongguo zhi lu" (*Tianxia* thinking and China's road to modernity), *Sixiang yu Wenhua* 8 (2008): n.p.

35. For an example, see Daniel A. Bell, *The China Model: Political Meritocracy and the Limits of Democracy* (Princeton, NJ: Princeton University Press, 2015).

36. See Yasheng Huang, *Capitalism with Chinese Characteristics: Entrepreneurship and the State* (Cambridge: Cambridge University Press, 2008); Ding Xuliang, *Bianlun "Zhongguo moshi"* (Debating the "China model") (Beijing: Shehui Kexue Wenxian, 2011).

37. The most striking example is Gan Yang, *Tong san tong* (Unifying the three traditions) (Beijing: Sanlian Shudian, 2007). *Translators' note*: See the selections from Gan Yang's book translated in chapter 1.

38. See Harvard-Yenching Institute, Joint Publishing, eds., *Rujia yu ziyouzhuyi* (Confucianism and liberalism) (Beijing: Sanlian Shudian, 2001).

39. Chen Zuwei has vigorously defended the ideological position of liberal countries in his article "Zhengdangxing, quanti yizhi yu zhishan lun" (On legitimacy, unanimity, and the acme of perfection), in *Ziyouzhuyi zhonglixing ji qi pipingzhe* (Liberal neutrality and its critics), ed. Ying Qi (Nanjing: Jiangsu Renmin, 2008), 367–405.

40. For an explanation of "constitutional patriotism," see Jan-Werner Müller, *Constitutional Patriotism* (Princeton, NJ: Princeton University Press, 2007).

CHAPTER 3

A CHINA BEREFT OF THOUGHT[1]

RONG JIAN

TRANSLATED BY GLORIA DAVIES

Translator's Introduction

Rong Jian (b. 1957) was, like the other intellectuals translated in this volume, destined for a life of scholarship when the Tian'anmen demonstrations of 1989 got in the way.[2] In the late 1980s, he was a doctoral student in Marxist philosophy at Renmin University in Beijing and an active critic of the then popular notion that China needed a "new authoritarianism" (see the essay by Xiao Gongqin translated in chapter 9) to navigate the choppy seas of economic and political reform. In January 1989, Rong published a ringing condemnation of these ideas in a piece entitled "Xin quanweizhuyi zai Zhongguo shifou kexing?" (Can new authoritarianism work in China?) in the Shanghai newspaper *World Economic Herald*. The piece made Rong famous and changed his life; the political firestorm that followed the Tian'anmen demonstrations meant that he was unable to defend his dissertation. Rong subsequently followed the path of many Chinese intellectuals who left the academy and "plunged into the sea" (*xiahai*) of private entrepreneurship, becoming a successful art dealer.

Rong continued to follow intellectual trends in China, if from a distance, and in the 2010s reentered the public sphere with numerous essays published on the website Gongshi Wang (Consensus Net). The essay translated here is of a piece with those writings.

It takes some nerve to title one's essay "Meiyou sixiang de Zhongguo" (A China bereft of thought), for this is, surely, an extravagant claim. Yet as we will discover in Rong Jian's essay, he is utterly dogged in his ambition to make the claim stick. He knows he is being deliberately polemical, and as he points out early on, the title is likely to trigger a reaction in people before they have even started on the essay. The reaction, in turn, begs the question as to what the author means by *sixiang*, "thought."

In mainland China, *sixiang* refers to two quite different modes of thinking. As part of the term *Zhongguo sixiang*, "Chinese thought," *sixiang* refers to key ideas and arguments constitutive of what we might best describe as "intellectual inquiry" as it has been practiced in the Chinese-speaking world. Hence, "modern Chinese thought" or "contemporary Chinese thought" would include philosophy, theory, and other varieties of conceptual thinking as they have developed in the Sinophone humanities and social sciences. However, as part of the phrases *dang de sixiang* (Party thinking) and *sixiang gongzuo* (thought work), *sixiang* is synonymous with ideology, specifically the ideology of the Chinese Communist Party (CCP). Because China's Party leaders are accustomed to presenting their ideas as the nation's "guiding thought" (*zhidao sixiang*), they also pretend to occupy the vanguard of "Chinese thought." Doing so allows them, among other things, to justify censorship in terms of protecting the nation from the harm of dangerous and subversive ideas that are at odds with their own.

Rong does not distinguish between these divergent senses of *sixiang* in his essay, preferring instead to highlight the interdependence of intellectual inquiry and Party thinking. His attention-grabbing title serves as an answer of sorts for the big question he tacitly poses and around which his entire essay revolves: "What has Chinese Communist Party rule done for Chinese thought?" He argues that the CCP's authoritarian power and the makeshift ideas it calls "Party thinking" have so handicapped China's capacity for independent inquiry as to render the country "bereft of thought."

The question as to how authoritarian power has affected scholarship and inquiry in China is seldom openly discussed, but the effects of authoritarian power are everywhere evident, as in the exercise of self-censorship and the resulting characteristically oblique nature of mainland intellectual discourse. If the need not to attract unwanted state attention is particularly important for those who write and publish for their living, Rong's unusual candor perhaps reflects his independence from both the university sector and academic publishing in mainland China. Censorship of his *sixiang* would not deprive him of his main source of income.

The timing of Rong's essay is interesting. He first presented it at a seminar in January 2013 at the Unirule Institute of Economics in Beijing. It was then published on Gongshi Wang on March 26, 2013, and has since appeared on many other websites hosted inside and outside China. The first half of 2013 was a time of intense speculation in mainland intellectual circles about the newly incumbent Party general-secretary Xi Jinping (b. 1953), who had taken up this top leadership role in November 2012. Many had hoped that the plain-spoken Xi, unlike his ineloquent predecessor, Hu Jintao (b. 1942, who spoke mostly in Party slogans), would implement reforms that would make the Party-state system not only more accountable but also more hospitable to constructive criticism. It was in this generally positive ambience that Rong presented his seminar at the Unirule Institute.

However, all such expectations of greater intellectual freedoms would be dashed by mid- to late 2013. In August 2013, Xi revealed his determination to control and shape public culture to be stronger than Hu's when his administration introduced new harsh penalties for "rumor mongering." The arrest and televised humiliation of self-styled "liberal" social commentators whose observations about common daily injustices had offended the Party-state and whom it now identified as "rumor mongers" soon followed. From then on and up to the present, mainland universities have been subjected to increasing political restrictions, and outlets for independent inquiry have been shut down. Gongshi Wang was arguably the last leading online forum for intellectual debate standing by mid-2016, and it was closed down later that year. (The bold and influential magazine *Yanhuang Chunqiu* [China through the ages] was silenced in July 2016 via the ousting of its editorial board.)

Rong's essay initially fared somewhat better. In early 2017, it was still accessible on several mainland-based blogs, including Rong's column on the Caijing website. However, by 2018 no trace of it could be found on the mainland Internet. A similar fate has befallen websites operated by the Unirule Institute. On January 20, 2017, the Cyberspace Administration of China in Beijing shut down the institute's two websites for allegedly breaching Internet regulations.

Prior to this shutdown, Rong's presentation in 2013 had appeared on Unirule's main website, listed as the 469th presentation in the institute's fortnightly seminar series. There is no mention of it on the institute's current Chinese-language website, www.unirule.cloud, hosted outside China. The institute's list for 2012 ends with seminar 468, and its list for 2013 begins with seminar 470. The omission of Rong's seminar is neither noted nor explained.

The Unirule Institute is renowned for its defense of intellectual independence. Founded by three economists, Mao Yushi (b. 1929), Sheng Hong (b. 1954), and Zhang Shuguang (b. 1956), who are widely regarded as leading liberal intellectuals, this think tank has so far survived Xi's continuing crackdown. However, it has faced increasing pressures. On July 10, 2018, Unirule staff were evicted from their Beijing office. On October 20, the Haidian branch of Beijing's Administrative Bureau for Industry and Commerce informed Unirule's directors that the institute's business license had been suspended. (Unirule had registered as a business to avoid the problems encountered by nongovernment research organizations in China.) In November, Sheng, Zhang, and a third

Unirule researcher, Jiang Hao were prevented from leaving Beijing to partici-
pate as invited speakers at a four-day seminar commemorating forty years of
China's reform and opening up, held at Harvard University's John K. Fairbank
Center for Chinese Studies.

This ongoing harassment of Unirule staff is indicative of the Xi administration's determined efforts to bend mainland public culture to its will. At a two-
day meeting on "political and ideological work" at Chinese universities on
December 8, 2016, Xi demanded that mainland educators redouble their efforts
in disseminating "advanced ideology and culture" so as to instill students with
Party thinking. Educators, he said, must show "resolute support for the Party-
state's governance."[3]

The Party-state's success in greatly diminishing independent inquiry in
mainland China since then makes Rong Jian's essay "A China Bereft of Thought"
all the more instructive, for he considers the range of deleterious effects, past
and present, that have resulted from "academic production" in China being
"shackled to political power."[4]

A China Bereft of Thought

Author's Note

The text below forms part of my research on the history of modern Chinese
thought. It is my personal perspective on the production and dissemination of
thought in China since the Hundred Days Reform of 1898. The essay is themati-
cally rather than chronologically organized, and the focus of my analysis is
the mindset of Chinese intellectuals in different historical periods toward revolution, reform, and scholarly discourse.

At the start of this year [2013], I was invited by the Unirule Institute of Economics to speak at their 469th fortnightly discussion forum, and I presented
what I had uncovered to date from researching this topic. I would like to thank
my host, Professor Zhang Shuguang, and Professors Zheng Yefu, Xu Zhang-
run, Lei Yi, Ma Yong, and Fang Deling for their excellent and inspiring comments on that occasion.

〜

I would like to thank the Unirule Institute very much for giving me this opportunity to express my views. I have been posting my writings online for a year
but have seldom taken part in academic discussions. As Professor Zhang said
in his introduction, I "took the plunge" into business some twenty years earlier. However, an unexpected catalyst last year led me to post a series of articles

online. I had no idea that my writings would provoke such a strong response. As a consequence, I reconnected with several old friends and made new ones. All of this has prompted me to contemplate things anew. After I "took the plunge," I did not stop reading and writing—in fact, I read a great deal. In 2003, I resolved to find the time to write one long essay each year. The several lengthy essays I have given to the many teachers assembled here were all written in the past year or two. My presentation today draws on these essays.

Chinese Thought and Its Evolution Before and After the Reform Era

The past century of Chinese thought has been a topic of abiding interest to me. With the question of Chinese modernity as my starting point, I have examined and contemplated the changes that have occurred in Chinese thought in the period from the Hundred Days Reform of 1898 to the 1930s. I have sought to analyze and assess the three major currents of thought in modern China— liberalism, Marxism, and conservatism. When I first completed this essay, my plan was to continue my research into Chinese thought since the founding of the People's Republic to provide a general account of this period of history through which we are still living. As luck would have it, the Unirule Institute invited me to speak on this topic, which forced me to quicken the pace of my research. I hope that today's discussion will allow me to deepen my still incomplete understanding.

The title of my talk, "A China Bereft of Thought," is likely to offend many people, who may react and ask, "Where, then, would you put those scholars who conduct research on Chinese thought?" The scholars present here are clearly thinkers, so how can China be without thought? Moreover, there is no shortage of thinkers in China who have produced substantial research over the years. In judging China to be "bereft of thought," I mean the overall situation, in the sense of thought as something that the nation as a whole has produced. Of course, I shall also evaluate the state of thinking in the Chinese academic world. The subheading for "A China Bereft of Thought" is "The Situation of Thought in China Around the Start of the Reform Era." The outline below is approximately ten thousand words long. The finished work is likely to be four or five times longer. Let me elaborate my views on this topic in five sections.

How Should We Examine the State of Chinese Thought and Its Evolution?

My way of approaching this topic may differ from those of the scholars present here. After years of working in business, I have perhaps acquired a highly individualistic view of things in some respects. What type of problem-consciousness should one have when examining the situation and evolution of Chinese thought?[5] I raise this question because it is the first thing we must consider when discussing the production, dissemination, and utility of Chinese thought. In my view, from the end of Qing rule mainland Chinese society underwent great and turbulent changes. It underwent the experience of unification first under the Beiyang government [1912–1928], followed by the Nationalist government ([Guomindang], GMD) and then the Chinese Communist Party (CCP).

At the same time, wave after wave of foreign ideas poured into China to produce a never-ending series of clashing theories. Every idea and theory in the world soon acquired a Chinese version. To this day, clashes in China between Left and Right and between "isms" remain fierce and irreconcilable. And so what path should China take? The question has led to raging debates and a plethora of articles in academic circles. But do these debates actually concern Chinese thought, or are they debates about the influence of foreign ideas in China? This question provokes the following questions: In the past century, has China actually produced its own thought? Has the Chinese Revolution produced its own thought? Has the reform process in China produced its own thought? How has the existing field of thought in China been formed? What, ultimately, constitutes key elements of this field of thought? What actual influences has it had on social change in China?

In this regard, my topic is not an interrogation of Chinese thought over the past century (or since the late Qing) as such. Rather, I am exploring what happens to the production and dissemination of thought under an oppressive state power. In reflecting on the work of career academics, I am also undertaking a process of self-examination. I will attempt to answer these questions from three perspectives. First, has the Chinese Revolution produced its own thought? Second, has China's reform process produced its own thought? Third, has Chinese academic discourse produced its own ways of thinking? I see these as three enormous questions, and I would be interested to know how other scholars see them.

Let me outline my three perspectives on the topic. The first perspective is historical. What types of ideas have helped to form Chinese thought over the past century? Although Professor Qiu Feng [b. 1966, pseud. Yao Zhongqiu] is not here today, I think this question is closely linked to his research interests. Let me begin with an evaluation. As an imperial ideology, Confucianism was subjected to an unprecedented attack when the dynastic system ended. I published an article of some forty thousand characters on this topic titled "The Chinese View of History and the Problem of Chinese Modernity" in a journal edited by Deng Zhenglai [1956–2013].[6] In this article, I wrote about three discursive shifts in Confucianism: the first corresponded to the political shift in the Han period during which Confucianism became the study of classics; the second was the metaphysical turn of Neo-Confucianism of Song and Ming times; and the third was the shift to "plain learning" [*puxue*] achieved during the Qing.

My study of Confucianism's three discursive shifts is a critical response to the argument put forward by the New Confucians about three stages of Confucian development. New Confucians argue that the first stage was Han classical learning; the second stage was Neo-Confucianism of the Song and Ming periods; and the third stage is modern New Confucianism. This approach takes Confucianism to be a metaphysical entity. Why do I examine Qing-era "plain learning" as the end stage of Confucianism's development? The reason is that after Confucianism became "plain learning," it was divested of both a political mission and a metaphysical impulse. The greatest achievement of Qing-era "plain learning" was its establishment of a Confucian understanding of procedural justice, derived from "evidential scholarship" and other forms of empirical sciences that were entirely different from Han classical learning and Song-Ming Neo-Confucianism. I have borrowed the legal concept of procedural justice here to highlight how in its heyday "plain learning" was based in a series of procedures involving textual research and exegesis; its aim was to verify the legitimacy and propriety of the Confucian texts being examined. It was a mode of inquiry that required neither a political nor a metaphysical purpose. This led ultimately to the formation of a system of academic evaluation in Confucianism. In my view, this was a value-neutral and formal discursive system based in instrumentalist reasoning.

The departure of Qing "plain learning" from politics can be read as the abandonment by Qing-era scholars of both the Confucian tradition of "applying one's learning in statecraft" and the related disposition of assuming responsibility for society. We can also see this phenomenon as an essential condition for the development of academic independence in Qing times. The avoidance of substantive justice issues in Qing "plain learning" was a natural outcome of academic discourse oriented toward procedural justice. In my view, by the time of Qing "plain learning," interest in constructing procedural justice was already displacing issues of substantial justice. This form of scholarship no longer gave heed to political and metaphysical concerns. However, with the revival of New Text classicism during the late Qing, things changed again. "Plain learning," which had flourished during the reigns of Qianlong [1735–1796] and Jiaqing [1796–1820], retreated when the Qing Empire went into decline.

A new intellectual trend appeared, leading to the revival of the statecraft tradition in the name of New Text classicism. Zhuang Cunyu [1719–1788] and Liu Fenglu [1776–1829], representing the Changzhou school of New Text classicism, revived the study of the *Gongyang Commentary*. This branch of learning prospered when it was further promoted by Gong Zizhen [1792–1841] and Wei Yuan [1794–1856].[7] Finally, Kang Youwei's [1858–1927] method of "using antiquity to advocate reform" (*tuo gu gai zhi*) brought the inner tensions of Confucian political culture to an extreme point, resulting in the Hundred Days Reform as the very last movement of institutional reform in imperial China. I consider Kang Youwei's interpretation of New Text classicism to be Confucianism's last struggle to remain politically relevant. It appeared to emulate Han-period scholarship in hopes of restoring its authority in opposition to Qing "plain learning." It instead augured the end of Confucianism as a political mission. By the late Qing, Confucian thinking was no longer a useful and effective resource for political reform.

Professors Ma Yong [b. 1956] and Lei Yi [b. 1956] are the real authorities on these matters. I am merely offering my own assessment here. On this point, can we use Kang Youwei's attempts at reconstructing and establishing New Text classicism as an analogy for understanding present-day efforts by Qiu Feng, Jiang Qing [b. 1953], and others to reformulate Confucianism for our times? Kang Youwei certainly achieved a great deal. As Qiu Feng is not present today, I do not know how he would view this issue. Personally, I think that after Kang Youwei, Yan Fu [1854–1921], and Liang Qichao [1873–1929], a fundamental, indeed revolutionary, change took place among scholars who had been educated in the premodern Confucian tradition. These were people who had looked out into the world and who could not help but perceive Western ideas as the basis for China's institutional reform. In other words, the so-called great changes unprecedented in three thousand years refer not only to the sweeping changes that took place outside China—which led European nation-states ultimately to arrive in China via India and Southeast Asia and to encroach on the Chinese hinterland—but also to the collapse of imperial China's ideology.

The political and academic legitimacy of Confucianism was fundamentally shaken. It had collapsed for good as an orthodoxy. From a historical perspective, the end of Confucianism's historical mission (which was also its political and ideological mission) saw the introduction of liberalism to China. The intellectual change represented by Yan Fu's and Liang Qichao's ideas was in fact a turn toward Western liberalism. The ideas they introduced were unlike anything in the Confucian tradition, such as those of law, progress, the nation-state, society, liberty, and science.

After the May Fourth [Movement of 1919], this intellectual openness became even more comprehensive. All of the world's "isms" flowed into China during this time, with socialism, Darwinism, anarchism, unionism, and Marxism all competing for the attention of Chinese readers. Eventually, three main intellectual currents were formed: liberalism, Marxism, and traditionalism with Confucianism at its core. The key words for liberalism were *liberty, constitutional government, reform of the national character, emancipation of women, education as the foundation, improvement*, and *scientific principles*; for Marxism, the key words were *class struggle, violent revolution*, and *seizure of political power*; the key words for traditionalism were the ones that were already an integral part of premodern scholarship. We must note that although Confucianism's political role had ended, it continued to matter as an academic discourse. These three major currents of thought formed the intellectual ecology of the day.

It is worth noting that all three were essentially controlled by the intellectual Left. At universities and in other "intermediate zones" (*zhongjian didai*), leftist discourse was the mainstream, whether as left-wing liberalism or Marxism, and the ideas of the extreme Right had little chance of survival.[8] In the ensuing rivalry between these three currents of thought, the discourse of Marxism proved the most authoritative, not only in academe but in public culture. Before the 1930s, the rise of Marxism in China was not the work of political power because the CCP was not yet the ruling Party. Marxism's intellectual dominance was owed to its systematically ordered set of concepts and the cogency of its explanation of Chinese society and Chinese social development. From 1929 to 1931, there was intense debate among Chinese academics about the nature of Chinese society and Chinese social development. This was a debate that involved practically the whole of China's intellectual world. Disagreements were fiercest between the GMD Left, the Marxists, and the Trotskyists. However, the arguments of these three rival factions were formulated in a common Marxist vocabulary, reflecting the evident authority of Marxist explanations of Chinese society at that time.[9] Meanwhile, liberalism and Marxism adopted the same critical position against Confucianism.

If we consider the intellectual situation of Republican-era China from the purview of a history of ideas, it is evident that liberalism and Marxism, as the two dominant intellectual currents, were derivative discourses that explained and assessed Chinese phenomena and made forecasts about changes in China using a Western vocabulary. The Chinese intellectual world no longer used an indigenous language of ideas. Confucianism had lost its explanatory power for addressing Chinese problems, and even if someone chose to speak in a Confucian idiom, no one would listen. If you wanted to sound authoritative, you had to imitate Western discourses—liberalism or Marxism, these two were necessary for you to properly recognize and understand China. From our vantage point today, these two discourses posed difficulties back then and still pose difficulties for us today.

The Evolution of the CCP's Guiding Thought

For the CCP, having Marxism as the Party's guiding thought was of the utmost importance because it was this ideological foundation that enabled the Party to be victorious. As the CCP went from being a revolutionary Party to the governing Party, its guiding ideology gradually developed a genealogy—from Marxism-Leninism/Mao Zedong Thought through Deng Xiaoping Theory to the Three Represents [discussed below] and the Scientific Outlook on

Development. I believe that the newly installed leader would also be required to propose his own theory, without which he would be unable to secure his place in history. My question is: What impact did these different arguments, which together form the Party's Marxist genealogy, have on the CCP? And how did they affect the process of social transition in China?

As I mentioned earlier, in the debates over the nature of Chinese society that took place in the 1930s, Marxism already commanded discursive authority and significantly shaped the intellectual ecology of the time. The CCP was the main organizational vehicle of Marxism then. How did it use Marxism? The way I see it, during the CCP's Yan'an period, the Chinese Communists had a very rudimentary understanding of Marxist theory. The so-called Marxist theoreticians of the day were merely dabbling in Marxism. Mao Zedong [1893–1976] was learning and applying Marxism simultaneously in those days. For instance, he asked Ai Siqi [1910–1966] to give him lectures in his cave every night, and he would apply what he learned overnight the very next day. This Marxism of the ravines clearly lacked the wherewithal to compete with the theoretical prowess of the Internationalists led by Wang Ming [1904–1974]. Mao was distressed by this. At the time, he had written two major essays: "On Practice" and "On Contradiction." Both subsequently underwent several revisions. In other words, the CCP of those years had not produced any proper theoretical works. These two essays by Mao indicate his level of theorizing.

However, the CCP's theoretical inadequacies not only did not hinder the organization's robust development but helped to facilitate it. Overall, the ideological mobilization pursued by the CCP in its Yan'an period was based largely on practice alone. This involved a kind of pragmatic, strategic, or opportunistic thinking that was most visible in the integration of the various strands of thinking within the Party into a half-baked Marxism, which then became Party ideology. The CCP used "the principle of the masses" (*dazhongzhuyi*) (what we now call populism, *mincuizhuyi*) to mobilize large groups of people; nationalism to legitimize the Party's use of weapons; and Western sayings about democracy and freedom both to destroy the legitimacy of the GMD and to win the support of democratic political organizations.

Different wordings were used to achieve different objectives and to resolve different problems. This proved a very effective strategy for the CCP in the prosecution of its armed struggles. As a consequence, the CCP appeared to be well equipped with a range of theories and to have borrowed from different intellectual resources to establish Marxism as an orthodoxy. In reality, the Party's theoretical approach was defined by entirely pragmatic interests. The same pragmatism guided the formation of the Party's ideological line after 1949. Mao's attitude toward the Soviet Union was shaped by his understanding of Marxism, which could be considered an entirely Chinese stance. A pragmatic approach to theory persisted under Deng Xiaoping [1904–1997] and Chen Yun [1905–1995] in the reform era. In effect, Party theory does not involve any discussion of theory; it consists only of methods. There is no discussion of value outlooks but plenty of interest in the applicability of ideas. Deng Xiaoping's "black cat or white cat theory" and Chen Yun's saying "Look only to facts, not to books or what the higher-ups say" exemplify this one-thread-running-through-everything (*yiyi guanzhi*) line of thought.[10]

Accordingly, we must ask why they don't believe in theories and have no faith in ideals. If Marxism is your guiding thought, why don't you put Marxism into practice? As I see it, the CCP has no difficulty with using populism, national-ism, and Western concepts of liberty and democracy simultaneously to handle different types of practical problems. It has preached but never properly fol-lowed Marxist teachings. This is because the Party knows only too well that Marxist theory is useless, and this is the crux of the problem. Thus, by Deng's era, he was keenly aware that Party doctrine was in jeopardy and so simply avoided the topic altogether. He talked about not arguing, not quibbling over whether a theory is right or wrong, not choosing a side, and with these types of issues forming his basic attitude. He spouted Marxism but did not believe a word of it. Mao once said, "Very few in our Party truly believe in Marxism-Leninism."[11] I think there's a lot of truth in this remark.

After Deng Xiaoping, the Party's guiding thought showed few signs of inno-vation or development. The "Three Represents" is a half-completed thought. The proponents' original intention was to build a new value system for the Party, but when they drew fire in the form of a "ten-thousand-word riposte" from the Left, they retreated from their ambition to overhaul Party thinking and never raised the issue again. The Scientific Outlook on Development is merely a tool of instru-mental rationality. It contributes nothing to the actual concerns people have about values.[12]

From this, we can see that the CCP's style of government has not required a guiding thought. The Party pays little heed to the approved wording appear-ing in its own constitution. This is hard for anyone to understand. As a ruling political party, the CCP is one of a kind. It has neither a set of guiding ideas nor a value system; it possesses no program of government; and its constitu-tion is placed on a high shelf, merely for display. By comparison, when the Republican Party in the United States was in government during the 1980s, it put the ideas of Margaret Thatcher and Ronald Reagan into practice. In the countries of northern Europe, democratic socialism is practiced. You could say that even North Korea practices an ideology introduced by Kim Il-sung. What I mean is that in these countries, whether socialist or capitalist, there's an align-ment between theory and practice.

Conversely, what we have in China is a total disconnect between theory and practice, where what is said is not only different from but often the opposite of what is done. Someone once told me that all of China's problems stem from the fact that the capitalism that is being practiced is being preached as socialism.

This paradox has persisted for a long time and has remained unresolved to this day. Perhaps there's a reluctance to resolve it. Let me now turn to how we might assess the consequences of a mode of government that requires neither theories nor ideas.

Approaching the Problem Via the Situation of Academic Production in China

From an academic perspective, the "plain learning" of the Qing era was the first meaningfully modern attempt at establishing a knowledge system in China. Both Hu Shi [1891–1962] and Liang Qichao wrote about this. What "plain learning" produced was akin to a form of procedural justice in scholarship, which had the direct consequence of treating thought as something set apart from real life and as if questions of substantive justice did not matter at all. Let's now consider the importance that twentieth-century Chinese Liberals accorded to intellectual independence. When Cai Yuanpei [1868–1940] headed Peking University, he emphasized the importance of the university's responsibilities and social effects. Under his leadership, the university became a crucial vehicle for academic independence.

The production and dissemination of ideas in China that followed in the 1930s was an important stage in the development of modern scholarship in China. What, then, is the problem with these developments? First, from the twentieth century on, Chinese liberal thought derived all of its resources from the West. Chinese Liberals have had enormous difficulty in adapting their ideas to local Chinese experience. Second, Chinese academic production has enjoyed a certain degree of independence at different times because of people such as Cai Yuanpei who established the autonomy of the university. But Chinese academics have also remained dependent on political power, and this has been so from Hu Shi to Guo Moruo [1892–1978].

The GMD and the CCP alike treated intellectuals as people who ought to serve the Party's ideological needs. After the CCP formed a government, it no longer offered any explanation for why academic production should serve political power and the needs of Party ideology. Before the Reform Era, China was basically bereft of thought. In fact, you weren't allowed to think, you were confined to producing annotations of or professing your faith in Marxism. From the launch of the reforms to the present, academic production has continued to be shackled to political power and the Party's ideological needs. To this day, there is no place for independent inquiry in Chinese academic production.

This is the first key issue I have discerned from my investigations of the situation and development of ideas in China over the past century or more, considered as a history of ideas.

A Revolution Without Thought

To elaborate on what I mean by "a revolution without thought," I pose four questions.

What Kind of a Revolution Was the Chinese Revolution?

First, if we describe the Chinese Revolution as a one-off peasant revolution, we must ask how it differs from previous peasant uprisings. Since peasants are the common subject of all such uprisings, why did the Communist-led peasant uprising flourish under the harshest conditions, enabling the CCP to seize political power in a very short time? Did the CCP lead a peasant revolution? The biggest difference between the Chinese Revolution and previous peasant uprisings is that the Communist leadership attracted large numbers of educated people to join the Party and support its cause. It provided its followers with a cogent set of ideas and theoretical guidance. But what theories did the leaders use to mobilize and organize those they led? We need to pose the question in this manner.

Second, if we describe the Chinese Revolution as a Communist revolution, what relation does this revolution bear to Marxist teachings? In fact, very few in the Party were well schooled in Marxist thinking or knew the original arguments. The twenty-eight Bolsheviks led by Wang Ming played no part in the progress of the Chinese Revolution. Thus, those who knew their Marxism and had a systematic understanding of it had no influence over the Chinese Revolution. In fact, they were ostracized and were ultimately purged from the core of the Party. How should we assess the relationship between Chinese Communists and the Comintern? At first, China took the Soviet Union as its teacher. Later, it turned its back on the Soviet Union to claim its own independence. In this way, we could say that the divergence between China and the Soviet Union is not a divergence within Marxism. What sort of divergence is it, then? Therefore, we should ask if the Chinese Revolution was really a Communist revolution.

Third, was the Chinese Revolution a nationalistic revolution? If it was, then how should we understand the actions of Chinese Communists during the Sino-Japanese War? How should we understand China's alignment with the Soviet Union in the early years of the People's Republic of China and its reconciliation with the United States some two decades later? How should we understand Mao's theory of "Three Worlds?" Was this a nationalistic narrative or an account of internationalism? If we say that the Chinese Revolution is a nationalistic revolution, then what ideas furnished the revolution with an ideological foundation?

Fourth, in evaluating the Chinese Revolution, we must ponder the insistence of the orthodoxy that this was a revolution of workers and peasants, led by members of the working class. Who made up the so-called working class? Extant Party accounts are full of praise for those who took part in urban uprisings precisely because these acts of rebellion involved workers. However, the facts make clear that workers did not play the main role in the Chinese Revolution. The working-class leadership was a retrospective fabrication.

Fifth, we must ask if the Chinese Revolution should be considered part of the world revolution. What was its global significance? How would an understanding of changes then under way in the world order enable us to gain perspective on the Chinese Revolution? It turns out that we do have a basic judgment of the Chinese Revolution: namely, the victory of the Chinese Revolution is said to have rapidly altered the political structure of the world after World War II. The socialist camp led by the Soviet Union and China is said to have resisted the capitalist camp led by the United States and England, and these two major camps are said to have existed in opposition, with an iron curtain between them. However, after China fell out with the Soviet Union, the socialist camp became nonexistent. Viewed in terms of the various factors leading up to their occurrence, the Chinese Revolution had several things in common with Russia's October Revolution. However, the differences between them were far greater. To evaluate the Chinese Revolution using the Russian model is clearly inappropriate. The Chinese Revolution was even more complex than Russia's and with considerably greater ideological ramifications. How should we view these differences? This is a significant issue we must consider.

What Theoretical Resources Do We Draw on for Our Historical Perspective on China's Revolution?

Regardless of how we understand the nature of the Chinese Revolution today, we must first take stock of the various intellectual resources that gave shape and form to the Chinese Revolution and on which it relied. Over the long term, the view of China's history as a revolutionary history overtook everything, and the discourse of revolution came to be seen as the most legitimate. And so this perspective on history as a revolutionary history controlled how we understood the dynamics of revolution in China. Our understanding of war, violence, murder, and the seizure of power was formed within the discourse of revolution: a discourse that granted legitimacy to all of these actions.

Accordingly, we must ask how the CCP's perspective on revolution was formed. As I see it, this perspective was never ideologically or theoretically pure. As mentioned earlier, when the CCP claimed to be unifying Party thinking through Marxism, it was actually using populist ideas to mobilize the masses, drawing on ideas of nationalism to justify armed conflict and military separatism, and invoking democracy to oppose the GMD's authoritarian rule. The Party's attitude to the use of theory was strategic and opportunistic. In other words, the Chinese Revolution does not represent the triumph of a given theory, nor was it the unique product of a particular set of ideas. In fact, by separating practice from theory, the CCP became a tremendously flexible organization. At any given moment, it could use whichever banner was available to it to say what it wanted to say, according to the needs of the situation.

In contrast, the GMD did have its own set of ideas, and it did want to realize Sun Yat-sen's Three Principles of the People. This proved to be a problem precisely because the CCP's approach was evidently superior. The four types of argumentation used by the CCP, outlined earlier, could all be used to attack the GMD where it was most vulnerable. For example, the CCP was able to claim a high degree of ideological unity, and it did so by invoking Marxism. The CCP was also adept at using populist language to mobilize those who were at the bottom of society, which happened to be the GMD's weakest link. Jin Guantao [b. 1947] once noted that the GMD proved capable of mobilizing only the middle class and the elite, thereby leaving the lowest level of society entirely to the CCP. Through highly effective mobilization of the masses, the CCP achieved strength in numbers. Before long, the CCP also gained the upper hand over the discourse of democracy. Around 1945, it was the basic practice of *Liberation Daily* in Yan'an and *Xinhua Daily* in Chongqing to publish a daily editorial using *liberty, democracy, freedom of speech*, and *opposition to one-party dictatorship* as key words. With the CCP taking charge of the discourse of democracy in this manner, the democratic parties were basically won over. As regards nationalism, we must acknowledge the contribution of the GMD. It clearly succeeded in defeating the Japanese but created a greater enemy in the process. In sum, the CCP's historical perspective on revolution has made extensive use of four different discourses, and of these four, Marxism was by no means the primary discourse.

How to Understand and Evaluate Mao Zedong Thought

There is no doubt that the victory of the Chinese Revolution was the victory of Mao Zedong Thought. Mao determined the direction and mode of the revolution to the extent that it's difficult to say whether the Chinese Revolution could have been won without him. Hence, it is important for us to have a basic judgment about Mao's ideas. The genealogy that the Party has created for its guiding ideology consists of a huge pile of ideological doctrinal statements that have become clichés. Everything is in the Party's language; there is little of Mao's own ideas. So, what did Mao really believe?

As I am no expert in the study of Mao's thought, my analysis is based on direct observation and intuition. First, Mao had an anti-intellectual attitude, as many people have mentioned. He was a rural junior intellectual of the Wang Yangming [1472–1529] type who gave priority to insight and believed that revolution must first erupt in the depths of one's soul. He had a lot in common with Hong Xiuquan [1814–1864, the leader of the Taiping Rebellion]. He hated the traditional knowledge system. He was contemptuous of intellectuals all his life. To him, they were utterly foul creatures and couldn't hold a candle to workers and peasants. Mao drew mainly on his knowledge of ancient Chinese books and history. Second, Mao was an activist. The emphasis he placed on practice and action indicates he was a natural-born activist. This emphasis on practice meant that having the right strategy was crucial. His aim was to achieve the maximum effect of action. He would make use of any means to achieve his goal, which meant that he followed no creed. He was opportunistic and given to sudden changes. He believed in the adage that while the winner gets to be crowned king, the loser is despised as a bandit.

Third, Mao's knowledge of the West was virtually zero. He was utterly contemptuous of the theories associated with liberalism. In his Yan'an period, Mao expressed admiration for Franklin Delano Roosevelt's ideas about democracy but purely as a discursive strategy. In his later years, he was completely baffled by why Watergate caused Richard Nixon [1913–1994] to step down. To his dying day, he could not fathom the mysteries of Western democracy. Fourth, Mao's anti-intellectual attitude determined the position he took toward Marxism. Ultimately, he was not a Marxist even though he had to claim allegiance to Marxism-Leninism. He was tentative toward Stalinism. Mao said of his ideas that they were Marxism plus Qin Shihuang [259–210 BCE, China's first emperor], and this self-evaluation is accurate. He sought to bring the established systems of ethics and morality, politics, and scholarship under his control. He attempted to make politics synonymous with indoctrination. He had a monopoly on interpreting Marxism and on knowledge production. Every one of his utterances was exalted as a true principle.

If we look at the words on the page, the extent to which Mao understood Marxism was, at best, a form of Leninism and Stalinism. He lacked basic understanding of the writings of Marx himself. It's quite likely that there were no works by Marx in Mao's study. Moreover, he rarely quoted from Marx. For these reasons, he should not be called a Marxist.

How Should We Evaluate the Effects of "a Revolution Without Thought?"

Given the three areas discussed earlier, we can conclude that the Chinese Revolution led by Mao was a revolution bereft of thought. The theoretical resources on which this revolution drew were quite unlike what the revolution promoted as its ideology in which Marxism occupied the dominant position. The ideology was instead contained in a hybrid discourse that drew from different ideas, values, and methods. The success of the Chinese Revolution was advanced by four kinds of discourse that were motivated respectively by realistic, pragmatic, strategic, and opportunistic concerns. There were no clearly defined ideas or theories; the needs and goals of a given moment instead decided the types of ideas or theories that were proposed.

How, then, should we evaluate the consequences of a revolution bereft of thought such as this? I think we must first recognize that this was a revolution that lacked a clear ethical-moral boundary. It was one where the ends justified the means, enabling people to adjust their strategies for survival and develop as they pleased. This was a highly adaptable revolution that was not weighed down by moral values and concerns. It lacked a clear theoretical direction, and it brimmed with utopian imaginings and longings. Speaking practically, it was a revolution that proceeded blindly and, as such, a revolution that lost its way.

This is my basic evaluation of the Chinese Revolution. Because it lacked theory and thought, all of the different periods of the revolution were defined by strategies that aimed to increase one's strength in relation to the enemy's. The choice of theory or thought was thus contingent on what would provide maximal benefit to oneself, and the chosen policy or strategy would then be treated as absolutely essential to the life of the Party.

After 1949, Yan Xishan [1883–1960] produced a systematic summary of the reasons for the Chinese Communist Party's defeat of the Nationalist Party.[13] I agree with most of what Yan wrote, particularly the point he made about how the Chinese Revolution led by Mao was one where the ends justified the means and all available means were accommodated to achieve an anticipated end. When Mao found it necessary to speak of democracy and freedom, he would hold forth on democracy and freedom. When the democratic parties sent a delegation to Yan'an in 1945, Mao told Huang Yanpei [1878–1965, then leader of the China Democratic Federation] that democracy was essential for changing the "periodic law" of history. However, armed struggle was Mao's clear response to Chiang Kai-shek [1887–1975], for which he used populist methods to mobilize the masses.

For these reasons, the Chinese Revolution as a revolution bereft of thought not only shaped the direction and mode of social change in the first half of China's twentieth century but also brought an end to the constitutional framework introduced in 1946 by the Common Program [in negotiations with the GMD and other parties about the fate of postwar China]. The CCP's implementation of a series of institutional arrangements after it took power was similarly affected. Social change continued to be trapped in the orbit of revolution until the end of the Cultural Revolution, when the system was on the brink of collapse. As a consequence, revolution retreated, and reform appeared.

A Reform Without Thought

This topic concerns our evaluation of China's history of the past thirty years. First, let us consider the political and intellectual contexts against which the reforms took place. The nature and significance of China's reforms during the 1980s can be likened to the "Duke of Zhou's institutional reforms" [eleventh century BCE] and "Shang Yang's Legalist reforms" [fourth century BCE]. The Duke of Zhou's "system of rites and music" enabled the *fengjian* (feudal) system to be established. It allowed the emperor, as Son of Heaven, and the regional rulers to control "All Under Heaven" (*tianxia*) [the known world, the realm]. This brought about the first historical transformation of Chinese society. Most historians today share this view. On the *fengjian* system of the Western Zhou period [trad. 1122–771 BCE], Wu Jiaxiang [b. 1955] has provided an analysis in his book *Gong tianxia* (Public state, 2013).[14] Qiu Feng has also written on the legacy of the Western Zhou *fengjian* system. In 2008, I wrote a lengthy article on "the problem of Chinese 'feudalism.' "[15]

The first social transformation occurred in the Western Zhou period and was completed under the Duke of Zhou. Essentially, the federation-style system of Xia [trad. 2205–1766 BCE] and Shang [trad. 1766–1122 BCE] times in which different autonomous tribes formed alliances with a central authority gave way to the more organized feudal system of Western Zhou in which there was both a horizontal and a hierarchical distribution of power. This power system was both binary and multicentered. Shang Yang's [390–338 BCE] Legalist proposal for change furnished the Qin state with the foundational basis for unifying China. This became the second historical transformation of Chinese society that established a centralized system of autocratic rule. This unitary power structure was vertically defined so that power moved upward toward greater centralization.

In fact, the reforms that occurred in the 1980s had their roots in the Self-Strengthening Movement of the late Qing, as did the whole series of institutional reforms that grew out of this movement over a century or more. These interrelated developments constitute the third historical transformation of Chinese society. The goal of the late Qing reforms was ultimately to turn imperial China into a modern democratic republic. A system of constitutional democracy had to be established to integrate nation and state. A federal system had to be built to integrate central and local relations. A cultural system of universal values had to be instituted so that Chinese culture could become integrated.

Thus, when we consider the reforms that were launched in the 1980s, we must remind ourselves that they were part of a model of change within the history of the third transformation of Chinese society, and we should recognize their deep historical implications.

How then did the momentous reforms of the 1980s begin? What were the ideas that guided and brought them into being? Under what conditions did these reforms, which were to have completed the third historical transformation of Chinese society, occur? First, we must see that they began with de-Maoization (*fei Maohua*). *De-Maoization* is a very general term that the ruling Party clearly does not recognize. However, during the 1980s most of the Party membership saw that Mao's Cultural Revolution had already collapsed. Expressions related to the Cultural Revolution such as "taking class struggle as the key link" and "continue the revolution under the dictatorship of the proletariat" had lost their legitimacy and had fallen outside the scope of what the Party found acceptable. Within the Party, people were keenly aware that if they continued along this path, the Party and the country would be doomed.

"De-Maoization" began with critical evaluations of the "Two Whatevers."[16] Then came the theoretical conference of 1979 and the great debate over "practice as the criterion of truth" as well as the burgeoning Movement to Liberate Thinking that spread across the whole of Chinese society.[17] These activities amounted to a settling of accounts with the legacy of Mao Zedong Thought, and they constituted a liberation of thinking within the Party and a reflective engagement with the inner logic of Marxism. We can also see them as a struggle between two different varieties of Marxist discourse.

Previously, only people such as [leading Maoist ideologues] Chen Boda [1904–1989], Kang Sheng [1898–1975], Zhang Chunqiao [1917–2005], and Yao Wenyuan [1931–2005] had the right to interpret Marxism. Moreover, the power of interpreting Marxism ultimately belonged to Mao alone. As a consequence, the Movement to Liberate Thinking meant taking the power of interpretation back from Mao. However, contestations over how to understand Marxism soon produced divisions within the Party. The ensuing debates over humanism and alienation were in effect a struggle over who had the authority to explain Marxism, with [influential Party theorist] Hu Qiaomu [1912–1992] assuming that this authority belonged unquestionably to him. His dispute with [the Party's cultural czar] Zhou Yang [1908–1989] should be understood as a contest over authority. To occupy a position of authority in relation to Marxism was of crucial importance because Marxism remained the Party's primary tool for unifying Party thinking. Marxism also furnished the primary evidence for the Party's legitimacy to govern.

This is also why Deng Xiaoping made Marxism the first of the "Four Cardinal Principles" that he proposed. The legitimacy of Communist Party rule comes from two sources. The first is violent revolution, and the second is

Marxism. Deng Xiaoping was basically uninterested in theory and thought, and his defense of Marxism was pragmatically motivated. He was concerned to maintain the stability of the regime. Whether he believed in Marxism is another matter altogether.

Second, let me propose the following basic view: the reforms of the 1980s began with the people lower down "crossing the river by feeling the stones" [i.e., tentative experiments]. Once they had felt the stones, they sought approval for their findings from the people higher up. Once a given finding was approved, it was allowed to be widely disseminated. As a consequence, the reforms were launched in the complete absence of a given theory or a given set of ideas. The slogan of reform itself was what there was. During that time, there was a certain breakthrough in Deng's thinking. Theoretically speaking, the programmatic document "On the Reform of the System of Party and State Leadership" [a speech Deng delivered on August 18, 1980] was the most thoroughgoing statement of the Party's existing ideological framework in the thirty years of the Party-state's existence to that point in time. Nothing since then has come close to the importance of Deng's words in this document. However, once it was released, the document was put away on the top shelf because even Deng was not keen to implement his own proposals.

He felt that the proposals were difficult to achieve as the resistance to them was too great. To attempt to implement them by force would lead to many unintended consequences. Thus, I consider the reforms of the 1980s in a situation in which practice produced a dramatic theoretical change—by exceeding the limitations imposed by the existing theory—as opposed to one in which practice was guided by theory. What was the greatest limitation? It was Marxism, the first of Deng's Four Cardinal Principles. Clearly, this was a highly dogmatic Marxism. The substance of reform was the opening of a very small space in the planned economy by means of which the people lower down could "cross the river by feeling the stones." In other words, during the reforms of the 1980s, theory trailed practice while also constraining practice. The reforms were bereft of theory and were indeed a process of "crossing the river by feeling the stones." Accordingly, there was nothing to serve as theoretical guidance for a methodical approach to the implementation of the reforms.

Third, let us consider the theoretical genealogy of reform once debate was no longer allowed. In Deng's speeches during his Southern Progress in 1992, besides affirming the economic-reform path of marketization, he made the momentous decision that there was to be "no debate" [about socialism versus capitalism], which effectively ended theoretical discussion [on the relative merits of these two modes of development]. As I see it, on the one hand Deng stopped debate because he was unable to overturn the theoretical edifice of Marxism that provided Communist Party rule with its sole source of legitimacy, which was why he had to make it the very first of his Four Cardinal Principles.

On the other hand, Deng saw clearly that Marxism was a huge obstruction to the smooth implementation of China's economic reforms.

I think Deng understood that the Marxism of the Party-state was a huge impediment for its own progress. The Party could not abandon the deity of Marxism, and its members were not well versed in the Marxist classics, and even if they were, the Marxist classics were not helpful for the present realities in China. Deng thus chose simply to sidestep Marxism altogether and to insist that there be "no debate."

In this, we see Deng's cleverness at work, but it was also his only option. His pragmatism came in handy here. Deng said he wanted to blaze a trail for China, but the trail he took was shaped by the obstructions that Marxism put in the path of China's reforms. That said, Deng's "no debate" directive had a positive effect on nonofficial and local reforms. It allowed people, as it were, to signal left and turn right, which reflected the divergence between theory and practice. This divergence has dogged the entire process of reform in China such that progress needs to be measured in terms of the degree to which practice has effectively exceeded the limitations imposed by theory. Deng's "no debate" directive can be said to have produced three versions of Party theory. The first is the theory of "socialism with Chinese characteristics" credited to Deng and an updated version of his black-cat/white-cat remark from 1962.

The second is the Three Represents proposed by Jiang Zemin [b. 1926], which sought the backing of universal values for Party theory but failed to develop further once it encountered resistance. The third is the Scientific Outlook on Development advanced by Hu Jintao. Each of these three versions of Party theory prevailed for a period of ten years and represented the approach of the respective administrations led by Deng, Jiang, and Hu. Deng's pragmatism meant that his theoretical propositions lacked a value orientation. Development was the hard truth that preoccupied him. When Jiang promoted the Three Represents, he wanted to introduce social values and concerns but did not proceed. By the time of Hu's Scientific Outlook on Development, values had taken a huge step backward, for this concept was purely instrumental. Hu's Scientific Outlook lacked social values and concerns. Overall, these three versions of Party theory lacked clarity.

Fourth, in relation to intellectual debates, the Party-state adopted a position that was neither left nor right. Within the Party, there have been two factions, the conservatives and the reformists, since the 1980s. Because these two factions stopped debating each other in the 1990s, disagreements came to be seen in terms of siding with the Left or the Right. The policy orientation and decisions of this period as well as the divisions between Left and Right emerging in society all contributed to this development.

For example, people saw the economic reforms implemented under Deng and the complete expansion of these reforms under Jiang as the work of the

Right. Conversely, Hu's subsequent move to advance the state sector at the expense of the private sector was considered as having a leftist complexion. The point is that although all of these top Party leaders tended left in their theoretical outlook in the strategies they adopted, they were neither left nor right. When they felt it necessary to assert their power, they suppressed the Left and the Right alike. What they sought was a form of theoretical equilibrium.

The foregoing, I believe, indicates a fundamental lack of theoretical thinking on the part of the governing Party. It lacks a guiding ideology that is genuinely aimed at unifying theory and practice. To this day, the governing Party confines itself to the utilitarian and opportunistic mode of thinking that prevailed under Mao. This one-thread-running-through-everything mode of thinking has proven to be a serious intellectual hindrance to the deepening of reforms in China.

Genuine reform requires the clarification of one's guiding ideas, for such clarification would indicate that the mooted reform has a theoretical goal to which one has made a clear commitment. To properly determine the path and policies of reform, one needs to have a clear idea of the direction one is taking and the kind of value perspective one must defend. In other words, the principles of social development or the universal values to which one subscribes must be clearly articulated. One simply cannot afford to be vague or adopt an ambiguous attitude where everything is contingent on the needs of a given moment. We have now reached the terminus of a process of reform that is bereft of thought. It's time for reform to be equipped with an unequivocal guiding ideology. At present, no such guiding ideology can be discerned, and we are still relying on vague statements such as "Don't take the old road. Don't travel a deviant path."[18]

What road, then, should we take? So far we have been given neither a definition nor a sufficiently clear theoretical outline to assess. As a consequence, all of us, the Left and the Right alike, are speculating as to what the governing Party has in mind. No one knows for sure. All that we can be sure of is that without a properly stated position, China's reform path will remain unclear.

Academic Production "Bereft of Thought"

Let me now consider academic production from three aspects.

The State of Inquiry Since the Launch of China's Reforms

I would summarize post-Mao intellectual inquiry as follows: intellectual production in the 1980s, academic production in the 1990s, and the production of "isms" in the 2000s and thereafter. These three phrases are sufficient to encapsulate the production, dissemination, and effects of ideas in China of the past three decades or more. I did not coin these phrases. In the 1990s, people used the expression "The thinkers retreated and the academics came to the fore" to signal the difference between the 1980s and 1990s. We need to establish what people understood by "thinkers" and "academics" in this expression. What did inquiry or thinking mean in the 1980s?

As I see it, inquiry (*sixiang*) took two forms in the 1980s: one involved thinking about Marxism in self-reflective, self-critical, and self-renewing ways. A new kind of Marxism was used to attack the old approach to Marxism. What was this new Marxism? It took the form of what people referred to as humane and practical Marxism. It was an innovative way of reworking Marxism from within. The other line of inquiry in the 1980s was the whole range of things people were saying about liberalism and democracy derived from Western formulations. In short, self-reflection on Marxism and the renewed acquisition and interpretation of liberalism were the two main endeavors of the 1980s. Both Marxism and liberalism belong to Western thought. They have not developed out of Chinese experience, nor have they undergone theoretical refinement and innovation in China. This is important to bear in mind when we consider the intellectual legacy of the 1980s. Marxism and liberalism dominated academic inquiry in China at the time to the extent that I cannot think of a distinctive area of inquiry outside these two domains.

In the 1990s, a process of academic professionalization began where, as mentioned earlier, "the thinkers retreated and the academics came to the fore." The philosopher Li Zehou [b. 1930] has written about this. The main feature of this academic professionalization was a burgeoning variety of disciplinary specializations. The metanarrative of Enlightenment, no longer sought after, was displaced by discipline-based research, and important academic achievements in fields such as economics, history, and law were soon evident. As my training was in philosophy, I had an interest in developments within it. Marxism was previously the dominant discourse in departments of philosophy, and it was a discourse produced by rereading and repeating existing arguments presented in various philosophical textbooks. By the 1990s, however, different varieties of Western philosophy had entered China. Every few years China's philosophical journals would feature a range of new terms and notable thinkers. The 1990s also provided a prime opportunity for Confucianism's revival. Formerly attacked when antitraditional forces held sway, Confucianism now prospered as tradition gained authority. Should we consider the 1990s to be a decade in which scholarship flourished? At the very least, we can say that, compared to the 1980s, the 1990s appeared to be a scene of academic flowering across different disciplines.

By the twenty-first century, debates in mainland intellectual circles, whether over ideas or over academic issues, had deteriorated into ideological contests.

Everyone sensed that inquiry was once again becoming politicized. All manner of "isms" appeared, of which the most influential were liberalism, social democracy, statism, neoauthoritarianism, neoconservatism, nationalism, populism, patriotism, classicism, and Confucian constitutionalism. All of these varieties of ideas took a side—whether on the left or on the right—and had an impact on how people saw China. The opposition between Left and Right had become irreconcilable. "Left" and "right" were no longer considered merely differences of opinion or perspective. They had instead become strongly held positions, and clashes between ideological opponents were increasingly intense.

"Left" and "right" now mark two opposing sides in society with a clear boundary between them, such that people can make out straight away from what you've said whether you're on the left or the right. On social media, bloggers with a large following also make their positions very clear and are utterly uncompromising when waging verbal war with their rivals. This is a new phenomenon in China that has appeared only in the past decade. When I say that academic production in China is bereft of thought, I am referring to this shift from academic endeavors of the 1990s to the ideological contests of the 2000s and since. Let us now consider how the mechanisms and inner workings of academic production in China have led to this situation.

The Main Mechanisms of Academic Production in the Reform Era

With academic production in the 1990s located mainly in state-run institutions, the state could exercise a great deal of control over it. The scholars who are present here seem to have evaded the state's control. They are the few who have survived despite the system. The state exercises control mainly through its bureaucratic management of mainland Chinese universities. Moreover, the institution of publishing in China lacks independence, and every form of knowledge production must satisfy the standards set by the state. If the intellectual content of a given manuscript fails to meet the state's standards, it will be excluded from the normal publishing channels.

The state has provided massive subsidies for academic production within its system. It has basically taken control of academic production by determining which topics are of national importance. The state has made a clean sweep of things by restricting university professors and research personnel to work only on these topics. Those who accord with the state's diktat will reap varying levels of benefits for their academic production. This is the basic mechanism of exchange between the state and the academy. The rapid expansion of the state's financial resources has resulted in an unprecedented level of state control over intellectual and academic endeavor, exceeding what the dynastic regimes of premodern China achieved. Today, power has corroded academic production across the entire nation such that thought and scholarship—considered as a national product—are ultimately ideologically constrained to serve the state as its tool.

Under these conditions of strict control, however, the market-led process of reform, especially from the 1990s on, had opened a new channel for market-able academic products. This is a development outside the Party-state system and one that led to the publication of several good works of intellectual inquiry and scholarship. That said, this market for academic products was and remains unable to fully free itself from state control. To run a profitable business, pub-lishers had to avoid a clash with the authorities. They used inventive strategies to publish their academic wares. In the 1990s, these publishing practices pro-duced a modest change in the ecology of mainland intellectual life, as did the emergence of nonofficial academic institutions such as the Unirule Institute.

The productive capacity of this nonofficial academic sector is severely lim-ited because it receives neither state nor commercial support. This sector is in a situation of negative growth. Many of its academic institutions have encoun-tered difficulties, making it impossible for them to continue. Having to fend for themselves has already led several to run out of steam. How can academic institutions, beholden to state power, produce works of intellectual indepen-dence? Even thinkers and intellectuals operating on the fringes of or outside the Party-state system are unable to fully escape it. One can either stop doing intellectual work or revise one's work to accord with the standards for publish-ing laid down by the state. In this regard, the academic flourishing of the 1990s was hollow for it obscured the deficiencies of intellectual life in China.

Vacuous Academic Production

Let's begin by noting that state control over academic production in China has meant that academics must be ever mindful of the types of products the author-ities favor. We may describe the state as well disposed, at best, toward the expansion and renewal of those forms of knowledge that serve a functional, methodological, practical, or technological need: the kind of knowledge that is devoid of both ultimate concerns and intellectual creativity. Academic publi-cations that have resulted from state-funded research are mostly garbage. These publications not only provide no assistance whatsoever to China's intellectual advancement but also have had the opposite effect of destroying people's capac-ity to think and to defend the values they hold dear.

The growing vacuousness in mainland intellectual life is also the result of ideological clashes among academics. These are clashes over the use of Western ideas in China rather than home-grown Chinese theories. The war of words between China's Left and Right essentially revolves around Chinese under-standings of the differences between the Left and the Right in the United States. Both sides draw on Western intellectual resources to discuss Chinese issues, yet their arguments are a clear departure from Western thinking, value perspectives, and approaches. As a consequence, many people have been at a loss for words. These Chinese debates over isms are neither centered on China nor faithful to the Western ideas they employ, which is why Chinese academics have found themselves unable to make any progress.

Finally, let us consider the Confucian revival Mr. Qiu Feng has been studying. On the surface, it would appear to be the reconstruction of a knowledge with China at its very core. At present, however, its prospects of becoming the intellectual mainstream in China are dim. The Confucian narrative contains elements of constitutionalism and can lend itself to politicization. However, the important thing for us to observe is whether and the extent to which it has any impact on present-day society in China. In this regard, Jiang Qing's so-called political Confucianism and Qiu Feng's constitutional Confucianism appear to me, even at their very best, incapable of surpassing Kang Youwei's re-reading of the early classics to promote a New Text revival.

Academic production that is bereft of thought is cut from the same cloth as revolution and reform pursued without thought. Together, they reflect a China that is bereft of thought. Following the total eclipse of traditional Chinese thought centered on Confucianism, the production and dissemination of Chinese thought has had to draw on the intellectual resources of the West for a century or more. This process occurred alongside the subjection of Chinese thought to systematic state control. Thus, Chinese thought was reduced to a useful tool. It became a loincloth covering up the state's imposed ideology. If we reflect on the situation and development of Chinese thought over the past century, we are bound to ask ourselves the question: Can we rebuild a thinking China?

To Rebuild a Thinking China

Based on the foregoing analysis, let me reiterate that both the Chinese Revolution and the reforms undertaken since 1978 have lacked an intellectual soul. Neither revolution nor reform has benefited from clear theoretical guidance. Neither was motivated by ultimate concerns. People instead espoused conflicting forms of theory and practice that were riven with contradictions, and this was because pragmatism and opportunism guided the actions that were taken. The stated theoretical programs and guiding ideas have been merely rhetorical and a form of strategic discourse. The future of China lies in rebuilding a China rich in thought, in restoring the unity of theory and practice, and in developing values that accord with human justice.

The first thing we must do is to build proper mechanisms for producing thought. These mechanisms require freedom of speech and an independent publishing system. They are also contingent on the demise of the present system whereby the state controls the production of thought. These mechanisms also require the abolition of state-imposed standards on intellectual production and a clear distinction to be drawn between thought and ideological propaganda. The producers of thought must be allowed the freedom to discuss, write, and publish their arguments as they see fit. This would ensure that thought can be independently produced and disseminated. State funding for intellectual production should be based on academic measures, and the system must ensure equal treatment for all academics. Only when there is freedom of speech and freedom of publishing will Chinese thought genuinely flourish. Only then will China become a great civilization and a country rich in thought.

Next, we would need to establish a marketplace for ideas. The Nobel laureate in economics Ronald Coase [1910–2013] once gave China this piece of advice: "A vibrant market for ideas is both a precondition for scholarly excellence and an indispensable moral and epistemic foundation for an open society and a free economy."[19] A market for ideas implies that intellectual products can circulate freely, that there are no restrictions on their dissemination. This is especially pertinent in the era of the Internet, in which an open market for ideas is the precondition for the flourishing of ideas.

From a market perspective, the dissemination of ideas requires us to invalidate the idea of the state's power over the market. To a certain extent, thought is power's natural enemy, for thought both criticizes and defines power. Ideas that have relied on people in power for their dissemination may enjoy preferential treatment during a period of authoritarian rule, but such ideas lack the vitality to endure beyond the period of authoritarian patronage. The credibility of a given theory cannot be sustained by power. Rather, it rests on the capacity of that theory to solve real problems. Moreover, the dissemination of ideas within the market for ideas is propelled by demand. Only those ideas that satisfy the spiritual needs and ultimate concerns of ordinary citizens can exert an influence on their actions and behaviors. People will surely reject those ideas that go against their normal needs.

Third, this market for ideas implies the fullest exchange of ideas with all varieties of ideas jostling for attention. It allows a system capable of accommodating a plurality of ideas to be established, to produce a true situation of a hundred flowers blooming and a hundred schools of thought in contention. The flourishing of thought alone ensures that intellectual products will be diverse and innovative.

Fourth, we must establish thought that is anchored in Chinese subjectivity. This is a huge topic. In saying this, I am not proposing a departure from the broad road of world civilization, nor am I calling for a rejection of universal values. Rather, we need to build a discursive system suited for discussing

China's past, present, and future, premised on a world civilization and universal values. This is an issue of abiding interest to me. The two journals I have distributed today contain articles I have written on the concept of a Chinese historical perspective. As I see it, there are four aspects to consider in relation to thought that is anchored in Chinese subjectivity. First, this form of thought must take a Chinese historical perspective as its principal guide. What I'm calling a Chinese historical perspective is essentially a way of discerning how Chinese history differs from European history in terms of its developmental features and human experience. On this basis, we would develop a Chinese yardstick to rediscover and rewrite Chinese history as a history that has long been obscured by European history. This would thus allow us to distinguish between Chinese and European historical perspectives.

Second, Chinese thought that is anchored in Chinese subjectivity must accord with Chinese experience past and present. Third, awareness of real-life Chinese problems must guide our thinking. Fourth, our goal is to advance universal justice and happiness for the whole of humanity. These are the four aspects of what I am calling thought that is anchored in Chinese subjectivity.

The issues I have raised here today are underdeveloped and require more work. For a long time now, the governing Party has enjoyed a monopoly on ideology and the production of thought. It has turned Marxism into the key source of its political legitimacy. However, the Party leaders are well aware that there is no market demand for Party thinking and that Party thinking is in fact useless. Yet they continue to rely on the formulations that make up Party thinking to justify their being in power. This is a problem for the Party leadership. Nonofficial thinking produced within society is critically oriented and resistant to the Party's formulations. Most nonofficial thinking draws on Western knowledge paradigms, and liberalism and social democracy should be considered, in this regard, as belonging to the same knowledge system.

At present, many people are asking if we can resolve the opposition between nonofficial and official modes of thinking. Is Qiu Feng's constitutional Confucianism an attempt to provide us with an alternative path? Is it a third path that would serve as an intermediary between Western-informed nonofficial thinking and Party thinking? Methodologically, it is an advisable path to take, but the question of what formulations we would use to understand and explain Chinese problems requires much more work. For scholars, the present situation of Chinese thought and the problems it faces have become increasingly clear. Everyone should be able to analyze these problems from their own perspective and propose solutions to these problems. The production of independent ideas of positive value is contingent on free and open debate among thinkers and on their capacity to exchange their ideas to the fullest. It is by these means alone that together we can advance Chinese thought.

Appendix: My Response to Expert Critiques

The comments from my fellow scholars were most relevant. As both Lei Yi and
Ye Fu have pointed out, I have yet to address such questions as "What is Chinese autonomy?" "What is thought that is anchored in Chinese subjectivity?"
and "What is Western discourse as a system?" I am also aware that if we want
to depart from Western formulations and concepts, then we would have no way
of expressing ourselves and no words with which to form our thoughts. I mentioned the need for us to construct a Chinese historical perspective. Is it valid
to speak of a Chinese as opposed to a European historical perspective? This will
also require more work. When my presentation was published, someone criticized me for producing a statist narrative and using statist rhetoric.

China's development for the past two thousand years has indeed been state
led. We cannot deny this. China's state-led structure, understood as an organizational system, has remained intact to this day. This enduring state-led structure is the object of my inquiry. The question is, Should it be regarded as a
form of statism?

This is where we must consider the differences between Chinese and Western understandings of the concept of the state. The Western concept of the state
entails a narrative that includes the ideas of constitutionalism, democracy, and
liberty as these ideas have emerged and developed in the West, reflecting the
history of their usage over time. If we now choose to assign a "universal value"
to these ideas and transplant them in China's discursive terrain, we will indeed
encounter a whole raft of enormous difficulties arising from the shift of these
ideas from a Western to a Chinese discourse.

Professor Zhang Shuguang mentioned just now that in proposing a need for
thought that is anchored in Chinese subjectivity, I seem to be ignoring the fact
that the work of scholars such as Qiu Feng is already premised on the idea of a
Chinese intellectual tradition extending over two thousand years. He thus finds
unconvincing my attempt to establish a new way of exploring Chinese thought
as anchored in Chinese subjectivity. What I am calling thought anchored in
Chinese subjectivity or a Chinese historical perspective is merely an abstract
proposal at present. I am still uncertain as to how to develop these concepts
intellectually or to reach an empirical conclusion about them. It would be absurd
to treat Qiu Feng's work as our only source of information on what constitutes
China's intellectual tradition. At present, there is little new thinking besides the
accumulated Western and Confucian intellectual resources already available
to us. This is the predicament of intellectual production in China today that I
have tried to address in my lecture today.

When I pointed out that we don't seem able to take a step without leaning
on the crutch of Western thought, I am including myself as someone for whom
Western thought is indispensable. My critics have pointed out my reliance on

Max Weber's concepts of procedural justice and instrumental rationality, which are clearly Western in origin. On this point, we need to ask the question whether we are up to the task of productively transposing Weber's concepts into Chinese intellectual discourse.

The bigger issue, however—and this is what Ye Fu raised—is whether our existing range of theories is adequate for explaining China's present-day problems. The criteria and measures we use must be able to explain Chinese realities. Otherwise, these theories would lack vitality. When we consider the ideas that have flooded into China for the past century, we should judge them for their effectiveness. Whether it be liberalism or Marxism or any other ism, we should be asking whether and how effective an ideology has been in solving Chinese problems. Assessing liberalism in this way would not make us feel optimistic about its prospects in China—of that I am certain. This is because liberalism has encountered and will encounter restrictions from the political system in China. However, we should also consider whether theories of liberalism create their own conceptual limitations. I dealt with this question in my article "The Third Wave of Chinese Liberalism," in which I reflected on the types of changes that liberalism would have to undergo and the types of discursive adjustments that would need to be made before a liberal argument could provide an effective response to the problems in our midst.[20]

I find myself in agreement with Ye Fu's comment that I am ultimately asking only one question. My question in fact goes beyond asking why it is that China lacks great ideas and great thinkers. There are many thinkers in China, and many excellent thinkers are present at this seminar here. My question is in fact a criticism of the system in which we find ourselves. For several years now, I have devoted my energies to promoting the social critical tradition in Marxism, with the aim of critiquing the existing power structure in China. This is a power structure unlimited in any way by institutional and legal restraints, let alone by moral constraints. Indeed, we would not be able to find an enduring set of ideas, beliefs, meanings, or values within this power structure.

Thus, if this power structure continues to develop, it will gravely endanger China. Hence, my question should not be read as asking what tasks we have yet to complete within Chinese scholarship or that I am implying that Western critical discourse is not effective in explaining Chinese problems. I instead want us to be alert to the fact that the political system and institutions that have developed out of the Chinese Revolution and the process of post-Mao reform are the result of pragmatic, opportunistic, and strategic actions taken in response to the problems of a given time. There really are no theoretical norms or a program, no ultimate concerns or a general direction to speak of. My main goal is to provide a critique of the flaws of the system. In this regard, I have focused on the structural and intellectual causes of these flaws.

Translator's Notes

1. Rong Jian, "Meiyou sixiang de Zhongguo" (A China bereft of thought), Gongshi Wang, March 25, 2013, Chinese text available at The China Story, https://www.thechinastory .org/wp-content/uploads/2017/02/Rong-Jian-%E8%8D%A3%E5%89%91-%E6%B2%A1 %E6%9C%89%E6%80%9D%E6%83%B3%E7%9A%84%E4%B8%AD%E5%9B%BD.pdf.

2. For a very useful brief biography of Rong, see "Rong Jian," The China Story, n.d., https://www.thechinastory.org/key-intellectual/rong-jian-%E8%8D%A3%E5%89%91/.

3. See the Xinhhua website's report on Xi's talk at Xinhua Wang, December 8, 2016, http://news.xinhuanet.com/politics/2016-12/08/c_1120082577.htm.

4. This translation was supported by the Australian Centre on China in the World at the Australian National University and the School of Languages, Literatures, Cultures, and Linguistics at Monash University. Rong Jian's essay was the subject of a translation practicum undertaken by students enrolled in the master of translation course at Monash University in 2015. I thank the students for sharing their views on the challenges of translating this text.

5. The frequent use of the term *wenti yishi*, "problem-consciousness," in Chinese intellectual discourse indicates a widespread view that effective problem solving comes from asking the right questions.

6. Rong Jian's article "Zhongguo lishi guanyu xiandaixing wenti" appeared in the journal *Zhongguo Shehui Kexue Jikan* (Chinese Social Sciences Quarterly) in 2013 and is readily available at Siyu Wang, http://www.m4.cn/opinion/2013-04/1205901.shtml.

7. All of the figures Rong names here were prominent Confucian scholar-officials deeply involved in New Text scholarship and activism. On the New Text and the *Gongyang zhuan*, see note 9 in chapter 1.

8. Republican-era CCP discourse used the term *zhongjian didai* for areas perceived as under neither socialist nor capitalist control and thus ideological battlegrounds.

9. This "social history debate" is recounted in Arif Dirlik, *Revolution and History: Origins of Marxist Historiography in China, 1919–1937* (Berkeley: University of California Press, 1989).

10. The expression *yiyi guanzhi* first appeared in *The Analects* (4:15) of Confucius: "The Master said, 'Shen, my doctrine has one single thread running through it.' Master Zeng Shen replied: 'Indeed.' The Master left. The other disciples asked: 'What did he mean?' Master Zeng said: 'The doctrine of the Master is: Loyalty and reciprocity, and that's all'" (*The Analects of Confucius*, trans. Simon Leys [New York: Norton, 1997], 17).

11. Rong misquotes Mao here. What Mao was reported to have said on April 23, 1975, was: "Few in our Party really understand Marxism-Leninism." Quoted in "Shiyi da shangde zhengzhi baogao" (Political report to the Eleventh Party Congress), August 20, 1977, http://cpc.people.com.cn/GB/64162/64168/64563/65449/4526440.html.

12. These are the signature slogans of China's top leaders: since 2000 Jiang Zemin's "Three Represents" (the Party represents the most advanced productive forces—capitalists are OK; the most advanced cultural forces—intellectuals, too; and the interests of the whole people—so, no more class struggle), and Hu Jintao's Scientific Outlook on Development, which defies any clear summary.

13. Yan Xishan, "Gongchandang heyi xizhuan Zhongguo dalu" (How did the Communist Party capture the Chinese mainland?), August 10, 1949, https://blog.boxun.com /hero/201110/jjp/2_1.shtml. Yan was a militarist and governor of Shanxi Province in Republican-era China.

14. Wu Jiaxiang, *Gong tianxia* (Public state) (Guilin: Guangxi Shifan Daxue, 2013).

15. Rong Jian, "Lun Zhongguo 'fengjianzhuyi' wenti, dui Zhongguo qianxiandai shehui xingzhi he fazhan de chongxin renshi yu pingjia" (On the problem of Chinese "feudalism": A fresh recognition and evaluation of the nature and development of premodern Chinese society), *Wen shi zhe* 4 (2008): 5–21.

16. "Two Whatevers" refers to the following official statement that appeared in a joint editorial of the CCP's three leading outlets, *People's Daily, Red Flag*, and *People's Liberation Daily*, on February 7, 1977: "We will resolutely uphold whatever policy decisions Chairman Mao made and unswervingly follow whatever instructions Chairman Mao gave." The name was a derogatory reference to Mao's immediate successor, Hua Guofeng (1921–2008), used by Deng Xiaoping and other critics of Hua to highlight his unsuitability to lead post-Mao China as an unthinking Mao loyalist.

17. On these developments, see Xu Jilin, "The Fate of an Enlightenment: Twenty Years in the Chinese Intellectual Sphere (1978–98)," trans. Geremie R. Barmé and Gloria Davies, in *Chinese Intellectuals Between the Market and the State*, ed. Merle Goldman and Edward X. Gu (London: Routledge, 2002), 183–203.

18. In his final political report to the CCP Congress in November 2012, Hu Jintao, as the party's departing general secretary, stated: "We cannot take the old road of seclusion and stagnation, and we must not change our banner to travel along a deviant path." See also David Bandurski, "CCP Congress Enters the Weibo Era," China Media Project, November 8, 2012, http://cmp.hku.hk/2012/11/08/28719/.

19. The original statement appears in Ronald Coase and Ning Wang, *How China Became Capitalist* (Basingstoke, U.K.: Palgrave Macmillan, 2013), 203. Rong appears to be quoting Coase from Deng Yuwen, "Kesi de zhonggao, sixiang shichang shi Zhongguo zhuanxing chenggong de guanjiang" (Coase's warning: A market for ideas is the crux of China's successful transition), *Yifengwang*, September 7, 2013, http://news.ifeng.com /opinion/sixiangpinglun/detail_2013_09/07/29403576_0.shtml.

20. Rong Jian, "Zhongguo ziyouzhuyi disan bo" (The third wave of Chinese liberalism), 2012, China in Perspective, https://www.chinainperspective.com/ArtShow.aspx?AID =180003.

CHAPTER 4

ORIGINAL INTENTIONS START WITH THE PEOPLE[1]

GUO YUHUA

TRANSLATED BY DAVID OWNBY

Translator's Introduction

The text translated here is one of Guo Yuhua's (b. 1956) recent social media posts that, like many others, was quickly removed from the Internet. The post was prompted by Beijing municipal authorities' decision to remove a significant part of Beijing's "low-end population" (*diduan renkou*, migrant workers) as part of a city cleanup campaign in late 2017, a campaign that made headlines outside of China as well. Guo used this "campaign" as part of a broader criticism of the heavy-handed, top-down style of political leadership that, she insists, has changed little over the years, despite four decades of "reform and opening." Her use of the notion of "original intentions" in the title and elsewhere in the post is meant to be ironic. Party authorities use the term to suggest (among other things) affinities between Party rule and Confucian benevolence, both of which are grounded in "the people."[2] Guo's text thus also serves as an example of what can no longer be said in China (aside from the mention of the "Nazi overtones" in the removal of Beijing's "low-end population," Guo's text is "liberal" but not particularly radical).

"Original Intentions Start with the People"

It was at the end of 2017, the closing of a day at the beginning of winter. Triggered by a fire in the Daxing district on November 18, the entire city of Beijing plunged itself into a forty-day-long special exercise to root out and clean up hidden safety problems. The cleanup work naturally linked up with efforts to phase out nonmunicipal functions and reduce the population of migrant workers.[3] According to the previously announced upper-population limits in each district and the number of people to be relocated, Beijing would need to deal with more than 3 million outsiders. A movement aimed at cleaning up the "low-end population" quickly kicked into high gear, and even if that term was quickly dropped because of its Nazi overtones, the cleanup work continued to move forward like a thunderstorm.

The results of the campaign were immediately obvious: some migrant workers left with their families; others moved to even more marginal areas of the city; and a few lost souls wandered through the cold night streets. Beijing landlords suffered heavy losses as their renters vacated their buildings, and outside merchants who had catered to the migrants lost their shirts. Rents shot up on all grades of housing [as the affected population struggled to relocate]. Beijing residents also suffered: shops in the neighborhood closed down [as migrant workers left], which made buying groceries, shopping, and eating out difficult, especially for old people. Nannies who suddenly found themselves without housing had to go back to their villages. Taxi drivers couldn't find a place to eat. Many white-collar workers living in midlevel or low-level housing were anxious, fearing night raids by the police. A Tsinghua PhD who was already teaching in a university had to find new housing overnight because his rental unit was caught up in the cleanup.

The forty-day cleanup had hardly begun when another campaign began with the call to bring forth a beautiful "skyline" by destroying signs and billboards. There was heavy equipment all over Beijing, and billboards, building signs, and work-unit identification plaques all came tumbling down. This was even the case for well-known organizations such as *China National Geography* [magazine], China International Broadcasting Station, the Baidu Building, China Grain Reserve Management Company, China Agricultural University, Shangdi Office Center, Zhongguancun Enterprise Building, National Open University, Zhongguancun Kemao Electronic City . . . all of these signs disappeared.

According to the plan, some twenty-seven thousand illegal advertisements were to be torn down before the end of the year. It didn't take long for people to feel that destruction was proceeding at a dizzying pace, [and people asked one another,] "Do you still know the way home (or to work)?" I heard that the reasoning behind the destruction of signs was the following: the roofs of the skyscrapers and the billboards come together to make up what is called the "skyline," the city's calling card, as well as an important organized part of the city's landscape. Crafting a more beautiful landscape for Beijing required new regulations in order to accelerate the legal cleanup activities targeting the illegal signs.

We have to wonder if this is really a legal campaign to remove illegal signage or if the goal is rather to create a beautiful skyline? These are not the same thing. First, where is the campaign's legitimacy? When the signs were put up, did they not follow regulations? Who decides what is illegal and what is not? Next, what is the "legitimacy" of the beautiful skyline? The signage may be obscuring the skyline, but the skyscrapers are much taller than the billboards. Aren't they obscuring the skyline, too? Will removing the obstacles reveal a beautiful skyline? Will uniformity be beautiful? Is empty beautiful? Are the cities of the world, full of all sorts of signage, ugly? Should the government decide what is beautiful and what is not? Massive destruction leads to commercial losses, the waste of vast amounts of capital and resources, inconvenience for the citizens, and huge amounts of garbage. Who is finally benefiting from this? To my mind, this is not at all clear.

The third year-end misery was the changeover from heating with coal to heating with natural gas or electricity. This was something meant to benefit the people and protect the environment, and we cannot say that the original intention was not good. The government agencies responsible for the change certainly worked hard at it, but they, too, attacked the problem campaign style, ruthlessly promoting it throughout North China, establishing "coal-free areas," and promoting the "switch from coal to natural gas." In some areas, they went so far as to threaten coercion, warning that "whoever sells coal will be arrested; whoever burns coal will be arrested."

To control smog, reduce fine particulate matter, and preserve the blue skies of Beijing and Tianjin, government agencies certainly went all out, but did policy makers ever stop to consider what the negative consequences of the campaign might be? Especially for people in rural villages, who for many years have been burning coal and straw for heating and to cook their food? Are their heaters and pipes properly installed to handle the change? Is the supply of natural gas timely and adequate? Is the state supplement offered to those making the changeover sufficient to pay for the work that needs to be done? Are they sure that natural gas is safe? What might be the effects of the changeover on different regions, climates, and popular habits? This is a process that affects a large number of systems, and attacking it campaign style is sure to produce lots of problems. Some places gave up coal only to find that gas wasn't available or wasn't sufficient; many companies and enterprises were compelled to stop or limit production for this reason. Some peasant households made the changeover only to find that the heating didn't work and they had to endure the cold. This was particularly hard on the elderly and the children. Even primary schools in some villages were reduced to holding classes outside in the sun, and the children ran around trying to stay warm.

Only after the complaints of shivering people filled the streets, after the houses had been knocked down, the heaters shut down, the billboards, signs, and placards torn down, production stopped, stores closed, the daily routines of the people upturned, only then did the Environment Ministry issue its "letter concerning properly carrying out the work of coal management and ensuring that the masses comfortably get through the winter," pointing out that "in the case of projects or areas where the work is not yet completed, [the people] have the choice of continuing to heat with coal or changing to alternative methods." It was only at this point that the leadership began talking about "paying attention to cultural activities and human society" and "warming the people's hearts." It was only at this point that mainstream media began to insist that "we must not use extreme work methods that leave the masses' homes or hearts cold." Might this have been just a bit tardy?

The three things I just discussed—population, signage, and heating (environment)—are in fact one thing: they all have to do with the city; they all involve management through campaigns; and the underlying thought pattern is that of a planned economy. Obviously, the existence of a city is as complicated as natural ecology because city ecologies have always been pluralistic, based on mutual give and take and cooperation. People of different social classes live together in cities and make demands on one another in the course of economic and social life, and this mutual work and play constitute the ecology of city life. No one can live alone in a city, no matter what "level" he or she occupies, and when you clear away the "low-level population," the influence will be felt by the midlevels and the higher levels, as I argued earlier. Such changes in a city's ecology are bad for everyone.

Managing the diverse life of a city ecology through the mentality of a planned economy cannot work. As in the case of economic activity, even the most intelligent mind or think tank cannot understand everything, adjust everything, control everything. This is mission impossible. The function of government is not to manage and control everything but rather to protect the legitimate rights of enterprises and individuals through laws, regulations, and procedures and to provide the public commodities and services required by city life. For example, to manage the problem of urban smog, the government should scientifically establish and publicize standards, and any enterprise, government body, or region that is not ready to make the changeover from coal to gas (or electricity) can autonomously manage its transformation, achieving a balance between meeting the standards and coping with its capacities, making progress in a gradual fashion.

Given the complexity of city management, a one-size-fits-all, pedal-to-the-metal approach cannot work. In fact, we are still managing in a "Great Leap Forward" campaign style, a management tradition that China continues to employ. By "campaign style," I mean an all-out effort that ignores concrete details, noninstitutional and unscientific methods that ignore unfortunate consequences—all of which goes against standard procedure. We've seen this over and over again in campaigns in our lifetime, which in practice caused huge disasters, proving that this approach does not work. The reason that we keep doing this in China is that the mechanism is one of top-heavy coercion, with each level of government paying attention only to the top, rather than to the bottom, to say nothing of being responsible to the people.

The basic logic of campaign-style governance is, first, bureaucratic logic, with its emphasis on results and achievements; second, the logic of pleasing the ruler, which means extreme enthusiasm for the policy and competition to carry it out, which means that going too far is preferable to not doing enough; and, third, the logic of great unity, meaning unified planning that ignores differences of regions, situations, and professions and demands uniformity.

From this, it is clear that in terms of city development and governance, the problem is not that of "going too fast" or "going too far" or "lacking methodology." The problem is the basic thought patterns behind management thinking.

Another important problem created by the three urban initiatives discussed earlier has to do with considerations of the people's lives and the people's hearts. What is the point of a city? For whom is a city built? For whom does it develop? This looks like a simple question, something that goes without saying. Isn't the point of a city for people to live in it? Isn't the point of city management to make the people living there happy? But in actual practice it is precisely on this point that things have gone off the tracks, and we have forgotten our original intention. After the Nineteenth Party Congress [in October 2017], the [Chinese Communist] Party and the government frequently brought up the notion of "original intention[s]," and someone provided eight examples of the meaning of the expression to help the people understand it.[4] To my mind, the most important and most basic of them all is number six: "Persist in your original intention; continue to believe that the basis of the Party is the people; cling to the idea that everything is for the people, everything relies on the people. Fully develop the positive spirit, the initiative, and the creativity of the masses, and unstintingly develop undertakings that create happiness for the people."

The common people might wonder what the original intention actually was. Clearly, if we turn our backs on the original intention, then no matter how good it was at the outset, the result we produce will be a disaster. Smart people know that All Under Heaven is the people's All Under Heaven; the city is the city dwellers' city. If there were no people, why would we need a government, and if we pay no attention to the people's lives, then what's the point of the capital? City management must be based on the people. If the basis is not the life and heart of the people, then all governance plans, management measures, and concrete policies will miss their mark and wind up producing negative or even disastrous consequences. If the people are crawling on the ground, women and children sobbing and weeping, what a responsible government should do is surely clear as day.

Translator's Notes

1. Guo Yuhua, "Chuxin suozai yiren weiben" (Original intentions start with the people), originally published on Guo's blog on December 8, 2017, but shortly thereafter removed and the blog closed by authorities.
2. See, for example, Jiang Shigong's discussion of "original intentions" in "Philosophy and History: Intepreting the 'Xi Jiping Era' Through Xi's Report to the Nineteenth National Congress of the CCP," orig. pub. in Chinese January 2018, trans, David Ownby, Reading the China Dream, n.d., https://www.readingthechinadream.com /jiang-shigong-philosophy-and-history.html.
3. This "cleanup" was part of Xi Jinping's campaign to remake Beijing city so that it would be among the world's great capitals, in part by relocating "nonmunicipal functions" such as manufacturing, logistics, and wholesale markets to districts outside Beijing. See "Beijing to Continue Phasing Out Non-capital Functions in the Next Five years," *Global Times*, December 8, 2016.
4. Announced by Xi Jinping at the ninety-fifth anniversary of the founding of the CCP in July 2016 as *buwang chuxin* (never forget original intentions). A simplified version of the eight "original intentions" would be:

   1. Never forget original intentions: persist in Marxism-Leninism.
   2. Never forget original intentions: struggle for communism and socialism.
   3. Never forget original intentions: persist in the four self-confidences of socialism with Chinese characteristics, persist in the Party's basic line.
   4. Never forget original intentions: promote the strategic arrangement of "the overall plan for promoting economic, political, cultural, social, and ecological progress" and the "four comprehensives"; promote the overall construction of a moderately prosperous society.
   5. Never forget original intentions: do not swerve from reform and opening.
   6. Never forget original intentions: rely on the people for all things, progress toward the goal of creating happiness for the people.
   7. Never forget original intentions: follow the path of peaceful development.
   8. Never forget original intentions: preserve the progressive nature and the purity of the Party.

CHAPTER 5

"THE SHADOW OF COMMUNIST CIVILIZATION"

A Gongshi Wang (Consensus Net) Interview[1]

GUO YUHUA

TRANSLATED BY DAVID OWNBY AND JOSHUA A. FOGEL

Translators' Introduction

Guo Yuhua (b. 1956) is a well-known sociologist at Tsinghua University in Beijing. Academically, she is perhaps best known for her project, carried out with fellow Tsinghua sociologist Sun Liping (b. 1955) and others, on "communist civilization" (*gongchanzhuyi wenming*), which is the subject of this interview. The project, launched in the mid-1990s, uses an oral history approach to tell the story of life in village China, beginning with collectivization and land reform. Several villages were chosen in North and South China, and teams of scholars and students spent many months with the peasants over the years, building relationships and collecting data. Guo worked in Ji village in northern Shaanxi, and the results of her work were eventually published in her volume *Shouku ren de jiangshu: Ji cun lishi yu yizhong wenming de luoji* (The narrative of those who suffer: The history of Ji village and the logic of a civilization, published by the Chinese University Press of Hong Kong in 2013). As the title suggests, Guo's work reflects her embrace of "the people" and her engagement with Western theorists such as James Scott. In the China field, her work resembles that of Edward Friedman, Paul Pickowicz, Mark Selden, and Kay Ann Johnson on village China in its fiery condemnation of much of the impact of "communist civilization" on China's rural population.[2]

Guo's embrace of the people has made her a trenchant critic of China's authorities, as reflected in the journalist Ian Johnson's interview with her for the

New York Review of Books in 2018.[3] This critical stance has ultimately limited the diffusion of her work and hence her influence. Her book is banned in China (friends and colleagues "smuggle" in copies for her from Hong Kong), and the authorities frequently take down her posts on social media. In this instance, the platform on which the interview was published—the website Gongshi Wang (Consensus Net)—was dismantled by authorities in 2016, and although the interview is still available elsewhere on the Web, it is no longer conspicuously available as it was on the well-known site Gongshi Wang, where it appeared together with similar interviews with other figures such as the historian Xu Jilin (b. 1957). Like the move from the social media platform Weibo to Wechat, which diminished the impact of powerful Internet voices in China by confining them to smaller "friend circles," the "disappearing" of platforms such as Gongshi Wang disperses and thus muffles critical voices.

The Shadow of "Communist Civilization"

A Commitment to Collecting the Oral History of Village Life
in the Second Half of the Twentieth Century

The Origins of Oral History: "History Without the Voice of the People Is Not Complete"

Xu Shuming (journalist): Professor Guo, you've been continuously engaged in fieldwork over the past fifteen years. Could you briefly describe the background to your oral history project?

Guo Yuhua: This project started in the mid- to late 1990s. At the time, Professor Sun Liping was at Peking University, and Professor Shen Yuan [b. 1954] and I were at the Academy of Social Sciences.[4] Ying Xing [b. 1968] was still finishing his studies,[5] and there was also a small group of MA and PhD students. Our idea was to carry out research in oral history related to the larger history of Chinese village social life in the second half of the twentieth century, so Professor Sun and I took charge of the project. At the outset, the idea was to choose six villages in different regions throughout the country and then to separately collect interview materials from the villagers. We have been working for years to carry out the plan, but in fact we have worked on only four villages: Xi village in Hebei, Ji village in northern Shaanxi, Liuping village in Sichuan (now a part of Chongqing municipality), and Shiwan village in Dongbei (China's northeastern provinces).

Yuan Xunhui (journalist): Why choose these villages? Was it a random sample?

Guo Yuhua: At the time, our hope was to choose samples from different regions, from both South and North. The last two villages we chose were from the South, but our resources were inadequate in that the southern villages—in Guangdong or in Jiangxi—posed lots of problems, including that of dialects. In addition, after the participating students graduated, many wound up no longer working in the same area, which left us short-handed, and we finally just dropped the last two villages. In addition, even if we used the oral history approach in the four villages we worked on, more progress was made in some villages than in others. Fieldwork in Ji village was the most thorough and basically covered its entire history over the course of the second half of the twentieth century. Work in the other villages was oriented toward particular questions. In some, work on "land reform" was most comprehensive; in others, it was "collectivization." We had two goals for this oral history work at the outset.

First, China is presently undergoing a social transformation, and if we want to understand today's transformation, we first must understand the condition of China's society prior to the transformation. Many people think today's transition has arrived at a bottleneck, that the reforms are dead and the transition stalled. This means that research into the situation prior to the transition—from 1949 until the beginning of reform and opening—is all the more important, including the basic nature of the social system as well as its actual mode of operation prior to the current period. So to study any aspect of the contemporary situation in China, you have to pay attention to the transition, and to analyze the process of transition you need a sense of the historical context. In the past, sociology paid relatively little attention to history, and when we decided to make up for this lack and look back at history, we discovered another problem, which is that the history we had was only the official history, the historical narrative of mainstream ideology, which contained any number of twisted, hidden, or even fabricated elements, which meant that we had to treat history from a different angle. History needs different voices; a history with a single voice is clearly problematic and suspect. In past histories, whether official or academic, the historical experience of everyday peasants and women has been ignored. So our ambition at the time was to seek to understand the experiences of those people as well as their own understanding of this historical period. Whether you see this [project] as a return to this history or as a retracing, our goal was to collect and record this period of history because history without the voice of the people is incomplete history, nor is it the real history because history does not exist in one single mode.

Second, as scholars we need to have a basic understanding and judgment of Chinese society to frame our theoretical or academic explorations, so we proposed the idea of "communist civilization." Defining this idea requires understanding its logic in the organization and control of social life, which means grasping its mechanisms and logic through detailed historical materials and the stories of those who have experienced this civilization on the ground. What is especially urgent is to make clear the mechanisms and structures of this civilization through research focused on the process of its development. This has been our scholarly and theoretical pursuit.

At the time, we also knew that progress in the project would be extremely difficult because the mere task of collecting historical materials is already no easy task. Nor was our theoretical conclusion particularly well grounded, which meant that even if we managed to collect and record the materials we were looking for, it was by no means clear that we would be able to achieve our theoretical ambition, which meant that all we could do was make slow progress as we listened, recorded, and carried out our analysis.

This is the general background to our oral history research.

From "Leaders" to "Kin": Building Trust with Villagers

Xu Shuming: The hardest part of fieldwork is getting into the actual lives of the villagers. Did you run into this kind of problem in your fieldwork? How did you solve the problem?

Guo Yuhua: On this front it helped that we were interdisciplinary. Ethnography as practiced by anthropologists demands that scholars enter into the social life of those they are studying, which allows them to view and think about questions from the perspective of the locals.

Of course, doing this demands a long period of input and interaction. It takes more than just a couple of contacts for the peasants to warm up to you, trust you, and talk to you frankly.

Xu Shuming: Can you give an example?

Guo Yuhua: For example, the first time we went to Ji village, the locals were still fetching water in buckets from the well. Their caves were halfway up the mountain, which meant that they had to go down to the valley, fill their buckets, and then walk back up the mountain. There were a good many people in our research team, which meant that our landlord's water needs increased substantially, which meant more trips to the well. This made things harder on the landlord, which we felt bad about, so we started fetching water ourselves. I could only carry the buckets on flat land because there was no way to put them down once you started up the slope, and it was just too much for me. But because our team had only one man, I wound up carrying the buckets to the bottom of the hill, after which he carried them up to the caves, but it really wore us out.

In our second year of research, some people in the village had started to dig their own wells, after which they bought a pump and pumped the water up the hill, which meant that there was running water. We talked about this in our research team and decided that we would provide the money and our landlord the labor so that he could have a well dug in the valley below his mountain, where he planted potatoes. We hired a geomancy master because we didn't know where to dig and followed his advice. We researchers all thought this was funny [i.e., hiring the "superstitious" geomancer], but we were really lucky and found water on the first try. The quality of the water was also very good. So we installed a pump and water pipes, which we buried underground so that they would not freeze in the winter. This was a huge undertaking. We first had to build a reservoir for the water above their [the landlord's family's] cave and pump the water into the reservoir. Then we had to bury the pipes on the mountain so that the water would arrive in the landlord's home.

In fact, you don't have to do anything in particular to get along with the peasants. What's more important is to be friendly, earnest, and trustworthy in the course of interacting with them. As time went on, we got closer and closer to the villagers, and if a young person in the village wanted to go to Beijing to look for work, we would help them. We eventually wound up being something like relatives or kin. When we first got there, they viewed us as outsiders and from Beijing to boot, so they thought that we were part of the government. And no matter how hard we tried to explain to them that we were just teachers and students and not "leaders," it was no use.

In the gradual process of trust building, they would seek us out to help with some activities related to popular beliefs—for example, when they worshipped the Dragon King or Guanyin.[6] At the outset, they were a little hesitant, thinking that outsiders surely would not support these "backward superstitions." Once, when they were rebuilding a temple, they needed someone to write an inscription on a memorial tablet that they were having redone for one of the gods, and they couldn't find anyone in the village who was up to the task. At the time, I was in the village with Professor Luo Hongguang [b. 1957] of the Academy of Social Sciences Sociology Institute, and the former Party secretary of the village—who became the head of the temple committee after leaving that position and was thus in charge of the "religious affairs"—came to us and asked us timidly, "You are both PhDs. Can you help us write the characters?" Both of us automatically said, "Sure," after which we both realized that neither of us knew anything about calligraphy. I said, "We'd better start practicing," and borrowed brush and ink from our landlord's fourth-grade daughter. We started practicing on paper, but it was pretty awful. Calligraphy takes time, after all. We finally came up with an idea: I transferred a nice example of traditional calligraphy from my laptop, and it fit the bill perfectly. We finally traced the characters onto a piece of wood, and then I stayed up all night one night transferring the characters from the wood onto the tablets. I didn't let anyone see me and did it secretly in my room. When the sun came up, we put the tablets on the window sill, and when the former Party secretary saw them, he was very happy and exclaimed: "What beautiful characters! You really are PhDs!" We didn't dare tell him that we had traced them.

As things continued this way over time, they came to know that we were sincere and that we wanted to interact with them and be their friends, and obstacles to exchange melted away, and interviews became very easy.

Can Communism Be Called a Form of Civilization?

"Civilization" as Understood from the Perspective of Everyday Life
Xu Shuming: You just explained the origin of your oral history research in the hope of arriving at a new understanding of contemporary Chinese history. What is innovative about the analytical concept of "communist civilization" compared with the relatively mainstream history of nation building?

Guo Yuhua: The concept wasn't completely new. When we were starting out with the oral history project, we discussed this idea on numerous occasions, and both Sun Liping and I wrote essays about it, arguing that we needed a concept that would cover the period of history that we were planning to study. Some people defined it as the "culture of the Chinese Communist Party" (CCP), or "Party culture." But my feeling was that this was inadequate and defined the scope too narrowly. Of course, we can debate endlessly about the idea of "communist civilization," some people saying that there's no civilization there, only savagery. Here, I can offer two clarifications.

The first has to do with the notion of "civilization." In the past, understandings of civilization have been positive, and the emphasis has been on distinguishing civilization from barbarism in the belief that civilization brought enlightenment and awakening. But now we can see it as a neutral concept, the form manifested by culture at a certain point in its process of development. This is not a definition that we came up with. Norbert Elias [1897–1990] used the idea of "civilization" in this way in his book *The Civilizing Process* [1978].[7] He noted that when the English and the French looked down on one another, each saying the other's behavior was uncivilized, then "civilization" contained within it the idea of "civil" and served to affirm and brag about their own culture. But we decided not to start with a positive interpretation.

The second has to do with the concrete contents of civilization. In the past, when we talked about civilization, we always thought about huge material achievements (Great Wall, Egyptian pyramids) or the spiritual expressions of a civilization (thought, theory, artistic masterpieces). In addition to these, institutional civilization is another extremely important dimension, concerned with the institutional structure on which society rests as well as with the mode of operation attached to this structure. This obviously is another meaning of civilization. It is easy to overlook the ordinary people who live under the structure of a civilization—their daily lives, the way they behave, think, and talk, but all of these are related to civilization.

So our understanding of "communist civilization" is based on our observation of the daily lives of ordinary people, an understanding of civilization from the perspective of the grass roots. If we embrace only the positive, imposing understanding of civilization, we wind up ignoring the state of existence of most members of a society. Communist civilization is altogether different from Western capitalist civilization because its cultural basis, its institutional organization, and even its national character are all different. For this reason, using the idea of "communist civilization" to guide our analysis of the historical period that we want to study is both defensible and applicable in our research. Because we can construct a history out of the daily activities of common people, we should also be able to make clear the logic of a civilization through the words and deeds of common people.

"Communist Civilization" Is More Inclusive

Xu Shuming: The definition of and reasoning behind the concept of "communist civilization" are very close to Western sociological theories. How did you deal with the tension between Western social theory and the experience of Chinese history?

Guo Yuhua: Our hope was to go beyond Western social theory, which is based on research on capitalist civilization. Marx [1818–1883], Weber [1864–1920], and Durkheim [1858–1917] all looked at capitalist civilization and were concerned with its functionality, its weaknesses, and its prospects. We cannot simplistically apply Western theory because, after all, we're dealing with a civilization different from that of capitalism, and the theoretical goal of our work is to answer the most genuine and urgent questions about Chinese society. But we are not rejecting Western theory, which has its own legitimacy and proper place.

If Western scholars can produce theories based on work concerning their contemporary societies, why can't Chinese scholars working on China—a very particular country—produce their own theories in the same way? We are not the only ones to feel this way. Western scholars also think that China in transition is a goldmine for academic research, that the "social facts" produced in the process are stunning. Western societies are already well structured and stable and have been well studied. This is not the case for China, where daily changes leave scholars breathless. From this perspective, we can do a lot of theoretical work and engage in dialogue and exchange with Western scholars, together adding to the store of human knowledge.

Xu Shuming: By starting with the idea of "communist civilization" and only after building your theoretical framework through empirical research, do you not run the risk of limiting your academic research vision?

Guo Yuhua: No. "Communist civilization" is not a particularly rigorous, complete concept, nor have we attached a great deal of theory to it. When I discussed it with Sun Liping and Shen Yuan, we decided that what we called it was not terribly important—and we could even have called it "fish"; what was important was that it is an open system [i.e., the beginning of an exploration]. In my new book [*The Narrative of Those Who Suffer*], the "logic" that we attributed to communist civilization came from generalizations based on empirical research and fieldwork. The idea is based on two preconditions: first, it was different from Western capitalist civilization; and, second, in its process of operation it produced a complete set of mechanisms, logics, and techniques of power. We cannot simplistically reduce this to Party culture. Instead, it is more inclusive and more important because it is implemented in the social practice of ordinary people.

From "Not Identifying" to "Believing:" The Fascination of Researching Communist Civilization

Yuan Xunhui: As a new form of civilization, when communist civilization encountered Chinese tradition, did the two engage in exchange?

Guo Yuhua: Of course. In fact, we really can't say that communist civilization is a new form of civilization because it's hard to tell if it's old or new, and most of it consists of old and new ideas mixed together. It's an ensemble of intellectual concepts and practical logics that gradually came together as the CCP built its regime and consolidated its political power.

The fascinating part of this system is what we might call its "macrolevel social ideal," its "beautiful communist blueprint," which at first glance has nothing to do with the peasants. In fact, it's not just the peasants; probably most intellectuals didn't identify with this "blueprint" either. Outside of the small number of people who founded the CCP, what does this have to do with most people? From this perspective, it looks like these ideas would have had no chance of succeeding, but, in fact, in practice they influenced many, many people, who fought for it, sacrificed for it, and believed in it. In this sense, it's worth trying to understand how these ideas mobilized so many people, how they came to dominate the mental world of so many people, changed their lives, their social relationships, and even their spiritual worlds! This is what we want to understand and analyze.

The emphasis in our research on Ji village was squarely on these beliefs or this ideology and how all of this came to be integrated into the lives of the villagers. This is especially interesting given the conflicts between these concepts and the existing mentality of the villagers, who nonetheless finally came to "accept" the new ideas. Of course, what the villagers accepted was clearly different from what the CCP thought at the outset, but we cannot say that the villagers were not influenced at all because they were changed by the ideas in ways related to their way of life and their way of thinking—the entire structure of village society was changed. For example, in traditional peasant thinking there is the concept of unity (*datong*), as illustrated by the slogan "equalizing rich and poor" used in peasant uprisings over the years. There is a certain overlap between this traditional idea and communist ideals, and of course there are many ways to combine the two. These are what we might call "techniques of power." Peasants always need a belief, and the use of power allowed communist ideals to penetrate deeply into village society.

Yuan Xunhui: You just mentioned numerous activities related to popular beliefs in Ji village. When Communist activities were the most popular, were they still there?

Guo Yuhua: You could say they were forced out of existence—because beliefs, images, and ceremonies were replaced by the mechanism of communist civilization. For example, the peasants originally believed in the Dragon King or Guanyin, but the Communists said that all these were "feudal superstitions" that had to be eliminated. Land reform destroyed some, and at the time of collectivization and the Great Leap Forward they ceaselessly suppressed traditional village beliefs. And during the Cultural Revolution, practically all idols and village temples were demolished. They needed to be replaced at the time, and belief in the revolution and its leaders filled the void.

Yuan Xunhui: My grandmother believed in Buddhism. At the height of the Cultural Revolution, she still believed in Guanyin, the Goddess of Mercy, but circumstances would not allow her to worship openly, so she often awoke in the middle of the night at 3:00 a.m. and offered sacrifices in private by herself. Once political campaigns were over, popular belief and sacrifices returned, and, compared to traditional Chinese popular culture, communist civilization was perhaps only a temporary phenomenon created by political campaigns.

Guo Yuhua: You can't really say it was temporary because in the end many things changed fundamentally. For example, originally many popular ceremonies (such as carrying the Dragon King in his sedan chair to pray for rain, using divination sticks) were thoroughly replaced by political ceremonies at the most extreme moments. Even though they were forced out of sight, these ceremonies did reemerge once again, but they were not the same as they once had been; they had been transformed, merged with something of a different essence.

The Logic of Communist Chinese Civilization

The Lumpenproletariat Become the Initial Activists in Village Land Reform

Xu Shuming: In the Chinese Communist penetration of grassroots villages, land reform was a critical moment. There are documents that illustrate that after the Chinese Communists carried out basic land reform and redistribution, many peasants quietly returned the land to the landlords. How do you understand such behavior?

Guo Yuhua: That happened in Ji village, the one I worked on, and not only did they return the land, but they even returned all the redistributed property. This was not the case everywhere, and the peasants who returned land were genuinely honest, decent people, who despite being caught up in a revolutionary process nonetheless followed traditional ideas. In our fieldwork, we asked them: "Why did you return the land?" They replied: "If somebody had that [land], it was because they had worked for it." In other words, they were saying: "That's not mine." In their view, the land and property had been accumulated bit by bit through the property owner's diligence and ability. In Ji village, some landlord families had numerous cave dwellings, and the process of constructing these caves was exceedingly slow—for example, it could take a year to build one-half or one-third of such a cave, and when they had a bit more money the next year, they would continue the work. So the construction of a cave could take many years to complete. After the revolution arrived, the traditional rural village order was turned upside down overnight, and honest, decent peasants had a hard time accepting it. In addition, returning the land involved practical considerations, such as the worry that the land allocated today might very rapidly be returned tomorrow.

Yuan Xunhui: So, ultimately, people with money still held influence in local areas.

Guo Yuhua: Yes. On the one hand, the peasants worried that the Guomindang would return, and they wouldn't have a leg to stand on in the village. On the other hand, many landlords were the elders in lineages to which the peasants belonged, even lineage heads who may have been linked by blood ties— How could they steal from them? This is the reason that land reform in many villages ran into difficulties with mobilization.

Thus, during land reform, the most extreme, the most violent people were dishonest people, people the peasants called "black skins" (*heipi*), "savage demons" (*yegui*), or "bastards" (*hunzhongzi, zazhong*). These people had nothing and belonged to the lumpenproletariat. They were totally devoid of scruples, and it was they who became the initial activists in village land reform.

"Land to the Tiller" Was Only a Slogan

Xu Shuming: Regarding the Chinese Communist land-reform policy, Yang Kuisong (b. 1953)[8] has noted that at the time of the promulgation of [Liu Shaoqi's] May Fourth directive [1946] and the launch of land reform, the Chinese Communists had no intention of using land reform to expand the military because at the time the major Party policy was to cooperate with the Guomindang.[9] Yet, as you point out many times in your research, in village-level documents the goals of land reform and enlarging the military were linked together, which means that high-level policy and village-level practice seem utterly divorced from one another.

Guo Yuhua: No, it wasn't a divorce between top and bottom, but the differences in land reform in different localities were immense. Land reform in older base areas was basically a gradual process going from moderate to violent; in newer areas, it was implemented all at once and was relatively violent from the beginning. The main reason, though, was concern by the upper level to take stock of the situation, which produced differences in matters of timing. This also reflected the basic logic of communist civilization—namely, a pattern of action based on pragmatism or utilitarianism to reach the goal by any means necessary.

In the older base areas of northern Shaanxi during the period of Communist–Guomindang cooperation, relations between the Chinese Communists and the local gentry was extremely close for basic reasons of survival in the local areas, and the grain and housing provided by local gentry were essential to the Party. In Ji village, Mao even borrowed a set of the *Twenty-Four National Histories* from a local gentry household and never returned it, just compensating the family with a little bit of millet. Li Dingming [1881–1947], a gentry figure from a border region at that time, took part in the Three-Thirds System (*san-san zhi*).[10] He was greatly appreciated by the Communists for his implementation of the policy of "crack troops and simple administration," but ultimately he reportedly committed suicide by swallowing gold. This illustrates that the Communists' policy was based on expediency. During the War of Resistance, they needed a united front against Japan, and thus their land-reform policy was one of moderation and rarely challenged the landlords. When land reform began, the policy was to "reduce rents and interest," to test "trial requisitioning," and to encourage voluntary "contributions of land," all without coercion. After the May Fourth Directive, particularly with the promulgation of the "Outline of the Land Law," the policy underwent a fundamental change, and now it was to confiscate the lands of the landlord class to distribute them to landless peasants.[11] Policy was consistently dictated by the needs of the time.

Yuan Xunhui: The CCP has always been very "crafty." When the Communists entered my hometown in 1949, they absorbed several cultured gentry figures into the system. My grandfather was very active at the time, and he thought he was young and could make a major impact in the new regime. However, after the regime stabilized, it began to lose confidence in him and kept the gentry at a distance.

Guo Yuhua: This sort of thing happened repeatedly because the policy objectives of the Chinese Communists and the goals about which they boasted endlessly were not the same. During land reform, giving "land to the tiller" was a slogan calculated to best win over popular sentiment, and everyone took it as a worthy goal. Looking back on things now, "land to the tiller" was clearly not an objective, but rather a means of mobilizing people during the war, expanding the military, and winning over the people. By obtaining the support of the masses and investing manpower and physical resources, they would gain the support of the masses for the new regime after the establishment of the Communist government. After the regime stabilized and collectivization commenced, all the land allocated to the peasants was taken back. "Land to the tiller" and the idea that it was an objective was, needless to say, just a slogan or a means to an end and nothing more.

The Illusion of "Women's Liberation"

Xu Shuming: Women's policy was also like this. Women's liberation was a highly important item in what the Chinese Communists called "liberating all of China." The provisions in the Marriage Law gave women great freedom, enabling them to demand no-fault divorces. After collectivization, though, women were subjected to discrimination in positions within the work teams, and the work-point system was clear in its inequality to women. What is your assessment of the Chinese Communists' policy on "women's liberation"?

Guo Yuhua: On the question of "women's liberation," I differ from many scholars who have studied this topic. Many of them argue that during the revolutionary period women achieved genuine liberation, but once the period of reform and opening began, women's position once again declined. I completely disagree with this judgment. "Women's liberation" after 1949 was not real liberation in any genuine sense of the term; women were instead the passive objects of liberation. Liberation is a subjective process; one liberates oneself. If another bestows it on you, how can you call this liberation? Anything "given" by another person can just as easily be taken away, and because this was the case with women's liberation at the time, it was meaningless. During land reform, the Communists encouraged women's literacy and mobilized women to participate in political campaigns, but this "participation" was only an indicator of the revolution's success. Rather, you might say that women were mobilized.

What had the greatest impact on women's lives and production was cooperativization (*hezuohua*). For example, in Ji village before cooperatives were formed, women did not work in the fields because traditional roles in the division of labor dictated this. Only during a few days each year, such as during planting season, when there was insufficient manpower, would women help plant seedlings. In the division of labor, women had their own responsibilities, such as cooking, cleaning, caring for the elderly, raising children, weaving cloth for shoes and the like—indeed, the number of tasks was considerable. Cooperativization used a set of institutional arrangements to compel women to participate in collective-labor movements, claiming this to be the liberation of women's labor. However, when they went with men to till the soil, they still had to assume their traditional family chores. So was this liberation, or had their circumstances actually worsened? As I describe it in my book, women during collectivization endured starvation, sickness, and anxiety about their children, amid various sorts of pain and suffering, and had nowhere to go for help.

To a certain degree the so-called women's liberation was nothing but an illusion. The Guanzhong Plain in Shaanxi Province during collectivization was a very large site for cotton production, and cotton was an essential agricultural product for the country's industrialization. However, planting requires the investment of a huge amount of labor. At that time, women's labor capacity was mobilized, and women were treated as instruments of labor—Is this what liberation means? At the same time that the burden on them was made heavier, the work-points policy was highly unfair. Women's work points were always inferior to men's, no matter how competent they were. During cooperativization, the population of Ji village was divided into different teams, such as agricultural teams, and all team members were expert at sowing. The majority of women's labor power went into work on capital-construction teams; they were responsible for repairing terraced fields and providing supplemental labor on the plain. They [the Party-state] completely ignored the fact that women are relatively weak physically and, moreover, have to bear children, yet they were viewed and used as tools. And the compensation they received was also very low.

The crux of the issue was that women had no freedom to choose. They could not give up working for work points because without work points they could not get food. Isn't this forced labor? Have they not effectively transformed women into slaves of the nation? In a country where everyone is a slave and no one's human rights are guaranteed, how can you have women's liberation? Does participation in labor or collective labor mean liberation? I don't believe so.

Xu Shuming: This also reflects what many people thought at the time, which is that "women's liberation" meant that men and women should be completely equal and that there should be no differences at all.

Guo Yuhua: Right. How can men and women be the same? Can men take the place of women in childbirth and child raising? Some of the women in Ji village told me about their experiences bringing up their children. Because mothers worked in the fields, they were often unable to breastfeed their children, who screamed and cried from hunger. The mothers, too, suffered, with tears streaming down their faces. These memories were firmly etched in their memory.

"Belief" or "Fear": How Did the Chinese Communists Penetrate the Villages with Their Ideology?

Xu Shuming: There is a consensus in the academic world that the Chinese Communists' capacity to penetrate to the base of society is extremely strong, but do the peasants really believe the ideology of the Chinese Communist system? Or is it fear that leads them to feel that they have no choice but to acquiesce to the regime?

Guo Yuhua: Both are present. First of all, putting this system into effect necessitates an economic base: namely, a planned economy. The system of a planned economy is actually a form of control. The lifeline of the peasants' economy is firmly under control, and their necks are firmly in the clutches of the regime. What choice do their have? They even lack the freedom to withdraw. Just as Professor Qin Hui [b. 1952] has noted, the people's communes are not collective farms—they're concentration camps, and the major feature of a concentration camp is that you can't leave.[12] The fellow villagers in Ji village have an expression called *qianggu* (to muzzle or straitjacket).[13] It describes the system very well. Agricultural cooperativization is a *qianggu* process of cooperativization.

A few days ago I read a novel entitled *Meigui ba* (Rose valley), which talks about the great famine period [during the Great Leap Forward]. In one village, many people starved to death. There was only one family that not only did not go hungry but had extra food to help others. Because this family suffered from leprosy, it could not work with everyone else and divide work points. The villagers forced them to a valley, built them a house, and allowed them to work the land and grow food on their own. Because they had no contact with the outside world, at the time of the famine they had food and drink, and their lives proceeded apace. Although just a novel, it reflects very well the disasters this system inflicted on the peasants.

In addition to coercion, there is also ideology. Coercion and indoctrination work hand in hand, one supporting the other. On the one hand, peasants are constantly told that communism is good, while at the same time they have no other options. They have no choice but to accept. This is closely related to the national character of the Chinese people. To suffer a bit less, they opt for compliance or sometimes display a greater activism if they think they might benefit from it. With the passage of time, these patterns of behavior become natural.

Xu Shuming: Can we understand things in this way? People who entered this system early on are most likely to comply out of fear, but after living under the system for a long time, perhaps long enough for the next generation to be born, they evolve a heartfelt belief in the system over time. As the American political theorist Robert Dahl [1915–2014] has stated, the longer a regime remains in existence, the more legitimate it seems.

Guo Yuhua: There are certainly many people like the ones you have just described, but it does not describe everyone. During the Socialist Education Movement [in the early 1960s],[14] for example, many cadres who had been thoroughly loyal and devoted to the CCP were denounced as "greedy and selfish" and as "corrupt." The work teams made them suffer terribly, and they indeed may have harbored a grudge. There was a Party secretary in Ji village who was pressured to the point that he nearly hanged himself. This led him to reflect on society from a different perspective. Although he found it quite difficult to understand that the system could inflict such pain on him, he could only feel that it was unjust—this was the extent of his reflection. Nowadays, if you ask peasants to think back on that phase of history, they can see that Chairman Mao was not without error. Thus, we can't completely lose faith in the will of the people because even the greatest power cannot remain in perpetual opposition to the most legitimate and basic demands of the masses.

Xu Shuming: If an individual is attacked in the context of a political incident, leading him to rethink the nature of the system, can this be seen as the impetus for the dissolution of a system of planned economy?

Guo Yuhua: It's surely one of them. The most basic impetus is still the fact that the system itself was unsustainable. The peasants themselves had no enthusiasm. Whether they invested 120 percent or 20 percent of their labor, in the end their profits were only 20 percent. Everyone naturally wound up slacking off.

We carried out many interviews with the accountant in Ji village during collectivization. He said that many people stole items belonging to the collective. This phenomenon is worthy of analysis because everyone knows that theft is immoral. However, under these distinctive circumstances, the peasants understood theft as taking back things that originally belonged to them. Why should they hand over the fruits of their labor to the system or have them transferred to other areas? Because the state did not allow them to take such items, they stole them, but they didn't see what they were doing as theft and hence had no sense of moral guilt.

The system of people's communes had reached a dead end; there was universal consensus on this point.

The Shadow of "Communist Civilization"

Do the Peasants Cherish the Memory of the Mao Era?
Xu Shuming: Nowadays many peasants feel conflicted when they think back on the history of the collectivization period. On the one hand, the atmosphere in the rural villages during collectivization was good; everyone had a sense of public spirit, and they would certainly attack grassroots corruption. At the same time, the memories of famine at the time remain especially profound, and older people are teaching their children and grandchildren to treasure their present lives in which they lack for no basic necessities. How do we explain this ambivalence?

Guo Yuhua: Actually, there's no contradiction here. When those with personal experience criticize the inequities in contemporary society, they use the discourse of the socialist period, such as "Party cadres must be honest" or "All these corrupt officials we see today would have been executed under Chairman Mao," as if they cherish memory of the Mao period. This sort of reminiscence or memory is often cited by the New Left to prove that the peasants were happier in the old days. In fact, this is hugely misleading. When I was doing research in Ji village, we asked peasants: "Would you like to return to the Mao era?" The peasants immediately replied: "We'd fucking starve to death if we returned to that era!" We can clearly see here that the peasants do not genuinely long for those days. Trying to understand why, it appears that although they know that their own suffering is traceable to some sort of unjust arrangement, it is very hard for them to attribute this to the institutional framework of communist civilization. Peasants have a hard time carrying out a scholarly analysis of institutional arrangements; that's what scholars are for. But when you ask the peasants directly, it's all crystal clear.

The peasants' own narrative concerning the abolition of the communes can also bear out my views. The peasants of Ji village told us that as they saw it, there was still the same amount of land, the people were still the same people, and after the land was divided, they would have plenty to eat. They said: "I'll work for myself. I'll work as much as I want to. I'll make the decisions." "Once we're free, we'll be happy and complete." We did not put the word *freedom* in their mouths. When the peasants talk about that period, they are unable to restrain their emotions and naturally use that word. This is liberation in the true sense of the term.

Xu Shuming: The linguistic resources of those who lived through the era of collectivization are surely quite limited. When confronting the many different injustices of contemporary society, they can only use language from the Mao era with which they were familiar.

Guo Yuhua: That's right. Having gone through many years of training, not only the peasants but even we scholars often use language from the Mao period. For example, we speak of preliberation, postliberation, or the wrongly labeled rightists, among others, but what is "liberation"? Surely all the "rightists" were unfairly labeled? When you can see that even our language has become "alienated," the peasants' use of bureaucratic terminology becomes utterly normal. When speaking about events in their own lives, however, they did not adopt this language. They spoke of this person as "black skin" (*heipi*), "savage ghost" (*yegui*), or "half-breed/bastard" (*hunzhongzi*), in the way that peasants use these terms.

Yuan Xunhui: Were Party cadres more deeply influenced by this kind of ideological language?

Guo Yuhua: There were differences among the cadres. Ultimately, many cadres were uncultured sorts; some of them were even illiterate. They had a hard time accepting Communist discourse. Therefore, if the institutional constraints were ever taken off, they naturally reverted to their own language patterns.

For example, I just mentioned the old accountant. He was always using yin and yang and the five elements as well as astrological and astronomical phenomena to explain Chinese history, saying things like "All the emperors, the generals, and the ministers were celestial constellations; Chairman Mao was not a true constellation; he was a Turtle star (*biexing*), Chiang Kai-shek a Fish star (*yuxing*). Thus, Chiang Kai-shek went off to an island, and Chairman Mao defended the mainland." The peasants have many ways of their own to express themselves—only, it's often difficult for others to understand, even if they are serious. At the beginning, they did not want to talk with us and were always asking: "What do you really want? Why are you always asking us about these things?" I replied: "I would like to know your history and to know how these past years have been for you." They asked: "What do you mean?" I explained why ordinary people's history is important, too: "Your history isn't just important to your children, grandchildren, and posterity, but it's important to all of society." They slowly came around, and once they understood, they were especially keen on chatting (*lahua*) with us.

This old accountant believed that he had special speaking rights in the village. Thus, he always enjoyed seeking us out to have a chat. On one such occasion, he said to me: "The ones I most believe in are intellectuals." I asked why, and he replied: "All history is what intellectuals write down." You see! He understood what history was and understood that it had weight. He said: "Intellectuals are great." His meaning was that intellectuals were capable of recording and evaluating history, and his underlying meaning was that although rulers are powerful, they are judged by history. This old fellow's understanding of history is not inferior to that of historians.

In fact, the peasants face immense pressure to simply survive, and if they are to go on living in this environment, they need not only the capacity to survive but also above all the wisdom to survive. Peasant wisdom is enough to make us ashamed of our own ignorance. People with such wisdom are certainly capable of judging history.

What Is the Solution to the Dilemma of Governance at the Grassroots Level?

Xu Shuming: Villages presently lack a mechanism for cultural integration. Traditional culture was wiped out in the era of collectivization, and notions of class no longer fit in contemporary society. All of this creates numerous dilemmas in grassroots governance. What solutions do you see?

Guo Yuhua: This is an overarching problem, true for all of Chinese society as well as the villages. Although ideological propaganda has not diminished at all, it is already completely bankrupt, and even those spreading it don't believe a word of it. There are also people who are searching for answers from within China's cultural tradition, but I feel this is unrealistic. The essential ideas of traditional culture are basically only compatible with the imperial system, which is thousands of years old. I think that finding resources there for contemporary politics is going to be extremely difficult.

Of course, traditional village resources should not be abandoned by the people because they serve the needs of contemporary society, but this process certainly must come from the local masses themselves. This is especially true of traditional social organization and its norms because their emphasis on morality, order, and the rule of personal interrelationships may all be put to use in village administration together with contemporary democratic principles. I believe we can place our hope in the reinvention of the autonomy of popular society as we seek solutions to problems of the contemporary governance of the villages.

One strength is that of local society, and another is the tradition of commerce, which is also very significant. For example, in places such as Wenzhou and Guangdong. The history of commercial civilization is well developed, and people in such areas have personal experiences with commerce, such as a sense of business contracts. Commercial civilization and local social traditions, growing out of traditional culture, hold promise for producing contemporary political civilization.

But these two are not enough. They ultimately were not shaped by contemporary society. For example, local society traditionally had numerous lineage rules, which are not terribly useful in contemporary society. Thus, the crux of the issue is how we integrate cultural resources with contemporary social practice to shape and promote the healthy development of Chinese society.

Yuan Xunhui: The population mobility in rural China today is intense, and many traditional villages are being abandoned.

Guo Yuhua: This is true. Some villages are showing signs of cultural decay, so much so that villages overall are trending in that direction. The state, the market, and peasants themselves are all abandoning them unless land in a given area is chosen as an area for development. Yet land so designated may prove disastrous for the peasants.

Xu Shuming: Do you believe that urbanization is the answer for the development of rural villages?

Guo Yuhua: Urbanization would ordinarily provide a solution, but the problems with urbanization in China today are immense. All this kind of urbanization does is make the cities ever larger, like pancakes on the griddle. Expanding Beijing municipality from two ring roads to six is "urbanization" for the cities and not "urbanization" for peasants. All of the peasants' land and rural resources have been absorbed by the cities, with the exception of the peasants themselves. The peasants are treated as manpower but not as people. They can come to the cities and contribute their labor power, but only if they return to their hometowns can they receive various social protections. Professor Lu Xueyi [1933–2013] once noted: "Nice trees will be transported from the village to the city, so the trees are urbanized, but not the peasants."[15] Where does urbanization not require peasants? Can you carry out urbanization without peasants?

The Nature of Contemporary Chinese Society: "Post-totalitarian" or "Neototalitarian?"

Xu Shuming: In terms of Party policy concerning peasants, the expropriation of the collectivization period has continued right down to the contemporary era. The only difference is that during collectivization the land was confiscated and invested in the collective, and now the peasants are being squeezed through the selling off of the land [to commercial or industrial concerns].

Guo Yuhua: Many people today say that China is a post-totalitarian society. I completely disagree. I have discussed this notion with Professors Sun Liping and Shen Yuan, and we feel that "post" (*hou*) would mean that China is no longer a totalitarian society. I would say rather that it is "neototalitarian," but what does "neo" (*xin*) mean here? It means that power controls society completely by integrating all essential features of the market. In the era of the planned economy, there was no economic life outside the plan, and there was no private property. The present market economy is a market economy (controlled by) political power. The state completely controls the pulse of the economy, which can be a very frightening thing. The trend toward "the state advances, and the people retreat" is not only an economic problem, but it further means a return to the era of total control. Not only is this the old road—it's a bad one.

The Difference Between "Communist Civilization" and "Chinese Characteristics"

We Must Destroy "Sinocentrism"

Xu Shuming: You have tried using the term *communist civilization* to explain the logic of China's historical evolution. Hu An'gang [b. 1953][16] and others have used "Chinese characteristics" to explain China's developmental experience. Where does your thinking differ from theirs?

Guo Yuhua: Although the notion of a "Chinese model" or "Chinese characteristics" aims to conceptualize a Chinese model at a theoretical level, these ideas also, as I noted earlier, evince a positive attitude toward the reality of contemporary China and betray a certain yearning to achieve a final victory over capitalist civilization. The point of the notion of "communist civilization" is to see through the internal logic and essence of this system. Only when we have a clear understanding of the mechanism can we make a clear judgment. The supporters of the "Chinese model" are a little blind, but it surely cannot be that everything labeled "Chinese characteristics" is good and that as long as we follow a "Chinese way" that is different from that of Western countries, then everything will work out.

Why do we appreciate the analytic power and the insight that come from the idea of "communist civilization"? Our true goal is to study it and analyze it and not simply to embrace Chinese tradition, the Chinese model, and thus worship it as a god while arguing that any difference proves our superiority. We always say that we can't fall into the trap of "Western-centrism," but is it then rational to uphold "Sinocentrism"?

Xu Shuming: Can what you have dubbed "communist civilization" develop into a generalizable theory?

Guo Yuhua: We most certainly do not stress any sort of theoretical universality (note that this is not "generalizability"). "Communist civilization" is a puzzle for us, and to a large degree our goal is to gradually deconstruct it. The essence of sociology lies in the power of criticism; it can't just sing the praises of and glorify power. No matter how good a government is, sociology must still must look at whatever problems exist in society; it is by nature explanatory and critical. There are scholars who insist that we also take a critical stance vis-à-vis Western capitalist civilization. This is necessary, but it is not the mission of Chinese scholars because we do not live in Western societies. This is a responsibility that Western intellectuals must assume, and our focus is on diagnosing the ills of Chinese society.

China's social problems are not the result of excessive westernization. Everyone feels that he or she is distinctive and uses this as a pretext for not assuming the most basic universal values. Should we not admit this? World trends today are not toward unity, but toward pluralism and coexistence. How do we get to pluralism and coexistence? If everyone insists that he is unique and refuses to accept common values and norms, then how can we coexist? If we want China to coexist in harmony with the rest of the world, the basic premise is that everyone accepts the same rules of the game. Universal values are the cultural basis of the rules of the game. I have penned two essays that discuss this issue—"Universal Values Are Basic Common Sense" and "Just How Unique Are the Chinese People?"[17] As long as we are part of humanity, we aren't that distinctive. We must recognize humanity's basic values. Otherwise, couldn't extremist religious organizations justify their terrorism by claiming to be distinct?

In addition, rules of the game are the product of mutual discussion and competition. Everyone makes compromises and concessions, and dispenses with some of their distinctive traits, thereby forming a consensus of values we can all accept. Would this not be universal values?

If We're Not Yet Modern, How Can We Talk About Deconstructing Modernization?

Xu Shuming: There are some believers in the "Chinese model" who claim that right-wing scholars harshly criticize contemporary China, while at the same time indiscriminately accepting a system of values based on Western theory. They call this the behavior of "Western slaves." How would you respond to this?

Guo Yuhua: Chinese and Western intellectuals are facing different issues. Many Western intellectuals are nowadays engaged in postmodernism and deconstructionism. What they want to deconstruct are precisely the Western values that preach convergence, and they advocate values that are more plural. However, Chinese society is different. It has not yet constructed modernity. How can we talk about deconstruction? Even if Western scholars carry out the deconstruction of contemporary social values, the most basic of values—such as democracy, freedom, brotherly love, human rights, the rule of law, and so on—will still exist as a foundation, and these are things that China still lacks.

For example, in research on contemporary labor issues, some scholars blame everything on neoliberalism. They claim that the Chinese labor situation is the worst in the world, and the root of the problem is the globalization of capital supported by neoliberal ideology. I would like to first ask: Where is Chinese liberalism? If China still has no liberalism, what is this *neo*liberalism they're criticizing? The crux of the problem of Chinese labor lies in social inequities in the structure of power. To be sure, the globalization of capital has had an influence, but it is not a direct cause. Where else in the world can bosses get away with mistreating workers like this? Only in China! In addition, workers in other countries have recourse to resistance or strikes after being mistreated. Can Chinese workers do this? If they were to strike, they would run afoul of the government's policy of "maintaining social stability." These are "Chinese characteristics"!

A little while ago I gave a lecture at China's Central University for Nationalities on the topic "China's special characteristics as the factory of the world." China is the world's factory and clearly a world factory with Chinese characteristics. The nature of capital is to exploit and mistreat workers, but in the absence of China's structure of power the damage done by capital could never reach such a level. When workers at the Foxconn Technology Group committed suicide by jumping out of a building instead of resisting, people thought this was very strange. If they were unsatisfied, why didn't they quit? But if they were to quit their jobs, what future could these young people expect? With cities that don't welcome them and villages they can't go back to, where was their future? Their despair and suicide are easily understood.

It Is Not the Responsibility of Scholars to Sing Praises

Xu Shuming: There are scholars who have said we need to point out the various problems in national development, but we also need to acknowledge our successes, and by affirming these positive achievements, we can arrive at our own theoretical system.

Guo Yuhua: We certainly need to affirm social progress, but we mustn't praise things to the stars. Economic life in the country now has made major improvements, but what are the reasons for it? Some people conclude that they are gifts of the Party and the government, and they expect the common people to be constantly moved to tears of gratitude. This is confusing cause and effect. First of all, were you raised by your mother and father? Or were you raised by the Party and the government? Are the improvements in the lives of the people the results of their diligence and striving? Or were they a gift from someone? Next, who raised the Party and the government? Wasn't it the taxpayers?

China's basic problem all along is that it's never been clear who "raises" whom, which gives rise to all sorts of praise for famous leaders and miracle stories. Under normal relations between officials and the people, when the government comes up with a decent policy, people should affirm it, but they can also wonder whether there might not be something even better. Are the "masses" who are continually and profoundly grateful really citizens?

Maybe if someone has to do the work of singing praises, then the media, artists, and official propagandists who are already doing it are enough. We don't need sociologists joining the chorus. The responsibilities of sociologists are to seek out social problems and identify solutions. This certainly does not mean that China's future is bleak, but our basic duty demands that we maintain a critical consciousness, a spirit of reflection, and if we continue searching for the impetus and pathway for society to forge ahead, then this is enough.

Xu Shuming: People are always bringing up nationalism these days, arguing that this kind of positive propaganda for the government is something that all patriots should engage in.

Guo Yuhua: This is harmful to the state. Nationalist propaganda has nothing to do with discussing problems, to say nothing of coming up with rational solutions. From the get-go, they use terms like *traitors* (*hanjian*) and *slaves of the West* (*xinu*). Recently, even the official media have begun to use these terms. This reflects a trend toward vulgarization in the mainstream media. The result, however, has been to produce the opposite effect. This sort of propaganda is unconvincing.

Yuan Xunhui: The problem facing us now is that the language of the old propaganda is very old-fashioned, and many people, in particular younger people, don't believe any of this stuff. They don't even want to talk about it. It looks to me as if they hope to break through this by developing things on the Internet. Unfortunately, they have come up with clumsy writers such as Wang Xiaoshi [b. 1971] and Zhou Xiaoping [b. 1981]—the logic of their writing and the facts aren't persuasive, producing the opposite effect of what is intended.[18]

Translators' Notes

1. Guo Yuhua, "'Gongchanzhuyi wenming' de yinying—Gongshiwang zhuanfang Guo Yuhua" (The shadow of "Communist civilization": A commitment to collecting the oral history of village life in the second half of the twentieth century), interview by Xu Shiming and Yuan Xunhui, Gongshi Wang (Consensus Net), 2013. Consensus Net was suppressed by authorities in October 2016, but a version of this interview is still available at http://ptext.nju.edu.cn/c7/2d/c13327a247597/page.htm.

2. Edward Friedman, Paul Pickowicz, Mark Selden, and Kay Ann Johnson, *Chinese Village, Socialist State* (New Haven, CT: Yale University Press, 1991); Edward Friedman, Paul Pickwicz, and Mark Selden, *Revolution, Resistance, and Reform in Village China* (New Haven, CT: Yale University Press, 2007).

3. Ian Johnson, "'Ruling Through Ritual:' An Interview with Guo Yuhua," *New York Review of Books*, June 18, 2018, https://www.nybooks.com/daily/2018/06/18/ruling-through-ritual-an-interview-with-guo-yuhua/.

4. Sun Liping is a well-known professor in the Sociology Department of Tsinghua University as well as a famous public intellectual. Professor Shen Yuan is deputy chair of the department. His research touches several fields in social theory. In recent years, he has developed research projects on new economic sociology, state and society relations, the birth and development of civil society, urban social movement, and social intervention.

5. Ying Xing is professor of political science at Tsinghua University and specializes in the historical sociology of the early CCP movement.

6. On the Dragon King, see Adam Chau, *Miraculous Response: Doing Popular Religion in Contemporary China* (Stanford, CA: Stanford University Press, 2005).

7. Norbert Elias, *The Civilizing Process*, rev. ed. (Oxford: Blackwell, 2000).

8. Yang Kuisong is a well-known historian at East China Normal University in Shanghai who works on the history of the CCP.

9. This famous directive announced a radicalization of Party land policy from rent reduction to "land to the tiller." It is translated as Liu Shaoqi, "Directive of the CCP CC on Settling Accounts, Rent Reduction, and the Land Question," in *The Rise to Power of the Chinese Communist Party: Documents and Analysis*, ed. Tony Saich (Armonk, NY: M. E. Sharpe, 1996), 1280–85.

10. Li Dingming, not a CCP member, was a leading representative of the gentry of the Suide area of northern Shaanxi who served in the Communist-dominated base-area government as a vice chair under the Three-Thirds System of representation in which one-third of government personnel would be Communist, one-third would be members of other parties, and one-third would be unaffiliated. This was the moderate United Front policy of the Yan'an period (1937–1947).

11. "Outline of China's Land Law," October 10, 1947 (in *Rise to Power*, ed. Saich, 1295–98), dictated equal distribution of all the land in villages and resulted in a wave of violent expropriation and retaliation against village elites that was not curtailed until spring 1948. The policy flip-flop supports Guo's interpretation.

12. Qin Hui is an influential historian and public intellectual in China, now retired from Tsinghua University. For his remarks on communes and concentration camps, see Qin Hui, "Jitihua hu beijitihua" (Collectivizing and collectivized), Ai Sixiang Wang, 2008, http://www.aisixiang.com/data/21328.html.

13. As with many local sayings, the term *qianggu* comes from one of China's famous traditional novels, *Journey to the West*, and refers to the golden band (*jingu*) around the Monkey King's head that was used to control him.

14. Also known as the "Four Cleanups" (*siqing*), the Socialist Education Movement was launched by Mao in 1963 to "clean up" the Party's politics, economy, organization, and ideology, particularly at the village and local level. The movement is now considered the first stage of the Cultural Revolution.

15. Lu Xueyi was a sociologist associated with the Chinese Academy of Social Sciences and an expert on rural China.

16. Hu An'gang is a professor of economics at Tsinghua University. A firm supporter of the CCP, he believes Chinese socialism is superior to all other systems.

17. These two essays, which are no longer available on the Chinese Web, are "Pushi jiazhi ben shi changshi" and "Zhongguoren daodi you duo teshu?"

18. Both Wang Xiaoshi and Zhou Xiaoping are popular pro-Communist bloggers and essayists, well known for their antipathy to the United States and the West generally.

CHAPTER 6

ADVANCING CONSTITUTIONAL DEMOCRACY SHOULD BE THE MISSION OF THE CHINESE COMMUNIST PARTY[1]

CAI XIA

TRANSLATED BY TIMOTHY CHEEK, JOSHUA A. FOGEL, AND DAVID OWNBY

Translators' Introduction

ai Xia (b. 1952), a retired professor from the Central Party School in Beijing, offers a robust defense of liberal democratic values and institutions but does so in the language of the Chinese Communist Party (CCP). She earned her PhD in law at the Central Party School in 1988 and until recently served in its Department of Party Building and Education Research. She is a prolific writer on Party theory and a noted commentator on public affairs—using social media to weigh in on notable cases of corruption or Party repression of intellectuals. Her book *Quanqiuhua yu Gongchandangren jiazhiguan* (Globalization and Communist values, 2002) received a prize in the Party education system. She thus speaks as a notable establishment intellectual.

Cai Xia offers her essay as a repost to Professor Yang Xiaoqing (b. 1946). Both are responding to the public debate that exploded in January 2013 when a New Year's editorial in *Nanfang Zhoumo* (Southern weekend) advocating constitutional government was removed by Party authorities. Yang, not a well-known figure, made the case that constitutional government did not fit China's national conditions. Cai Xia and others begged to differ. Cai makes these familiar liberal arguments (bar the role of the CCP in bringing about democracy) entirely on the basis of the classics of Marxism-Leninism/Mao Zedong Thought, plus additions by later Party leaders such as Jiang Zemin (b. 1926) and Hu Jintao

(b. 1942), the CCP general secretary when this essay was first drafted in 2011. There is even a passing reference to a speech by Xi Jinping (b. 1953) in 2010 (on the rise but not yet supreme leader then). Nonetheless, the careful and detailed review of the history of socialist revolutions, their professed commitment to democratic values, and their sorry track record in establishing instead party dictatorships will strike Anglophone readers as the last thing to expect out of the Party School. In fact, Cai Xia's core premise is that democratic politics defined by freedom of speech and human rights is not only *not* antithetical to the socialist revolution predicted by Marx but its fulfillment. Hence, the topic of her essay: it is the CCP's historical mission to bring about constitutional democracy in China.

This assertion confronts the reader with a challenge: How can a Party theorist in the top Party School of the country say this? Are the careful citations to the Marxist-Leninist-Maoist cannon a cover, or are there resources in the Marxist-Leninist cannon for conceptualizing the need for and how to establish constitutional democracy? However one answers these questions, it is clear from this essay and its continuing availability on the Chinese Internet as well as from Cai Xia's ongoing public life that such thinking is thinkable and such speech is possible without reprisal. The key to her greater freedom of speech, of course, is both her position in the establishment and her reliance on the intellectual resources—and the style of writing, what Geremie Barmé calls "Party New Speak"—she uses to make her case. In short, Cai Xia presents liberal democracy, which she calls "constitutional democracy," not as the repudiation of the Communist Party and its revolution, but as its fulfillment. In the language of forces of production, class structure, and ideology, she argues that this is the task for the CCP in the current period.

Her essay has two other notable characteristics. First is the emphasis on thought (*siwei*), ideology (*sixiang*), and consciousness (*yishi*), which are the hallmarks of ideological thinking in Communist Parties in general and echoes a strong theme in modern Chinese intellectual life. However, although correct thinking is important to Cai Xia, she considers it but a step toward good governance. It is the doorway to institutional reforms, and it is through institutions that changes are made according to Marxist theories of governance. In this, Cai Xia maintains the dynamic dialectic in Marxism between ideology and organization. Second, the essay emphatically embraces universal laws of society and governance—primarily Marxist laws of economic and social development but equally "the universal laws of democratic politics." And this means, she maintains, learning from the theory and experience of other countries. Thus, Cai Xia presents an example of how the scientific and internationalist stream of Marxist-Leninist thought can indeed make the case for constitutional democracy.

Advancing Constitutional Democracy Should Be the Mission of the Chinese Communist Party

I recently read an article by Professor Yang Xiaoqing [b. 1946] of Renmin University, Beijing, and I was shocked by the article's opposition to the idea of constitutional government.[2] The progressive trend in the development of human politics and civilization is toward democratic governance and constitutional rule as the legal basis for democratic politics. This is the realization of the objective rules of political life everywhere as well as the most basic demand and the most basic common sense. The disaster that Hitler's fascism inflicted on humanity in the absence of constitutional protection can never be forgotten. Thus, I reprise my essay of 2011 in hopes of launching a discussion with Professor Yang Xiaoqing.

The full text of the article from 2011 follows:

If a country hopes to advance toward modern civilization, the modernization of politics must be an important part of the project. The Chinese Communist Party (CCP) has created a new China through a victorious revolution over the ruins of despotism, thus bequeathing to the CCP a multifaceted historical mission. One aspect of this mission is to lead in the construction of modern state institutions and to use socialist constitutional democracy to shore up and guarantee the great revival of the Chinese people. For a significant period of time, the people thought that the victory of the revolution would mean that the people would be masters of their own lives. However, the CCP has held power for sixty years, and the rapid changes that have accompanied the reform and opening of the past thirty years have particularly illustrated that we still have a long row to hoe in our strenuous efforts to establish a state system of modern constitutional democracy.

Revolution Can Overturn a Despotic Regime and Still Find It Difficult to Establish New Institutions of Political Democracy

Three-quarters of China's twentieth century has been engulfed in blood and shaken by the great tide of the Chinese Revolution. The Republican Revolution of 1911, the New Democratic Revolution of 1919–1949, and the Cultural Revolution of the 1960s are fundamentally different in nature, but all had democracy as a rallying cry.[3] From the time of its birth, the CCP has written into the guiding principles for which it struggles the achievement of the people's democracy and took initial steps toward democratic practice in the anti-Japanese base areas during World War II. After taking power in 1949, the Party engaged in difficult efforts to bring about popular democracy. To this day, however, how China will finally implement constitutional democracy remains a mystery. The paradox of history is that revolution can overthrow an old regime, but it can't exorcize the ghosts of despotic government. Revolution can shatter a world but has difficulty establishing a new, modern democratic state.

In Chinese culture, revolution has a sacred quality. In ancient Chinese texts, we find the term *Tang-Wu "revolution,"*[4] and in the early twentieth century there was the Revolution of 1911. Democracy is the mainstream of twentieth-century human political civilization, and it, too, has a sacred quality in terms of political legitimacy. Finding the link between revolution and democracy was a necessary requirement in the Chinese people's search for a way forward in the early twentieth century. The influence of the October Revolution in the Soviet Union drove progressive Chinese intellectuals to accept Marxism. In Marxist theory, revolution is class warfare, and democracy is the most important goal to achieve in class struggle. In the *Communist Manifesto,* we read: "The first step in the revolution by the working class is to raise the proletariat to the position of ruling class, to win the battle of democracy."[5] Under the guidance of Marxism-Leninism, Chinese Communists now take democracy as the core discourse of revolutionary ideology and revolution as the necessary path to the realization of democracy.

Democracy is the core language of revolutionary ideology. The CCP wrote the idea of the realization of people's democracy into the political program of the revolution, so that democracy became a political weapon in the struggle for legitimacy between irreconcilable class enemies. During the period of the revolutionary war, the CCP used all means to expose the one-party despotic rule of the Guomindang, and publications such as the *Xinhua Ribao* (New China Daily) and others in Yan'an published large numbers of editorials and criticisms advocating constitutional democracy, even affirming and praising American democracy.[6] In the anti-Japanese base areas under their control, they carried out democratic constitutional measures, such as universal suffrage and the "Three-Thirds System."[7] In 1940, Mao Zedong stated explicitly: "What is constitutional government? It is democratic government."[8] When talking about people's democracy in the anti-Japanese base areas, he pointed out that "freedom of speech, press, assembly, association, political conviction, and religious belief, and freedom of the person are the people's most important freedoms. In China only the Liberated Areas have given full effect to these freedoms."[9] In 1949, New China was established, and CCP members proclaimed that the revolution's victory and the establishment of the CCP regime were the realization of the people's democracy: "The Chinese people have stood up."

Revolution is the only path to realize democracy. Old China was a society under despotic rule in which the Chinese people had no democratic rights to speak of. This compelled Communists to carry out a violent revolution to realize democracy. The revolution brought the Communists to political power, and once in power the Communists similarly resolved all difficult problems "in the name of the revolution." This included resolving ideological differences on socialist construction both inside and outside the Party, overcoming the problem of the minority of Party cadres who were divorced from the masses, the phenomenon of bureaucratic privilege, and the so-called spontaneous trend toward capitalism among the peasantry. During the Cultural Revolution, which used Mao Zedong's "theory of continuing the revolution under the dictatorship of the proletariat" as a guide to mobilization and development, slogans such as "great democracy" (*da minzhu*) and "mass dictatorship" (*qunzhong zhuanzheng*) were all the rage for a time. In fact, these [developments] amounted to a Chinese-style "tyranny of the majority," and they dragged the country into a decade of chaos and caused the people untold catastrophes.

History makes clear that revolution takes shattering the old regime as a condition for the establishment of people's democracy. However, revolution most certainly is not the natural "midwife" of democracy. Before 1949, the revolution promoted progress in Chinese society, but after 1949 what we call the "revolution" moved in the opposite direction from democracy.

Why Did Revolution in "New China" Go Against Constitutional Democracy?

The Chinese Communist Party established New China through violent revolution on the ruins of autocracy, and guiding the construction of the new China has been the basic mission of the CCP as the ruling party. However, the "construction" that New China needs is not only economic and cultural but at a more basic level also the construction of a modern political community that will put New China into the category of modern democratic countries. But if we look squarely at reality and take seriously the lessons of the history since the Party took on this mission as the ruling party, we have to admit that even today this mission has not been fully accomplished. The reasons why this mission has still not been completed, despite sixty years of the CCP as the ruling party, reflect the complex interaction of objective factors from China's social history and current realities as well as the limitations of the Party's understanding of national construction and the influence of the Soviet Communist Party's ruling system.

Long-Term Negation of the Market Economy Inhibited the Conditions for Constitutional Democracy

Generally speaking, democracy is first of all the expression of the form of a country's political life, which is safeguarded by the modern state system. Marx pointed out: "Democracy is a categorical concept of state systems."[10] When the

CCP established a new political community after taking power, this was actually more of a transformation of the traditional autocratic state in the direction of a modern democratic state. From the perspective of political civilization, we can say that the establishment of a sound constitutional democratic state system has been the fundamental trend of human political development in modern times. Even though each state's historical path to constitutional democracy has differed according to the national characteristics of each, all of them at least needed an economic base in the form of some kind of modern market economy. For a long time, the CCP understood democratic politics only in terms of class struggle and for a relatively long time did not recognize that a market economy is the indispensable basis for developing democratic politics. It instead suppressed and rejected elements of a market economy because it identified market economies with capitalism.

In Europe, it was on the basis of the full development of the market economy that civil society arose and promoted modern politics while progressively strengthening the democratic system. In the *Communist Manifesto*, Marx and Engels vividly describe the economic processes of city dwellers' becoming the earliest members of the bourgeois class; of the discovery of North America, which stimulated the rise of commerce, transatlantic shipping and industry; and of the expansion of market demands leading modern industry to replace artisanal production, and they point out that the bourgeoisie, at each step of economic development, also made corresponding political achievements.

> The bourgeoisie keeps more and more doing away with the scattered state of the population, of the means of production, and of property. It has agglomerated population, has centralised the means of production, and has concentrated property in a few hands. The necessary consequence of this was political centralisation. Independent, or but loosely connected provinces, with separate interests, laws, governments, and systems of taxation, became lumped together into one nation, with one government, one code of laws, one national class-interest, one frontier, and one customs-tariff.[11]

This economy established the basis for the modern political community and also provided its needed social resources. Constitutional democracies created on the basis of national market economies now had their fundamental meaning and practical contents: the rational separation of state powers under a constitution, likewise the prevention of the monopolization of productive forces through a constitutionally mandated rational separation of powers, the limitation of the powers of the state through the power of society, and the protection of the individual rights of the citizen and property rights from harassment or expropriation by state power. The realization of plural democracy and social harmony, mutual understanding, and cooperation were thus achieved through the recognition of free will and equal rights on the basis of a plurality of interests and the protection of citizen rights by law. It is clear that a market economy is the indispensable economic foundation of constitutional democracy, and the constitutional democratic system is the necessary political arrangement for a market-economy society.

The historical starting point of China's transition from an autocratic state to a modern political community is not the same as in European society. The economy did not give rise to our politics; politics produced our politics. China made the transition from a traditional autocracy to a modern democracy in the context of the savage invasion of foreign capital and the danger of national extinction. During the half century from 1898 to 1949, from the Hundred Days Reform through the Revolution of 1911 and down to the New Democratic Revolution led by the CCP, all embodied the search for a modern political order. Yet political progress could not rely solely on politics but needed the support of genuine economic and social strength. Due to the tragic history of the Chinese nation in modern times, however, Communists could not self-consciously face this question, which meant that Chinese society failed to build a modern market system and the conditions surrounding it.

Due to the resistance of its highly developed autocratic political system, it was difficult for Chinese society to develop a market economy in the modern sense until the middle of the nineteenth century. And the market economy in Chinese society before 1949 was a deformed market economy branded by the colonial economics of a savage and heartless invasion and penetration of foreign capital. The elimination of this deformed market economy in the socialist transformation undertaken after the Communists came to power was completely correct. However, the Communists had a dogmatic understanding of the Marxist discourse on commodity economy in which they mistakenly equated the market economy with capitalism, and so they used state power to impose a planned economy that restricted and eliminated the market elements in society. The fundamental laws of the development of political civilization clearly show that a market economy is the necessary basis for constitutional democracy. In a certain sense, without a market economy there can be no pluralization of social interests or the requirements for the respect and protection of rights or the growth of civil society or the checks and balances of power necessary for the realization of constitutional democracy. When the establishment of the modern state system is divorced from the growth of actual society, democratic politics can be only propaganda for a political ideology.

Precisely because we lack the fertile soil of the market economy in which to grow democratic politics, even though the constitution declares that the people are the masters of the nation, in fact in actual political life it is difficult for the political rights of a people's democracy to manifest themselves or for individual members of society to live out those rights. Furthermore, the political ideal of a pluralistic "people's republic" has been displaced by "majoritarian democracy" because of the partial nature of constitutional government that has been subsumed by the "representational" role of the ruling party to the point that the leadership for political reasons changes and ignores citizen rights. And society can do nothing but submit. Going a step farther, "majoritarian democracy" can easily in the name of the revolution become "majority tyranny."

There Has Been Insufficient Recognition by the Party Since Taking Power of the Arduous Nature of Establishing a Modern State System

Ruling parties promote the political development of society under the constraints of specific conditions, such as the political ecosystem of the society in which the ruling party operates, a country's political traditions, the structure of the state political system, and the like. Developed countries in the West have gone through several centuries of bourgeois democracy and have already established a set of relatively complete modern state institutions. The ruling parties of these states wield power within an established national democratic system, restrained by the mechanisms of that system. But the CCP first led the revolution to overthrow the old autocratic system and then became the ruling party in leading the establishment of a new state power.

The difference between Old and New China is not solely limited to differences in their class nature but also extends to the distinction that Old China was one of the traditional autocracies, and New China ought to be counted among the ranks of modern democratic politics. Democratic state systems and autocratic state systems have essential differences. Marx, when comparing monarchy with democracy, particularly pointed out: "In monarchy the whole, the people, is subsumed under one of its modes of existence, the political constitution; in democracy the constitution itself appears only as one determination, and indeed as the self-determination of the people. In monarchy we have the people of the constitution, in democracy the constitution of the people. . . . Only the specific difference of democracy is that here the constitution is in general only one moment of the people's existence, that is to say the political constitution does not form the state for itself."[12] According to Marx's theory of the state, the new-style state system, which is "only one moment of the people's existence," needs the constitutional form to elaborate the people's democratic rights and to formulate and implement a legal system to protect people's rights and freedoms. Thus, it is a great historical responsibility of China's ruling Party to use the constitutional democratic system to establish and advance the progress of China's political civilization.

However, the CCP's heightened insistence on the class domination of people's democracy comes at the cost of an insufficient concern for concretely establishing a democratic system. Communists typically understand the overthrow of the previous rulers in terms of violent revolution, smashing Old China's state apparatus, and assume that the day of revolutionary victory is the same as the achievement of democracy. Actually, this is not the case. Due to the profound influence of millennia of autocracy, even though the previous rulers have been overthrown, autocracy has been dismantled in "form" but not in "spirit." At the same time, the high concentration of power in the planned economy, the political control of class struggle as the guiding principle, the hierarchical system of the administration, and so on—all have caused the old imperial politics, status consciousness, and the belief that privileges go with position to seep into the new political system. Their actual operation in the new system is hidden, but their influence is profound and makes the establishment of the new state system of people's democracy imperfect in "form" and causes its "spirit" to gradually dissipate.

Deng Xiaoping has pointed out: "From old China we inherited a strong tradition of feudal autocracy and a weak tradition of democratic legality. Moreover, in the post-Liberation years we did not consciously draw up systematic rules and regulations to safeguard the people's democratic rights. Our legal system is far from perfect and has not received anywhere near the attention it deserves."[13] As a consequence, even though after taking power we erected the institutional framework for people's democracy, still we lack a constitutional arrangement with a reasonable separation and limitation of powers, nor have we been able to institute a system with sufficient concern for the procedural side of state operations. This is not only because the difficulty in effectively operating democratic institutions has reduced democracy to a formulaic slogan but also because the creation of the new, overly centralized state power, the cult of personality, and the systemization of status privileges have allowed autocratic traditions to deeply influence the political life of the Party and the state. This made it difficult for the Party, after taking power, to resolve the many complicated contradictions in political and economic development, finally ending in the Cultural Revolution—the great crisis of Chinese society. Because of this, Deng Xiaoping reflected deeply on the years before reform and opening, saying: "We should have mustered all our resources to develop the economy, and, second, we should have substantially extended democracy."[14] He believed that "now it is essential to state clearly that we must continue to eliminate the influence of feudal remnants in our ideology and politics and that we must carry out a series of effective reforms in our institutions. Otherwise, our country and people will suffer further losses."[15]

The Profound Influence of the Former Soviet Communist System of Governance on the CCP

As indicated in the previous citations, classic Marxist writers in their research on different state systems have used logic to identify the fundamental differences between monarchy and democracy, but they have not clearly delineated a concrete model for a "people's state system." They later just relied on the great attempt of the Paris Commune to create a workers' government and put forth a number of important principles.[16] After the October Revolution, Lenin carried out an innovative exploration with regard to establishing a socialist state regime and for the first time concretized the theoretical abstraction of the "people's state system" in actual political operations. Looked back on now, the form of the Bolshevik government that took shape under Lenin's leadership was in part the accidental result of special historical circumstances, in part the fruit of immature ideological viewpoints, and in part the result of betraying the thinking of classic Marxist authors to suit the political needs of the moment.

This is all understandable. New inventions are never flawless, to say nothing of the great historical innovations pursued by the Soviet Communist Party. However, Stalin later fixed and absolutized Lenin's provisional measures as universal Marxist principles. By the same token, he dispensed with Lenin's correct thinking, deviated from the basic principles of Marxism as concerns the people's state system, and suppressed and struck out at different views inside and outside the Party, thus transforming the Soviet Communist Party into a one-man dictatorship. Not only did this inflict extreme harm to the reputation of the socialist state, leading to its branding as a totalitarian regime, but it also seriously compromised the construction of democratic legal institutions in other socialist states.

For example, around the time of the October Revolution the Bolsheviks had a different attitude toward holding a constitutional congress and participating in a multiparty coalition to govern. In the party platform for 1903, the Bolsheviks clearly advocated implementation of a constitutional congress with universal suffrage, but after the organization of the Soviets created by the Russian revolutionary masses, Lenin considered it a regime comparable to the Paris Commune of 1871, and he said: "We do not want a parliamentary republic." After the October Revolution, Lenin contemplated having the Bolsheviks lead a multiparty coalition, and initially the highest organ of the Soviets was to bring such a multiparty system into existence. The Bolsheviks had hoped to use the Soviet representative assembly to supersede the results of a constitutional congress. But the actual contrast in strength among the domestic Russian parties made the Bolsheviks unable to cancel the election of a constitutional congress, and in the subsequent elections they were moreover unable to gain a majority of seats. With the backing of the armed might of workers and soldiers, the Bolsheviks overruled the election of the constitutional congress, and as a result they dissolved it. Afterward, in a series of serious problems, the contradictions between the Bolsheviks and the political parties grew ever more intense and ultimately led to a thorough rupture in the multiparty coalition, and the Bolsheviks established one-party rule.[17] In a reprisal move, Lenin denounced the opposition parties who had criticized the Bolsheviks as "one-party dictatorship," saying: "Yes, it is a dictatorship of one Party! This is what we stand for, and we shall not shift from that position."[18] The aim of persevering with "one-party dictatorship," of which Lenin spoke here, was the principle of the Party retaining leadership of the Soviet regime. However, the complicated political situation at the time in Russia ultimately brought about "one-party rule." This was a fierce course of action under special conditions and certainly was not the same as the principle of maintaining party leadership. Stalin fixed this in practice and propagandized it as the realization of Marxism's basic principles, which had a profound impact on the Chinese people.

We equate the principle of upholding party leadership with the form of "one-party rule." This establishes a monopoly on power and a system of governance in which the party rules the state. After the CCP took power, there developed high-level inter-Party differences in the execution of the socialist transformation of industry, large-scale People's Communes, and the Great Leap Forward, while at the same time the design of the post-1954 state political system failed to provide a legal avenue by which the highest leaders of the CCP could engage in the decision-making process for important national affairs, so that demands by the highest Party leaders to increase Party leadership over the state took the form of calls to revive the "unified leadership" of the war period, with no separation between Party and state in the postwar regime, in which the Party replaced the state in a "unified" leadership system and exercise of power. At the same time, because the Party's top leadership was viewed as the personification of the Party, strengthening the power of individual leaders also increased their political control over the Party and state. Moreover, under the direction of "leftist" thought such as "take class struggle as the key link," beginning in the second half of the 1950s, the construction of our country's democratic and legal systems stagnated and even retreated. Not only did this lead to the demise of the National People's Congress, but the ruling party also directly commanded the government, directly exercised state functions, influenced the normal operation of the country's political life and social governance, and alienated the ruling party itself from the government. In other words, the ruling party was nationalized [i.e., became the country], Party organization took over the administration, the Party leadership took on ever greater power, and leading cadres gained ever greater centralized powers and special privileges.

Construction of a modern political community must be protected by a constitutional system, and only the identification of all of society with the constitution will give the state the legal guarantee for long-term peace and stability. For a long time, however, we have ignored the construction of constitutional democracy and relied on political achievements and the leadership's charisma to consolidate the legitimacy of the ruling power. This meant that the base of the regime had a political fragility that was difficult to overcome, hidden under the shadow of a supposed "crisis of the Party and state." Following rapid social changes and the accumulation of contradictions and conflicts, the ruling party's anxiety with respect to all this grew increasingly profound, which ironically led the ruling party to strengthen individual authority and the degree of political control, which further magnified the flaws of "rule by men," which in turn weakened constitutional and legal authority. Objectively speaking, it is clear that continuing in this manner led state politics into a vicious cycle that betrayed trends toward democracy and ultimately may well have led to even greater political dangers.

Deng Xiaoping had a crystal-clear understanding of the serious consequences caused by institutional issues. As he put it, "It is true that the errors we made in the past were partly attributable to the way of thinking and style of work of some leaders. But they were even more attributable to the problems in our organizational and working systems. If these systems are sound, they can place restraints on the actions of bad people; if they are unsound, they may hamper the efforts of good people or indeed, in certain cases, may push them in the wrong direction. Even so great a man as Comrade Mao Zedong was influenced to a serious degree by certain unsound systems and institutions, which resulted in grave misfortunes for the Party, the state, and himself. . . . The problems in the leadership and organizational systems are more fundamental, widespread, and long-lasting, and they have a greater effect on the overall interests of our country. This is a question that has a close bearing on whether our Party and state will change political colour and should therefore command the attention of the entire Party."[19]

Marx once explained: "It was most difficult to form the political state, the constitution, out of the various moments of the life of the people."[20] Without a doubt, Marx's viewpoint here is correct. Having experienced the bumpy road of national construction under conditions of the planned economy and the bitter lessons of ten years of the Cultural Revolution, at the outset of the period of reform and opening Comrade Deng Xiaoping raised the issue of reforming the Party and state leadership system: "Since the Third Plenary Session of its Eleventh Central Committee [in December 1978], the Party has stressed that there can be no socialist modernisation without democracy, that democracy must be institutionalised and codified in law and the Party must conduct its activities with the limits permitted by the Constitution and the laws of the state."[21] "To eliminate surviving feudal influences, we must stress the need to effectively restructure and improve the systems of the Party and state in such a way as to ensure institutionally the practice of democracy in political life, in economic management, and in all other aspects of social activity and thus to promote the smooth progress of modernization."[22]

In sum, although New China is already more than sixty years old, we still have yet to fulfill our duty to complete the construction of state institutions. When today we talk about the reform of political institutions and about building a socialist democracy with Chinese characteristics, its essential content will be to carry out this historical task that should have been carried out long ago—building a modern political community so that, with the support and protection of constitutional democratic institutions, the Chinese people will continue the historical path toward modern civilization. This, then, is the historical dimension of the mission of Party rule, a heavy historical duty that Communist Party members cannot shirk.

Promoting the Ruling-Power Thinking Required for Constitutional Democracy

The process of constructing a modern political community is the process by which the ruling Party carries out the integration of society.[23] In all of this, furthering the construction of constitutional democracy is the key and the guarantee. If we want to complete this historical mission well, then the ideology of the ruling Party must make a profound change, a change from social revolution to building democratic governance.

Completing the Transformation of Thinking in a Political Party from Revolution to Democracy

There is a major difference between revolutionary thought and democratic thought. Building a modern political community requires that the ruling Party self-consciously carry out profound changes in its ideas about governance, leave behind the ideological stereotype of violent revolution, and establish proper intellectual conditions for modern state institutions. The CCP led the revolution to eradicate despotic rule and pursue people's democracy. However, for quite a long time the ruling Party has been in the habit of using revolutionary thinking to deal with problems and has been unable to firmly establish the fundamental thinking needed for a democratic politics.

In the process of political development of human society, revolution is an intense social conflict in which various social forces engage in conflicts over competing interests, whereas democracy is the trend of political development, the mechanism by which social contradictions are peacefully managed and social conflicts reconciled. In the course of social conflict, revolution is a "zero-sum game," a struggle that usually results in a fight to the death or common ruin. Democracy, then, is a "win-win game" played without harming the bottom-line interests of both sides and in which each side can accept the result. The nature of these games is completely different, so the characteristic modes of thought concerning revolution and democracy are clearly distinguishable. For example, revolution, on the one hand, emphasizes, "Either the East Wind prevails over the West Wind, or the West Wind prevails over the East Wind," refusing to accept any compromise or middle path and persistently rejecting the adversary. Democracy, on the other hand, advocates "live and let live," forgiving, agreeing, yielding, and insisting on mutual benefit. Or, for example, revolution, on the one hand, does not recognize the human rights of political opponents and even takes the physical extermination of an adversary as a basic demand of revolution. Democracy, on the other hand, recognizes that political opponents should have the same human rights guarantees, and the power struggle to achieve individual interests is carried out on the basis of the legal system. Similarly, revolution places its hopes in the fundamental subversion of the social system in order to bring about a just society. Revolution is a revolt that seeks to wreck all legal institutions; but democracy stresses legal standards to ameliorate the social order and to promote social justice, and so on.

If we complete a profound transformation of the ruling Party's political thinking, we will then be able to open the ideological space for moderate understanding and a suitable context in which to deal with problems. Then we may bravely forge new paths for resolving various contradictions and guide popular participation in politics, with dialogue and consultation, compromise and collaboration, all in an orderly fashion, while exploring how to deepen reform and bring about flexibility and stability, which will bring about the peaceful promotion of democratic politics.

Overcome the Influence of Traditional Political Culture; Establish the Point of View of Modern Democratic Political Authority

The Chinese Communist Party was born in China, and so it bears the weight of traditional political culture. In terms of how the ruling authority views power, these influences are relatively complex. For example, to whom does power belong? Modern democratic politics has always stressed that "sovereignty resides in the people." However, within the Party some have been deeply influenced by the ideas from China's traditional culture that "those who conquer the land rule the land." When they talk of upholding the Party's ruling position, they always stress the twenty-eight years of armed revolution [1921–1949] that achieved it. But, in fact, the Party has already ruled for sixty years, and during that time nearly all of the Communists who fought those bloody battles have passed from the scene. If today's Party cadres simply rely on the blood of revolutionary martyrs to justify their inherited positions, it will be difficult for many people in society to identify with them. Moreover, the rapid infestation of inner-Party corruption has eroded the ruling Party's political authority and the government's credibility. Some leaders within the ruling Party have noted social dissatisfaction, and so they frequently cite "the dynastic cycle" to admonish Party cadres.[24] In fact, "the dynastic cycle" is a rule governing society and political power in agricultural civilizations. To use this to admonish Party cadres really reflects the deep influence of traditional political culture on the ruling Party.

First, the notion of "the dynastic cycle" implies that "authority is in the hands of those in control" and not authority in the hands of the masses. This is contrary to the idea that "sovereignty resides in the people." According to the logic of democratic politics in which "sovereignty resides in the people," the idea that state power resides in the people is fundamental. The constitutional system stipulates and guarantees that the citizens produce the government by regular elections, and through this the government exercises state power in the service of the interests of the people, and democratic supervision of the government is exercised by the masses, thus establishing a rough equality between state authority and citizen rights. Thus, those in power dare not act willfully, and society operates in an orderly fashion. For this reason, the change of governments in modern democratic politics and the transfer of power are different from "the rise and fall of political regimes" and even more from "the dynastic cycle."

Next, in traditional agricultural society, every cycle of the rise or fall of a "regime" was the result of human action, and every cycle of the "rise and fall of regimes" was the result of large-scale social unrest and collapse that plunged the people into the abyss of misery. By way of contrast, the more modern democratic politics is strengthened, the more changes in government and the increase or decline of a particular ruling authority do not bring on social unrest or collapse, and society continues to live and work in peace. The people are not affected by the advance or retreat of government officials or the ruling authority but are protected by the constitutional order.

Furthermore, how do Party cadres in the ruling Party treat their personal use of power? General Secretary Hu Jintao has repeatedly stressed that we must "exercise power for the people, identify ourselves with them, and work for their interests."[25] This is, of course, correct. But if we do not discuss who possesses power or where power comes from, it will be likely that we will fail to throw off the influence of China's traditional culture of enlightened monarchs and upright officials, whereupon the idea of "exercis[ing] power for the people, identify[ing] ourselves with them, and work[ing] for their interests" can become "gifts to" the people and not rights or powers that the people have. In a speech presented in 2010, Comrade Xi Jinping clearly proposed the premise that "power is bestowed by the people." This places the Party's view of governing power squarely within the meaning of modern democratic politics.

Thus, one of the logical starting points of modern political states is "sovereignty resides in the people," and the basic form of democratic conferral of power is the general election. The two most basic points for establishing a state democratic constitutional system are: genuine general elections and the separation of powers with checks and balances. Without general elections, the separation of powers is false and cannot produce true checks and balances. Elections without a separation of powers merely produce the transfer of power centers: whoever has power can use that power to profit themselves. The separation of powers has three layers: first, the separation of the ruling Party and the state; second, the separation of state and society; and third, the separation of the center and localities. Genuine elections have two aspects: competitive elections within the Party and national democratic general elections. Because we have not had true general elections or the separation of powers for a long time, there are some people within the ruling Party who have changed. They mouth the platitude that power is the people's, but in their hearts they think, "Power is mine." Because of this, to establish a modern political community according to the ideas of democratic politics, we must conform to the development of society's political civilization and put our efforts into constitutional reform. We must use the strengthening of constitutional government and its effective operation to regulate the ruling Party and government and the relation between the ruling Party and society, to guarantee the orderly progression of democratic politics, and in this process to find new space for the political development of the ruling Party. This will not only put the CCP's ruling authority on the legal footing of modern democratic political principles but also gain it more political leeway and strengthen the ruling Party's leadership initiative.

Working to Get Rid of the Traditional Consciousness of Having People Serve as Tools, Showing a High Level of Respect for People, and Preserving Human Rights

Treating people as human beings is a prerequisite for recognizing the value of constitutional democracy and building a modern political community. Traditional Chinese culture took the idea of "holism" as its core ideal, with each individual serving merely as a tool or a means for realizing the goals of the whole community—people had no independent existential value. Under the particular historical conditions of the Chinese Revolution, the existential circumstances facing all ethnicities and classes of that time directly determined the individual's living conditions. Ethnic interests, class interests, and individual interests were united in a particular whole, which justified making individuals serve as the means or the tools to implement the goals of the collective. To a certain extent, this strengthened traditional culture's influence over us, and it made thinking of people as a means to an end clear and concrete, while the notion of people as an end in themselves remained vague and indistinct.

Precisely because despotic political culture uses people as a means to achieve its objectives and does not respect or protect the value of human beings or basic rights and even less acknowledges that both sides in a political competition should have their rights protected, then when the CCP was leading the revolution and was confronted with the cruelty, repression, and carnage of a despotic regime, they had no choice but to adopt an armed struggle. In the face of bloody massacres, it used violent slaughter to resolve social contradictions. As a result, when we now reminisce about the revolution, we are necessarily drenched in violence and blood, and over time the extreme idea of life-or-death struggle has become sanctified.

The core of politics contains options, and in its search for values politics constructs the modern political community using both instrumental rationality and value rationality. To speak of democracy, we must first treat people as people, honor the life and existence of each and every individual as well as the rights and interests that every person should have. However, even today some local governments treat people only as political symbols, accounting figures, and instrumental tools for the sake of gross domestic product and official achievements. This reliance on the coercive power of public authority, the forced requisition of land, and forced demolition of housing among the masses have triggered numerous bloody incidents.

From the perspective of society, the most basic difference between the modern political community and the traditional political community is the distinction between subjects and citizens. Subjects are the tools of power, whereas citizens are the masters of power. Citizenship in a democracy is the manifestation of their status as masters. One of the most important and most cherished of civil rights is the right of free speech. Freedom of thought is the most fundamental manifestation of a human being's life and existence, while speech is the expression of thought. Democratic governance must realize and safeguard freedom of speech, and through the right of free speech it will promote participation in public decision making and public authority through social supervision. After all, democracy can be understood as an institutional system that allows people to control public power and peacefully manage social conflicts for the sake of living with dignity and for the promotion of human freedom and overall development. As Marx once said, only when we arrive at a communist society—that is, what he thought of as mankind's beautiful, ideal society—will we truly have advanced to a historical time in which people are truly human. Before then, everything is human prehistory.

The fundamental purpose of constitutional democracy is to create the necessary political conditions for human freedom and overall development. The reason why China's road to democracy remains so bumpy after a century of republican rule and constitutional government stems from the failure to genuinely establish the conditions for this way of thinking. If the ruling Party is to guide the construction of a modern political community, then it must create a consciousness that respects people and guarantees their basic rights and through institutional reform make constitutional democracy into the political way of life of the Chinese people.

Abandon the Constraints of Ideological Thinking About Democracy,
Strive to Absorb the Best of Humanity's Political Civilization

As the political life of human society progresses from barbarism and ignorance toward civilization, the essential question to answer is how to make it possible for all people throughout the world to live and live well. The progress of democratic politics in practice is a process of exploring the full capacities of humanity in political life, a process of the continual enrichment of democratic practice, a process of continual improvement of individual political life and the civility of society. Thus, we can divide humanity's explorations in democratic politics into three periods of democratic theory and practice: ancient, modern, and contemporary. Terms such as *bourgeois democracy* and *proletarian democracy* are reflections of the practice of democratic politics in the class structure and social conditions from the eighteenth to the mid–twentieth centuries. But now, with the fundamental transformation of the hierarchical class structure and the expansion of democratic politics brought on by the progress of productive forces, to persist in understanding and handling the question of democracy in terms of a life-and-death struggle of class antagonisms and absolute opposition patently shows historical limitations. We must abandon stereotypical ideological thinking about democracy. Only then can we truly open up the ideological space to absorb the experiences and lessons offered by the democratic practice of the people of various countries around the world and so be able to develop China's democratic politics more reasonably and with fewer twists and turns.

Just as the economic life of mankind has its rules, so does political life. Democratic theory sums up and generalizes the laws that have emerged in the course of democratic practice. This is why throughout history most democratic theory is not scholarship produced by academics silently meditating in their studies but has instead been formulated through the practice of political life itself. For example, from the perspective of instrumental rationality, democratic politics is the political mechanism for peacefully managing political conflict and for reconciling social contradictions. Thus, democracy needs a legal system. From the perspective of value rationality, democratic politics is the ultimate embodiment of the values that support human rights. Thus, democracy needs the rule of law. Today, democracy is a complex concept, and it needs to be integrated with the constitutional rule of law.

Democratic politics is itself a process of unceasing exploration and improvement, and in the process of using current democratic theory to resolve problems, new problems are created even as old ones are resolved. To resolve new problems, new theory is created. From the classical theory of direct democracy to representative elite democracy, Robert Dahl's [1915–2014] plural democracy, participatory democracy, consultative democracy, and even Takis Fotopoulos's [b. 1940] inclusive democracy, all these schools of democratic thought have been produced in the process of advancing democratic practice and have, in turn, influenced democratic practice.

To maintain a scientific attitude, to treat democratic theory and practice in a scientific spirit, we must acknowledge the universal laws of democratic politics. The objectivity and the universality of these laws illustrate that in democratic politics there are things that are surnamed neither Mr. Capitalism nor Mr. Socialism, and what we find instead is different developmental phases of the social histories of different countries and the particular features of the concrete problems they faced. I believe we can advance along the road to constitutional democracy in China by recognizing and respecting the law's preconditions as we absorb and study the experience and lessons of democratic practice in various countries and rationally engage the contradictions and conflicts in contemporary Chinese society.

In sum, the construction of a modern political community requires profoundly transforming the governing ideas of the Chinese Communist Party, moving away from the blinkered thinking of violent revolution and the influence of traditional political culture, and boldly advancing ideological rejuvenation and creation to fully absorb and gain from the beneficial experience of political civilization from all humanity so as to advance on the road of developing socialist democratic politics with Chinese characteristics.

Notes

1. Cai Xia, "Tuijin xianzheng minzhu yinggai shi Zhongguo Gongchandang de zhizheng shiming" (Advancing constitutional democracy should be the mission of the Chinese Communisty Party), Aisixiang Wang, March 30, 2013, http://www.aisixiang.com/data/64416.html.

2. *Translators' note*: Cai Xia is referring here to Yang Xiaoqing's contribution to the heated debate on the issue of constitutionalism in early 2013, following the well-known case of the censoring of the New Year's editorial on the topic in Nanfang Zhoumo (Southern weekend). See Yang Xiaoqing, "Xianzheng yu renmin minzhu zhidu zhi bijiao yanjiu" (Comparative study of constitutional government and the people's democratic system), *Nanfang Zhoumo*, May, 22, 2013, http://theory.people.com.cn/n/2013/0522/c40531-21566974.html. For the context, see Joseph Fewsmith, "Debating Constitutional Government," *China Leadership Monitor* 42 (2013), http://media.hoover.org/sites/default/files/documents/CLM42JF.pdf.

3. *Translators' note*: All Chinese would recognize the use here of the term *nahan* for "rallying cry" (also rendered "call to arms") as the title of the first collection of essays by Lu Xun (1881–1936), China's most famous writer of the twentieth century.

4. *Translators' note*: The expression *Tang–Wu geming* refers to the first ruler (Tang) of the Shang dynasty, who overthrew the Xia dynasty, and to the first ruler (Wu) of the Zhou, who overthrew the Shang. The term *geming* acquired the meaning "revolution" only at the turn of the twentieth century; before then it meant "changing the mandate" to rule.

5. Karl Marx and Friedrich Engels, *Gongchangdang xuanyan* (Communist manifesto), in *Makesi Engesi xuanji* (Selected works of Marx and Engels) (Beijing: People's Press,

1972), 1:272. *Translators' note*: The standard English translation used here is *The Communist Manifesto* (New Haven, CT: Yale University Press, 2012), 91.

6. *Translators' note*: Cai says, "*New China Daily* . . . in Yan'an," but *New China Daily* was published in Chongqing by the Communists during the war, while in Yan'an the core Party paper was *Jiefang ribao* (Liberation daily).

7. *Translators' note*: The "Three-Thirds System" was a United Front policy of the Yan'an era, mandating that one-third of elected government personnel come from each group: Communists, non–Communist Party members, and unaffiliated.

8. Mao Zedong, *Mao Zedong xuanji* (Selected Works of Mao Zedong) (Beijing: Renmin, 1966), 2:732. *Translators' note*: We have taken the official translations for quotations from Mao from *Selected Works of Mao Tse-tung* (Peking: Peking Foreign Languages Press, 1965), 2:408.

9. Mao, *Mao Zedong xuanji*, 3:1070 [*Selected Works of Mao Tse-tung*, 3:243].

10. Karl Marx, "Makesi 'Heige'er fazhexue pipan' " (Marx's critique of Hegel's *Philosophy of Right*), in Marx and Engels, *Makesi Engesi quanji*, 1:316. *Translators' note*: This quote comes from a long section in Marx's critique of Hegel that discusses the idea of democracy in contrast to monarchy. The standard translation gives this quote as "Democracy is the generic constitution," followed by "monarchy is a species, and indeed a poor one." See Karl Marx, *Critique of Hegel's "Philosophy of Right" (1843)*, trans. Annette Jolin and Joseph O'Malley (Oxford: Oxford University Press, 1970), 29, https://www.marxists.org/archive/marx/works/download/Marx_Critique_of_Hegels_Philosophy_of_Right.pdf.

11. Marx and Engels, *Gongchandang xuanyan*, 1:255 [*Communist Manifesto*, 78].

12. Marx, "Makesi 'Heige'er fazhexue pipan,' " 1:280–81 [*Critique of Hegel's "Philosophy of Right*," 29–30].

13. Deng Xiaoping, *Deng Xiaoping wenxuan* (Selected works of Deng Xiaoping) (Beijing: People's Press, 1994), 2:332. *Translators' note*: For the English translations of quotations from Deng, we used Deng Xiaoping, *Selected Works of Deng Xiaoping*, trans. Bureau for the Compilation and Translation of Works of Marx, Engel, Lenin, and Stalin, Central Committee of the Communist Party of China (Beijing: Foreign Language Press, 1984), 2:315.

14. Deng Xiaoping, in *Makesi, Engesi, Liening, Mao Zedong, Deng Xiaoping, Jiang Zemin lun minzhu* (Marx, Engels, Lenin, Mao Zedong, Deng Xiaoping, and Jiang Zemin on democracy), ed. Democracy Research Center, Chinese Academy of Social Sciences (Beijing: CASS Press, 2002), 245. *Translators' note*: For the English translation given here, we used "Resolution of the CCP Central Committee on the Guiding Principles for Building a Socialist Society with an Advanced Culture and Ideology" (September 12, 1986), *China Report* 23, no. 2 (1987): 259.

15. Deng Xiaoping, *Deng Xiaoping wenxuan*, 2:335. *Translators' note*: The English version of the quotation here is adapted from Deng Xiaoping, "On the Reform of the System of Party and State Leadership," August 18, 1980, http://en.people.cn/dengxp/vol2/text/b1460.html.

16. *Translators' note*: In *The Civil War in France* (1871), Marx summarizes the basic practices of the workers' government of the Paris Commune and points out that the important principles of the new-style people's regime. For example, with the system of universal suffrage and fusion of powers, representatives are selected by the electorate with responsibility and can be replaced. Government employees are public servants of society, and they can receive only a worker's salary. Such employees are under the conscientious supervision of the people, and so on.

17. See Li Yongquan, *Eguo zhengdang shi* (History of Russian political parties) (Beijing: Zhongyang Bianyi, 1999), 220–96, for a comparatively detailed discussion and analysis of the changes before and after the Bolsheviks thought to seize power.

18. Vladmir Lenin, *Liening quanji* (Complete works of Lenin), 2nd ed. (Beijing: People's Press, 1984–1990), 37:125. *Translators' note*: For the English translation, we relied on Vladimir Lenin, *Collected Works of Lenin*, 4th ed. (Moscow: Progress, 1972), 29:533, https://www.marxists.org/archive/lenin/works/1919/aug/05.htm.

19. Deng Xiaoping, *Deng Xiaoping wenxuan*, 2:333 [*Selected Works of Deng Xiaoping*, 316].

20. Marx, "Makesi 'Heige'er fazhexue pipan,'" 1:283 [*Critique of Hegel's "Philosophy of Right,"* 31].

21. Deng Xiaoping, in *Makesi, Engesi, Liening, Mao Zedong, Deng Xiaoping, Jiang Zemin lun minzhu*, 245. *Translators' note*: The English translation comes from Deng Xiaoping, "Resolution," *China Report* 23, no. 2 (1987): 259.

22. Deng Xiaoping, *Deng Xiaoping wenxuan*, 2:336 [English in "On the Reform of the System, " per note 15].

23. *Translators' note*: In the subhead to this section, Cai uses the term *zhizheng siwei*, which we have translated as "ruling-power thinking," though it literally means "governance thinking" or "ideas on governance," a term much used in the work of Xi Jinping.

24. *Translators' note*: Here Cai is using a phrase loaded with historical weight, *zhengquan xingshuai zhouqi lü*, which means "the cycle of rise and fall of regimes," though for clarity we render it as "the dynastic cycle." This phrase refers to the repeated rise and fall of dynasties in traditional China and was famously discussed by Mao Zedong and the noted democratic intellectual Huang Yanpei (1878–1965) when Huang visited Mao in Yan'an in July 1945. Mao suggested that the CCP could escape the rise and fall of regimes that had hampered earlier Chinese regimes by implementing constitutional democracy.

25. *Translators' note*: Hu Jintao made this pronouncement in a speech on July 1, 2011, commemorating the ninetieth anniversary of the founding of the CCP. The speech and its English translation are given at http://www.china.org.cn/learning_english/2011-07/06/content_22930201_7.htm.

CHAPTER 7

"I AM A CHILD OF THE NINETEENTH CENTURY"

The Last Twenty Years of Wang Yuanhua's Life[1]

XU JILIN

TRANSLATION BY DAVID OWNBY

Translator's Introduction

Xu Jilin (b. 1957) is a well-known historian of modern Chinese intellectual life and a public intellectual who has had a considerable impact through his writings on social media. He is generally characterized as a Liberal but portrays himself as a "bat figure" (*bianfuxing renwu*), by which he means that he is "neither fish nor fowl," being politically liberal (support for individual rights, constitutions, and rule of law), economically socialist (support for equality), and culturally conservative (support for Confucian values as part of an eventual Chinese "civil religion"). However deeply felt, the evolution of Xu's "bat persona" has accompanied the decline of liberalism as a major intellectual force in China. Like Liu Qing (b. 1963) and other Liberals, Xu has had to recast certain liberal arguments in light of China's rise and the ascension of the New Left and the mainland New Confucians. His "eulogy" for Wang Yuanhua translated here, along with a similar text written following the death of Li Shenzhi (1923–2003),[2] is part of Xu's reflection on the fraught relationship between Confucianism, socialism, and liberalism in the historical experience of important Chinese intellectuals of the twentieth century.

Wang Yuanhua (1920–2008) is little known in the West, even if he is a hero to many Chinese Liberals, because Wang, like his better-known counterpart Li Shenzhi, was deeply steeped in traditional Chinese culture, joined and loyally served the Chinese Communist Party (CCP) for decades, and in later life developed an independent, critical, "liberal" voice grounded in humanism.

Wang joined the CCP in 1938 and worked in the realms of propaganda, thought, art, and culture. After the revolution, he served in the Shanghai Writers' Association and did editorial work for different newspapers and magazines. He was caught up in a major purge against Hu Feng (1902–1985) in 1955,[3] who had dared to argue that Mao Zedong's theories of art and literature were too narrow and repressive. Wang was incarcerated and interrogated for some time and was not finally rehabilitated until 1981, which meant that he had sixteen years to reflect on his thought and experiences. Once rehabilitated, he published a series of books—often composed of notes, commentaries, and brief essays—that were immensely influential among Chinese intellectuals because of his willingness to use his personal experience to question received wisdom.

Whereas Liu Qing reflects on the fate of Chinese liberalism from a theoretical perspective in his essay in this volume (chapter 2), Xu Jilin uses Wang's experience and reflections to ground Chinese liberalism in the soil of modern Chinese history. Wang, like Li Shenzhi and others, came to his "liberal" stance after considerable personal pain and suffering, which brought him to reflect deeply on his prior ideological beliefs and commitments. Furthermore, as Wang questioned his earlier commitment to revolution, his thoughts turned more to the humanism of traditional Chinese civilization than to the classics of Western liberalism. This is the point of Wang's embrace of Du Yaquan (1873–1933),[4] a figure of ridicule during the iconoclastic May Fourth period because he dared to suggest moderate solutions that found a place for both the past and the present, the Chinese and the foreign. Such moderation was important for Wang and remains so for Xu, who often argues that Chinese scholars must set aside petty ideological differences in the search for a consensus that can help to create the basic values Chinese society currently lacks.[5] In the end, Wang Yuanhua represents a personality type, a commitment to independent thinking and personal integrity that to Xu Jilin serves as a Chinese "contribution" to liberal theory that draws on the moral stance of the traditional Chinese scholar-official.

"I Am a Child of the Nineteenth Century"

On May 9, 2008, at 11:40 p.m. in a room at Shanghai's Ruijin Hospital, Wang Yuanhua quietly departed this earth. Three days later the Sichuan earthquake occurred, and throughout China tears were shed for those killed and injured. Wang had struggled with his own suffering in his old age, and being spared the horrible news that followed his death might be seen as the fortunate side of his own misfortune. At the funeral ceremony, Wang lay peacefully among the fresh flowers, his expression as calm as ever; I could hardly believe that he was gone for good. A sadness overcame me that I could not control.

When I met Wang, he was already elderly, without much time left. The twenty years around the turn of the century were difficult times. I was lucky enough to witness the last years of Wang's life from a close vantage point. While he was alive, he would discuss affairs of state or talk about the Way (*dao*) in a manner that seemed completely ordinary. But after his death, as his familiar silhouette slipped over the horizon, I suddenly felt a huge lump in my throat, a hole that could never be filled. The loss was not just personal but belonged to all of Chinese culture.

During the period of mourning, I reread Wang's writings, with the idea of working my scattered memories into a larger canvas that might convey Wang's thought, spirit, and frame of mind in his later years.

In death, Wang's body was draped in the flag of the Chinese Communist Party, with its hammer and sickle. He entered the Party at the age of eighteen, in 1938, a year marked by constant warfare, especially in bloody, occupied Shanghai, where Wang was living. Like Li Shenzhi, Wang joined the revolution in the wake of the December 9 [1935] movement, on fire to save the country. Like Li, Wang was an "old-style Communist Party member." "Old-style" was what Li Shenzhi called himself. New-style Communist Party members join the Party for material gain; the Party is a tool in their efforts to climb the hierarchy and make money. Old-style Communist Party members poured the loves and hatreds of a lifetime into the Party, and their identification with the Party, their idealism—all of this is hard for later generations to grasp.

Not only was Wang "old-style," possessed of a burning idealism, but he also had an independent will and a theoretical mindset. Prior to liberation, the Communist ranks were essentially composed of intellectuals and peasants. There were two important waves of intellectuals who joined the Party: the first was in the early 1920s, when the Party was being established, and all of the founders of the Party were intellectuals, even well-known members of the elite. The second wave came in the wake of the December 9 movement of the 1930s, when their passion to save the country compelled young intellectuals to join the revolution in droves. Wang belonged to the underground Party culture committee in Jiangsu, made up of a particular group of intellectuals. Looking just at the leadership, we find Sun Yefang [1908–1983] as committee secretary and Gu Zhun [1915–1974] as vice secretary.[6] Both figures were theoretical and thoughtful, and both were important leading intellectuals within the Party. Wang Yuanhua was fortunate in that once he joined the revolution, he was groomed in such an atmosphere of theoretical richness. The Jiangsu cultural committee was, for the young Wang, no different from a university and molded his character for life. Wang was of course a Communist Party member, but in his own eyes he was first an intellectual, a Communist Party member with an intellectual temperament. In a personal letter to Li Rui [1917–2019] written in his later years,[7] Wang exclaimed, "I joined the Party more than half a century ago and am embarrassed to have never completed an intellectual task or responsibility. In such turbulent times, to have never done anything to encourage myself and others is enough to keep me up nights when I think back on things."[8]

When Wang was young, he had a heroic spirit and liked to read Friedrich Nietzsche [1844–1900], Lu Xun [1881–1936], and Romain Rolland [1866–1944].[9] He believed that this filthy world would be saved by Mara poets with transcendent wills.[10] At the time, his favorite figure was Lu Xun, and when he fled Beiping after it fell to the Japanese, all he took was a small image of Lu Xun that he had drawn himself; Lu Xun was his idol. His favorite book was Romain Rolland's *Jean-Christophe* [1913], which he greatly admired, believing that every word and act of this idealist represented critical righteousness and artistic truth. The essays that Wang wrote as a youth were excellent, with a bookish flavor, full of vim and vigor, and earned him a bit of fame within the Party. The young Wang was proud of his determination and his talent; right after liberation, one of his coworkers, Xia Yan's [1900–1995] secretary, Li Ziyun [1930–2009],[11] described him as haughty and insulting, somewhat overwrought.[12]

Pride goeth before a fall. Wang was caught up in the vortex of the anti–Hu Feng movement of 1955. He suffered two years of isolation and investigation, receiving nothing but cold glares and serious denunciations. He later remembered: "My mind was in shock. The thing that for years I had made out to be beautiful, even sacred, was destroyed in an instant."[13] During his isolation and investigation, he read a great deal—no more stories of heroes but rather philosophical works, including those of Mao Zedong, Lenin, Marx, and Hegel, returning to the classics. His personal failures and the wisdom of the philosophers made him thoughtful, and he was transformed from a radical literary youth into a thinker with a capacity for deep reflection.

Wang went through several periods of deep reflection in his life. To my mind, the most important were those of the mid-1950s and the early 1990s, periods that coincided with sudden changes in the political situation, leading Wang to reconsider his basic beliefs. His life during these periods was isolated from current affairs, and he nursed his wounds in an atmosphere of loneliness, calmly examining sacred beliefs he had previously held, wondering whether they would survive his reflection. In 1950s China, dogmatism was in full force, and while Wang was in prison, he painstakingly read Hegel's *Shorter Logic* and finally grasped the origin of the dogmatic theory of knowledge: in the passage from emotional knowledge to rational knowledge, there is also an intellectual stage in which we make abstract generalizations about things. But if the intellectual stage becomes absolute, replacing dialectical rational knowledge, then one can fall into rigid dogmatism—for example, recognizing only man's class nature and denying his basic human nature and his richly diverse personality or discussing only the universal aspect of a thing while ignoring its particularity. These reflections, rooted in classical German philosophy, were undoubtedly seen at the time as heterodox and could not be publicly discussed until the thought liberation of the early 1980s. In 1982, like Wang Ruoshui [1926–2002],[14] Wang Yuanhua gave a talk entitled "An Exploration of a Number of Theoretical

Questions in Marxism" at the conference planned by Zhou Yang [1908–1989][15] to mark the hundredth anniversary of Karl Marx's death. This leading document in the movement to liberate thought, which later fell afoul of the anti-spiritual pollution campaign [in 1984], not only reintroduced Marx's theory of alienation but also set out Wang's thoughts about intellectual issues. During the thought-liberation movement and the New Enlightenment of the 1980s, Wang was a leader in the world of thought and was ahead of his time, but Wang's rethinking at this time was not thorough enough and still contained a good many habitual notions.

The early 1990s constituted the most important turning point in Wang Yuanhua's life. During that period, Wang's normally busy living room was much quieter. Wang moved to the South, living for a time on Baiteng Lake in Zhuhai. In letters that he wrote to me during this period, Wang described his state of mind: "I'm cut off from the outside world here, as if I were in another world. I once enjoyed this kind of calm in my youth. In front of where I live is a small flower garden with grass, flowers, and trees. When the weather is nice, I sit in the yard looking out into space and the cloud formations. This takes away the mind's volatility and imposes a sense of calm."

Having suffered the unforgettable wounds of time, Wang drew lessons from his painful experiences and undertook the most important reflection of his life. He later often explained himself like this: "I started to write when I was young but did not really enter the world of thought until the 1990s. . . . The 1990s were my age of rethinking, and it was only then that I did a thorough examination of my own thoughts and assumptions, accumulated over a long period of time."[16] In the works Wang published in his later years, he liked to use words such as *thought* and *reflection*. Some people don't like to reflect and think that they are always right. One of Wang's scholarly colleagues got nervous at the very idea, abruptly arguing, "What should I rethink? There's no reason for that." Wang saw rethinking as part of an intellectual's penchant for worrying over things (*youhuan yishi*)[17] and as the basic feature of his own life.[18] Just as Lin Tongqi [1923–2015] said,[19] rethinking was for Wang not just a way of thinking but also a way of life. Such a lifestyle was surely not without pain because the object of rethinking was not other people, but rather the self that once thought it was right.

Wang had many feelings about the May Fourth Movement and once said that he was a child of May Fourth. As part of a generation of intellectuals that came after May Fourth, he had drunk deeply at its well, and the most profound aspects of his thought and personality were full of the spirit of the Enlightenment. Yet prior to the 1990s he had not understood that there were negative elements hidden in May Fourth thought. When in the late 1980s criticism of May Fourth by Chinese scholars abroad filtered back to China, in a fit of pique Wang wrote an essay called "On Tradition and Anti-tradition: In Defense of the May

Fourth Spirit." But his solitary reflections at Baiteng Lake led him to a new appreciation of the tragedy of twentieth-century radicalism and to a bitter search for the historical origins of such thought. Not long after his return from the South, I was asked to request that Wang write a foreword for *The Collected Works of Du Yaquan*. Not long after that, he telephoned me, saying, "Little Xu, that Du Yaquan is really something. The problems we're thinking about today, he had already thought about them back then!" In the summer of 1993, in Shanghai's extreme heat, Wang took off his shirt and painstakingly read Du Yaquan's essays on thought during the May Fourth period. Three months later, he produced his essay: "Du Yaquan and the Debate on Problems in Eastern and Western Cultures," an essay with an immense impact in China and abroad.[20]

This essay opened a curtain on Wang's thoughts in the 1990s as he discovered that the intellectual origins of twentieth-century radicalism emerged first in the anarchism of the late Qing–early Republican era and that it was latent in the Enlightenment thought of the May Fourth period. In Chen Duxiu's [1879–1942] May Fourth–period writings on the debates between Eastern and Western cultures,[21] Wang found a kind of dogmatic personality. In the past, Wang had fiercely defended May Fourth and the Enlightenment, but now he felt that some negative elements within the Enlightenment mindset required rethinking, such as primitive evolutionism, radicalism, instrumentalism, and situational ethics.[22] As a son of the May Fourth who in addition had been much influenced by Hegel, Wang originally believed that human rationality could become all knowing and all powerful. Directed by rationality, people would be capable of destroying an old world and building an ideal new world. Yet the human and Chinese tragedies of the twentieth century coldly illustrated that vast numbers of sins had been committed in the name of rationality. Wang suddenly realized that "the spirit of rationality and human strength brought mankind out of the medieval dark ages, but once rationality was deified to the point that we believed it to possess the final truth, then in the name of truth we could brand as heterodox all those who opposed or disagreed and those who were not transformed could be eliminated."[23] Although he had once been a dedicated follower of Hegel, in the 1990s one of the first objectives of his rethinking was to cleanse himself of the poison of absolutism and dogmatism found in Hegelian thought. At the same time, he also invested a great deal of energy in a painstaking reading of Rousseau's *Social Contract* [1762], reflecting on the inner connections between Rousseau's theory of the general will and totalitarian ideology.

Wang repeated many times that it was not until the 1990s that he himself was "enlightened" and that his rethinking had only just begun, leaving him with too much research to do. The ups and downs of his life and the many important events he experienced made him an important historical witness. I urged him many times to write his memoirs. He replied in a letter:

I am not self-reflexive enough, and although I'm old and rigid, I still have to study, I have to study. As long as I have breath, my heart will not die. At present I am writing this and that. I haven't yet thought about my memoirs. I feel like first I need to finish up these little projects. Maybe you think that I'm abandoning the fundamentals to tend to nonessentials, but everybody has his own way of thinking. I know that what I'm writing is not worth much, but I never thought to make a name with my writing, and I don't want to use my essays to seek after anything (even if it is the respect of others). Crickets chirp and crows caw because they have to. When I ask myself what it is that I want to write, it's not purely academic, nor do I want to use scholarship to discuss politics. But I'm not just writing to amuse myself or to cheer myself up or to flaunt some sort of naturalistic style. I have always believed in the notion that knowledge is power.

Wang was too modest. The "odds and ends" that he mentioned in his letter were precisely the important "rethinking" essays that he published after 1993.

What is too bad is that Wang's "enlightenment" came a bit late! After the 1990s, his energy was no longer what it once was, and writing an essay often took too much out of him. Especially once he passed eighty, his health declined, and he was often hospitalized, afflicted by all sorts of illnesses and suffering. Although his thought was not as sharp as before or his memory as clear, his reflections remained profound, even if his aging body brought him down. He was no longer able to write long essays and expressed his fresher thoughts through notes, interviews, and talks. He was also a perfectionist, and every character had to be weighed and considered to find the best, most perfect way to express the ideas—he was almost pitiless with himself. He did not write all that much when he was old, but every word was a pearl, everything coming together to express the force of his ideas and will.

The elderly Wang's state of mind was often in pain. Physical suffering was less important; what really tortured him were spiritual concerns. In a letter to one of his students, he wrote: "I remember that Lu Xun said, right before he died, in a letter to a young person, that 'to live truly is to suffer,' and I find that this is indeed true."[24] Wang's pain finds its origins in the mentality of worrying practiced by China's scholar-officials. He was once an idealist full of utopian imaginings, believing in historical evolution, believing that civilization always progresses. He believed that he was part of a transitional generation and invested all of his hopes in the younger generation. But in the last twenty years of his life, from a rational perspective he saw through the deification of historical evolution, and he never again ignored the utopian aspects of any ideology. Wang was both happy and concerned about the huge changes that occurred in China after the 1990s. The world that he saw in his final years was not the world that he had hoped for; reality had become exceptionally utilitarian, fragmented, and vulgar. It was not a world that captivated people.

From what I observed at close hand, what the aging Wang most worried about was three things: the divorce of thought from scholarship, the factionalism of the intellectual world, and the decline of ancient world civilizations.

The separation of thought and academics was a phenomenon of the post-1990s scholarly world. This problem did not exist in the 1980s because during the New Enlightenment period, thought and academics were blended together, mutually embedded. Reading a few pages of the journal *Dushu* [Reading] from that period will suffice to make that clear.[25] The New Enlightenment of the 1980s was both a rational movement and a movement of Sturm und Drang. In fact, feelings ran stronger than rationality. In the context of the history of Chinese scholarship, the 1980s were like the Song dynasty,[26] with people of every stripe freely discussing ideas and principles, all of it chock full of the traditional scholar-official notion of making the world a better place. Although both "respect for morality" (idealism) and "inquiries into the Way" (intellectualism) were valued, morality trumped inquiry. After the 1990s, with the huge changes in the intellectual world, some of those involved in the Enlightenment returned to the academy from the public square, relinquishing the search for truth for academic scholarship, so that "inquiry" suppressed "morality" and intellectualism replaced idealism, which evolved toward paper shuffling. . . . Ji Xianlin [1911–2009] and Li Shenzhi, two great academic scholars with principle and vision, can stand as spiritual symbols of the bifurcation of "inquiry" and "morality." As the great master of a generation of national studies, Ji is widely seen as the representative of Qing-style studies, of academics for academics' sake, of seeking knowledge for knowledge's sake, and he ultimately became the model of today's widely educated scholar. Li Shenzhi inherited the Sturm und Drang tradition of May Fourth and deeply felt that the personality of the 1990s scholar was listless, having lost critical passion. To mobilize the scholarly spirit and point out the future direction, Li took up the great banner of liberal ideology and sought through his own moral practice to serve as an example and carve out a new escape route to an ideal world.

Faced with the split between academic research and truth, Wang was quite concerned. In the battle between arid scholarship and moral engagement,[27] Wang occupied the middle ground. In terms of scholarly style, he was partial to "inquiry," but in terms of spiritual concerns he also was concerned with "morality." Wang deeply understood that thought and scholarship were better when combined than when separated. Academic study without deeper intellectual engagement is like the minor technical skills of an artisan's subordinates, while thought without an academic basis often winds up being conceptual slogans without foundation. Upon reflection, Wang proposed the formula "scholarly thought and thoughtful scholarship." In his old age, the senior scholars he most respected were Gu Zhun, the great theorist who was full of knowledge and who embodied the model of "scholarly thought;" and Chen Yinke [1890–1969],[28] who, in addition to his great learning, addressed the world with exceptionally deep concern, thus fulfilling the model of "thoughtful scholarship." To combine thought and scholarship in one pursuit is the scholar's highest goal. Wang himself sought to apply himself to such a project, through knowledge, scholarship, and self-cultivation coming to master literature, history, and philosophy, achieving first-class results in pursuit of truth, scholarship, and the art of writing. In the academic world, people talked about the "southern Wang [Yuanhua] and the northern Qian [Zhongshu],"[29] and in the thought world they talked about the "southern Wang [Yuanhua] and the northern Li [Shenzhi]." Even if Wang himself did not accept such accolades, this one nonetheless illustrates his great achievements in the two realms of scholarship and thought.

In our current age of scholarship for the sake of scholarship, what does Wang finally symbolize? If we see Li Shenzhi as a descendant of Wang Yangming [1472–1529] and Ji Xianlin as an inheritor of Qian Daxin [1728–1804], the great Confucian scholar of the Qianlong-Jiaqing era [1735–1820] of the Qing dynasty,[30] then we might see Wang Yuanhua as a contemporary version of Dai Zhen [1727–1777].[31] According to Yu Ying-shih [b. 1930],[32] Dai Zhen's mode of study valued essence rather than breadth, and his ultimate goal was to understand the Way. He used the teachings of the ancients to seek out truth and argued that behind truth was efficacy. In Qing scholarship, there was a conflict between emphasis on breadth and emphasis on insight. In the academic style of the Qianlong-Jiaqing era, there was breadth but not insight, which often yielded useless details. As for those who still followed the scholarly styles of the Song and Ming, their priority was great insight, which often wound up in empty abstraction. The reason that Dai Zhen transcended his era was that he was a hedgehog in an age of foxes, possessing the talents of a fox (the breadth of evidential scholarship) but the vision of the hedgehog (and a hedgehog's embrace of insight).[33] Wang's accomplishments approach those of Dai Zhen. In the summer of 2006, I went to a conference in Tunxi, Anhui, and visited the Dai Zhen Memorial Hall. I discovered that Wang Yuanhua had written the couplets to accompany the general title, "Of Great Breadth and Deep Essence." The left-hand couplet read, "Develop deep thought by teaching classical truths," and the right-hand couplet read, "Universal meaning is profound and will sustain careful thought." This may have been Wang's formula for self-encouragement.

Another thing that greatly troubled Wang Yuanhua was the factionalism in the post-1990s academic world and its partisan "Party spirit." In the Enlightenment camp of the 1980s, noble colleagues shared common ideals and faced common enemies. Even if there were internal debates, there were also mutual support and shared struggle. The Enlightenment camp began to divide in the mid-1990s over differences in intellectual backgrounds and ideological quarrels as well as questions of material interest. Wang was very concerned about the state of the scholarly world and was often wounded by the conflicts and mutual recriminations. He would wake up in the middle of the night wondering why Chinese intellectuals could not develop reasonable, normal relationships instead of acting like prima donnas or jackals.[34] What he hated most were those who formed a faction in the name of some mysterious something, ran up a banner, and attacked all of those who were different or on the slightest pretext accused someone of representing a certain "ism" or faction—judging all scholars from their own little group's point of view. Wang was above the partisan positions and the ideological wars. His "middle way" and his rethinking sometimes incited gossip and were sometimes misunderstood by outsiders as a "transformation" in which he joined the national studies group or the conservative group—there were many such accusations. This made Wang angry, and he often sternly pronounced: "There is a tendency now in the scholarly world to form groups and factions, but I am not joining either the 'mutual aid group' or the 'cooperative society.' I'm staying alone until the end."[35]

Although pained by the factionalism in the academic world, Wang also resembled Hu Shi [1891–1962][36] in his later years and increasingly came to feel that tolerance was more important than freedom. Tolerance doesn't mean being two-faced or abandoning one's own standpoint for that of other people; it instead means listening to the voice of the other, seeking out mutual understanding. In a letter to me in 1993, Wang described the conflict in the intellectual world between radicals and conservatives in the following way: "Please listen to an old man's sincere words: in scholarship we should adopt a democratic practice in which we are both extremely open-minded (accepting other people's viewpoints) and unyielding (holding to our own truths)." Wang's way of friendship was to disregard shared viewpoints and the closeness of positions in favor of the closeness of the minds. His friendship with Lin Yusheng [b. 1934][37] and Yu Ying-shih is a charming tale of enemies turning into friends. Both Lin and Yu had originally criticized Wang's essay "On Tradition and Antitradition: In Defense of the May Fourth Spirit," from 1988, which had led to bitter exchanges between Wang and the two. Later on, when they met at an international conference in Hawaii, they became intellectual bosom buddies. In recalling these events, Wang said: "For such a thing to occur, I think that on both sides there must exist a genuine search for truth and a respect for intellectual democracy and free discussion. Only then can one forget oneself for the common good and treat people equally rather than looking down on others and seeking victory."[38]

When Wang was alive, his living room was full of famous as well as ordinary people; everyone was welcome. He had an accepting heart and a charisma that brought people together. No matter what was said, as long as it was reasonable and spoken with a purpose, Wang was always willing to listen closely. But if you knew Wang well, you saw that behind his moderate rationality there was also a radical side. He often said: "I'm from Hubei, and my personality has a certain Hubei wildness." He had a fiery spirit, and on certain questions of importance he might explode in a rather extreme fashion. Friends who didn't know him well were often shocked when this happened, because it was something that one did not sense in reading his writings. Why was there such a distance between his writing and his personality? Wang once revealed to me what he had learned through writing: "One should never write when agitated because when you do, what you write is more emotional than rational. Wait until you have calmed down and use your knowledge. That's the only way to come up with even-handed arguments." And it's true that Wang's writings are calm and reserved, their power contained. Yet behind the seemingly rational writings was a flood of uncertain emotions. Wang's true nature may well have been externally soft (peaceful) and internally hard (fiery).

The deepest impression Wang made on people was his eyes, which were extremely bright, expressing dignity and incisiveness, as if they penetrated the surface of what they saw to discern its true meaning. In his last few years, he had already seen through the dusty world and its tawdry dramas. After seventy years of political life, with its rude ups and downs, plus his careful reading of the classics and history and his deep grasp of human nature, Wang had no more facile political beliefs and paid little attention to the politics of the day. Heroes came and went on the political stage, but the hard facts of history hardly changed at all. Looking toward the future, Wang often revealed an ineffable preoccupation. His perspective had, for some time, transcended that of a particular period, nor did he believe that institutions could change everything. In his view, even if we created a democratic system, it could still change for the worse if we still lacked humanistic spirit and public morality.[39] Wang often mourned the decline of traditional Chinese civilization, especially that of the humanistic spirit. His earliest worries concerned a mass culture that had gotten out of control. As part of the intellectual elite, he was not opposed to mass culture in and of itself but rather worried about its deleterious effects on art appreciation and the spiritual life. He often said: "Art cannot be judged according to traditional and modern, Chinese or foreign, old or new; the distinctions are rather between lofty and petty, beautiful and ugly, eternal and vulgar."[40] There are good things in mass culture, but if it dominates culture, it lowers the standards of art. If the sole goal is to be popular and trendy, then the taste of the market replaces art. Wang was most opposed to kitsch, and he often cried: "A society whose culture is led by what is trendy has no true, deep spiritual life."[41] Sadly, Wang's voice was too weak; he could not reverse what had already happened, and he could only watch as traditional humanistic culture and civilization declined day by day.

In 2002, on Lin Yusheng's recommendation, Wang read Harvard professor Benjamin Schwartz's [1916–1999] essay "China and Contemporary Millenarianism," which affected Wang deeply. Schwartz, basing himself on the spirit of ancient prophets and deeply preoccupied by the fate of the civilization of mankind, warned humanity just before he died, saying that the consumerism and materialism bequeathed to mankind by technological progress and new scientific developments already constitute a sort of material millenarianism, and the accumulated humanistic spirit of the axial civilizations is in decline.[42] On reading this essay, Wang understood that the decline of the humanistic spirit is not only a particular feature of contemporary China but also a collective threat faced by the civilizations of all mankind. Wang then wrote a short essay devoted to this theme, pointing out with great concern that "today's China truly has no reason to feel excited about the spread of universal Western notions of consumerism and materialism."[43] In subsequent years, Wang became increasingly concerned about this, even obsessed with it, and he talked about it virtually every time I went to see him. I vaguely came to feel that Wang shared with the elderly Wang Guowei [1877–1927][44] and Chen Yinke a sadness and desolation born of a fear of civilization's imminent decline. Wang had lived into the twenty-first century but was not optimistic about mankind's future, and in a letter to Lin Yusheng he noted with great concern: "Isaiah Berlin said that the twentieth century was a terrible century, but observing how things look now, the twenty-first century may well mark the eclipse of culture."[45] "Each time I think of this, it truly makes me sad. I am already old and no longer search for anything, but when I think of future generations, and when I think of our long cultural tradition, and that it might cease to exist—I can hardly bear such a catastrophe."[46]

Unwilling to look back on the twentieth century and convinced that the prospects for the new century were bleak, Wang in his final months and years began to recall the nineteenth century, which is really not that far past. In 2001, in an important interview entitled "A Dialogue Between Spiritual Civilization and the Twenty-First Century," he publicly declared: "I have more feelings for the nineteenth century than for the twentieth. Even now, my favorite literature is Western literature from the nineteenth century. . . . Spiritually, I am a child of the nineteenth century and was raised on the nourishment of nineteenth-century writers."[47]

Why did Wang pine for the nineteenth century? What did the nineteenth century mean to him? For Wang, the first meaning of the nineteenth century was breadth. Culturally, the nineteenth century was a "wide-open field,"[48] people's hearts and minds were wide open, rivers flowing into the seas, East and West absorbing one another. Hu Xiaoming, one of Wang's best students, once said to Wang: "You have been greatly marked by the cultural spirit of the nineteenth century. Your spirit and nature in your later years are like those of the generation just preceding May Fourth—Liang Qichao [1873–1929], Yan Fu [1854–1921], Wang Guowei— . . . at the time they were considering how to develop traditional studies and integrate new knowledge, believing that East and West were basically similar. Things changed after May Fourth, when something approaching belief took over."[49] Wang agreed. At one point, he had been the son of May Fourth and threw himself into the Enlightenment project in defense of it. In the 1990s, reflecting on May Fourth, he came to understand that the movement that had represented the spirit of the twentieth century had a narrow character. And when he reconsidered the turn of the twentieth century and late Qing scholars from Liang Qichao through Yan Fu and Wang Guowei, he found that they did not emphasize the gulf between China and the West but rather worked toward communication among civilizations. The figures that Wang appreciated in his later years, such as Du Yaquan and Chen Yinke, all possessed this nineteenth-century breadth and attitude of acceptance. This was an attitude of cultural self-consciousness, the attitude of a great civilized country, neither arrogant nor self-denigrating.

There was another reason that Wang liked the nineteenth century, and it was that the Enlightenment ideals of the nineteenth century were full of the spirit of humanism. Living quietly in occupied Shanghai at the beginning of the Anti-Japanese War period with nothing to read, Wang had only nineteenth-century European literature for spiritual nourishment. From the English Dickens and the Brontë sisters, the French Balzac and Romain Rolland, and the Russian Chekhov and Dostoevsky—these writers, brimming with the humanistic spirit, molded Wang's soul. He said: "I like that nineteenth-century literature is always revealing people's feelings and worries about their fate. This underscores the importance of spiritual life and affirms mankind's worthy feelings."[50]

The core of the humanistic spirit is to view people as the goal, to respect the personality and dignity of each person. Wang accorded great importance to dignity. In political violence such as the anti–Hu Feng campaign and the Cultural Revolution, Wang had been grievously harmed and was exceptionally sensitive to questions of dignity. He once said: "You can't insult a person's dignity. . . . Thought is a strange thing. Thought cannot compel others to accept it, and thought cannot be destroyed by violence."[51] Human dignity comes from human spirit, and from the beginning people are thinking animals. In a letter to one of his students, Wang once wrote: "In my life, and especially during the Cultural Revolution and other campaigns, I experienced too much cruelty, callousness, brutality. For this reason, I hope your generation will no longer be insulted and can preserve your own human dignity."[52] In past political campaigns, human dignity was assaulted at the level of power, and today it is suffering from the vulgarity of the market. This was painful for Wang, and he repeatedly brought up the tomb inscription Chen Yinke wrote for Wang Guowei: "Independent spirit, free thought." Wang's goal was to encourage the people of the present generation, to inspire himself and others. By independence and freedom, he meant not only in the face of despotic power but also in the face of the power of the market and money.

In Wang's view, the literature and philosophy of the nineteenth century were full of human spirit and dignity. Even if in his later years Wang abandoned Hegel, nonetheless Hegel's embrace of the power of human thought and spirit, his insistence that "the strength of spirit cannot be underestimated or ignored," remained for Wang the rule by which he lived his life. Wang lived in a turbulent yet furtive age, when all kinds of dangers and temptations followed close on one another, yet he frankly admitted that "I am someone who works with his pen, and what I would most like to do is to fulfill my responsibility as a Chinese intellectual and leave behind something of use, something that is not tawdry or falsely intellectual. And I also hope in any situation to be able to not surrender my will, not besmirch my person, not seek after fashion, not hide from danger." Even if Wang, in his later years, did nothing earth shattering, nevertheless in his words and in his actions he chose some courses and avoided others. This may look ordinary, but in today's scholarly world, how many people can say as much?

Wang lived for thought and died for thought. His was a spiritual existence. When he entered the hospital for the last time and understood that he had little time left, he said, "I am a believer in spirit only, and now I am transforming from a spiritual person to a biological person. I have no more to fear from this world." He told his relatives and asked for assurance that in the final stages they not agree to any traumatizing, life-saving measures. He believed that to experience the end of life stuffed full of tubes or with the body opened up was not in accord with human nature. Human life requires dignity, as does human death.

Wang finally left with his dignity. This son of the nineteenth century guarded his dignity throughout his life.

Notes

1. Xu Jilin, "'Wo shi shijiu shiji zhi zi'—Wang Yuanhua de zuihou ershinian" (I am a son of the nineteenth century: Wang Yuanhua's last two decades), September 2008, Ai Sixiang Wang, http://www.aisixiang.com/data/20738.html.
2. Xu Jilin, "Li Shenzhi: The Last Scholar-Official, the Last Hero," in *Rethinking China's Rise: A Liberal Critique*, ed. and trans. David Ownby (Cambridge: Cambridge University Press, 2018), 191–210. Li Shenzhi was a noted Chinese establishment intellectual, rising to prominent positions in such institutions as the Xinhua News Agency and the Chinese Academy of Social Sciences. He was dismissed for his blunt criticisms of the government after the violence in June 1989 and emerged in the 1990s as a prominent and vocal exponent of Chinese liberalism. He was often described as "China's Havel."

3. Hu Feng was an important literary figure in the Chinese Communist movement and the object of a fierce purge in 1955. Hu argued that Mao's theories on art and literature were too confining and ignored the real lives of workers and peasants. He was subsequently jailed for some twenty years.

4. Du Yaquan was a writer and thinker who sought to reconcile East and West and avoid extremes. His views were rejected during the May Fourth period but have been revisited by Chinese scholars in the past decades.

5. See, for example, Xu Jilin, "Modern Politics Is Live and Let Live," 2013, Reading the China Dream, https://www.readingthechinadream.com/xu-jilin-modern-politics .html.

6. *Translator's note*: Sun Yefang was one of Communist China's best-known economists, serving in a variety of important posts in the 1950s. He eventually came to advocate market reforms, which earned him the criticism of the Left. Gu Zhun originally trained as an accountant and subsequently converted to communism. Imprisoned for political reasons under Mao, he "reinvented" liberalism while in confinement, and his writings later made a major contribution to the emergence of liberalism in post-Mao China.

7. *Translator's note*: Li Rui was a well-known CCP member of the same generation as Wang Yuanhua. Li served briefly as Chairman Mao's secretary in the 1950s but was jailed in the late 1950s after criticizing the Great Leap Forward. He became an outspoken liberal in the post-Mao era.

8. Wang Yuanhua to Li Rui, n.d., in Wang Yuanhua, *Qingyuan shujian* (Notes from the Green Garden) (Wuhan: Hubei Jiaoyu, 2003), 153. *Translator's note*: The "Green Garden" was the name of Wang's library in his Shanghai residence.

9. *Translator's note*: Lu Xun was a prominent figure in the May Fourth Movement and remains modern China's most important literary figure. Romain Rolland was a French idealist and man of letters who opposed war and embraced Joseph Stalin as the "greatest man of his era." He is much admired by Chinese intellectuals.

10. *Translator's note*: "Mara poets" were iconoclastic, romantic figures celebrated in Lu Xun's early translations of Eastern European revolutionary poetry.

11. *Translator's note*: Xia Yan was a famous playwright and screenwriter who served as China's minister of culture for part of the 1950s. Li Ziyun was a well-known writer and editor in the People's Republic of China.

12. Li Ziyun, "Wo suo renshi de Wang Yuanhua" (The Wang Yuanhua I knew), *Tianya* 7 (2000), http://www.zwszzz.com/qikan/bkview.asp?bkid=126045&cid=389114.

13. Wang Yuanhua, "Ji wo de sanci fansi lichen" (Remembering the process of my three reflections), in *Qingyuan jinzuoji* (Recent writings from the Green Garden) (Shanghai: Wenhui, 2004), 13.

14. *Translator's note*: Wang Ruoshui was a CCP member who spent much of his career as an important journalist, responsible for theory and propaganda in the influential *People's Daily*. In the post-Mao era, he sought to contribute to reform by writing about Marxist humanism and the possibilities of "alienation" in socialist China. He died in exile in the United States.

15. *Translator's note*: Zhou Yang was a well-known literary theorist and an important figure in the politics of literature in China from the 1930s onward.

16. Wang Yuanhua, *Jiushi niandai riji* (Diary from the 1990s) (Hangzhou: Zhejiang Renmin, 2001), 528.

17. *Translator's note*: For more on *youhuan yishi* in general, see Gloria Davies, *Worrying About China: The Language of Chinese Critical Inquiry* (Cambridge, MA.: Harvard University Press, 2009).

18. Wang Yuanhua, *Jiushi niandai riji*, 78.
19. *Translator's note*: Lin Tongqi was a Chinese scholar of intellectual history who worked frequently with Wang. Lin was an affiliate of the Harvard-Yenching Institute from 1985 until his retirement.
20. Wang Yuanhua, "Du Yaquan yu Dong Xi wenhua wenti lunzhan," 1993, Ai Sixiang Wang, http://www.aisixiang.com/data/related-3728.html.
21. *Translator's note*: Chen Duxiu was a major intellectual figure in the May Fourth Movement and a cofounder of the CCP in 1921.
22. Wang Yuanhua, "Dui 'Wusi' de sikao" (Reflections on "May Fourth"), in *Jiushi niandai fansilu* (Reflections from the 1990s) (Shanghai: Shanghai Guji, 2000), 127.
23. Wang Yuanhua, "Renwen jingshen yu ershiyi shiji de duihua" (A dialogue between spiritual civilization and the twenty-first century), in *Qingyuan jinzuoji*, 8.
24. "Wang Yuanhua zhi Wu Qixin" (Wang Yuanhua to Wu Qixin), n.d., in Wang Yuanhua, *Qingyuan shujian*, 117.
25. *Translator's note*: *Dushu*, founded in 1979, is reform-era China's most important intellectual journal.
26. *Translator's note*: Xu's reference is to the Song dynasty (960–1279), a dynamic, creative period in Chinese intellectual history, culminating in the establishment of Neo-Confucian texts and institutions.
27. *Translator's note*: Literally "Han learning" and "Song learning."
28. *Translator's note*: Chen Yinke (the last character in his name is sometimes read "que") was a well-known Chinese historian and humanist.
29. *Translator's note*: Qian Zhongshu (1910–1998) was a famous literary scholar and writer best known for his novel *Wei cheng* (Fortress Besieged, 1947). Qian was also a multilingual translator and accomplished scholar.
30. *Translator's note*: Wang Yangming was a major figure in the history of Neo-Confucian philosophy, much admired for reacting to the rigidity of Song thought and scholarship by arguing that anyone could become "a sage" through his own efforts. Qian Daxin was a well-known figure in the "evidential scholarship" that dominated this period.
31. *Translator's note*: Dai Zhen was a wide-ranging Confucian scholar who criticized an overemphasis on scholarship for scholarship's sake and argued that human emotions should be recognized as part of the search for truth.
32. *Translator's note*: Yu Ying-shih is a well-known Chinese American historian of Chinese intellectual history.
33. *Translator's note*: Xu Jilin is, of course, borrowing these metaphors from Isaiah Berlin's book *The Hedgehog and the Fox: An Essay on Tolstoy's View of History* (New York: Simon and Schuster, 1953).
34. Wang Yuanhua, *Jiushi niandai riji*, 474.
35. Wang Yuanhua, *Jiushi niandai riji*, 452.
36. *Translator's note*: Hu Shi was a central intellectual during the May Fourth Period and later and is seen as one of the major figures in Chinese liberalism.
37. *Translator's note*: Lin Yusheng is a prominent Chinese American historian of Chinese thought.
38. Wang Yuanhua, *Jiushi niandai riji*, 85.
39. Wang Yuanhua, *Qingyuan jinzuoji*, 52.
40. Wang Yuanhua, *Jiushi niandai riji*, 189–90.
41. Wang Yuanhua, *Qingyuan jinzuoji*, 7.
42. *Translator's note*: Benjamin I. Schwartz, "China and Contemporary Millenarianism: Something New Under the Sun," *Philosophy East and West* 51, no. 2 (April 2003):

193–96. A Chinese translation of Schwartz's essay is included in Wang Yuanhua, *Qing-yuan jinzuoji*, 142–50.

43. Wang Yuanhua, "Guanyu 'Zhongguo yu dangjin qianxinianzhuyi' de jijuhua" (Remarks on "China and Contemporary Millenarianism"), in *Qingyuan jinzuoji*, n.p.

44. *Translator's note*: Wang Guowei was a prominent Chinese intellectual devoted to research in the Chinese humanistic traditions. He killed himself in 1927 as revolutionary Guomindang troops entered Beijing.

45. "Wang Yuanhua zhi Lin Yusheng" (Wang Yuanhua to Lin Yusheng), n.d., in Wang Yuanhua, *Qingyuan jinzuoji*, 204.

46. "Wang Yuanhua zhi Lin Yusheng" (Wang Yuanhua to Lin Yusheng), n.d., *Caijing* 143 (October 3, 2005): n.p.

47. Wang Yuanhua, "Renwen jingshen yu ershiyi shiji de duihua," 2.

48. Wang Yuanhua, "Rengran you hen chang de lu yaozou" (There is still a long way to go), in *Caijing niankan, shijie 2003* (Financial yearbook, world edition 2003) (Beijing: Caijing Zazhishe, 2003), n.p.

49. Wang Yuanhua, *Qingyuan jinzuoji*, 2, 51–52. *Translator's note*: Liang Qichao was an important figure in late Qing–early Republican history who used his role as the founder of modern Chinese journalism to transmit knowledge about Western culture and institutions to his readers. Yan Fu was an important figure in the late Qing reform movement best known for translating many important works of Western liberalism and social science into Chinese.

50. Wang Yuanhua, in *Qingyuan jinzuoji*, 2–4.

51. Wang Yuanhua, *Jiushi niandai fansilu*, 355.

52. "Wang Yuanhua zhi Wu Qixin," in Wang Yuanhua, *Qingyuan shujian*, 117.

PART III

LEFT VOICES

CHAPTER 8

MAO ZEDONG AND HIS ERA[1]

QIAN LIQUN

TRANSLATED BY DAYTON LEKNER AND SONG HONG

Translators' Introduction

This text is drawn from the first of a series of lectures given at National Chiao Tung University in Taiwan in 2009. Qian Liqun (b. 1939) was professor of Chinese literature at Peking University until his retirement in 2002. He remains an active and leading proponent of May Fourth humanism in post-Mao literary and cultural criticism, with a focus on Lu Xun (1881–1936)—China's most famous left-wing writer of the twentieth century—and the plight of the intellectual in twentieth-century China. Qian is generally considered a voice from the left, though he does not share the postmodern concerns of the New Left.

This talk is a call, in Qian Liqun's own words, for a "thorough critique and assessment of Mao Zedong Thought and culture," which Qian sees as persisting as the major cultural and intellectual undercurrent of contemporary China.[2] Without such an appraisal, he argues, China will remain under the influence of Mao Zedong—not the man, but the deeply ingrained social and intellectual practices that were formed during his rule. These practices, as Qian argues throughout the piece, shape thought and action at all strata of contemporary Chinese society: from Chinese Communist Party elites who perpetuate the oligarchic system established by Mao to those outside the establishment who draw on the heretical strands of his thought and to workers who deploy his populist egalitarianism. In this deeply reflective work, Qian admits that any such "clearing up" (*qingli*) must also be a critique not only of his generation (which he sees as complicit in the propagation of Mao culture) but also of Qian himself—who is no less complicit. Qian claims ownership of this Mao Zedong culture, both for himself and for his generation, and in the process illustrates the extent to which divisions between the Party and intellectuals and between the propagators and followers of Maoism are largely illusory and finally misleading. His own confession (*jiaodai*) of culpability serves as a starting point for a critique and an attempt to purge what he calls the "cancers" of Mao Zedong Thought and culture.

At the same time, however, as we translated, we could not help but notice that the text itself is in many ways an artifact of the Mao era. In fact, Qian's writing is so redolent of what Li Tuo (b. 1939) calls the "Mao genre" (*Mao wenti*) and Geremie Barmé calls "New China NewSpeak" (*Xinhua wenti*)[3] that it serves at once as critique and homage. Perhaps most striking is Qian's adoption of Mao's rhetorical strategy of positioning himself with and among the people. A member of the intellectual elite by education, career, and status, Qian yet identifies himself (whether categorically or rhetorically) as part of that most elusive and nebulous group, the *minjian* (loosely, "among the people," but Qian's floating use of the term is in this translation rendered as "folk," "grassroots," "popular," "heterodox," or "outside the establishment," depending on context). As we translated, we felt Qian's internal contradiction—of both loathing and loving the subject of his talk and of embodying the Mao Zedong culture he wishes to exorcize.

For the reader, the result is a deeply layered experience as Qian both critiques and speaks from within the Mao Zedong Thought and culture that is his subject. In four sections, Qian establishes Mao's sweeping influence (as thinker and doer, as icon, as poet, and as culture) on his own life, his generation, contemporary China, and twentieth-century history. In the closing sections, he argues that the "critique and assessment of Mao Zedong Thought and culture" are necessary as part of a grander project: the summation of the global experience of the twentieth century. The past century, Qian argues, has seen the dissolution of two great myths—the myth of the West as purveyor of universalist-liberal capitalism and the myth of communism as its counterpart. These myths, according to Qian, are two utopian dreams that have been shown to be misguided. With the monkey (and tiger) of Mao off his and his nation's back, Qian hopes that the Chinese experience can combine with the global experience and form the basis of a new kind of critical thought, one that transcends the cultures of both capitalism and socialism. But here again Qian finds himself channeling Mao's utopian urges. As Qian himself says, it is not so easy to "walk out from under the shadow of Mao Zedong."

A Few Questions Concerning Mao Zedong and His Era

To begin with, let me express my thanks to National Chiao Tung University and the Institute of Social Research and Cultural Studies for inviting me to come and teach. It is a personal gratitude I feel and an emotional one because I have a kind of "blood bond" with Taiwan. During regime change sixty years ago, as the whole nation underwent division and turmoil, my father and I parted ways in Nanjing.[4] He moved to Taiwan in 1948, and my mother and many brothers and sisters and I remained behind in mainland China. My father passed away in 1972 and is buried near here on Mount Yangming—we were never to meet again. I visited Taiwan in 1995 and 2007, but both were hurried trips. This time I have had the chance to teach for three months, and I made a point of choosing the topic "My Sixty Years with the Republic and Mao." It is a subject laden with my own personal motives because it is also sixty years since I was separated from my father. I wanted, through teaching this class, to recount to my father all my diverse experiences of the past sixty years. So today, as I teach, I feel as though he is here, listening to every word. This is a dream I have had for many years, so I thank you for giving me the chance today to fulfill it.

I also have another dream, which is to take this opportunity to have a heartfelt exchange with the younger Taiwanese generation. I have, in this life, always communed with the young and have maintained a close spiritual connection with six decades of young mainland Chinese. First are those born in the late 1940s and 1950s, the generation of the Cultural Revolution, the Red Guards, and the Educated Youth. Then came those born in the 1960s and 1970s, known in the mainland as the "June Fourth" generation. Finally come those born in the 1980s and 1990s, known as "post 80" and "post 90."[5] I have a close spiritual relationship with these generations born from the late 1940s to the late 1990s—of this I am proud. Now, in coming to Taiwan I don't know whether I will be able to make use of this opportunity to establish a dialogue of the heart and an exchange of ideas with young Taiwanese. This is what I yearn for, and at the same time I can't avoid feeling a little anxious because although I have abundant experience conversing with young mainland Chinese, I have none with young Taiwanese.

So, in coming to Taiwan, what should I talk to these young Taiwanese about? This is a question I discussed at length with Professor Chen Kuan-hsing [b. 1957][6] and many other friends, finally settling on two individuals as central subjects: Lu Xun [1881–1936] and Mao Zedong. I arranged two classes, one held on Tuesday evenings (tonight's class) that focuses on Mao and one held for undergraduate students on Thursdays at Tsing Hua University that will focus on Lu Xun. Why choose these two people? The decision is related to a theory of mine: I have previously raised the concept of the "twentieth-century Chinese experience" and emphasized the great importance of a summation of this experience.[7] Contemporary China, whether the mainland or Taiwan, confronts many problems. In facing such problems, both spiritual and intellectual resources must be sought, for which the intellectual mainstream in mainland China advocates one of two paths—one looking to the West and one looking to ancient China. I believe both sources to be very important, but between them is lost something that I see as paramount: that is the twentieth-century Chinese experience—which of course includes the experience of Taiwan.

It is this experience that most tightly enfolds us but is neglected on the mainland and, I suppose, to an even greater degree in Taiwan. To understand this twentieth-century Chinese experience, one must start from three people: Sun Yat-sen [1866–1925], Mao Zedong, and Lu Xun.[8] The twentieth-century Chinese experience is concentrated and embodied within these three figures. Beginning with them will facilitate a concrete grasp of the twentieth-century Chinese experience and confronting the many problems facing us today. In Taiwan, everyone is familiar with Sun Yat-sen but somewhat estranged from Mao Zedong and Lu Xun. This, of course, is related to the Cold War split of the two sides of the Taiwan Strait beginning in the 1950s. On the Chinese mainland, however, Mao Zedong and Lu Xun have had profound influence. Whether one's assessment is positive or negative, whether one is enamored with them or not, their existence cannot be ignored. In discussing or researching the twentieth-century Chinese experience, we absolutely cannot skirt these two figures.

Beyond the important status of these two people, my desire to speak about them is also personal. In my younger years, I grew up under their constant influence—they were my two spiritual teachers. Because of this, I have had to untangle my relationship with them through academic research. My research on Lu Xun from one angle is a kind of sorting out of my relationship with the author, the results of which have already been published and read by a few friends. On Mao Zedong, however, my research has remained in a state of primal chaos and never made public, except for a small section. Long ago I wanted to research Mao Zedong. In early 1986, in writing the afterward to *Xinling de tanxun* (Soul-searching), I felt I had already completely resolved my relationship with Lu Xun and wanted to turn my hand to clearing up my relationship with Mao Zedong.[9] I made several attempts at this endeavor but in the end shelved them. Why over such a long period of time have I not carried out this work? At root, the problem is me; I haven't yet been able to sort out my relationship with Mao; it's too complicated, too tangled. Further, from beginning to end I have not been able to locate my own moral standpoint. I don't know how I should evaluate Mao Zedong.

Mainland China's attitude toward Mao Zedong is either black or white: one group of people sees him as a national hero, while another group sees him as a national villain. I don't happen to be able to take such a clear-cut position. This is because although I cannot overlook the disasters that Mao brought upon the entire nation—disasters of which I have personal experience—neither can I shake off the allure that he holds for me deep in my heart. So my research has never advanced, and it was only just before this visit to Taiwan that I pulled out my scattered notes and leafed through them. But, confronted by this mess of material, I have no idea how to begin. So in talking to you about Mao, I do so awash in contradiction and confusion, my account itself reflecting these same qualities. This is not the case with my work on Lu Xun, for although this relationship is also highly complex, in reading my work you can see that my standpoint is quite clear.[10]

This kind of contradiction and confusion reflects an inner truth of my own, but whether it reflects a truth of history I cannot be certain. Therefore, in teaching this class I hope to faithfully relay to you all the observations and experiences of a historical witness; I hope to arouse some interest in you, and perhaps among you a few will go on to your own research on Mao. The teaching materials I have prepared for this class as well as the selections of Mao's writings I suspect will be new to those present here today. I'm extremely curious as to what sort of reaction you will have upon reading Mao Zedong's works. Maybe because of this some of you will become interested in Mao and go on to research him. Once you have researched Mao and reached your own conclusions, then my mission will be complete. I hope that at that time you all can forget everything that I have told you today. My class is a bridge, and I hope that you all can "cross the river and tear down that bridge," that in your own research on Mao Zedong you can leave my account behind.

The above may serve as my opening remarks. Below, I would like to speak on four topics.

My Relationship with Mao and the Mao Era

This is perhaps a coincidence of history. I was born in Chongqing in January 1939, and Mao established his position as leader of the Chinese Communist Party (CCP) in Yan'an in spring of the same year. In the past, it was mistakenly believed that his position was established in 1935 at the Zunyi Conference,[11] but over the past few years there has been a breakthrough on this question by historians of Party history. Here I take the opportunity to introduce a book written by He Fang [1922–2017] entitled *Dangshi biji* (Notes on Party history).[12] He Fang served as secretary to Zhang Wentian [1900–1976] and can be considered as involved in the history of that time. According to He Fang's highly persuasive research, at the Zunyi Conference in 1935 it was decided only that Mao would enter the highest level of Party leadership, in particular that level concerned with military command. Zhang Wentian remained general secretary and not, as was believed, in name only. Until at least 1939, Zhang Wentian's position as general secretary carried real leadership power, with Mao acting as only one member of the central leadership. The actual establishment of Mao's leadership position within the Party took place in the second half of 1938. In July of that year, the leader of the Comintern, the Bulgarian Georgi Dimitrov [1882–1949], representing the Comintern, informed Wang Jiaxiang

[1906–1974], then in Moscow and preparing to return to China, that "the leadership organization should be headed by Mao Zedong," to create "an atmosphere of close unity." Dimitrov also passed on a directive from Stalin for "each nation's party to propagandize its own leader and to establish their power and prestige."[13] This makes clear that it was the Communist International that appointed Mao leader of the CCP. In September of that year, Wang Jiaxiang relayed this directive at the CCP Politburo Conference, and at the Sixth Plenum of the Sixth CCP Central Committee in October 1938[14] Mao for the first time represented the Central Politburo by delivering the political report to the Congress. According to CCP practice, it is the leader who usually gives political reports; doing so thus meant that Mao had at that time obtained the qualifications and status of leadership.

Even more importantly, at this meeting Mao raised for the first time the concept of the "Sinification of Marxism," stressing that "a Communist is a Marxist internationalist, but we can put Marxism into practice only when it is integrated with the specific characteristics of our country and acquires a definite national form."[15] It is here that Mao raised his own theoretical flag for the first time, one that was pivotal for two reasons. First, it became the key political weapon in his prosecution of intraparty struggle (primarily in opposing the "dogmatists" led by Wang Ming [1904–1974]). Second, as the historian Gao Hua [1954–2011] has pointed out, it proved to be of great benefit for the CCP's effort to establish roots in Chinese society by "pouring the vitality of nationalism into the Chinese Communist movement" and "altering the then popular notion of the CCP as only a product of foreign ideology."[16] Further, for Mao himself, this report established a firm foundation for his leadership, both organizational and intellectual, within the CCP.

Thus, by the spring of 1939, Mao had in practice already become the leader of the CCP Central Committee.[17] So we could say that at this time the CCP began to enter the Mao era, and it just so happens that I was born at this time. Ten years later, in 1949, when I was ten, Mao became the leader of the People's Republic of China (PRC), and the PRC then entered the Mao era, which lasted right up until Mao's death in 1976, at which time I was thirty-seven. The years from ten to thirty-seven are one's golden age—my childhood, my youth, my middle age were all lived under Mao's rule. My intellectual makeup, my ideas, the path of my life—all took form and were established under the direct influence of Mao Zedong.

More importantly, when Mao launched the Cultural Revolution, I became a staunch Maoist (it wasn't only internationally but also inside China that such Maoists existed), which means that I actively participated in the Cultural Revolution led by Mao; this is something that sets me apart from many other intellectuals. It reflects a particular characteristic of our era, and we grew up through revolution, a revolution that drew the most ordinary, most marginal people into the tide of history, something perhaps harder to directly experience in Taiwan. When the Cultural Revolution broke out, I was in Guizhou, in a remote village deep in the mountains, but there was revolution even there. Our generation has a flesh-and-blood relationship with history, these historical campaigns directly influenced our lives, our bodies, our emotions, and our spirits. Our "little selves" (*xiaowo*) and the historical "big self" (*dawo*) were all tangled together[18]—this is something that sets us apart from the students I teach and from those present here today. What strikes my students when they read my book *My Retrospection and Reflection*[19] is that, for them, history is something external, a subject that needs to be understood. For us, however, this is not the case: history is simply oneself.

My generation has an extremely tangled relationship with the history and revolution led by Mao Zedong. Each person carries a great dilemma within, a dilemma particular to each intellectual. The greatest problem of revolution is that it constricts the space for freedom of the individual. A great number of intellectuals felt this and sought without success to break from its tethers—from this there comes confusion. But I am an intellectual of a different stripe: I actively sought to participate in, not break free from, revolution. My distress came from lacking the qualifications to participate, as described in Lu Xun's story *The True Story of Ah Q* in which the titular hero is barred from revolution or able to carry out revolution only according to the direction and design of others; he has his own way of thinking and critical awareness but is not permitted to act on them—from this state comes great confusion. We, too, had our own style of thought, perhaps not consistent with Mao Zedong; but it remained only thought, and we were unable to realize this thought and influence the course of history. These dilemmas are likely foreign to you, my audience. But even when pushed aside and suppressed, I still resolutely and actively threw myself into the revolution and in the process entangled myself irrevocably with the Mao era and revolutionary history. After Mao died and the Cultural Revolution drew to a close, as a staunch Maoist I faced the dilemma of reconsidering what I knew of Mao Zedong. But walking out from under his shadow has been an extremely difficult process.

My complicated relationship with the Mao era can be presented in two ways. On the one hand, I am shaped by that era. Mao Zedong culture has already seeped into my flesh and into my soul, and its traces cannot be altered. No matter how I struggle, critique, or examine myself, I remain an incorrigible idealist, romantic, and utopian. On the other hand, I am even more a self-conscious rebel of the Mao era. My historical mission is to turn on my old comrades, to carry out the thorough sorting through and critique of Mao as only those of the same generation can do. I've both been influenced by and revolted against Mao and have done my utmost to transform myself into the complete rebel. Of course, this standpoint of mine isn't permitted in the post-Mao era or by those today who remain infatuated with Mao's time, and I am unable to please either side. So I feel intense empathy when I read Lu Xun, in whose "The Shadow's Farewell" we find "The darkness will swallow me, but light will make me disappear. Yet I'm unwilling to hover between the two; I'd rather sink into the darkness. . . . I shall, when I have lost track of time, make a distant journey alone."[20] I feel that this is precisely my position and predicament. Lu Xun at that time was himself befuddled by his entanglement with several thousand years of traditional Chinese culture. He was both a resolute critic of traditional culture and at the same time the most outstanding scion of this culture—it's this complicated relationship that inspires my empathy. Lu Xun called himself the last intellectual of traditional China—please allow me to brag and tell you that I am the last intellectual of the Mao era.

For me, sorting out and critiquing Mao Zedong culture is a kind of painful sorting out and critiquing of myself, and at the same time it is a kind of self-redemption. I have already settled up my relationship with Lu Xun. If I can do the same for my relationship with Mao, then I can meet my maker with a clear conscience and account for my life. In Lu Xun's "Tremors of Degradation," he writes of a certain "old lady": "In the dark of the night she walks endlessly, she walks and walks to the boundless wilderness . . . and in an instant reconciles everything: devotion and estrangement, affection and vengeance, nurture and annihilation, blessings and curses. . . . Thereupon she thrusts both hands toward heaven, and from between her lips spills forth an utterance born from the margins between human and animal—not of this world, and thus without words."[21] This is a fitting expression for my complicated feelings toward Mao Zedong culture: at once "blessing" and "cursing"; "estranged" and "devoted"; "vengeful" and "affectionate." Because of this, my account of Mao Zedong simply cannot be as decisively authoritative as that of many others, nor can it be coldly objective. My critique is burdened with complex emotions, perhaps limiting it, but at the same time rendering it unique.

You may have noticed that in my account so far I have repeatedly used two concepts: Mao Zedong Thought and Mao Zedong culture. What do I mean by "Mao culture"? This is the second question I wish to address.

A Few Fundamental Features of Mao Zedong Thought and Culture

Mao Zedong was no ordinary man. He is characterized by six traits that I have previously summarized. First, as Karl Marx once said, we cannot stop at interpreting the world, for we must also transform it. As a Marxist, Mao was not only a thinker who interpreted the world but also an agent who transformed it. Marxists believe that theory and practice must be reconciled, that thinkers and doers must bond as one—this is what distinguishes Mao. In general, the philosopher and the activist are distinct from one another, a division of labor existing between the two. To raise a simple example, in the French Revolution Jean-Jacques Rousseau [1712–1778] was considered a philosopher, whereas Maximilien de Robespierre [1758–1794] played the role of activist. Theory and practice are driven by different kinds of logic: theory is concerned with the absolute and is thus uncompromising, but practice must be negotiated; thought is visionary, whereas practice emphasizes the existing. If a person is both a thinker and a doer, then he will hold a great advantage, but if he is unable to correctly resolve the different logics of thought and practice, then from time to time he will bring disaster upon society.

In *Abundant Suffering: Don Quixote and Hamlet Head East*, I put forward a proposition: "The realization of a thought implies the destruction of both the thought itself as well as the thinker."[22] Rousseau's thought became Robespierre's dictatorship, undergoing a total transformation in the process. The ideals of the Encyclopédistes became realized as capitalist society; the otherworldly ideal of Marxist communism, once realized in this world, became a disaster. This is a complicated question, and I can only broach it here. If students are interested, we can discuss this more in private. For now, I would only like to emphasize one point: because Mao's thought transformed into a practice that influenced people's lives and fates, in observing, discussing, and researching Mao Zedong Thought, we cannot consider it only in its textual form but must pay even more attention to its practical form—that is, to examine Mao's thought in its practical impact, its outcome, its influence, to look at the practical significance beyond his writing.

The second characteristic of Mao resides in the fact that he was also a poet and wielded a poet's romantic and impractical way of thinking in his leadership of China. To govern a nation with a poet's logic and vision can lead only to great catastrophe. In reading Mao's works, you'll notice they are extremely enchanting. Packed as they are with the imagination, passion, and the utopian ideals of a poet, they are endlessly moving. But as soon as such ideas are transformed into practice, they will often bring about disaster. Mao often exhibits just such a conversion: romanticism at the theoretical level mutating into despotism at the practical level. Of course, this is an extremely involved process, one that requires concrete research and description.

Third, neither was Mao a run-of-the-mill activist, for he was the nation's paramount ruler. In previous comparisons of Lu Xun and Mao, I've suggested that although Lu Xun may have had his extreme side, he was not a national leader, and thus his extremes did not go on to influence the destiny of others. As an example, Lu Xun once called Liang Shiqiu [1903–1987] a worn-out lackey of the capitalists,[23] but Liang Shiqiu was not undone by this reprimand from Lu Xun. Of course, we can say that Lu Xun had his right to speak, but Liang Shiqiu had this same right; each could, in practice, exercise his own right to criticize the other without either inflicting a mortal injury. But Mao was different because he wielded tremendous political and economic power, and along with this came the absolute power of his speech. Every word and action decided the fate of others; any lapse influenced the nation's path to development.

From this we arrive at the fourth characteristic of Mao: he was not the leader of a normal country, but the leader of a totalitarian nation. His power was neither supervised nor restricted. In democratic countries, it seems there are limits to authority, corrective mechanisms to temper the mistakes of national leaders, and disasters thus rarely reach the irreparable stage. The calamity brought about by Mao's mistakes, in contrast, could be addressed only after his death.

Fifth, even among totalitarian rulers such as Stalin, Mao set himself apart. Such dictators usually control only the bodies of the people; dissidents, heretics, and opponents are at most sent to prison or labor camps and thus are neutralized corporeally. Mao, however, sought also to remold thought. He once said that two types of people existed in Chinese tradition: heroes and sages. Heroes were extremely talented in some areas, such as politics and economics; sages existed to influence people's thought. Mao sought to position himself as a hero but desired even more the role of sage.[24] He wanted to effect spiritual control over people, to conquer the popular will, to influence and remold people's thought, to have his dictatorship permeate people's minds, and he created an array of systems and methods to do so. This is both awesome and dreadful, and it is without precedent.

Finally, what he sought to rule and transform is the nation with the largest population in the world, with an influence both widespread and far-reaching. In other words, for half a century Mao Zedong Thought dominated the way of life, fundamental thinking, and behavioral patterns of the one-third of the world's population represented by the Chinese people. Mao was completely conscious in the use of his own thought to remold China and the world as well as the spiritual world of the Chinese people and, further, to establish, according to his own way of thinking, a complete set of organizational structures for social life that extended from the center down to the most basic level of localities. This is not simply a phenomenon of thought, but one of matter and organization.

In this way, Mao Zedong Thought fundamentally transformed the modes of thought, emotions, behavior, and language of mainland China, leaving a profound impression on the national spirit, character, and temperament and thus forming the culture and spirit of a generation, which we can only describe accurately as "Mao Zedong culture." To put this in another way, apart from Confucianism, Daoism, Moism, Legalism, and other schools of the Chinese tradition, mainland China also has Mao Zedong culture. Of course, it has a tight link with traditional Chinese culture, which I won't discuss today, but it also represents a new kind of culture external to the Chinese tradition. This Mao Zedong culture, having passed through a long period of organized, planned, and guided inculcation, has already come to form the national collective unconscious in mainland China, a new national character.

We absolutely cannot underestimate the success and consequence of Mao Zedong Thought in its remolding of the people and intellectuals of mainland China. I remember when the previously closed-off PRC began to open again to the world, many foreigners had quite a surprise when meeting mainland Chinese people again after so long. They discovered that the current Chinese individual had undergone a great transformation from the Chinese person of their historical memory. For example, the *Doctrine of the Mean* invoked in Chinese tradition is now nowhere to be found in mainland China.[25] That Chinese people have become belligerent, fanatical, and fierce is due precisely to this remolding by Mao Zedong culture. Of course, there has also been positive change; that the mainland Chinese people now have greater self-confidence is related also to Mao's influence. A few Taiwanese friends, including some here today, tell me that they sometimes feel that the way their mainland fellows think, behave, and speak is a little odd and hard to fathom. I normally reply by saying that the reasons, of course, are complex and need concrete analysis, but that one reason is simply that mainlanders have undergone the influence of Mao Zedong Thought and culture, and they [the Taiwanese] haven't. The issue lies in the fact that although the younger mainland Chinese generation haven't personally experienced the Mao era and perhaps haven't even read any of Mao's works, Mao Zedong culture has already infiltrated the national character and has never been fully analyzed. This means that its influence continues to be passed on from generation to generation.

More pertinent is that some of the concepts as well as ways of thinking, behaving, feeling, and communicating of both those who currently wield power in China and those who seek to rebel bear remarkable similarities to Mao's ways. I have even discovered a few "little Mao Zedongs" among dissidents and leaders of social movements; this has some positive aspects, but even more negative ones. We simply cannot underestimate the deep and lasting influence of Mao's successive lessons to "cultivate successors," "combat and prevent revisionism, and oppose peaceful evolution" and of the later Red Guard and Sent-Down Youth movements. The generation that has grown up through long-term exposure to and the creeping influence of these campaigns has today become the leading and central force behind mainland China's government, economy, thought, culture, education, and various fields of study. This also applies in practice to the leadership and nucleus of opposing factions. The influence of Mao Zedong culture on thought and ideology, spirit and personality, whether positive or negative, will profoundly affect the realities and developmental path of China. In my view, researching this influence is a very good entry point for an examination of the many problems facing China today.

This kind of sorting out and critiquing of Mao Zedong culture cannot help but clarify and critique the national ideology, spirit, and culture of an entire era; without this kind of conscientious and deep national self-reflection and critique, it is fundamentally impossible for China to get out from under the shadow of Mao Zedong. Lu Xun in his day said: Whatever kind of citizen you have, that will be the kind of government you have.[26] This should remind us that if we fail to fundamentally remold the national character shaped during the Mao era, then a reincarnation of the Cultural Revolution in some other guise is not beyond the realm of possibility.

Now let's discuss the second characteristic of Mao Zedong culture and talk about the relationship among its several aspects.

First is its relationship with the Communist Party. The Chinese authorities assert that Mao Zedong Thought is a product of the collective wisdom of the CCP, and I think this reflects reality.[27] The creation and development of Mao Zedong culture is not the act of Mao the individual but involves the collective participation of CCP members. So in researching Mao Zedong, we cannot stop at studying Mao the individual but must also research other CCP leaders, such as Liu Shaoqi [1898–1969], Zhou Enlai [1898–1976], Deng Xiaoping [1904–1997], Lin Biao [1907–1971], Chen Yun [1905–1995], and others. Their relationships with Mao were extremely complex. They not only participated in the creation of Mao Zedong culture but also on many particular issues were at odds with Mao. Mao Zedong culture was formed through interaction with such people, interaction that includes cooperation and complementarity as well as restriction and conflict.

But Mao Zedong culture does not belong to the Party alone, for the Chinese people (including intellectuals) also participated in its creation and development as they both shored up and reaped benefits from this culture. We cannot view Chinese intellectuals simply as subjects and victims of the Mao era; they were also active participants in history. They bear their own responsibility for the history that unfolded in China in the twentieth century. Mao Zedong culture, from thought to realization (that is, the realization of thought), had to pass through many intermediaries. The role played by CCP cadres and members at various levels as well as by other intellectuals in this intermediate process was in no way negative or passive and certainly had its own "creative contribution."

Also worth attending to is the relationship between Mao Zedong and the masses. Mao Zedong culture emphasized mass campaigns and mass participation and deployed the masses to carry out class struggle and construction. But the masses were made up of different interest groups, and each of these groups sought to interpret Mao Zedong Thought according to that group's interests. So there was a mutation from Mao's initial expectations to the final practice of the masses—a phenomena most obvious during the Cultural Revolution.

History was a result of a combination of forces (Mao Zedong, the CCP, the intellectuals, the masses); although Mao represented the overall driving force, he was, in the end, not omnipotent. It is only in the complex interaction between these forces that Mao Zedong culture took shape.

I want to raise one point in particular, one central to the focus of my research: that is the relationship of Mao Zedong Thought to popular heterodoxy.[28] Over recent years, I have constantly been engaged in the research of popular thought and popular resistance movements during the sixty years of the development of the People's Republic and in the process have discovered an extremely interesting phenomenon: These renegades have, on the whole, been roused by Mao Zedong. In the Mao era, it was very difficult for the people to be exposed to other modes of thinking; the sources of thought were quite limited. Mao's works were the only ones that could be read. But Mao's thought itself contains an element of heresy. He claimed to have a "monkey spirit" (houqi)[29] and often called for breaking through and revolt against the current system. To those dissatisfied with or holding a critical awareness of the status quo, it is in this Mao that they often find inspiration and even encouragement. In this way, for heterodox thinkers on the mainland (to some extent including myself), the primary spiritual godfather is none other than Mao Zedong.

Of course, Mao's imparting of heretical thought was done to realize ever more effective control over the nation, the society, and the Party. But this thought, once received by the people, developed by its own logic and was difficult for Mao to control. For example, at the outbreak of the Cultural Revolution, the promotion of the slogan "Doubt everything" to eliminate superstitious faith in the Party bureaucracy rested upon a bottom line—that Mao himself was not to be subjected to such doubt. But those of us who took on this "doubt everything" way of thinking carried it out to its logical ends: a skepticism of Mao. At this point, Mao acted to suppress such rebels who crossed the line; he was completely unambiguous about this. Here, Mao's "tiger spirit" (huqi) was expressed,[30] and conflict with heterodox thinkers was unavoidable as they all in the end became Mao's opposition. This also became another kind of interaction.

What I have said so far orbits about one point: Mao Zedong culture took form through the interaction of all kinds of complicated interactions, and it is only through the concrete observation of these manifold relationships, from inside the Party to outside, from the top to the bottom, that one can grasp their complexity and their abundance.

Mao Zedong in Contemporary China

Lu Xun once said: "Those previously on top seek restoration, those currently on top seek to maintain their position, and those never yet on top seek reform.

So it has been. So it is!"[31] These three kinds of people will be present in any society, and contemporary China is no exception. What is fascinating is that Mao Zedong holds an influence over all three; all three brandish Mao's flag.

"Those previously on top seek restoration." All those with a vested interest in the Mao era now pine for Mao. In 2007, on the eve of the Seventeenth CCP National Congress,[32] more than one hundred old cadres presented a memorial in which they made a clear-cut criticism of Deng Xiaoping and Jiang Zemin, decrying their betrayal of Mao. These old cadres called for a return to the Maoist line as well as a relaunching of the Cultural Revolution. This intellectual current is now extremely popular in China, and these "old leftists" are the ones who trumpet it.

"Those currently on top seek to maintain their position." As I see it, the political line implemented by the Chinese authorities is a continuation of the Self-Strengthening Movement's "Chinese learning as essence, Western learning as means."[33] But now it is Mao Zedong thought, culture, and organization that serves as "Chinese learning" and thus as "essence." The absolute authority of the single-party dictatorship—subject to no restriction, limitation, or supervision—that was established in the Mao era now acts as a lifeline to the current rulers of China. They absolutely will not abandon the system of one-party rule established by Mao.

More concretely, there are three points of inviolability. The first is that freedoms of speech, association, and publication will not be granted to the public; there may be a loosening, but never a total release. This is particularly true for the freedom of association, for which the CCP must remain "the one and only." In 1949, the speed at which the Guomindang (GMD) collapsed (and in fact the current state of corruption of the CCP is no less severe than that of the GMD of that time) was due simply to the existence of opposition factions such as the CCP—if the people were unhappy with the GMD, they chose the CCP. Today, however, no matter how discontented the people are with the status quo, there is no alternative in which to place their trust; they can only hope for the transformation of the CCP itself. Second, the Party's control of the military—that the military must remain under Party and not state control—is another iron-clad principle established and passed down by Mao.[34] Third, in the Party's system of bestowing authority, power must be granted only by the Party; it is not permissible for the people to grant such authority through the process of elections.

These three points are absolutely inviolable. But below these three immovable and central principles of Mao Zedong culture there remains much flexibility—herein resides "Western learning as means." A great deal of Western technology, management theory, experience, and even institutions can all be actively and enthusiastically absorbed on a grand scale. Of course, this at the same time implies the forsaking of a few of Mao Zedong's principles. Mao, for example, used class struggle to control the nation, whereas the current regime takes economic development as its core. In today's parlance, we could call this "No Sturm und Drang" and no more large-scale class struggle among the masses. This policy has been highly effective and is an important guarantee of China's swift rise. We have also seen an end to Mao's economic romanticism (although not a total end because it is sometimes still in effect), the key features of which are that development must be rapid and the economy managed through mass campaigns. These two principles have largely been abandoned by the current regime, but this regime from time to time also gets a little "hot-headed" and wants to take a little "Leap."[35] The third principle that has been relinquished is political romanticism, including Mao's utopian ideals and theories of social equality. But by and large the course pursued today is "Maoist learning as essence, Western learning as means." It is a line that has indeed helped China to develop, but it has also brought about many serious problems—problems that Mao himself would have never wished to see.

"Those never yet on top seek reform." All those whose interests have been encroached upon seek reform, and they, too, make use of Mao Zedong. There are currently two kinds of forces that place their trust in the person of Mao. The first are those who resist at the grass roots, in particular workers. In the Mao era, the status of workers was extremely high; in choosing a partner, women saw workers as second only to members of the People's Liberation Army. At that time, the pay for a high-level craftsman was very close to that of a professor. Workers' lives were hard, of course, but in status at least they were equal. During reform and opening, however, large-scale unemployment and layoffs meant that workers lost these benefits. Ill equipped for resistance (and for this intellectuals must accept some responsibility, having never provided the worker with critical resources), they were left with only Mao's flag to brandish. This has changed a little of late. Following the introduction of "rule of law" discourse, workers have gradually pursued legal avenues to defend their rights. Initially, however, it was Mao Zedong Thought that served as the crucial resource.

In China's grassroots society, the deification of Mao Zedong has taken place to a staggering degree. In countless taxicabs dangle icons of Mao, warding off evil spirits. I investigated a little the question which among China's many emperors and generals could become deities and which could not. Zhuge Liang [181–234] and Guan Yu [d. 219] were deified, but Qin Shihuang [259–210 BCE], Han Wudi [141–87 BCE], and Liu Bei [161–223] did not make the grade.[36] There are two prerequisites for such a deification: one must have either preternatural wisdom or a divine ability to ward off misfortune—Mao Zedong had both. Further bolstering Mao worship are those intellectuals who over recent years have taken a Maoist turn. Some have, for example, proselytized the "three new traditions" (*xin san tong*), which advocate establishing a new national ideology through the aggregation of Mao Zedong, Deng Xiaoping, and Confucius

[551–479 BCE].[37] These intellectuals see themselves as "imperial tutors" and their "three new traditions" as "schemes for public security" offered to the current regime.[38] After the recent abrupt rise of China's economy, there is now a push to strengthen Chinese soft power. What China has to offer in this realm, other than Confucius, is Mao Zedong. In the present statist stream of thought, Mao's status is extremely prominent, and he also carries influence among certain groups of young people, some of whom are even intent on establishing a "Maoist Party."[39]

Here, I would like to point out to all of you a divergence between myself and some young scholars in our approach to Mao Zedong and the socialist revolution. I once wrote an essay entitled "How Do We Look Back on That Period of Revolutionary History?,"[40] in which I suggested that the Chinese political, intellectual, cultural, and academic spheres of the 1980s exhibited two shortcomings. The first was an absolute refutation of the socialism of the Mao era. The second was a failure to carry out an earnest assessment and rational critique of Mao Zedong Thought and culture. The combination has left my students' generation completely estranged from the Mao era and from its revolution. Since the 1990s, in confronting the problems associated with the return of capitalism in Chinese society, some among this generation attempt simply to retreat once more to the socialist experiment of Mao's time, hoping to eke out from that revolutionary era some resource for a critique of the current era. As I see it, this is understandable.

Between myself and the young scholars of my students' generation, there is both concord and divergence on this point. I, too, stand for the deployment of certain rational elements of the Mao era as critical resources, but I believe a vital prerequisite to such a deployment is a thorough critique and assessment of Mao Zedong Thought and culture; only after this has occurred can some kernel of wisdom be rescued. After all, what we are faced with is a problem not of method or attitude, but of real politics: many aspects of Mao Zedong thought and culture continue to this day and are practically put to use in the system of one-party dictatorship in China. If we blindly idealize, even glamorize Mao Zedong Thought and culture, then we are at risk of identifying with, intentionally or not, the most important "legacy" handed down to us by Mao: the system of one-party rule currently in effect in China. And the position of the intellectual as independent critic is essentially lost.

Without a rational assessment and critique of Mao Zedong Thought and culture, its cancers will be anointed along with its charms and passed down in this spirit. The effect will likely be catastrophic. Speaking personally, such cancers are already internalized as a kind of poisonous gas deep within myself. Because of this, I must hold fast to the fundamental position of "making a serious accounting of myself in the process of critiquing and assessing Mao Zedong Thought and culture."[41]

My students, however, believe that there is no need for their teacher to spend his days in reflection and repentance. They see a teacher with many good qualities and see these qualities as endowed upon him by Mao Zedong. This is in some ways true. The key reason for this generational gap rests in the fact that the challenges we face are different: my challenge remains to cast off the influence, not only historical but actual, of Mao Zedong; their challenge lies in the fact that they are totally estranged from the Mao era; they know nothing of it, so they must start from scratch to seek out its reasonable elements. Therefore, between teacher and student there is a divergence of opinions and ideas. But, I have to say, I am most antipathetic to their "price theory." They agree that the Mao era was replete with problems but believe that these were a price that had to be paid. Whenever I hear this price theory, I get all fired up; do they really know what price was paid? The death of millions or even tens of millions. In my view, the death of one person is one too many, let alone tens of millions. Can we be so blasé as to use "price" to "settle this up"? They haven't personally experienced that time and think they can look upon it objectively—"people died, so they died." This touches upon another key problem: the life of a person, in my view, is of the utmost importance.

I have many haunting memories, and my students criticize me for always wallowing in my personal recollections, for being unable to break free from them. But I still want to remind these young scholars: in summing up the thought and culture of the 1980s, there is one great lesson to be learned. The attempt to directly apply Western modernity without thinking through the problems of China, to believe that China's developmental trajectory is simply to follow the road of Western modernity, will result in immense confusion. In the same vein, we absolutely cannot directly apply an unexamined Mao Zedong Thought and culture to respond to the problems of contemporary China. This would lead not only to great confusion but also to catastrophe.

Mao Zedong's Global Influence

This lesson is related also to the status and influence of twentieth-century China. In this century, the world experienced three great historical shifts. The first we find in the two world wars and in the Korean, Vietnamese, and Syrian wars as well as in other conflicts that sprang from them. Second is the rise of nation-states as many colonial and semicolonial territories broke from the metropole and found independence. Third is the birth, development, crisis, and reform of the Communist movement. China played a key role in each of these three great shifts: it was closely connected to all but World War I; it was an archetypal twentieth-century nation-state; and the transformation undergone by China has played a critical role in the Communist movement. In twentieth-century history, China occupies a uniquely important place, and for half a century China was under the leadership and influence of Mao Zedong. Thus, in the twentieth century Mao clearly occupied a pivotal position not only in China but also in the world. In discussing global issues of this century, Mao cannot be ignored. How we assess him, however, is another question.

As well as being a nationalist, Mao concerned himself also with issues that transcend national boundaries (of course, Marxism is itself an international way of thinking that crosses these boundaries). By Mao's own account, in his youth the topics he reflected upon and discussed were the great questions of humanity, the world, the universe, and human nature. One such problem was how to confront the various contradictions produced by industrial civilization—a global problem of the twentieth century. In response, Mao envisioned a divergent and utopian ideal that has been called by some scholars a "non-Western path to modernization." The pros and cons of this conception of a non-Western modernization will be discussed later, but the mooting of the idea itself exerted considerable influence on the world. When the intellectuals of Western nations grew discontented with Western civilization, Mao was waiting to entice them so that to this day Maoists live on in the West. I can understand the pull that Mao has for them; I lived through that time. But because I lived through that time, I know also of its pitfalls. The trouble with these Western Maoists is that although Mao fused utopianism and despotism, they see only the utopian and (intentionally or not) play down or overlook the despotic. I think the naive thought of these Western Maoists is related to our own failure to have a thorough assessment of Mao Zedong Thought. For Chinese intellectuals, this is a historical responsibility.

I once gave a talk in Korea in which I suggested that two myths ran through the twentieth century. The first was the myth of the West, and the second was the myth of communism. As the century came to a close, both myths were gradually debunked. That was in 1995, and today in 2009, as we look back, the trend is even clearer. The collapse of the Soviet Union and the Eastern Bloc, the Tian'anmen incident—all of these have exposed the problems of socialism. At the same time, the current global financial crisis has brought the internal contradictions of capitalism to the fore. Perhaps this is a historical opportunity, offering us the possibility of transcending the cultures of capitalism and socialism and pursuing a third, more equitable kind of culture. We should now, I believe, sum up the global experience of the twentieth century, including the Chinese experience, and of course also the Taiwanese experience. Can we, upon this foundation, establish a new kind of critical thought? In this, Taiwan's position may be more advantageous, connected to both sides and thus perhaps able to provide a clearer view of any one problem. This was also a key reason for my coming to Taiwan to teach. I wanted to discuss with the Taiwanese academic world how we may, on the foundation of a summation of the twentieth-century Chinese and global experience, establish a kind of critical theory that has the ability to elucidate both the past and the present. This is the current intellectual, cultural, and academic task before us, and the foundation on which it must be established is mutual understanding. In this there is much room for cooperation.

In the little time remaining, let me say a few words about how I plan to teach this class, which in itself implies a research methodology. I attempt to estab lish a three-dimensional narrative space: at the upper layer is Mao Zedong space, in the middle is the space of the intellectuals, and at the base is where I and other thinkers outside the establishment, along with the ordinary people, reside. I will try to narrate this period of history through the interaction of these three layers. This approach stems from a reflection on the current historical narrative and its focus, "only on historical events and not people or only on key figures and not ordinary people or only on collective politics and not the world of the individual spirit."[42] In response to these major deficiencies of the dominant historical narrative, I want to tell the story of Mao, of the intellectuals, of the heterodox thinkers, of the ordinary people, and of myself all within one time and space, not only describing the historical process but also revealing the spiritual world of the people involved in that history. It is an attempt to speak [not only] of Mao's internal contradictions but also of the damage to the spirit, the intellectual confusion, and psychological struggle of those who lived under Mao's totalitarian system as well as the humanistic problems that lurk in the background.

Another point about which I am concerned and about which I have thought is the identity and position of the researcher. In China, the academic world often sees the historian as a judge of history and a pundit of historical principle. Behind this lies an impulse to execute political, historical, and moral judgement on the subject of research as well as a determinist and an essentialist view of history. I have no interest in this and instead define myself as a narrator of history. Such narration, of course, includes an interrogation, and my questions are twofold: First, why do historical figures under particular circumstances and in particular contexts make this or that choice? According to what kind of logic and under what psychological and emotional state did he or she make this historical decision? Second, what consequences, perhaps unforeseen by those involved, have such historical decisions brought about? Therefore, my demands on myself are also twofold: the first is to have a sympathetic understanding, and the second is to face up squarely to consequences. I hope that proceeding in this way will perhaps evoke a compassionate spirit and render Mao Zedong a tragic figure of history.

Therefore, my primary duty is to tell stories, to create a historical narrative. Of course, this does not mean that I am totally without a standpoint; in the process of drawing together a story, a point of view is natural, but I don't excessively critique or sum up and leave narration and explanation as my key task. In this narrative, I hope to include as much historical specificity and sensibility as possible. I think also that this narrative style might also be better suited to all of you because what I want to relate is totally unfamiliar to you. In one sense, you came here to hear me relate stories, and I hope by way of these stories to help you understand the history of the People's Republic, to help you gradually enter into that particular historical context, to touch the spiritual worlds of historical figures, and to give you a sense of history. With this, my goals will be met.

Today's class serves as a sort of "preface," and I will stop here for now.

Notes

1. Qian Liqun, *Mao Zedong shidai he hou–Mao Zedong shidai, 1949–2009, ling yizhong lishi shuxie* (The Mao Zedong era and the post–Mao Zedong era, 1949–2009, another historical view) (Taipei: Lianjing, 2012).

2. The key term here is *qingli*, which generally means "clear up" or "dispose of," even "cleanse [a wound]," but it also carries the political meaning from the Mao years of "settling political accounts" in revolutionary struggle. This single term reflects the layers of meaning in Qian's prose. We variously translate *qingli* as "critique and assessment," "sort out," "untangle," or "clear up" according to context.

3. See Li Tuo, "Ding Ling bujiandan: Mao tizhi xia zhishifenzi zai huayu shengchan zhong de fuza juese" (Ding Ling is not simple: The complicated role that intellectuals played in the production of discourse under the Maoist regime), *Jintian* 3 (1993): 236–40; and Geremie Barmé, "New China NewSpeak," *China Heritage Quarterly* 29 (March 2012), http://www.chinaheritagequarterly.org/glossary.php?searchterm=029 _xinhua.inc&issue=029.

4. My late father was Qian Tianhe [1893–1972], also called Qian Zhilan, courtesy name Antao, from Hang County, Zhejiang. He was among the pioneers of modern Chinese agricultural science. He held a series of posts, including chairman of the Department of Sericulture at Nanjing University; director of the Academia Sinica Museum; bureau chief for agriculture and farming, Ministry of the Economy; and adviser on the Far East region to the United Nations Food and Agriculture Organization. In 1948, he served as leader of the agriculture group for the Chinese Rural Rejuvenation Committee before following the Guomindang government to Taiwan. In 1952, he was promoted to the Committee for Rural Rejuvenation, then retired in 1961. He passed away in 1972 due to heart failure. See "Qian Tianhe zhuanlüe" (Biographical sketch of Qian Tianhe), in Qian Tianhe, *Qian Tianhe wenji* (The collected works of Qian Tianhe) (Beijing: Zhongguo Nongye Keji, 1997), n.p.

5. *Translators' note*: "Post 80" refers to the first generation of Chinese to grow up entirely in the reformist era as well as through the first years of the one-child policy. The "post 90" generation were the second generation to grow up (mostly) as only children and the first of the post-Tian'anmen era.

6. *Translators' note*: Chen Kuan-hsing is professor at the Institute of Social Research and Cultural Studies, National Chiao Tung University, and a noted left-wing commentator and critic active in the Inter Asia Cultural Studies group. His major work in

English is *Asia as Method: Toward Deimperialization* (Durham, NC: Duke University Press, 2010).

7. *Translators' note*: See Qian Liqun, "Refusing to Forget," trans. Eileen Cheng, in *One China Many Paths*, ed. Wang Chaohua (London: Verso, 2003), 292–309.

8. *Translators' note*: Some people think that Hu Shi (1891–1962) is also a central figure.

9. *Translators' note*: *Xinling de tanxun* (Soul-searching) (Beijing: Beijing Daxue, 1999) is considered Qian Liqun's representative work on Lu Xun.

10. *Translators' note*: Qian Liqun has written extensively on Lu Xun, repeatedly arguing for his continued relevance as a critical and heterodox voice in contemporary China. His major work on Lu Xun, besides *Soul-Searching* (see note 9), is *Zoujin dangdai de Lu Xun* (Approaches to a contemporary Lu Xun) (Beijing: Beijing Daxue, 1999). In English, see Qian Liqun, "The Historical Fate of Lu Xun in Today's China," trans. Todd Foley, *Frontiers of Literary Studies in China* 7, no. 4 (2013): 529–40.

11. *Translators' note*: The Zunyi Conference was an expanded meeting of the CCP Central Committee Politburo held January 15–17, 1935, in Zunyi, Guizhou. During the meeting, Mao was added as a member of the Politburo Standing Committee but not made leader.

12. He Fang, *Dangshi biji, cong Zunyi huiyi dao Yan'an zhengfeng* (Notes on Party history, from the Zunyi Conference to Yan'an Rectification) (Hong Kong: Liwen, 2008). *Translators' note*: He Fang is also an expert on international relations of the period. *Notes on Party History*, written later in He's life, sums up a lifetime of personal experience and six years of reading and reflecting on CCP history. A major focus is on the Yan'an Rectification Campaign, but the Zunyi Conference is also covered, and he both describes and evaluates Zhang Wentian.

13. Wang Jiaxiang, "Guoji zhishi baogao" (Directive of the international) (September 1938), *Wenjian he Yanjiu* 4 (April 1986), quoted in Yang Kuisong, *Mao Zedong yu Mosike de enen yuanyuan* (Mao Zedong and Moscow, gratitude and grudges), 4th ed. (Nanchang: Jiangxi Renmin, 2006), 66.

14. *Translators' note*: The Sixth Plenary Session of the CCP's Sixth Central Committee was held from September 29 to November 6, 1938. Mao presented the political report "The New Stage in the Development of the National War of Resistance Against Japan and the Anti-Japanese National United Front." The congress ratified Mao as representative of the political line of the Central Politburo in the Party's Central Committee and criticized Wang Ming's "rightist deviationism." For translations of Party documents such as the one referred to here, see Tony Saich and Benjamin Yang, *The Rise to Power of the Chinese Communist Party* (Armonk, NY: M. E. Sharpe, 1996).

15. *Translators' note*: Qian Liqun gives specific citations to Chinese editions of Mao in this text, but we give published English translations of the same. Mao Zedong, "The Place of the Chinese Communist Party in the National War," in *Mao's Road to Power: Revolutionary Writings 1912–1949*, vol. 6: *The New Stage, August 1937–1938*, ed. Stuart R. Schram (Armonk, NY: M. E. Sharpe, 2004), 538–39.

16. Gao Hua, *Hong taiyang shi zenyang shengqi de: Yan'an zhengfeng yundong de lailong qumai* (How the red sun rose: The origin and development of the Yan'an Rectification Campaign) (Hong Kong: Chinese University of Hong Kong Press, 2000), 180. Mao announced the "Sinification of Marxism" in 1939. According to Yang Kuisong, this reflects a "middle zone" between America and Russia in 1946; China's own road to development in 1956; the expansion of "middle-zone" thinking in the 1960s; and, finally, in the late Cultural Revolution his "Three Worlds" theory. See Yang Kuisong, *"Zhongjian didai" de geming, guoji da beijing xia kan Zhonggong chenggong zhi dao*

(A "middle zone" revolution, the CCP's road to success in an international context) (Taiyuan: Shanxi Renmin, 2010).

17. According to Zhang Wentian's memoirs, in the spring of 1939 he had already "relocated the Politburo Conference to the Yangjialing area of Yan'an where Mao lived. I was only chairman for appearances, with all major decisions taken by Mao" (quoted in Yang, *Mao Zedong yu Mosike*, 67).

18. *Translators' note*: Qian is alluding here to early-twentieth-century debates on the relationship between individual and community or nation-state, which were rendered by debate participants such as Hu Shi as *xiaowo* (little self) and *dawo* (big self), respectively.

19. *Translators' note*: This is Qian's memoir: *Wode jingshen zizhuan* (literally, "My spiritual biography," but the Chinese edition carries the English title "My Retrospection and Reflection" (Guilin: Guangxi Shifan, 2007).

20. Lu Xun, "Yecao, Ying de gaobie" (Wild grass, the shadow's farewell) (December 8, 1924), in *Lu Xun quanji* (The complete works of Lu Xun) (Beijing: Renmin Wenxue, 2005), 2:169.

21. Lu Xun, "Yecao, Tuibaixian de chandong" (Wild grass, tremors of degradation), July 13, 1925, in *Lu Xun quanji*, 2:210–11.

22. Qian Liqun, *Fengfu de tongku: Tang Jihede yu Hamuleite de dongyi* (Abundant suffering: Don Quixote and Hamlet head east) (Beijing: Beijing Daxue, 2007), n.p.; for a closer analysis, see chapter 5, 84–93.

23. *Translators' note*: Liang Shiqiu was a noted literary intellectual famous for opposing the class-centered deployment of literature as propaganda as well as Rousseau-inspired romanticism. Such a stance positioned him squarely in opposition to Lu Xun.

24. *Translators' note*: See Mao Zedong, "Classroom Notes" (October–December 1913), in *Mao's Road to Power*, vol. 1: *The Pre-Marxist Period, 1912–1920*, ed. Stuart R. Schram (Armonk, NY: M. E. Sharpe, 1992), 19–22.

25. *Translators' note*: The *Doctrine of the Mean*, or *Zhongyong*, is considered one of the "Four Books" of the Confucian classics. It councils moderation.

26. Lu Xun, "Huagaiji, tongxun" (Inauspicious star, dispatch) (March 20–April 3, 1925), in *Lu Xun quanji*, 3:22–23. *Translators' note*: Qian paraphrases slightly here. A direct translation of Lu Xun's words would be "With the people as they are, a good government is impossible; even if good government were obtained, it would easily collapse."

27. *Translators' note*: The official confirmation of this relationship is given in the CCP Resolution on History, June 1981. For an English translation, see *Beijing Review* 27 (July 6, 1981): 10–39, https://www.marxists.org/subject/china/documents/cpc/history/01.htm.

28. *Translators' note*: Qian uses the term *minjian*, which literally means "among the people" but has been translated here into English as "folk," "popular," and "grassroots." It can mean "nonstate," and that meaning is rendered here as "heterodox." On *minjian*, see Sebastian Veg, *Among the Silent Majority: The Rise of China's Grassroots Intellectuals* (New York: Columbia University Press, 2019).

29. *Translators' note*: For a brief discussion of Mao's "monkey spirit," see Geremie R. Barmé, "A Monkey King's Journey to the West," *China Heritage Quarterly*, January 1, 2017, http://chinaheritage.net/journal/a-monkey-kings-journey-to-the-east/.

30. Mao Zedong: "I have within me a tiger spirit, which is dominant, and also a monkey spirit, which is secondary" (Mao Zedong, "Gei Jiang Qing de xin" [A letter to Jiang Qing], July 8, 1966, in *Jianguo yilai Mao Zedong wengao* [Mao Zedong's manuscripts since the founding of the state] [Beijing: Zhongyang Wenxian, 1998], 12:72).

31. Lu Xun, "Eryi ji, xiao zagan" (And that's that, some miscellaneous thoughts) (December 17, 1927), in *Lu Xun quanji*, 3:555.

32. *Translators' note*: The Seventeenth CCP National Congress was held December 15–17, 2007, in Beijing. The major slogan of the congress was "holding high the great banner of socialism with Chinese characteristics," and its stated guiding thought was "Deng Xiaoping theory and the Three Represents." Some old cadres felt these policies abandoned the spirit of Maoism.

33. *Translators' note*: "Chinese learning as essence, Western learning as function" (*Zhongxue wei ti, Xixue wei yong*) is the formulation by which the late Qing reformer Zhang Zhidong (1837–1909) articulated a balance between cultural conservatism and institutional and technological reform.

34. *Translators' note*: Qian here invokes a famous dictum on Party power from Mao. The original, found in Mao's essay "Zhanzheng he zhanlüe wenti" (Problems of war and strategy, 1938), reads: "Our principle is that the Party controls the gun, and must never allow the gun to control the Party." Translated in Schram, *Mao's Road to Power*, vol. 6: *The New Stage*, 548–59.

35. *Translators' note*: An allusion to the Great Leap Forward, an immense disaster, as archetype of the economic and developmental romanticism of the Mao era.

36. *Translators' note*: Zhuge Liang was statesmen and strategist of the Three Kingdoms era (220–265) who became a symbol of strategy and wisdom in Chinese folklore; Guan Yu was a general who was posthumously idolized and identified with the guardian Bodhisattva Sangharama; Qin Shihuang was the first emperor to unify China in 221 BCE; Han Wudi was "martial" emperor of the Later Han dynasty; and Liu Bei was the founder of the Shu-Han dynasty.

37. *Translators' note*: In the "three new traditions," Qian is referring to a line of thought popularized in Gan Yang, *Tong san tong* (Unifying the three traditions) (Beijing: Sanlian Shudian, 2007), selections from which are translated in chapter 1 of this volume.

38. *Translators' note*: The phrases Qian uses here are drawn from Han dynasty statesman Jia Yi's (200–169 BCE) work, thus comparing these fundamentalist Maoists with early Chinese autocracy and the scholar-official tradition.

39. *Translators' note*: Qian identifies two such Maoist parties, the Maoist Communist Party and the China's Workers (Communist) Party, and discusses them further in chapter 14 of *Mao Zedong shidai he hou–Mao Zedong shidai*.

40. Qian Liqun, "Ruhe huigu naduan geming lishi?" (How do we look back on that period of revolutionary history?) (December 16, 2007), in *Huozhe de liyou* (Grounds for living) (Guilin: Guangxi Shifan Daxue, 2010), 250–56.

41. *Translators' note*: Qian's use of medical metaphors here echoes Mao's own rhetorical habit, most obviously found in the cry to "cure the disease and save the patient" (*zhibing jiuren*). For a recent discussion of the centrality of this language to Party discourse, see Cristian Sorace, "Communist Party Immunology," in *China Story Yearbook 2016: Control*, ed. Jane Golley, Linda Jaivin, and Luigi Tomba (Canberra: Australian National University Press, 2017), 100–107.

42. Qian Liqun, "'Yiwang' beihou de lishiguan yu lunliguan" (The historical and ethical position behind "forgetting"), in *Liushi jieyu* (Sixty stories of calamity) (Fuzhou: Fujian Jiayou, 1995), 56.

CHAPTER 9

FROM AUTHORITARIAN GOVERNMENT TO CONSTITUTIONAL DEMOCRACY[1]

XIAO GONGQIN

TRANSLATED BY TIMOTHY CHEEK

Translator's Introduction

Xiao Gongqin (b. 1946) is professor of history at Shanghai Normal University, with cross-appointments at Fudan and Shanghai Jiaotong, among other institutions. He is often identified as one of the main representatives of new authoritarianism or neoconservatism in the reform-and-opening period, arguing that a strong central government and a steady hand at the top of the political order are necessary for China to avoid falling into the extremes of "political romanticism" of either the Left or the Right, as has so often happened over the course of China's modern and contemporary history.

The essay translated here is a notable defense of such new authoritarian policies, which the author views precisely as what Deng Xiaoping's policies have achieved for China since the Cultural Revolution. Originally published in *Dongfang Zaobao* (Oriental morning post) on January 18, 2012, in the special section on the twentieth anniversary of Deng Xiaoping's Southern Tour talks, this short essay offers a congratulatory history of Chinese Communist Party reforms in the post-Mao period, describing a five-stage model of economic and political development that starts with authoritarian order, stimulates economic prosperity, enforces social justice, and trains the populace in the civil society habits for constitutional government. Although Sun Yat-sen is not mentioned, the historically minded will immediately think of the "political tutelage" he proposed in the 1920s and that Chiang Kai-shek's (1887–1975) Nationalist government claimed through the 1940s.

Although Xiao is orthodox in his support of the government, his analysis is informed and reasoned, drawing from international political science theory and comparative examples from around the world. It is important to note as well that Xiao's neoauthoritarian prescriptions are essentially instrumental and not ends in themselves. In other words, Xiao imagines a future China with a healthy civil society and some kind of democracy. This distinguishes him from statist thinkers who celebrate the achievements of China's state as glorifications of state capacity.

The Five Logical Steps from Authoritarian Government to Constitutional Democracy: A Macrohistorical Perspective on Deng Xiaoping's Reforms

Now that China has become prosperous, our next task must be to take up the project of the people's livelihood (*minsheng*). Only when the will and spirit of the people are unhindered can the self-organization of society develop. And only then can we avoid a frustrated and anxious "mob" politics confronting a lawful government. Only then can we overcome populism and build a civic culture. All of this is the necessary prerequisite for China to move toward constitutional democracy and a renewed civilization. This is also the goal to which the political elite of China's new generation, inheriting the mantle of Deng Xiaoping's achievements, should devote itself, thus ushering in the arrival of a new era of democratic civilization.

China's Path Out of Ultra-Left Politics

Fortune and misfortune regularly appear together in human history. China, too, learned positive lessons from the great disasters of the Cultural Revolution. It is no exaggeration to say that the ultraleftism of the Cultural Revolution also awakened the Chinese people from at least a half-century of fanatical obsession with the utopianism of the planned economy. It was precisely an era like the Cultural Revolution that produced the fantastic stories of the Guizhou village where the day's work points of two able-bodied laborers couldn't buy a single egg, where poverty reached the extent to which women in villages around Longxi (Gansu) had no pants to wear. According to agricultural statistics from 1978, the average annual income of peasants nationwide was less than 75 Renminbi.

Such shocking facts of extreme poverty provoke profound anxiety, but only those who genuinely suffer—and not august power holders—emerge transformed. In human history, generally, the august power holders remain above the fray. In the great calamity of the Cultural Revolution, however, the founding leaders of the revolution suffered terrible blows just as the ordinary masses and intellectuals did. The marginalization and predicaments they experienced freed them from the fetters of the ideological doctrines of ultra-leftism. And like the proletarian masses, they were able by plain commonsense reasoning to gain a vivid understanding of the ultraleftist calamity that China had suffered. In fact, after Deng Xiaoping was reinstated to his position as vice premier in 1974, he argued with Jiang Qing [1914–1991][2] at the conference to study Dazhai. When Jiang Qing heard the report on village poverty, she said: "That is just a single case." Deng Xiaoping could not resist the retort: "Even one case is a serious problem." When he responded to Jiang Qing in this way, Deng's commonsense rationality awoke, and he cast off the fetters of his previous dogmatic faith.

After his reinstatement, Deng was conscience stricken about the erroneous line that the Chinese Communist Party (CCP) had pursued. On an inspection tour in the Northeast, he said: "Our people are too good. They have already forgiven us for such great crimes. People in other countries would have long since given up on us." According to the *Chronological Biography of Deng Xiaoping*, at the Party Central Committee meeting to decide on the rehabilitation of Liu Shaoqi [1898–1969], Deng felt compelled to say, "We have made a few more errors than Comrade Liu Shaoqi."[3] We can say that it was precisely the extreme to which the elderly Mao's utopian Cultural Revolution developed that activated history's "pendulum effect," prompting many Party elders to abandon utopian thinking and rediscover common sense and experience. This brought them a great awakening. When they once again took up the reins of power, Chinese history welcomed a new beginning.

Deng Xiaoping's rethinking finds a concentrated expression in volume 3 of *The Selected Works of Deng Xiaoping*. Deng Xiaoping Thought is summed up there in four pithy sentences: (1) Socialism is not poverty; socialism enriches the people. (2) To achieve prosperity we must develop the productive forces. (3) To develop the productive forces we must embrace reform and opening. (4) While carrying out reform and opening, we must uphold the Four Cardinal Principles and preserve political stability.[4] Deng's first three sentences are the crystallization of his reflections on ultraleftist thought, and the political function of the last sentence serves to defend the legitimacy of the neoauthoritarian politics of reform and opening.

Once the old revolutionaries had become reformers, they possessed special advantages that the young reforming elites did not. First, the authority, the personal prestige, and the personal connections within the establishment of these old hands who knew the ropes—all invaluable political resources—allowed them to lead institutional reform in the manner of enlightened patriarchs. They were able to reduce massively the cost of political reform, and when reform encountered setbacks, they had sufficient political room to maneuver. The political experience accumulated over long revolutionary careers enabled these old revolutionaries to remove the resistance to and assaults on reform by radical liberals outside the establishment and by conservatives inside it. They were able to preserve the necessary political stability during reform and opening.

Second, once the revolutionary elders had taken charge of the reforms, China's developmental path was firmly set, and China moved in the direction of an enlightened and developmental neoauthoritarian politics rather than the populist democratic politics idealized by radical intellectuals. This was because they had a profound memory of the great democracy of the Cultural Revolution and had no wish to repeat the disastrous policies of street populism. But this was also due to Deng Xiaoping's political experience and perceptiveness. He realized that during the early stages of development, Western-style, complete democracy would affect political stability and in the end lead to the failure of reform. He spoke about this many times. In addition, there were deeper causes, including Deng Xiaoping's own personal history, memories of the revolution, and ideas and emotions forged in the revolutionary era. These merged in him to form an instinctual rejection of any plan to directly apply Western-style pluralistic liberal politics to carry out reform. No matter what the reason, once Deng Xiaoping set out the policy of combining the Four Cardinal Principles and reform and opening, history decided that China's future basic road would be one of enlightened authoritarian politics and not the romanticism and political shock therapy of radical pluralistic democracy chosen by the callow, politically inexperienced Gorbachev.

We can see in Deng Xiaoping's reforms the historical trajectory of the transition from the omnipotent planned economy to an enlightened authoritarian politics: in the realm of economic reform, the Chinese people did not start out with a comprehensive blueprint for reform based on ideal principles. Rather, they felt for stones as they crossed the river, in Deng's famous phrase. They faced actual problems by addressing them on the basis of feasibility and cost–benefit analysis. They completed the transition to a competitive market economy step by step by implementing the agricultural responsibility system (that is, dismantling the communes and returning land to household production), township and village enterprises (the famous TVE workshops), the open share/stock system, the establishment of special economic zones (SEZs), the opening (of the economy) to the outside world, the transformation of state-owned industries (SOEs), entrance to the World Trade Organization (WTO), and so on.[5]

In the political realm, we can see that after the end of the 1980s the government used an iron fist to marginalize the radical liberals. For a time after this, Party conservatives were active. However, during his talks on his Southern Tour in 1992, Deng Xiaoping made use of his supreme authority to point out: "We should be on guard against the Right, but more importantly we must defend against the Left." His stance deprived the extreme leftist forces of their discursive authority. The basic spirit of Deng's talks on his Southern Tour was an endorsement of policies that would preserve the Party's hold on power, while the economy continued its opening to the outside world, the idea being to use the practical results of economic development to ensure the legitimacy of the CCP's political power. Then both the radical liberals outside the establishment and the conservative political forces within the Party were marginalized and withdrew from the center of political life.

In the realm of ideology, we can observe a series of creative developments from Deng Xiaoping onward: the significance of "the comprehensive understanding of Mao Zedong Thought" and "practice is the sole criterion of truth" lay in stripping the "Whateverists" of their discursive initiative;[6] "the initial stages of socialism" concept legitimized market economics in the ideology of the ruling party; the "Three Represents" emphasized that after discarding the promise of utopian egalitarianism, the CCP would maintain its position as the ruling party, leading the people of the entire country as long as it upheld advanced productive forces, moved culture forward, and protected the basic interests of the whole people.[7] In this sense the "Three Represents" have become the milestone marking the transformation of the CCP from a revolutionary party to an enlightened neoauthoritarian ruling party. "Harmonious society" signals an ideological innovation, a shift from revolutionary language based on the philosophy of struggle to a new, enlightened value system that can contain a plurality of interests and ideas. These creative ideological formulations (*tifa*)[8] embrace the novel contents of reform and opening while preserving the continuity of the Party's ideological history. They also make up the ideological basis of enlightened authoritarian politics.

In sum, in the twenty years since Deng's talks on his Southern Tour, China has undergone multifaceted reforms in economics, politics, and ideology. Through a process of "trial and error and step-by-step consolidation," we followed a process of systemic renewal in which we transformed ourselves from "a totally controlled society" to a diverse society of "enlightened authoritarianism and a competitive market economy." The Chinese people were hence liberated from the planned economy of household registration (*hukou*) and from the system's work unit (*danwei*) ownership, and through the market mechanism they became free to pursue their individual interests. The stimulation of the competitive power of the Chinese people, the emergence of contracts to manage exchanges between economic agents, and the rise of competition between regions meant that China bid farewell to the inherent limitations of its traditional society, which gave way to the new competitive civilization now taking shape in China.

Why This Kind of Neoauthoritarianism Can Give Us an Edge

A Taiwanese entrepreneur who has an enterprise in Kunshan used this metaphor when he was speaking with colleagues back in Taiwan: "China engages in the market economy much like it waged guerrilla warfare in the past. In the front-line headquarters, each department works together, makes their decision, double-checks their calculations, and builds the whole kit and caboodle. You can't find that kind of efficiency in any other country in the world." This is a mode of operation that ingeniously combines centralized mobilization and market competition. This is one more important reason for the emergence of the China miracle.

As a matter of fact, from the perspective of political science we can say that China's new political system since Deng Xiaoping's Southern Tour talks represents a "post-totalitarian authoritarian politics"—or, in plain language, a new kind of enlightened autocracy. Here we use enlightened autocracy as a value-neutral concept in political science. Its characteristic trait is that it continues to use the political resources and mobilizational methods of the "totalitarian system" to protect the development of a market economy. In this sort of authoritarian politics, state control and mobilizational capacity are strong, while social autonomy is relatively weak. This is a "strong state/weak society" model.

Since the Southern Tour talks, China's economy has developed massively, and Deng Xiaoping's contributions to the establishment of this neoauthoritarian system cannot be denied. In general, the authoritarian politics of late-developing countries in the process of economic modernization can be divided into three types. The first type is a "patrimonial system" that turns the state into private property in a hereditary system in which politics is based on cliques that degenerate into patriarchal rule. This is undoubtedly the most backward model of development. Many countries in Latin America and Africa unfortunately fall into this category. The second type is "decentralized plural politics." India is an example. The characteristic of this kind of state is that it has implemented Western-style competitive multiparty democratic elections before achieving modernization. The state essentially lacks the ability to make comprehensive plans and the integrative capacity to promote economic transformation and to mobilize resources. Rather, under this pluralistic system, parasitic interest groups are able to use legislatures to obstruct systemic reform and the rationalization of the distribution of social benefits. The third type, to use the words of the American political economist Professor Atul Kohli [b. 1949], is "cohesive capitalism," represented by South Korea, Japan, Singapore, and Taiwan. More concretely, politics are centralized, cohesive, while the economy is guided by the market. A cohesive government can effectively formulate industrial policy beneficial to economic development. It can forcefully control and

effectively use finances and guard against financial risk. The active cooperation between government and entrepreneurs facilitates joint planning for economic development and resource integration. The strengths of resource integration and systemic mobilization characteristic of "cohesive capitalism"
cannot be found in the other models of economic development. This system is
different from the liberal laissez-faire doctrine of India's weak government
as well as from the new hereditary states in Latin America and Africa.

From the perspective of comparative politics, we can see that the Deng
Xiaoping model is a new species in political theory. Its efficacy in government-
directed economic transformation, its ability to mobilize resources, its ability
to control society and resolve unforeseen incidents, and its capacity to deal with
unavoidable risks—all exceed the capacities of "cohesive capitalist" countries.
This is an enlightened autocracy with a high-level integration of resource mobilization and market competition. This is the key to China's success.

Deng Xiaoping's System from a Century's Historical Perspective

Over the past century, in the process of facing the challenges of modernization
since late Qing times, China has made six political choices: the enlightened despotism of the late Qing reforms, the multiparty democracy of the [Republican]
Revolution of 1911 and its immediate aftermath, the strongman politics of Yuan
Shikai [1859–1916], the authoritarian politics of the Nationalist Party, the totalitarian planning system of Mao Zedong, and the reform and opening of Deng
Xiaoping. In this broad historical perspective, the Deng Xiaoping model has
important characteristics and significance in the history of modernization.

In the late nineteenth century, the Qing dynasty's simple and crude authoritarian system was unable to respond to the challenges of modernization after
the midcentury Opium Wars. The late Qing's New Policies likewise were unable
to produce a new, enlightened autocracy and could not avoid being toppled by
the anti-Manchu nationalism of the Revolution of 1911.

Because of the endless fighting among the parties and the weak government,
the multiparty parliamentary politics set up after the Revolution of 1911 was
unable to surmount the combined dangers of the day, and so the contradictions
of a multiparty system dissolved into utter polarization. In other words, even
though Song Jiaoren's [1882–1913] political party and cabinet were established
by national elections, it was a divided and fragmented polyarchy that was completely unable to address the complicated tasks of political integration and
economic mobilization.

After 1914, Yuan Shikai dissolved Parliament and ran a strongman government. Although this might have been a new opportunity for social integration,
the intense cliquishness and patriarchal color of Yuan's government as well as

his effort to become emperor doomed his government to revert to a hereditary and sultanist politics that was fundamentally unable to address the needs of modernization.

After the success of the Northern Expedition in 1928, the authoritarian politics of a unified party-state that Chiang Kai-shek established came apart. On the one hand were the various sides in the wars on the central plains, and on the other the rise of the Communist Party. Together with the Japanese invasion, civil war, and finally its own corruption, Chiang's government was unable to avoid defeat in the national civil war.

Mao's post-1949 system enjoyed a combination of great organizational power and mass belief. But this belief became unmoored, and China fell into the great disaster of a self-defeating egalitarian utopianism, personal dictatorship, and the "extreme Left Cultural Revolution."

Deng Xiaoping's model of reform and opening arose to respond to the needs of the day in 1978. On the one hand, his model made use of the legacies of strong government from the revolutionary system as a lever to mobilize economic development, and on the other it used market economics to give play to the local energies of social actors, including individuals, enterprises, and groups. From the perspective of the previous five political choices, this effective integration of mobilizational levers and mechanisms of competitive market economy shows that the key to the successes of the Deng Xiaoping model has been precisely its ability to address these two needs of late-developing countries by organically integrating organizational and competitive strength.

The Five Steps to China's Modern Civilization

How do we get from the Deng Xiaoping model to the higher stages of modern democracy and culture? A large, late-developing country wanting to move toward a modern civilization based on democracy must, in the logic of development, meet a series of conditions: first, economic prosperity; next, social justice; and finally, the nurturing of civic culture.

It must be stressed that simple economic prosperity is not a sufficient condition for realizing democratic politics. This is because the prosperity of free-market economics in late-developing countries is often accompanied by two negative consequences. The first is "authoritarian political regression," manifested in the corruption of power, Mafiaization, and the collusion of power and capital. The second is the social inequality and polarization of rich and poor hidden behind economic prosperity. Globally, there are many late-developing countries that are now unable to solve these two great problems and have become mired in the trilogy of "social revolt/mass violent revolution/weak populist democracy." The "Jasmine Revolutions" of Egypt, Tunisia, and Libya in the Middle East are examples. After the euphoria of democratic revolutions overthrowing corrupt authoritarian regimes, these countries are now by degrees approaching the calamity of anarchy. This disaster has by no means concluded; it has only just begun.

From this we can see that if China wants to move toward democracy after economic development, it must first avoid falling into the twin traps of political corruption and social polarization. Only in this way can we avoid the vicious cycle between regressive authoritarian politics and weak pluralistic politics. It is necessary to seek out a new road.

According to this logic, we might argue that after neoauthoritarianism has achieved economic takeoff and the preliminary goal of economic prosperity, the next step is to use the great wealth and capital created by society in the process of economic development to support the people's livelihood as well as to resolve the contradictions of social injustice and the polarization of rich and poor. Only when social justice permits the will and spirit of the people to flourish will we have met an important precondition for future democracy.

Next we must rebuild civil society, but a society in which citizens organize themselves can be established only when the will and spirit of the people flourish. This is the only way to avoid creating a "mob" politics full of frustration and anxiety that will challenge the legitimate government. Civil society is the great school that fosters civic culture. Only with autonomy and through the social organization of good works can citizens cultivate the necessary political culture of tolerance, forgiveness, and reason and the capacity to engage energetically in public affairs.

It is precisely for this reason that after China has prospered, it must attack corruption and eliminate the collusion between power and capital to develop the people's livelihood and build civil society. All of these things are the necessary preconditions for China's pathway to a modern new civilization. This is also the goal to which the political elite of China's new generation, inheriting the mantle of Deng's achievements, should devote itself, thus ushering in the arrival of a new era of democratic civilization.

From a broad historical perspective, in the decade from the early 1980s through the Southern Tour talks Deng Xiaoping brought order out of chaos, kept reformers in power, and achieved political stability. He established the first substantial basis for China's development, accomplishing the first step in this Long March.[9] In the decade between the Southern Tour talks in 1992 and 2002, China's economy underwent a successful transformation, achieving economic takeoff and essentially realizing the goals of the second step.

With an eye toward achieving a high level of democracy in China, the state, in the relatively long period between the beginning of the twenty-first century and now and on the basis of the relatively flourishing economy created by the ruling party, has been able to use the enormous capital obtained through economic development to engage in a massive project to improve the well-being particularly of low- and middle-income groups.

Having improved the people's livelihood and achieved social justice, the next step is to put great effort into cultivating civil society, to let citizens acquire from society itself the civic culture necessary for democratic politics. This is the fourth stage. All four stages create the political, economic, social, and cultural conditions for the arrival of China's future democratic constitutional stage. In the fifth step, the maturation of civic culture will naturally produce socialism's era of high-level democratic politics.

In every ideal model of modernization, the state must be an active player. There are two kinds of state intervention by centralized governments in late-developing large states. If a strong state fuses with a utopian project or becomes part of an expansionist nationalism or merely becomes a tool to satisfy the interests of private parasitic groups, then this will be a calamitous misfortune for the people. If, however, there is a fusion of a strong state and practical reason, and if every effort is made to secure the welfare of the whole people and the goals of democracy, then, in the words of a foreign political scientist, this will be "a great force in the service of the good." Through a strong state developing a strong society, the century-long dream of democracy can be realized. Of course, this is just a tentative plan, but a plan entrusted with our most beautiful hopes.

You might ask, Why go through this five-step logic instead of going straight to democratic government? I think democracy, like seedlings, is something you cannot force to grow. It cannot transcend social conditions. This five-step program is an incremental-stage theory. In plain language, only if reformers are in power will there be economic transformation; only with economic transformation will it be possible to achieve economic takeoff; only with economic takeoff can the state accumulate vast economic power through taxation, undertake the project of addressing the people's livelihood, and realize an equal and prosperous society. Only when all of these goals are achieved will there be the conditions for creating the development of a healthy civil society. Only on this basis can civil society develop, democratic culture be nourished, populism be overcome, and the final step toward constitutional democracy be realized.

We must clearly recognize that democracy has necessary social, economic, and cultural conditions. Over the past century, we cannot say that the cry for democracy among China's masses and intellectuals has not been strong. But people subconsciously took democracy to be a kind of moral system, a simple tool with which to overcome despotism and corruption. They basically had no idea that democracy arose in the West through a series of social developments and is the product of the collective experience of a long period of trial and error. If we view democracy solely as a tool by which to realize moral government and yet completely neglect the conditions necessary for the achievement of democracy, then fledgling democracies risk falling into anarchy and political division. The ceaseless struggles of parties under the provisional constitution right after the 1911 Revolution are but one example of this sort of political anomie. Another possibility is the malignant spread of populism. In today's world, many late-developing countries have been caught in one or the other and cannot get out.

Notes

1. Xiao Gongqin, "Cong weiquan zhengzhi dao xianzheng minzhu de wubu luoji, da lishiguan shijiao xia de Deng Xiaoping gaige" (The five logical steps from authoritarian government to constitutional democracy: A macrohistorical perspective on Deng Xiaoping's reforms), *Dongfang Zaobao* (Shanghai), January 18, 2012, reprinted in *Chaoyue zuoyou jijinzhuyi: Zouchu Zhongguo zhuanxing de kunjing* (Beyond Left and Right radicalism: The path out of the predicaments of China's transformation) (Hangzhou: Zhejiang University Press, 2012), 115–24.
2. *Translator's note:* Jiang Qing was Mao's wife and a member of the "Gang of Four" who were later blamed for the excesses of the Cultural Revolution.
3. *Deng Xiaoping nianpu, 1904–1974* (Chronological biography of Deng Xiaoping) (Beijing: Zhongyang Wenxian Chubanshe, 2004), 1:604. *Translator's note*: Liu Shaoqi was deposed and virulently attacked during the Cultural Revolution.
4. *Translator's note*: The *sixiang jiben yuanze* (Four Cardinal Principles) are still in force in China today: keep to the socialist road, uphold the dictatorship of the proletariat, uphold the leadership of the Communist Party, and uphold Marxism-Leninism-Mao Zedong Thought. See Henry Yuhuai He, *Dictionary of the Political Thought of the People's Republic of China* (Armonk, NY: M. E. Sharpe, 2001), 435.
5. *Translator's note*: All are key institutions of China's economic reforms: TVEs were the first fruits of decollectivization in the countryside and the start of economic production outside the state plan; SEZs allowed the first private enterprises since Mao's time, beginning in the early 1980s; the number of lumbering SOEs was massively cut through privatization in the 1990s and 2000s (though under Xi Jinping this process has been somewhat reversed); and China joined the WTO in 2001.
6. *Translator's note*: The name "Whateverists" (*fanshipai*) refers to Party loyalists who in the late 1970s famously followed the dictum to follow "whatever Mao said" (generally attributed to Chairman Hua Guofeng [1921–2008]). The more pragmatic leadership that coalesced around Deng called themselves the "practice group" by contrast.
7. *Translator's note*: Most commentators summarize the "Three Represents," which General Secretary Jiang Zemin (b. 1926) proposed in 2000, as (1) to allow business leaders (capitalists) to join the Party, (2) to treat intellectuals better, and (3) to end class struggle.
8. *Translator's note*: *Tifa*, or formal political phrases or slogans, are central to CCP political life. Each of the formulations discussed in this paragraph was proposed by a top Party leader, from Deng Xiaoping to Jiang Zemin to Hu Jintao (b. 1942) to legitimize their policy innovations.
9. *Translator's note*: The Long March was the retreat of Communist forces in the 1930s and has become the metaphor for persistence and eventual success in Party discourse.

CHAPTER 10

LIBERALISM

For the Aristocrats or for the People?[1]

GAN YANG

TRANSLATED BY WILLIAM SIMA AND TANG XIAOBING

Translators' Introduction

G an Yang's basic profile has already been presented in the translation to selections from his book *Unifying the Three Traditions*
in chapter 1. The text translated here (composed considerably
earlier than that work) reveals another aspect of Gan's intellectual heritage: his
radical defense of mass democracy.

This piece was published in the influential Beijing journal *Dushu* (Reading)
in 1999. A culmination of Gan's engagement with liberal intellectual history—as
the author himself notes, his essays on Isaiah Berlin in 1989 were the first to
introduce key aspects of liberal theory to readers in the People's Republic of
China (PRC)—it was highly influential in the polemics between the Chinese
New Left and Liberals that began in the second half of the 1990s. In 2000, it
was reprinted in *Zhishifenzi lichang* (Intellectual positions), a collected volume
covering these debates, and has been republished many times since.[2] In the
translation here, we present the essay as it first appeared for mainland Chinese
readers and endeavor to preserve something of Gan Yang's grandiloquent and
at times haughty writing style.

Gan begins the essay with the charge that liberal discourse in China evinces
a pervading concern, born of a kind of intellectual conservatism, for promoting freedom for intellectual elites and the upper classes at the expense of democracy and equality for the masses. Stating the need to "reject using liberalism to
negate democracy; reject invoking the English Revolution to discredit the

French Revolution; reject citing Burke to discredit Rousseau; and reject using all of them to negate twentieth-century Chinese revolutionary history," Gan guides the reader through the work of a broad array of Western thinkers. His aim is to demonstrate that tension between elitist and mass forms of liberalism—which he dubs the "Tocqueville problem" in reference to the thought of Alexis de Tocqueville (1805–1859)—has been evident all throughout the Western liberal tradition and to a greater extent than contemporary proponents of liberalism and market reform are perhaps willing to acknowledge. There is no reason to expect "liberalism" to function any differently in China, Gan argues.

Although Gan's publishing and translation projects in the 1980s have led many to associate his name with a liberal revival in China, Gan rejects this association. He is open to the advantages of liberalism but has also been critical of the philosophy and its influence in China and steadfast in his defense of mass democracy and nationalism. Indeed, Gan later defended the "creative destruction" of the Maoist period as a necessary precursor for reform, anti-Western protests during the Beijing 2008 Olympics year as "voluntarily organized" celebrations of five thousand years of Chinese civilization, as well as reactions to a century of resisting foreign imperialism and sixty years of national self-strengthening since 1949. At times, Gan has even been a vocal proponent of Carl Schmitt (1888–1985), an antiliberal German philosopher from the Nazi period who has been popular among Chinese nationalists since the mid-2000s.[3] In sum, this essay shares with New Left thought a profound mistrust of liberalism, despite deep engagement with Western thought.

Liberalism: For the Aristocrats or for the People?

The basic trajectory of Chinese thought since the 1990s has evolved from the critique of radicalism of the late 1980s to conservatism and even ultraconservatism. The basic form of this type of conservatism typically manifests itself by disparaging and denying democratic equality in the name of liberalism, resulting in so-called liberalism being understood more as the privilege of the few rather than as a right possessed by all. In fact, many of the intellectuals who pontificate about liberalism today are talking about liberty for the bosses and liberty for the intellectuals—that is, liberty for the wealthy, liberty for the strong, and liberty for the capable. At the same time, they neglect even to mention that the starting point for the liberal theory of rights is the rights of all, and on this point it must be emphasized that this means particularly those who are unable to protect their own rights: the weak, the unfortunate, the poor, the hired hands, and the uneducated. If it is the case that "no error is more egregious than that of confounding freedom with free competition," as Frank Knight [1885–1972] of the Chicago School, who devoted his life to the study of the relationship between the market economy and freedom, sternly warned in his classic *The Ethics of Competition* [1935], then it is precisely this great error that has now become the collective faith of the Chinese intelligentsia.[4] That is, they have reduced the idea of freedom to that of freedom of the market, thinking that a free economy will automatically produce the greatest freedom. Within this version of freedom, democracy is an extravagance, equality is even more sinful, and the law of the jungle becomes the first principle of liberalism.

I refer to this collective faith as the "shared moral cancer of the Chinese intelligentsia" because it suggests that the Chinese intelligentsia have already almost lost the most basic sense of morality and justice. At the same time, this collective faith can also be called the "collective feeble-mindedness of the Chinese intelligentsia" because it reveals their inability to grasp the basic consensus in contemporary scholarship, which is that virtually any inquiry in the humanities and social sciences starts from the ideal of equal liberty, the notion that "each and every person is a free and equal moral individual." And yet in China this ideal of liberty is so rare as to have left hardly a trace on the Chinese intelligentsia. On the contrary, what they enthusiastically discuss is actually "unequal freedom." Especially absurd is that while the minority frenziedly plunders the assets and increasingly threatens the basic safeguards of the majority, we instead observe many people shaking their heads and wringing their hands about the "tyranny of the majority." Why not have the guts to do some soul-searching as to whether the Chinese intelligentsia is in fact using their intellectual privileges to support the minority's privileges in upholding the rights of all?

The phrase "Chinese intelligentsia" might not be completely appropriate because in fact more people nowadays already do not identify with the collective faith mentioned earlier. I am only pointing out mainstream tendencies and not addressing any particular individuals. Because the basic discourse of Chinese conservatism in the 1990s was not limited to the ideology of the market economy but had more to do with debasing democracy and equality in the name of liberalism, this essay will therefore focus once again on the relationship between liberalism and democracy.

The relationship or tension among liberalism, democracy, and equality is an old problem in liberal theory. Generally speaking, this tension cannot be resolved through one side prevailing over the other; that is, both "unequal liberty" and "illiberal equality" are unacceptable, and for this reason the crux of the matter lies in how best to maintain, in theory and in practice, the appropriate equilibrium in a tension of this kind. Because in past socialist experience the ideal of liberty has in general been rejected and the ideal of equality has at least in theory been approved, intellectual circles have accorded a particular priority to liberty. In fact, this has been a particular concern of mine in the past. In 1989, I published "The Idea of Liberty" and "The Enemy of Liberty" in *Reading*, and I was the first in China to introduce Isaiah Berlin's ideas on the differences between "negative freedom" and "positive freedom." Not long after going abroad, I published "Discarding 'Science and Democracy,' Establishing 'Liberty and Order.'" I also concentrated on raising the problem of the tension between liberty and democracy in an effort to describe the differences between the Scottish and French Enlightenments and the dividing line between the English Revolution and the French Revolution and to put forward "Establishing Liberty and Order" as the summary of what was at that time my political philosophy of "Euro-American liberty." This basic line of thought also ran through the other essays I published at that time, such as "Progress in Constitutional Drafting in Eastern Europe: A Survey," "A Critique of the Concept of Civil Society," and so on (both of which have since been published in my book *Beyond Radicalism and Conservatism*).

However, I have since become more and more conscious of the limitations of this line of thinking because it leads almost inevitably to a certain type of anachronism—that is, impulsively worshipping the English liberalism of the "predemocratic age," or aristocratic liberalism—and thereby neglecting precisely the process in which liberalism, especially English liberalism since the French Revolution, has gradually taken a key historical turn toward "democratic liberalism." The fundamental reason why Alexis de Tocqueville turned to the study of "democracy in America" and not "liberalism in England" was that he thought that English liberalism before the French Revolution (typically symbolized by the Glorious Revolution of 1688) was predemocratic liberalism and that this type of old-style, nondemocratic liberalism was already inadequate in helping liberals to face the challenges posed by the democratic age. Tocqueville went on to suggest that the arrival of the democratic age implied a "need for a new kind of political science" because the question for modern liberalism was not "reconstructing an aristocratic society, but . . . mak[ing] freedom spring from within democratic society."[5] In other words, liberalism in the age of democracy must move toward democratic liberalism. This is why Tocqueville expressed total approval of the contemporary principles for reform of "English radicals": to allow the citizens to take their rightful position as rulers and enable them to rule.

I call the change in liberalism from an aristocratic political form to a democratic political form the "Tocqueville problem" because in the history of liberal thought, Tocqueville was the first to focus on the question of transcending aristocratic liberalism and moving toward a democratic form of liberalism. This forces all those who claim to be liberals to answer the question: What is this liberalism that you brag about? Is it nondemocratic or even antidemocratic liberalism, or is it democratic liberalism?

I personally think that the Chinese intelligentsia's recent soul-searching on revolution and radicalism has reached its limit and indeed has started to turn in upon itself. Because Chinese intellectuals have not realized that liberalism under modern conditions can be only a democratic liberalism, they have reached a series of specious conclusions. For example, many believe that twentieth-century China went down entirely the wrong path, mistakenly imitating the French model instead of taking the English path. Recent studies of early-modern history have thus often asked in an ahistorical way how modern Chinese people could have gone wrong. For example, why did the Chinese not choose reform over revolution, gradualism over radicalism, freedom over equality, and why did they run fanatically after "positive freedom" instead of embracing "negative freedom"? Such an ahistorical study can lead Chinese intellectual circles only to a "liberalism of the predemocratic era," in the name of which they constantly belittle democracy and equality and praise conservatism, even ultraconservatism.

I think that today it is particularly necessary to propose the following: that we reject using liberalism to negate democracy; reject invoking the English Revolution to discredit the French Revolution; reject citing [Edmund] Burke [1729–1797] to discredit [Jean-Jacques] Rousseau [1712–1778]; and reject using all of them to negate twentieth-century Chinese revolutionary history since the Republican Revolution and the history of modern Chinese thought since May Fourth. Rather, all of these should be reexamined from the broad historical perspective of what Tocqueville considers the "advent of the era of democracy." We need not disavow radicalism and embrace conservatism but instead ought to "transcend radical and conservative" simultaneously!

Allow me to point out first that Isaiah Berlin [1909–1997], a figure already quite familiar to Chinese intellectuals, was moved neither by his profound reflection on "positive freedom" to reject the French Revolution nor through his explication of "negative freedom" to embrace Burkean conservatism. On the contrary, in his work *The Crooked Timber of Humanity* from 1990,[6] Berlin placed Burke in the ranks of the reactionaries, provoking a challenge from his friend, the Burke specialist Conor Cruise O'Brien. But on April 10, 1991, Berlin answered the challenge by stating unequivocally: "I cannot help but feel sympathy for the French Revolution, and to that extent some antipathy to the admirable Burke." And it was also no accident, Berlin notes, that many later reactionaries, such as Joseph de Maistre [1753–1821], cited Burke as their great master. Much of what Burke advocated was "deeply illiberal"—namely, his "respect for hierarchy; and for rule by a gentlemanly elite." Hence, Berlin asked: "Should one describe a man with such views as a liberal pluralist?"[7] On June 24 of the same year, he further explained that he stood on the side of the French Revolution, reasoning:

It does seem to me that it [the French Revolution] inspired people to attack prejudice, superstition, obscurantism, cruelty, oppression, hatred of democracy, and to struggle for various liberties. . . . In France the ideological divisions were always either for or against the French Revolution; and those against it were genuine reactionaries. . . . Hence, if I must line up, I line up with the Revolution—despite all the fallacies and the horrors.[8]

Berlin's confessional taking of sides after the Cold War was startling and revelatory. In terms of Chinese intellectual circles after 1989, I think it was purely coincidental that they should have simultaneously embarked on a critique of radicalism and utopianism and begun to question the French revolutionary tradition and Rousseau's thought. As necessary as it may have been then, in today's China we have to ask whether this soul-searching has not led toward yet another extreme: Has it not, on the one hand, moved from questioning the negative consequences of the French Revolution to totally disavowing the French Revolution and its momentous influence in modern China? On the other hand, in taking Burke's criticism of the French Revolution to be the true essence of "Anglo-American liberalism," does this stance not also imply that "respect for hierarchy and for rule by a gentlemanly elite" and similar "deeply illiberal" ideas are the sacrosanct, inalienable principles of "liberalism"?

In this respect, Berlin's criticism of Burke and his solemn warning that "all those who are against the French Revolution were genuine reactionaries" should be taken very seriously by Chinese intellectuals today. This is because his warning reminds us that the liberal critique of the French Revolution is not the same as the Burkean conservative critique; even less should it be tarred with the same brush as the wholesale repudiation of the French Revolution by the "reactionaries." Here, it must be mentioned that Berlin's position on the French Revolution comes from an oft-neglected special liberal tradition—namely, the French liberal tradition that Benjamin Constant [1767–1830] established after the French Revolution. It is not by chance that Berlin sees Constant and John Stuart Mill [1806–1873] as the "fathers of liberalism" because, in fact, Berlin's famous distinction between the two freedoms (negative freedom and positive freedom) originates from Constant's well-known thesis "The Liberty of the Ancients Compared with That of the Moderns" (1819). The most significant aspect of what can be called this "post-Revolutionary French liberalism" is that, on the one hand, its proponents summed up the historical lessons of the French Revolution, while, on the other, they themselves took responsibility to defend the basic principle of the revolution. Thus, while Burke stood with the ancien régime when he decried the "illegitimacy" of the revolution, French liberalism began first by affirming the revolution's "legitimacy" and on this basis proceeded to a critical examination of the revolution. It is therefore not surprising that Constant, after reading Burke's book *Reflections on the Revolution in France* (1790), noted bluntly that it "contained more absurdities than lines."[9]

The great historian of French liberalism François Guizot [1787–1874] introduced to Western historiography the concept of the "history of civilization" to
link "the past" with "the present." He emphasized that modernity as represented
by the French Revolution was not a total rupture from the past; rather, it was
the "legitimate inheritor" of civilizational progress. This liberal historiograph-
ical interpretation of "history" broke the conservatives' monopoly on explaining the "historical past." Guizot's father was guillotined during the French Revolution, forcing the seven-year-old son and his mother into exile overseas, yet
still he refuted the Burkean conservative critique of that revolution. He once
famously declared, in a line that is most representative of the French liberal
position on the revolution's "legitimacy," that despite the numerous errors and
crimes of the revolutionary period, it was still a "terrible but legitimate battle
of right against privilege, of legal liberty against despotism. . . . [T]o the Revolution alone belongs the task of regulating itself, of purging itself."[10]

In other words, only by first "standing on the side of the French Revolution"
can one truly critique and examine it. Guizot's student Tocqueville quickly took
this basic perspective and transformed it into the notion that "only by standing on the side of democracy" can you truly critique and examine democracy,
for, according to Tocqueville, the French Revolution was essentially a "democratic revolution," and thus the question of the French Revolution was, at its
core, a question of democracy.

Today's readers will not generally ask why at that time Tocqueville decided
to forego what was close at hand and to seek what was far away, going to America to investigate democracy rather than going to England to investigate liberalism. In fact, this question is not only crucial to understanding Tocqueville's
thought but also incredibly important to understanding liberalism's own development. According to Tocqueville, his decision to focus on America emerged
first from his belief that for postrevolutionary France and Europe the model
provided by England's so-called Glorious Revolution was not a useful example
to follow; in fact, it was just the opposite, for England's past revolution had
occurred in a predemocratic age, and as such its meaning was localized and
partial. The French Revolution, however, was global and universal, and so he
believed that the question going forward was not that of France imitating England, but rather that England sooner or later would have to follow the course
that France had taken. The only issue was whether England could avoid the terrible violence that had marked the French experience. After examining the
English reforms of the period, Tocqueville pointed out that the changes that
had occurred in the wake of the "Reform Bill" of 1832 were different than England's past revolution in that they were now already a part of Europe's democratic revolution and that in fact they were the continuation of the French Revolution in Britain: "The previous revolutions that the English have undergone

were essentially English in *substance* and *form*. The ideas that gave birth to them circulated only in England. . . . It is no longer so today: today it is the European revolution that is being continued among the English . . . Now, the English have indeed taken our [French] ideas. . . . They are European in substance, English in form."[11]

Here it should be pointed out that the concept of a so-called Anglo-American liberalism (I myself have used it in the past) is actually an extremely ambiguous and misleading term, for it greatly blurs the important differences that exist between England and America. In Tocqueville's age, America and England in fact represented two very different political choices. After the French Revolution, particularly after the fall of Napoleon in 1814 and the restoration of the Bourbon Monarchy through to Tocqueville's publishing of the first volume of *Democracy in America* in 1835, the intellectual atmosphere in France and in Europe resembled the intellectual world of contemporary China. It was full of comparisons of the English and French models and brimming with a desire to take England's Glorious Revolution of 1688 as a template. At the time, Burke's critique of the French Revolution had enormous influence over all of Europe, and it was seemingly very natural for people to use the English model as a means of thinking about the question of European reconstruction in the postrevolutionary period. If Tocqueville also saw the question in this way, then there would have been no need to go to America to investigate "democracy"; he would have gone to England to investigate liberalism.

Yet Tocqueville had early on begun to doubt this automatic tendency to glorify England, and in his important long work "Reflections on English History" [1828] he reached his own conclusions. The work offers a summary of English history from the Norman Conquest [1066] down to Tocqueville's age and was the product of considerable reflection. What is particularly meaningful is that Tocqueville provides a positive appraisal of England's Revolution of 1640, while his view of the so-called Glorious Revolution of 1688 is decidedly negative. He believes that the Revolution of 1640 was a victory for England's common people, which saw the establishment of a republic, whereas the Revolution of 1688 was a restoration of the feudal aristocracy, which rendered the Revolution of 1640 incomplete. Before he ends his work, Tocqueville stresses that he cannot see any benefit in the way that French people of his age hoped for their own Revolution of 1688, and he states that after summarizing England's history, he himself feels "prouder to be born on this side of the channel" (meaning France).[12] It is not strange, then, that two years later, when France's July Revolution broke out, and with many liberals in the country looking upon it as France's own Revolution of 1688, Tocqueville further affirmed his sentiment that "England could not be looked upon as a model" and left France for America.[13]

We should note that when Tocqueville returned from his travels in America but before he began formally writing *Democracy in America*, he decided that before he could begin writing, he had to go to England to investigate conditions there, to confirm his basic belief that even in England the system of aristocratic liberalism was no longer sustainable. The results of his investigations completely confirmed his premonition, that England itself was already in the whirlwind of democratic revolution: "If any fundamental change in the law, or any social transformation, or any substitution of one regulating principle for another is called a revolution, then England assuredly is in a state of revolution. For the aristocratic principle which was the vital one of the English constitution, is losing strength every day, and it is probable that in due time the democratic one will have taken its place."[14] After returning from this trip to England, Tocqueville hesitated no longer and threw himself wholeheartedly into writing *Democracy in America*.

What needs to be pointed out here is that it is not advisable to translate the famous title of Tocqueville's book as "American Democracy." Rather, it should only be translated as "Democracy in America," for just as Tocqueville himself emphasized, his book sought to express "a single thought," which was "the thought of the approaching irresistible and universal spread of democracy throughout the world."[15] In other words, Tocqueville's central question is above all the coming of the age of democracy, and he emphasized that the question of democracy is "universal and enduring." For this reason, he repeatedly emphasized that the question that his book raised "is of interest not to the United States only, but to the whole world; not to one nation, but to all mankind."[16] The reason why he became interested in the condition of democracy "in America" was that he believed that the precondition for the arrival of the "democratic age" in Europe was, without exception, the destruction of the aristocratic system and that this was a phase that the "democratic revolution" had to go through. Because America's history was short, it did not have an "aristocratic age," and as such the uniqueness of "democracy in America" was that it did not require the overthrow of an aristocratic order as its precondition. As such, it avoided democratic revolution of the European kind. Tocqueville believed that because democracy in Europe emerged only through revolution, many people had become accustomed to believing that there was a necessary relationship among democracy and chaos and revolution. Yet his investigations regarding America sought to tell us that the chaos that democracy brings is a temporary phenomenon belonging to a transitional period. It is not the essence of democracy, for the true relationship between democracy and revolution is surely that the more developed democracy is, the less chaos there will be, with revolution becoming less and less likely.

We know that Tocqueville entertained no notions of "democracy as a panacea"; on the contrary, he emphasized the inevitability of the approaching democratic era and the myriad complications it would produce. He anticipated how his analysis of democracy might be used both to defend and to criticize democracy, and he therefore set himself a two-fold objective: to remind democracy's defenders not to imagine democracy as infallible while convincing the detractors that democracy was not something to be feared. He hoped to "diminish the ardor of the former . . . and the terror of the latter . . . so that society could advance more peacefully toward the necessary fulfillment of its destiny."[17] Any more detailed discussion of Tocqueville's theory of democracy is beyond the scope of this essay, yet here one should at least note its most important premise: that the antithesis of democracy is *aristocracy*. All of Tocqueville's theory is in fact rooted in an analytical framework that takes democratic and aristocratic systems as opposites. Viewing democracy as something uniquely "modern," he asserted that neither the ancient Greek city-states nor the Roman Republic were democratic systems; rather, they were merely "aristocratic republics."

The greatest challenge of modernity is precisely that every person demands to be treated as an equal individual. The ancient Greeks and Romans could not accept this in theory, while the Christian Church of the Middle Ages could accept it *only* in theory as something unobtainable in "life on earth" and to be hoped for in the "afterlife." The reason that old-style European aristocratic liberalism could never adapt to the democratic era is that it was still rooted in an "unequal freedom"—that is, freedom as a privilege for the few rather than a right possessed by all. Tocqueville thus evoked the "equality of conditions" in his summary of modern democracy. That throughout his life Tocqueville saw Rousseau as one of his two most respected intellectual mentors (the other being Blaise Pascal [1623–1662]) and commented that he read a little of Rousseau every day is hardly surprising. His own exhaustive analysis of democracy as an "equality of conditions" in fact follows directly from Rousseau's critique of "inequality"; furthermore, this is especially true of the analysis of the basic characteristics of democracy in the second volume of *Democracy in America*, where even Tocqueville's writing style shows the influence of Rousseau's *Discourse on the Origin of Inequality* [1755].

Tocqueville's great contribution to democratic theory was that, unlike the earlier view of democracy as simply one form of the polity, he saw democracy as a process of profound, far-reaching change in all fields—from politics, law, and social structure through to thought, the emotions, psychology, cultural and intellectual activity. The second volume of *Democracy in America* is a detailed inquiry into democracy as an "equality of conditions" in relation to intellectual movements (in part 1), sentiments (part 2), mores (part 3), and the effect that democratization in all areas of society and culture has on politics (part 4). In Western intellectual circles, Tocqueville has received renewed attention in recent decades because he articulated the perpetually unfolding nature of democracy, something that has only become even more pronounced in the last half of this century. The so-called challenges of postmodernism, feminism, and so on are actually just increasingly intensified manifestations of what Tocqueville called the "democratization of culture"; they make the problem of "democracy" today even more complex.

Tocqueville's central concern is the constant tension between the mentality of modern humanity (what he calls "democratic man"), with his strong desire to pursue an "equality of conditions," and the "system" of democratic society. Yet he points out a paradox of modern democracy, which is that whereas "equal conditions" continuously permeate all other fields of society, democracy, by contrast, might never advance in the "political" field. On this point, Tocqueville famously concluded that people in the democratic age would cherish equality far more than they cherish freedom. The kind of "freedom" that Tocqueville insists on here is "positive freedom," or what Constant called "ancient liberty" (liberty of political participation).

I noted earlier in this essay that Berlin's theory of the two types of freedom was born out of Constant's differentiation between ancient and modern liberty; namely, Berlin's distinction between "negative freedom" and "positive freedom" is the same as Constant's "liberty of the moderns" (liberty in one's private life) and "liberty of the ancients" (liberty in political participation). Tocqueville's exposition on this theme can also be traced to the same origin as Constant's "two kinds of liberty" thesis. Constant had already noted that one of the greatest errors of the French Revolution was that the revolutionaries, taking their cue from Aristotle's idea that men are "political animals," understood liberty mainly as the "political liberty" of citizens participating in the public life of politics. They ignored the fact that the "liberty" sought by "modern man" mainly entails liberty in one's private life and the protection of individual rights. Constant therefore highlighted an inherent danger of the "liberty of the ancients," that public affairs and politics might infringe on people's private lives, yet he also emphasized that "the danger of modern liberty is that, absorbed in the enjoyment of our private independence, and in the pursuit of our particular interests, we should surrender our right to share in political power too easily." In other words, the twin danger of modern society is the "overpoliticization" of social life and its "overprivatization"; it is often the case that the former leads to the latter. For instance, "overpoliticization" during the French Revolution led to a widespread disdain for politics, which in turn gave way to an "overprivatization" culminating in Napoleon's rise to power. With this in mind, Constant stressed especially, first, that individual liberty is always safeguarded by political liberty and that if all citizens refrain from political participation and thus abandon effective restraints on public power, the final result will be the end of guarantees of individual liberty. Second, only when its citizens fully exercise their right to political participation will a people develop strength of character because "political liberty . . . enlarges people's spirits, ennobles their thoughts, and establishes among them a kind of intellectual equality which forms the glory and power of a people." Therefore, the relationship between the so-called two kinds of liberty—individual liberty and the liberty of political participation—is certainly not a mutually exclusive one; what is important is to "learn how to combine the two kinds of liberty."[18]

For Tocqueville, the threat that "overprivatization" in social life might lead to atrophy in political life posed an even greater problem. His declaration that the democratic age needed "a new political science" was made to address precisely this problem: that is, because people in the democratic age are naturally more concerned with "equality" in nonpolitical fields and are not concerned about politics, it takes a great deal of effort to prevent political dysfunction. Half a century later, Max Weber [1864–1920] highlighted exactly the same problem as Tocqueville, stressing in particular that an apolitical people are not qualified to participate in world politics. It would be fitting for me to end this essay with the concluding passage from Weber's "Suffrage and Democracy in Germany":

> "Democratization" in the sense that the structure of social estates is being levelled by the *state run by officials*, is a fact. There are only two choices: either the mass of citizens is left without freedom or rights in a bureaucratic, "authoritarian state" which has only the appearance of parliamentary rule, and in which the citizens are "administered" like a herd of cattle; or the citizens are integrated into the state by making them its *co-rulers*. . . . Democratization can certainly be obstructed—for the same moment—because powerful interests, prejudices and cowardice are allied in opposing it. But it would soon emerge that the price to be paid for this would be the entire future of Germany. All the energies of the masses would then be engaged in a struggle *against* a state in which they are mere objects and in which they have no share. Certain circles may have an interest in the inevitable political consequences. The Fatherland certainly does not.[19]

Translators' Notes

1. Gan Yang, "Ziyouzhuyi: Guizude haishi pingminde?" (Liberalism: For the aristocrats or for the people?), *Dushu* 1 (1999): 85–94.
2. Li Shitao, ed., *Zhishifenzi lichang, ziyouzhuyi zhi zheng yu Zhongguo sixiang jie de fenhua* (Intellectual positions, debates on liberalism, and the splintering of the Chinese intellectual world) (Changchun: Shidai Wenyi, 2000). An earlier version of the essay given here, published in the Hong Kong journal *Ershiyi Shiji* (Twenty-first century) in 1997, was translated by Xudong Zhang: see Gan Yang, "Debating Liberalism and Democracy in China," in *Whither China: Intellectual Politics in Contemporary China*, ed. Xudong Zhang (Durham, NC: Duke University Press, 2001), 79–101.

3. See Junpeng Li, "The Making of Liberal Intellectuals in Post-Tiananmen China," PhD diss., Columbia University, 2017, 90–95.

4. Frank Hyneman Knight, *The Ethics of Competition and Other Essays* (Chicago: University of Chicago Press, 1980), 52.

5. Alexis de Tocqueville, *Democracy in America*, trans. George Lawrence (New York: Harper and Row, 1966), 670.

6. Isaiah Berlin, *The Crooked Timber of Humanity* (London: John Murray, 1990).

7. Isaiah Berlin to Conor Cruise O'Brien, April 10, 1991, quoted in Conor Cruise O'Brien, *The Great Melody: A Thematic Biography of Edmund Burke* (Chicago: University of Chicago Press, 1992), 614.

8. Berlin to O'Brien, June 24, 1991, in O'Brien, *The Great Melody*, 613, 617–18.

9. Benjamin Constant, quoted in Stephen Holmes, *Benjamin Constant and the Making of Modern Liberalism* (New Haven, CT: Yale University Press, 1984), 210.

10. François Guizot, quoted in Stanley Mellon, *Political Uses of History* (Stanford, CA: Stanford University Press, 1958), 29.

11. Alexis de Tocqueville, *Selected Letters on Politics and Society*, ed. Roger Boesche (Berkeley: University of California Press, 1985), 106–7, emphasis in original.

12. Alexis de Tocqueville, *Journeys to England and Ireland*, trans. George Lawrence and K. P. Mayer, ed. J. P. Mayer (London: Faber and Faber, 1958), 39.

13. Seymour Drescher, *Tocqueville and England* (Cambridge, MA: Harvard University Press, 1964), 24.

14. Tocqueville, *Journeys to England and Ireland*, 66.

15. Tocqueville, *Democracy in America*, lxxxvii.

16. Tocqueville, *Democracy in America*, 286.

17. Tocqueville, *Selected Letters*, 99.

18. Benjamin Constant, *Benjamin Constant: Political Writings*, trans. Biancamaria Fontana (Cambridge: Cambridge University Press, 1988), 326–27.

19. Max Weber, "Suffrage and Democracy in Germany," in *Political Writings*, ed. Peter Lassman and Ronald Spiers (Cambridge: Cambridge University Press, 1994), 129, emphasis in original.

CHAPTER 11

REPRESENTATIVE DEMOCRACY AND REPRESENTATIONAL DEMOCRACY[1]

WANG SHAOGUANG

TRANSLATED BY MARK MCCONAGHY AND SHI ANSHU

Translators' Introduction

Wang Shaoguang (b. 1954) is emeritus professor of government and administration at the Chinese University of Hong Kong (CUHK) and a Schwarzman Scholar at Tsinghua University in Beijing. He earned his doctorate at Cornell and taught for several years in the United States before moving to the CUHK, where he spent most of his highly productive career. Wang is a prominent member of China's New Left, and his research agenda has from the outset been directly engaged with China's reform and opening, arguing for the development of "state capacity" and against the ravages of untrammeled free markets in dozens of well-researched, empirically based articles and books targeting concrete issues confronted by China's reform process.

More recently, as China has embraced its own "model" in which market forces interact in complex ways with state institutions, Wang's research focus has become more theoretical, moving away from specific challenges of the reform-and-opening era and toward a global defense of China's model of "democracy." Displaying his habitual energy, Wang has attacked his theme from multiple angles. His book *Minzhu sijiang* (Four lectures on democracy, 2008) traces the history of democratic thought and practices from ancient Greece and Rome down to the present day. In other volumes, such as *Zhongguo zhengdao* (China: The way of governing, 2014), he explores notions of traditional morality undergirding the practice of Chinese democracy (which he contrasts with the Western fixation on "political forms"). The text translated here, "Representative Democracy and Representational Democracy," tackles the same issue from a political science perspective.

Wang's criticism of "representative democracy" draws largely on Western scholars who highlight the shortcomings of Western (and particularly American) democratic practices: the role of money in elections and in the political process in general, the lack of accountability in representative democracy, and the fact that "representation" is in fact a modern betrayal of the original meaning of democracy as the people being masters of their own affairs. The argument that the system is more "electoral" than "democratic" and that the idea of "representation" is highly problematic would not necessarily sound out of place on American university campuses. What is perhaps new is Wang's robust defense of representational (i.e., Chinese) democracy. In past writings, he has called Chinese democracy "responsive"; the choice of "representational" presumably raises the stakes, suggesting that China's evolving one-party system should be thought of as genuinely representing and responding to the needs of the Chinese people, no matter how dissimilar such a system looks from Western models.

By "representational," Wang means that Chinese democracy, despite its lack of "democratic forms," manages to represent and respond to the wishes of the people in an effective manner. Representational democracy, in other words, is substantive democracy. He supports this claim with credible political science survey work that suggests that the Chinese people are more satisfied with this government than Americans are with theirs (the same data also seem to suggest that this phenomenon is true of many countries in Asia, allowing Wang to intimate that his findings concerning substantive democracy go beyond China).

Most of Wang's text, however, is devoted to explaining how and why Chinese democracy works. The key, according to Wang, is the notion of the "mass line," the idea that Chinese Communist Party and government cadres "go among the masses" to understand their needs and subsequently shape policies on the basis of their findings. Suspecting that some of his readers will be unconvinced by this claim, Wang goes to considerable effort to provide a compelling account of what may look like a conventional, even ossified, concept from the socialist past, tracing its textual history as well as the concrete forms that it is meant to take on: integration with the people, social surveys, involvement by leading cadres, and the like. To some extent, Wang appears to be reviving Maoism without Mao as he takes pains to describe the nuts and bolts of a political process that functions, in his telling, without the catalyst of Mao's charisma. At the same time, he argues that the mass line was largely abandoned in the first decades of reform and opening, to be revived by Hu Jintao (b. 1942) and especially by Xi Jinping (b. 1953), whom Wang depicts as being particularly devoted to the concept.

It is not clear whether Wang genuinely believes that the mass line has played a central role in China's rise or whether he hopes to convince China's leaders to cherish the mass line going forward as part of China's continued experiment in capitalist authoritarianism. In any event, his call to put Cold War clichés behind us and examine China's political order with fresh eyes is worthy of reflection.

Representative Democracy and Representational Democracy

Preface

Over the past twenty years, two worldviews have been in constant opposition. The first worldview is expressed in a popular saying often employed by the late British prime minister Margaret Thatcher [1925–2013]: "There is no alternative." According to statistics, Thatcher used this mantra in her speeches more than five hundred times, to the point that people gave her a nickname: "TINA." "There is no alternative" refers to the notion that aside from economic and political liberalism, the world has no other choices.

In the early summer of 1989, the American scholar Francis Fukuyama [b. 1952] raised Thatcher's "there is no alternative" to the level of historical philosophy, publishing an essay with the title "The End of History." In the essay, which had its moment of fame, Fukuyama proclaimed: "At the beginning of the twentieth century, the West was full of self-confidence in the ultimate triumph of liberal democracy, yet at its close seems to have returned to its point of departure: not to an 'end of ideology' or a convergence between capitalism and socialism, as earlier predicted, but to an unabashed victory of economic and political liberalism." Fukuyama boldly predicted "the end of history" because, in his eyes, humanity no longer struggled with "big questions" (such as the choice between capitalism and socialism); human society had already reached the end of its ideological evolution, and Western-style liberal democracy had irrefutably become the sole option for every country. Going forward, the only questions remaining were the technical details of how to implement Western-style liberal democracy. At the conclusion of his article, Fukuyama could hardly hide his sense of satisfaction as he deliberately expressed a victor's sense of loss over the fact that there was no one left to fight. According to him, the world after the end of history would be terribly boring: there would be no more art and philosophy, traces of them remaining only in museums.[2]

Today, even though Thatcher's "There is no alternative" and Fukuyama's "end of history" have already become standing jokes in academic and intellectual circles, their variants proliferate and circulate constantly. Though most people no longer use those particular expressions, many still firmly believe that the "today" of Western capitalist countries is the "tomorrow" of other countries (including China).

The second worldview is embodied in two different slogans used in the "rethinking globalization" movement: "one no, many yeses"[3] and "another world is possible."[4] What is rejected here is precisely the economic and political liberalism trumpeted by Thatcher and Fukuyama.

The opposition between these two worldviews is reflected first in their different perspectives on capitalism. After the financial crisis of 2008, the first worldview is already on the defensive. However, when it comes to the question of democracy, the first worldview seems to be as unyielding as before. Even though it is common for Western citizenries to lack faith in officials chosen through competitive elections, even though some Western thinkers have called for overcoming "electoral democracy"—advocating participatory democracy, consultative democracy, and sortition[5]—the majority of people still think that Western-style representative democracy is currently the only desirable and feasible democratic system and that differences between countries amount to different forms of representative democracies. Regardless of whether one employs a presidential or parliamentary system, power holders can emerge only out of competitive elections between different parties. This worldview is not only mainstream in Western countries but quite influential in other countries as well (including China).

This article's basic argument is that representative democracy is a gilded-cage democracy, which should not be nor can be the only form of democracy.[6] Conversely, though the *representational democracy* that China is practicing has many flaws, it has tremendous untapped potential, signifying that another form of democracy is possible.

Few will disagree with calling Western democracy "representative." However, if one calls China's political practice "representational democracy," many people in China and elsewhere will shake their heads. When those same people talk about China, they will without hesitation label China's political system authoritarian. The problem is that this label has, like snake oil, been applied indiscriminately in the past few decades. Not a single era has escaped this label, from the late Qing through the early Republic and the warlord period, then on to the reigns of Chiang Kai-shek, Mao Zedong, Deng Xiaoping, Jiang Zemin, Hu Jintao, and Xi Jinping. Chinese politics during this period has undergone earth-shattering transformations, and yet the label applied to Chinese politics has not changed at all. Is this not absurd? This is not academic analysis; it is an ideological smear. A simple label like *authoritarianism* explains nothing, and there is no way to distinguish [the current Chinese model] from other "authoritarian" regimes that have existed historically in China or abroad. As such, in the study of contemporary Chinese politics we see a wide range of variously qualified "authoritarianisms," including "dynamic authoritarianism," "adaptable authoritarianism," "participatory authoritarianism," "responsive authoritarianism," "highly legitimate authoritarianism," and the like, with no end in sight. These adjectives always sound as if they contradict the concept of "authoritarianism." If a political system is "dynamic," "adaptive," "participatory," "responsive," and "highly legitimate," would it not be more suitable to call it "democratic"?

This article defines China's political practice as "representational democracy" and will discuss the questions: What is representative democracy? What is representational democracy? How do they differ from one another? What are the characteristics as well as strengths and weaknesses of both? Yet before we discuss these questions, perhaps we should begin by addressing what appears to be a contradictory phenomenon.

A "Paradox"?

Mainstream Western ideology has a seemingly self-evident basic assumption: only leaders chosen through a system of competitive elections will enjoy legitimacy,[7] and authoritarian systems cannot possibly win the widespread support of the people. But a significant amount of empirical survey data indicates that the "authoritarian" Chinese system has continually received the support of an overwhelming majority of common people.

In recent years, the world's largest independent public-relations firm, Edelman International Public Relations Co., Ltd., has published the annual Edelman Trust Barometer, the latest of which was released in early 2013.[8] The report found that the Chinese public's trust in the government rose six percentage points in 2012, reaching 81 percent, ranking second only to Singapore and thus second among all surveyed countries. This is much higher than the 53 percent of public trust in the government in the United States. Taking an average from all the countries surveyed, public trust in government is a mere 48 percent.[9] As a matter of fact, over the years of the Edelman Survey, Chinese public trust in government has been among the highest worldwide.

The Edelman survey is not the only one to report this finding. Over the past two decades, regardless of who was conducting surveys (including foreigners who were skeptical of their predecessors' surveys), the manner of investigation (including the most rigorous random-sample surveys) or whether the survey was of rural or urban residents, the result was essentially the same: that the Chinese people have a high degree of trust in their government.[10] At present, scholars familiar with the survey data accept them without question. For instance, John James Kennedy concludes in an article in 2009 that "since the early 1990s, all surveys that examined public opinion about the Chinese Communist Party have shown that more than 70 percent of respondents support the central government and Party leadership. Regardless of changes in how various surveys asked the questions, the results were the same."[11] An article by Heike Holbig and Bruce Gilley in 2010 further claims that "while there are different views on the reasons for the stability of the Chinese Communist regime, there is broad consensus that the present regime enjoys relatively strong popular support."[12] All studies after 2010 have come to conclusions identical to that of these two scholars.[13]

We can draw two conclusions from this: either (1) an "authoritarian" system is much more popular with the people than are many "democratic" systems, or (2) a system that is highly supported by the people is nonetheless labeled "authoritarian." Together, these conclusions appear to be contradictory.

Those reluctant to abandon the label *authoritarian* have thought up a whole variety of excuses to resolve such contradictions. In their view, the government during the Maoist period enjoyed a high level of support from the people because of pressure tactics and ideological indoctrination; people supported the government after reform and opening because of the sustained growth of the economy and the drumbeat of Chinese nationalism.[14] In short, the Chinese people's strong support for the government is not because the system is good, but rather because of the temporary presence of favorable conditions. Their subtext is that no matter how much the Chinese masses support the present government, an authoritarian system cannot long endure.

Rigorous studies have shown, however, that these seemingly reasonable excuses are unfounded. After analyzing the data of the Asian Barometer Survey, Chu Yun-han, professor of political science at National Taiwan University, concluded that "the persuasiveness of these explanations is not as strong as many China experts in the West believe. There is no solid evidence which indicates that the Chinese government's public trust is highly dependent on its dazzling economic performance or relies on its manipulation of nationalist sentiment."[15] Similarly, the U.S.-based scholar Tang Wenfang and his American collaborators based their study on a systematic analysis of data, which refuted the same excuses as untenable.[16]

The resolution of such contradictions is, in fact, very simple. Scholars simply need to remove their "authoritarian"-tinted glasses. The reasons for such enthusiastic support of the Chinese system is obvious, as it is reflected in the three areas of demand, supply, and results: (1) demand—the Chinese people in general prefer representational (substantive) democracy to representative (formal) democracy; (2) supply—China has developed a set of representational democracy theories and modes of operation; and (3) results—the practice of representational democracy allows China's Party-state system to respond relatively effectively to social needs. In essence, the reason why the Chinese people are highly receptive to the existing system of government is that China has

Table 11.1 How Various Peoples Across Asia Understand Democracy

	Average	China 2008	Chinese Taiwan 2006	Singapore 2006	Mongolia 2006	Indonesia 2006	Philippines 2005	Cambodia 2008	Vietnam 2005	Thailand 2006
Formalistic Dimensions										
Opportunity to change the government through elections	31.9%	28.4%	28.2%	29.5%	20.5%	30.2%	31.0%	39.0%	42.6%	49.0%
Freedom to criticize those in power	13.4%	4.2%	4.5%	22.7%	32.1%	24.6%	19.6%	12.6%	6.6%	17.4%
Substantive Dimensions										
A small income gap between rich and poor	20.2%	28.9%	20.1%	19.8%	20.8%	12.3%	7.4%	4.0%	28.5%	18.0%
Basic necessities such as food, clothes, and shelter, etc., for everyone	34.5%	38.4%	47.3%	28.0%	26.5%	32.9%	42.1%	44.4%	22.4%	15.5%
Total	13,459 (100%)	4,070 (100%)	1,506 (100%)	954 (100%)	1,165 (100%)	1,417 (100%)	1,146 (100%)	941 (100%)	1,050 (100%)	1,209 (100%)

Source: Asian Barometer Study, 2013, http://www.eastasiabarometer.org/chinese/news.html.

practiced a new type of democracy that conforms to the aspirations of its own people—representational democracy.

How Chinese People Regard Democracy

The original meaning of democracy is that the people are the masters of their own affairs. Yet if one asked people from different cultures what "the people as masters" means and how to implement it, their understandings would diverge. In today's world, the overwhelming majority of people agree with the notion that "democracy is a good thing," but understanding what is "good" and what is "democratic" are very different. We must not take for granted that since we all like democracy, we must all be supporting the same thing. Many people in the West arrogantly believe that only their understanding of democracy is authentic and that there is only one correct understanding of democracy: this is a form of cultural hegemony. Empirical studies show that the concept of democracy in East Asia has unique features,[17] that the concept of democracy within the Confucian cultural sphere has its unique features,[18] and that the same is true for the concept of democracy in China.[19] If one does not look for the kind of democracy that the Chinese themselves understand but instead strenuously schemes to replicate in China the kind of democracy that Westerners understand, one cannot be called a "democrat" in any sense, because one is betraying the will of the people, which is contrary to the first law of democracy—that the people are the masters.

We can understand democracy in two ways, as formal democracy and as substantive democracy. The former concerns itself with so-called democratic features, whereas the latter concerns whether policy has produced results that meet the needs of the broad popular masses. Considering this, to which category does the Chinese people's understanding of democracy belong? The Asian Barometer Survey contains questions that precisely touch upon these two different kinds of understanding. When asked about the meaning of democracy, the respondents had four options: (1) that it was possible to change the government through elections; (2) that the freedom existed to critique those in power; (3) that the income gap between the wealthy and the poor was not large; and (4) that everyone enjoyed basic necessities such as food and clothing.

Table 11.1 compares the situation of nine countries or regions. What we see is that there are indeed close to 30 percent of mainland Chinese who feel that democracy above all means giving people the right to choose their political officials; there are 4.2 percent of people who understand democracy to mean freedom (for example, the freedom to critique those in power). If you add these together, those who chose these two kinds of formal standards [for what democracy is] come to roughly one-third of the people. More people were inclined to judge whether a political system was democratic or not by examining the results of governance. [According to table 11.1,] 28.9 percent of people took the ability to control disparities between the rich and the poor as the measure of democracy; close to one-fourth of the people believed that only a system that could guarantee that all people had the basic items required for survival—such as food, clothing, and housing—could be called democratic. More than two-thirds of people chose a substantive standard [for measuring democracy]. We can see that for the vast majority of Chinese people, "democracy" means substantive democracy rather than something that is a democracy in name only. What is interesting is that even though Chinese Taiwan has a different political system, the way Taiwanese people understand democracy is not terribly different from the way people on the mainland do.[20] In other nations in East Asia, more people prefer formal [i.e., Western-style representative] democracy, roughly 50 percent, with Thailand being the only country in which that number exceeds two-thirds of the population.

Perhaps some will suspect that those interviewed in table 11.1 were composed of a relatively large number of middle-aged people; for such doubters, it is young people who will perhaps be more inclined to accept "universal" democratic values—that is, formal democracy or procedural democracy. If this hypothesis is correct, then as time moves on, China will have more and more people who emulate "universal" democratic standards. What is the actual situation?

According to the data found in the most recent iteration (the third wave) of the Asian Barometer Survey, figure 11.1 displays democracy as it is understood by young people (born after 1980).[21] In mainland China, 30 percent of young people understand democracy as "good governance," while another 30 percent understand it as "social equality." Added together, they represent 60 percent of those surveyed. On the other hand, those who understand democracy as "procedural democracy" or "freedom" only accounted for 40 percent. In Chinese Taiwan the situation is about the same as in the mainland. Further analysis reveals that understandings of democracy among young people in China are not dissimilar to those held by adults.[22] Aside from the mainland and Taiwan, countries in which a majority of young people understand democracy in substantive terms include Japan, Korea, Singapore, Viet Nam, Thailand, Malaysia, and Indonesia; only Mongolia, the Philippines, and Cambodia are exceptions. Yet even in those three countries half of all people still understand democracy in substantive terms, on par with those who take a formal understanding of democracy.

In comparison with just their Asian neighbors, the Chinese people's substantive understanding of democracy is not exceptional. However, when that understanding is compared with Americans', its distinctiveness stands out. The data from table 11.2 come from polls conducted in America in 2010 as well as in China in 2011. They encompass two different groups given four choices, testing whether people understand democracy in a formal (Group A) or a

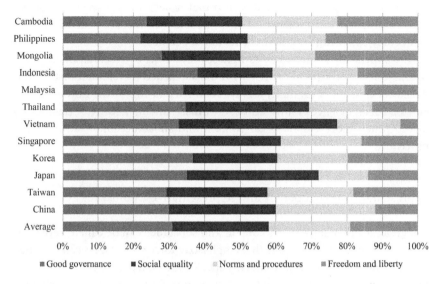

Figure 11.1 How Do Chinese Youth View Democracy?

Source: Asian Barometer Wave 3. From Yun-han Chu and Min-hua Huang, "East Asian Youth's Understanding of Democracy," paper presented at the conference "Democratic Citizenship and Voices of Asia's Youth," organized by the Institute of Political Science, Academia Sinica, and cosponsored by Asian Barometer Survey, National Taiwan University, September 20–21, 2012, Taipei, 5.

Table 11.2 Comparing Chinese and Americans' Understanding of Democracy

	Chinese	Americans
A. Regular and fair competitive elections are held to select government officials	53.57%	73.58%
B. How one gains the right to govern is not important; what matters is that the government takes the interests of the people as its priority and is competent	34.00%	26.17%
A. Ensure that two or more parties compete for the right to govern	15.36%	39.75%
B. The ruling party seriously considers ordinary people's opinions and suggestions	68.03%	58.89%

Source: Asian Barometer Study III, Mainland China Survey, 2013, (N = 3,419); USA National Survey, 2010, N = 810, cited in Jie Lu, *Democratic Conceptions and Regime Support Among Chinese Citizens*," Asian Barometer Working Paper no. 66 (n.p.: n.p., 2012), 72, http://www.asianbarometer.org/publications/abs -working-paper-series.

substantive manner (Group B). It is clear that Americans put greater emphasis on formal democracy, whereas Chinese people give more weight to whether democracy can bring tangible benefits to the people.

The conclusions reached by sample surveys done by research institutions within China correspond exactly with those reached by research institutions outside of China. For example, surveys conducted in 2011 by the Chinese Academy of Social Sciences found that the Chinese understanding of democracy placed much more emphasis on content and substance than on form and procedure.[23]

Representational Democracy and Representative Democracy

A democracy that emphasizes content and substance can be called "representational democracy," while one that emphasizes form and process can be called "representative democracy." Generally speaking, Asian peoples, including Chinese, prefer the former to the latter. Although their names differ only slightly, these two different kinds of democracy are in fact separated by a great gulf. Table 11.3 outlines the difference that exists between the two in three important dimensions.

For representative democracy, the most important concept is *daiyishi*. This term was one way of translating the English term *representative* into Chinese, popular during the late Qing and early Republican periods. Today this English term is often translated as *daibiao*.[24] Regardless of how it is translated, "representative" signifies a person selected by voters, who can be a legislator or the leader of the executive branch (for example, the American president). Yet calling these people "representatives" is often inaccurate, for in both the democratic theory and practice of many countries in Europe and America, people selected [for office] do not speak for the voters and are indeed not the representatives of the people.[25] It is precisely the opposite, in that once these people are elected, they can operate according to their own subjective judgment, for it has been claimed that "the voters are not angels; they do not necessarily have a healthy and rational judgment regarding public affairs. They often make mistakes, to the point of being led astray," and as such they require elites with "the capacity for political judgment" to keep them in line.[26] In other words, elections are merely a means by which common people grant power to political elites. The elected elites do not need to genuinely represent the people, for they only have to administer the affairs of the state in their place, thus replacing the people as "masters." Those who promote such a system state very clearly: these elected people "are absolutely not the representatives of the people; what democratic countries need is not representatives of the people but rather legislators elected by citizens!"[27]

Table 11.3 Representational Democracy and Representative Democracy:
Differing Points of Emphasis

Representational Democracy	Representative Democracy
Is the government representative?	How are political representatives produced?
Do policies reflect the basic needs of the people?	Are elections competitive?
Does the political system produce such substantive effects as social justice, good governance, welfare, and a high quality of life for the people?	Is the political system defined by such characteristics as civil rights, freedom, and formal systems and procedures?

If it does not allow the masses of the people to truly act as masters of the state but allows only a small group of elected elites (politely calling them "representatives") to serve as masters in their stead, then what exactly is "democratic" about the system? The way to defend representative democracy is to redefine the term: to call the kind of democracy that demands the people serve as masters "classical democracy" or "utopian democracy," but to define modern democracy as "representative democracy," a political system in which representatives are chosen through free elections.[28] Following this redefinition, the standard for measuring whether a political system is democratic or not changes as well: a political system in which there are free, competitive, multiparty elections is democratic; a political system in which there are not free, competitive multiparty elections is not.[29]

Why are governments created by free elections democratic? Two different theories are offered in support of this contention. One emphasizes the role of elections in granting authority (authorization theory); it deals with how politicians begin their political careers. The other emphasizes the role of elections in punishing elected officials (accountability theory); it deals with how politicians end their political careers.

According to authorization theory, during elections each political party puts forth its policy positions and promotes its candidates, while the people have the right to choose to support whichever party or candidate they want, and they will vote for the party and candidates of their choice. This system is of course democratic insofar as those who are elected start governing only after they have been invested with the authority of the people.

Yet authority theory is in fact grounded in three unstated but indispensable assumptions: first, that voters are rational and that they have a clear and comprehensive understanding of the various policy positions of the competing parties and candidates as well of the preconditions necessary to implement those policies and their possible consequences; second, that politicians will scrupulously abide by their promises and that when they take power, they will implement to the letter the policies that they promoted during the campaign; third, that implementation of the policies promoted during the campaign is in the voters' best interests. To actually realize any one of these three preconditions is incredibly difficult, and to realize all three at the same time is almost impossible. A large number of empirical studies have shown that voters are not necessarily rational and that in fact they are often politically ignorant.[30] In many circumstances, politicians are not willing, able, or inclined to act according to the platform presented during the campaign. Indeed, if policy were implemented according to the capricious nature of electoral language, in which candidates speak out of both sides of their mouths, it would not likely benefit voters.[31] What is even worse, modern elections are geared toward the rich, and parties and candidates must raise an inordinate amount of money to cover election expenses, without which they simply cannot run for office. What this means is that, for electoral parties and candidates, the most important people are not average voters but rather wealthy donors. Given that without wealthy donors there is no way to gain power, it is in fact these donors who truly "grant power."

Accountability theory is also premised on a series of hypotheses: first, that politicians will not necessarily honor their promises, and, second, that even if they do honor their promises, those promises will not necessarily benefit voters. Accountability theory further hypothesizes that in the case of the previously mentioned circumstances emerging, voters will certainly be displeased, and these unhappy voters will force these politicians out of power at the next election, choosing another group to replace them. This is what is called "demanding accountability," and its basis lies in voters' ability to force politicians out of power. If representatives want to stay in power over the course of multiple terms, if they do not want to give up power, then they must govern carefully while in power so as to win the voters' favor.

The problem is that all modern political systems are incredibly complex, and any given policy—from its inception, drafting, approval, and promulgation through to its implementation—will involve many different political parties, factions, departments, and officials. In addition, the positive and negative effects of the policy will be determined by internal and external factors. If voters are unhappy with the effects of a policy, they do not necessarily know whom they should punish. Politicians will of course find a variety of excuses and rationales in order to shirk responsibility, directing the voters' unhappiness toward other people and places.

Another problem is that accountability theory assumes that voters have the choice of many parties and politicians. If you are unhappy with A, then you can choose B; if you are unhappy with B, you can choose C. In reality, within a two-party system there are only two choices available. Even in a multiparty system, there is still a limited number of choices. In a situation in which alternatives are limited, voters are often faced with picking their poison.

Moreover, while politicians surely hope to win multiple terms, losing is hardly a disaster. In fact, after they leave the political arena, their profits will often be even greater. For example, in recent years in America fully half of the congressional representatives who lost their seats have joined lobbying groups, with much larger salaries than [they had] when they were in office.[32] Take, for example, Bill and Hillary Clinton, one a former president, the other a former secretary of state. Since they have left office, their annual speaking fees have been enormous.[33] In other words, those who leave the political world after serving for several years will have the possibility of gaining a highly lucrative future return on their investment. In this light, it seems to me that the latent threat of "demanding accountability" is nothing but a "paper tiger" to a clever politician.

All of this means that neither "authority theory" nor "accountability theory" can explain how so-called representative democracy is in fact democratic. Three authoritative scholars of representative democracy argue regarding this question that "the expectation of the founders of representative government was that the system they championed would through a variety of measures lead government to serve the interests of the people, but they did not precisely understand how it would work. More than two hundred years later, we still don't know."[34]

In contrast to representative democracy, the key concept of representational democracy is not "representative" (*daiyishi*) but "representation" (*daibiao*). According to the classic work *The Idea of Representation* by Hanna Pitkin [b. 1931], "representation" can be defined as that mode of operation that will realize the greatest benefit for the public; whether the subject representing the people is chosen through free and competitive elections is another question.[35] The basic assumption of representational democracy is that democracy can be realized through a variety of different representational mechanisms, and it is not the case that it must absolutely be the result of elections. As such, the standard for measuring whether a political system is democratic is no longer the existence of free and competitive multiparty elections. As Robert A. Dahl [1915–2014], the great theorist of democracy has said, "A crucial characteristic of democracy is that the government continues to be responsive to the preferences of its citizens, and that all citizens are completely equal politically."[36] Here, what is important is not the extent to which the representatives speak for the voters (representativeness) but rather the government's responsiveness to the people's preferences. Dahl's statement in fact established a standard by which to judge whether a political system is democratic: a standard of representational democracy. What must be further clarified are the "preferences" that Dahl speaks of. To my mind, the "preferences" referred to here are not the subjective wants of the people. No government, no matter when or where, can or should meet the boundless desires of the people. "Preferences" instead primarily refers to the people's objective needs and their opinions and suggestions having to do with those needs.

To distinguish between "authorization" and "accountability," we can call the theory we have just developed "representation."

China's Theory of Representational Democracy

In the past few decades, China has in fact already developed a theory of representational democracy. It is made up of four major parts, which can be divided by the answers to four key questions: Who is represented? By whom? What is represented? How is it represented?

Who Is Represented?

The answer given by Chinese representational democracy is: the people. All Chinese people are familiar with Mao Zedong's famous saying "serve the people"; this is the mission of the Chinese Communist Party (CCP); it is engraved on the East Gate as well as the Xinhua Gate of Zhongnanhai [CCP headquarters]. To "serve the people" does not mean that the people passively accept service. In fact, its true meaning is to build a better world through collective effort, together with the people.

So who are the "people"? In all nations, the internal connotations and broader implications surrounding the concept of "the people" (or "the citizenry") is always changing. On the eve of the founding of the People's Republic of China (PRC), Mao Zedong explained what he meant by "the people": "The masses of the people include the working class, the peasant class, the urban petit-bourgeoisie, and the national bourgeoisie who have been oppressed and harmed by imperialism and the reactionary regime of the Guomindang (which represents the bureaucratic-capitalist class as well as the landlord class), with workers, peasants (soldiers are mainly peasants wearing army uniforms), and other laboring people forming its primary subject."[37] Mao Zedong consistently understood "the people" as a political category that was historical and dynamic rather than as a general reference to the entire population of a given country. The one thing that did not change was that the subject of the people as he understood it from beginning to end was the great laboring masses who engaged in material production. Even if the internal connotations and broader implications of the concept of "the people" once again went through tremendous changes after reform and opening, its primary subject remained the great laboring masses, while at the same time bringing in all those patriots who upheld socialism and the unity of the motherland. The greatest historical contribution of the Chinese Revolution and the new China was to enable hundreds of millions to stride onto the political stage for the first time in history.

Emphasizing that the people are the object of representation is in sharp contrast to liberalism. The vocabulary of liberalism simply does not possess collective concepts such as "class" and "social groups," to say nothing of the concept of "the people." For liberals, only the individual in pursuit of his own private interests deserves to be represented.

Represented by Whom?

In mainstream Western theory regarding representation, it is only elected representatives (known as "political officials") who have the authority to represent others and make decisions on their behalf. But in the modern period, regardless of which political system we examine, there exist many unelected officials (known as "public servants") who truly do exercise political power. To say that they do not have the authority to represent others is in fact to negate the pressure on them to serve the people with all their hearts, as if everything will be fine if they follow standard procedure and go through the motions.

As for the question of who represents, the answer provided by representational democracy is: all those who exercise political power, including those representatives chosen through formal elections as well as other public servants who also possess genuine power. China calls all those who exercise some kind of power "cadres." Each and every cadre has a responsibility to represent the people's interests.

There is no doubt that cadres belong to the "vanguard" of which Lenin spoke, but this does not mean that they can act in an "elitist" manner, conducting their work in "elitist" ways. It is in fact just the opposite: those who have a responsibility to represent the people's interests must through various means become one with the great masses of the people and through this process unwaveringly remold themselves, for "it is the people, and only the people, that compose the force that can change world history";[38] for the "the masses are true heroes," while cadres at all levels "are often laughable in their naivety";[39] for "the masses have boundless creative power."[40]

This is to say that cadres at every level must "study amid practice and practice amid study." They cannot "see themselves as masters of the masses, as if they were aristocrats residing high above the commoners."[41] They "absolutely cannot pretend to know something when they don't, they must 'not be ashamed to ask those beneath them,' and they must excel at listening to cadres beneath them. They must first act as a student, then act as a teacher; they must first seek counsel from lower cadres and only then give orders."[42] This is in contrast with the role of the representative as imagined by "authority theory" and "accountability theory," which is that of a political elite above other people.

What Is Represented?

In Western-style representative systems, there are mechanisms for expression that enable people to express their desires (or preferences) and thereby produce a form of pressure on representatives in the hopes that they can thereby influence government policy. "Desire" is a relatively vague concept, which includes both the subjective wants and objective needs of the people. With a little bit of class analysis, we will see that the middle and upper classes of a society, those who have already solved basic questions of food and clothing, often express subjective demands (for example, reduced taxes, same-sex marriage, freedom of expression), whereas the lower classes of a society, those still struggling with poverty, often express objective needs (social safeguards, such as employment, medical care, education, and housing). In fact, the objective needs expressed by the lower classes are also the objective needs of the upper classes because the latter cannot do without clothing, food, housing, employment, medical care, and old-age care. It is only because they have money left over after seeing to the basics that the truth regarding these objective needs is hidden. We can thus see that the needs of society's lower classes are the needs of the entire society, while the demands from society's upper classes are not necessarily the demands of the entire society. There is one more difference between needs and desires: the former remain relatively stable over time, but the latter can change rapidly, even in a short period.

To enable the people to act as their own masters and to serve the interests of the greatest number of people, what representational democracy seeks to represent are the people's objective needs and not capriciously expressed demands or fashionable viewpoints.

Of course, objective needs are not set in stone. When the level of economic development is relatively low, the crucial needs are food and clothing. Once a society has reached a relatively high level of development, however, the importance of these survival needs diminishes, and other needs rise in importance: one wants to eat a little better, to wear clothes that are a little more attractive, to have more convenient transportation, to live in a more spacious and comfortable dwelling. When we're sick, we want medical care; when we get old, we want elder care; and the like. Representing the basic needs of the people must keep up with the times. This entails demanding that cadres at every level listen to the demands expressed by every level of society, even as they immerse themselves unceasingly in the lowest reaches of society, so as to understand the changing needs found there. In this sense, representation must be a dynamic process of construction.

How to Represent?

People often understand the mass line as the form of democratic decision making inherent in the Communist tradition, yet the mass line is also a method of representation imbued with the most Chinese of characteristics. In Chinese history, it was precisely the CCP that took the mass line as its own "basic political and organizational line" (see Liu Shaoqi's report on amending the Party's constitution presented at the Seventh Party Congress). It was the CCP that brought hundreds of millions of common people onto the political stage for the first time, and it was the [political] awakening of these hundreds of millions of people that was the precondition for the realization of democracy.[43] From this perspective, the American scholar Brantly Womack's assertion that the Chinese political system, with the mass line as a defining characteristic, is a "quasi-democratic system" makes sense.[44] The mass line is the core of Chinese representational democracy.

Several generations of CCP leaders have had much to say about the mass line. Mao's summary of the concept is most representative:

> In every aspect of my Party's practical work, if leadership is to be correct, it must come from the masses and go to the masses. This is to say, we must gather up the views of the masses (disparate and unsystematic views) and, through study, turn them into collective and systematic views, and then we must go back to the masses to disseminate and explain them, turning them into the masses' own views, enabling the masses to persevere and to see [these views] implemented in practice. From the practice of the masses, we must conduct examinations to determine whether these views are correct. We then must once again gather up the views of the masses and once again go back to the masses and persevere. This endless cycle will each time be more correct than the last, richer and more vivid than the last. This is the epistemology of Marxism.[45]

In representative democracies, the relationship between representatives and the people becomes closer during elections. Yet once representatives are elected and have the legitimacy to wield political power, they in fact come to possess free discretionary power; they can represent the people who elected them according to their own wishes. If during their terms in office representatives interact with the people, it is mainly with electioneering in mind, and their goal is to win favor in the eyes of the people so that they will win the next election. As such, they will do things that help secure and enlarge their electoral base and have no interest in doing things that do not, regardless of whether these latter things are beneficial for the people. For representatives, the object of their courtship are those people who participate in elections, the people with whom it is necessary to interact; and as for those people who do not participate in elections, they can ignore them altogether. And, indeed, those who do not participate in elections are often those at the bottom of society.

The mass line is different, for it demands that cadres at every level "love the great masses of the people and carefully listen to the voices of the masses; when one arrives at any region, one most become one with that region's masses, not placing oneself above the masses, but going deeply into [the life] of the masses."[46] "Go among the masses, learn from the masses, synthesize their experience and produce better and more orderly methods and principles, then go and tell the masses (to carry out propaganda), urging the masses to carry out such methods in order to solve their own problems, enabling them to gain liberation and happiness."[47] The "masses" spoken of here are "the great masses of the people," the same as "the people"; and "the people" refers primarily to peasants, workers, soldiers, and other laboring people.[48]

In order to address the shortcomings of representative democracy, some progressive scholars in the West have championed the concept of participatory democracy with the hope of producing more opportunities and channels by which common people can influence government policy.[49] Even when compared with the relatively more democratic notion of participatory democracy, the mass line still maintains its distinct characteristics.[50]

Figure 11.2 compares the concepts of the mass line and civic participation. It presents civic participation and the mass line in their ideal conditions. The first difference between the two is seen in the direction of the arrows on the figure. The arrow of civic participation moves from interest groups toward policy makers, meaning that interest groups have the right to wade forcefully into and deeply affect the process by which government makes decisions; yet this also means that policy makers do not have to step outside of their official chambers (see figure 11.2a). The arrow of the mass line moves from policy makers toward interest groups, meaning that within the process of government decision making, policy makers must let their guard down and work to engage deeply with various interest groups. This is a responsibility that policy makers are not allowed to shirk (see figure 11.2b).

The second difference between the mass line and civic participation regards the question of whether they include class analysis. The concept of civic participation often tacitly includes a pluralist assumption, imagining all interest groups as being evenly matched in strength, believing that they all can participate equally in the policy-making process and that in the end they will reach a kind of political balance (figure 11.2a). The mass line makes a distinction between the powerful who possess various kinds of resources and the weak who lack resources. The mass line in its ideal state of implementation entails policy makers engaging more with those weaker interest groups, listening more

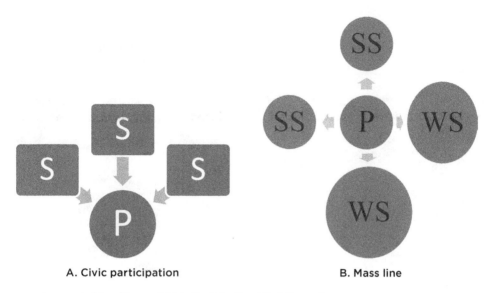

A. Civic participation   B. Mass line

Figure 11.2 Mass Line and Civic Participation: Ideal Operations

Note: P: policy maker; S: interest groups; SS: strong interest groups; WS: weak interest groups

thoroughly to their voices, for their interests require more thorough attention and their ability to actively influence policy makers is weaker. What this means is that the mass line is not neutral, but rather a process that favors common laboring people (figure 11.2b).

Civic participation and the mass line as they are actually implemented are perhaps quite different from their idealized forms. In civic participation, different social strata differ greatly in terms of their ability to participate in the policy-making process. Some classes have advantages in terms of money, knowledge, and social connections, and their desire to participate in politics can be strong, as is their ability to influence policy making; other classes spend their days simply getting by because they have no time or ability to exert influence on government policy (figure 11.3a). The inequality that exists among various classes' abilities to participate means that the lustrous halo surrounding the concept of "civic participation" can silently flicker out, with the necessary result being that [such a system] is more apt at expressing "wants" rather than "needs."[51]

In implementing the mass line there are relatively exacting demands placed on cadres at every level; they cannot simply sit and wait for the common people to come through their office doors but must actively engage with the broad masses of the people. If cadres have a weak sense of mass consciousness, if their mass consciousness has become dissipated, then I'm afraid that even if they get out of their offices to go among the people, they will "be suspicious of the poor and love the rich." They will suck up to powerful social groups, frequent

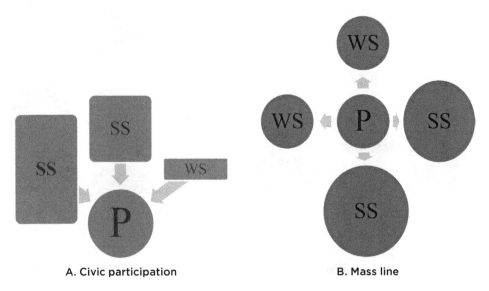

A. Civic participation   B. Mass line

Figure 11.3 Mass Line and Civic Participation: Actual Operations

ribbon-cutting events run by merchants, eat and drink lavishly with captains of industry. In short, they will be pulled this way and that and will wind up accepting bribes as they turn influence peddling into a bargaining chip. At this point, engaging with powerless social groups becomes a perfunctory task, a sham (figure 11.3b). This is the Achilles heel of the mass line, for it has an overreliance on the level of the cadres' enlightenment. Along with the mass line, there must be a comprehensive mechanism that forces cadres at every level to engage with the common masses at the base of society. One way to do this may after all be to forcefully promote the mass line, systematizing the means for carrying it out, speaking of the mass line every year, month, and day, ensuring that it is discussed and understood in every household, that it enters deeply into people's hearts, becoming an intense expectation of—as well as a firm demand on—cadres at every level.

Another method for forcing cadres to carry out the mass line exactingly would be to combine it together with civic participation. Though each of these has its own distinct characteristics, they are not mutually contradictory or exclusive. The relative strength of civic participation is that it is helpful for expressing the will of the people and for exerting pressure on policy makers; the relative strength of the mass line is that it is helpful for developing a sense of mass consciousness in cadres, to understand the feelings of the people, and to absorb the wisdom of the people. Not only are the two not in opposition, but they also in fact can be completely integrated, making an excellent combination that complements each other's strengths (figure 11.4). For example, the

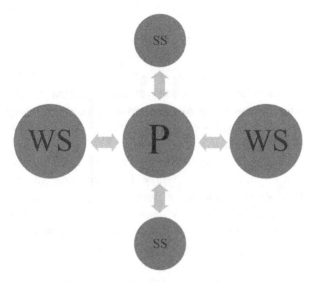

Figure 11.4 The Combination of the Mass Line and Civic Participation (The Practice of Chinese Representational Democracy)

government can on the one hand push cadres to carry out the mass line while on the other hand empower the masses politically, helping them to organize and to grasp the will and the ability to participate. If the government does this, the laboring masses can have a relatively large influence on policy makers as they express their needs, while at the same time the expression of reasonable demands by other social groups will not be ignored.

The mass line is not only the theoretical cornerstone of Chinese representational democracy but also the primary means of implementing it.

In his political report to the Seventh Party Congress, Mao Zedong pointed out that the mass line was one of the clear marks by which the Communist Party distinguished itself from other political parties. Whether during the revolutionary wartime period or during the period of socialist construction, the first generation of Party political leadership placed tremendous emphasis on the thorough implementation of the mass line. Mao Zedong was exemplary in this respect. Using Deng Xiaoping's words, we can say: "Comrade Mao was indeed great, was indeed different from us, for he excelled at discovering problems from within mass discussions and at presenting guidelines and policies to solve them."[52] At the beginning of reform and opening, the second generation of Party central political leadership continued to place important emphasis on the mass line. Deng Xiaoping once said: "The most basic work methods promoted by Comrade Mao are the mass line and seeking truth from facts. . . . As regards the current state of our Party, the mass line and seeking truth from facts are extremely important."[53]

One should openly admit that from the 1980s on, over a relatively long period of time, the rich heritage of the mass line has been forgotten by a considerable number of people. Though in official discourse sayings such as "trust the masses," "rely on the masses," and "serve the people" will sometimes appear (although less and less), in many places there are no longer specific measures designed to implement the mass line. This condition endured until around 2011, when changes finally took place. Major motivating forces in the rejuvenation of the mass line are perhaps the emergence of the Internet as well as continually increasing civic participation and pressure.

The year 2011 marked the ninetieth anniversary of the founding of the CCP. In his speech on July 1, General Secretary Hu Jintao said: "The unshakeable foundation of our Party is that we are from the people, rooted in the people, and that we serve the people." "Every single Communist Party member must keep the people in the highest of positions in their hearts; they must take the people as their teachers, grounding the enhancement of their political wisdom and the strengthening of their skills of governance deeply in the creative practice of the people themselves." Around this time, some provinces, cities, and districts began to raise the concept of the mass line again (for example, Chongqing, Guangdong, Shanxi, Jiangsu, Hubei, Tibet, and Yunnan) and to institutionalize and ensure its implementation. By the end of 2011, "go to the lowest reaches [of society], go to the masses" had become a national trend. Aside from the regions mentioned earlier, the leaders of the provincial Party committees of Hebei, Zhejiang, Anhui, Shaanxi, Guilin, Jilin, Gansu, and Xinjiang were going down to the lowest reaches of society, engaging with the masses "with zero distance between them," speaking to them face-to-face, and large numbers of front-line cadres were living in villages in order to conduct firsthand investigations, striving diligently to feel the pulse of the masses, getting as close as possible to their hearts and minds.[54] In 2012, even more provinces launched similar activities (for example, Qinghai, Guangxi, and Ningxia).

At the same time, many regions started to establish organizations for mass work (whose shortened names were abbreviated as mass work units). The first mass work unit emerged in 2005 in Yima City in Henan Province. It brought together representatives from various government departments, who were tasked with functions that bear directly on the interests of the masses, including departments such as the State Bureau for Letters and Calls, Civil Affairs, Labor, Social Assistance, the Judiciary, Science and Technology, Public Security, Land and Resources, and Urban Development. Such representatives were brought together to answer the complaints and demands of the masses face-to-face in one space. Not soon after, Yima's experiment gained recognition from central government leadership, and it was steadily expanded to eighteen prefectural-level cities and 158 counties (including municipalities and districts).[55] After this, Shandong, Hunan, Heilongjiang, Guizhou, and Liaoning

Provinces also established similar mechanisms at both prefectural and county levels. In June 2011, Hainan Province established the first provincial-level mass work unit in the entire country.[56]

In 2012, the Eighteenth Party Congress chose a new cohort of Party leaders. General Secretary Xi Jinping has always seen mass work as the lifeline of the CCP. Even early on, when he was serving as secretary of Ningde in Fujian Province [1988–1990], he established four routinized mechanisms for cadres to "go to the grassroots," including receiving the letters of complaints from the grass roots, meeting with people at the grass roots directly and dealing with their problems, conducting surveys and reports regarding the grassroots level, and promulgating policy at the grassroots level.[57] At the concluding ceremony of the special-topic seminar for leading provincial-level cadres in 2011, Xi Jinping demanded that cadres at every level use their own conduct as an example, cultivating within themselves a mass outlook, fortifying their mass stance, adhering to the mass line, deepening the emotions they feel for and with the masses, and innovating in the development of methods for mass work.[58] On the eve of the opening of the Eighteenth Party Congress, at the concluding ceremony of the special-topic seminar for leading cadres at the provincial level in 2012, Xi once again emphasized: "Our Party upholds our basic mission to serve the people with all of our hearts and minds; we uphold the work line of coming from the masses and returning to the masses; we uphold that the entirety of the Party's work is to realize the will, interests, and demands of the people; this is the greatest source of our Party's strength, a strength generated from close relations with the people."[59]

Xi Jinping was the leader of the working group tasked with writing up the report of the Eighteenth Party Congress. The term that appears with the greatest frequency in the report is *the people*, appearing altogether 145 times; this is without a doubt a revelation of his tremendous consciousness of the people.[60] A couple of weeks after the Eighteenth Party Congress, in order to strengthen the sense of popular consciousness that cadres at every level should have, the Politburo published "Eight Guidelines Regarding Connecting Closely with the Masses and Reforming Work Methods."[61] The Central Party School, the Academy of National Administration, and the Chinese Yan'an Cadre Academy have placed mass work within the ranks of the important courses for training cadres. On April 19, 2013, the Politburo made another decision: mass-line educational activities would commence in the latter half of that year, lasting for roughly a year in time, and would be executed across the entire Party from its highest levels down to its lowest.[62]

Figure 11.5 can perhaps help us gain a sense of the momentum surrounding the return of the mass line. The Baidu Index is a big-data analysis service based on searches on the Baidu engine as well as in *Baidu News*.[63] It can be used to display the "rate of user attention" and "rate of media attention" that certain

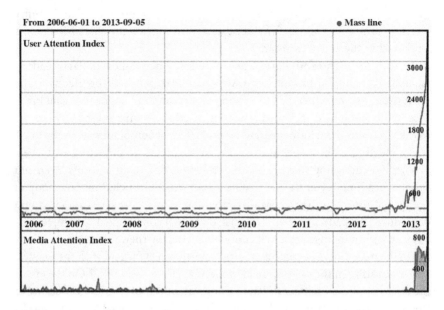

Figure 11.5 Baidu Index of the Term "Mass Line"

key words have received over a particular time period, directly and objectively reflecting hot social topics and netizens' interests. Figure 11.5 shows that before 2011 the Baidu Index number for the "mass line" remained below the average line (the dash line). Yet in the two subsequent years, the "mass-line" number passed the average line and, indeed, increased rapidly after the Eighteenth Party Congress, achieving unprecedented heights.

Through the practice of the past few decades, the mass line has already developed three different kinds of mechanisms. The first is a mechanism for understanding the sentiments of the people and absorbing their wisdom, which includes social survey work, front-line unit work, pilot projects, and strategies that start with one work unit but can be scaled up to an entire region.[64] The second is a mechanism for nurturing a mass outlook in cadres, which includes engaging with the poorest members of society and understanding their plight, the "three togethers" (eating together, living together, laboring together), being sent down, and the like.[65] Aside from this, there is also a series of accompanying mechanisms whose goals are to force cadres at every level to keep firmly in mind the mass line and to implement it, which include engaging in criticism and self-criticism at set times and at non–set times participating in rectification activities.[66] When these three mechanisms are active at the same time, the mass line can be thoroughly implemented.[67]

Among all of the mechanisms for implementing the mass line, one that deserves particular mention is the social survey, for this is a mechanism that is often used; though the tradition of social surveys continued during the years

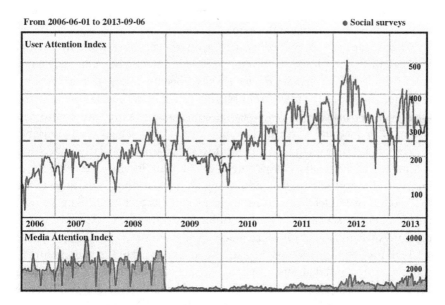

Figure 11.6 Baidu Index of the Term "Social Surveys"

in which the emphasis placed on the mass line wavered, they were not carried out frequently, and their investigations lacked depth.[68] Along with the return of the mass line, the emphasis placed on social surveys has increased tremendously, evidenced by the increase in the Baidu Index number for social surveys (figure 11.6).

Prior to his engagement with the mass line, Mao Zedong had already placed tremendous emphasis on social surveys and in fact conducted them himself. In the spring of 1927 in Hunan, he conducted investigations in five counties: Changsha, Xiangtan, Xiangxiang, Hengshan, and Liling. During the Jinggang-shan period, he conducted a wide range of investigation and survey work, including the two-county investigation of Ningqu and Yongxin, the Xunwu investigation, the Xingguo investigation, the Dongtang investigation, the Mukou village investigation, the survey regarding land allotment in southwestern Jiangxi, the investigation into the distribution of immature crops and land rent, investigations into the errors made in struggles over land in Jiangxi Province, investigations into the issue of rich peasants after land had been divided, investigations pertaining to the two initial land laws, the Changgang village investigation, and the Caixi village investigation.[69] After Mao became the leader of the CCP, he repeatedly impressed upon the entire Party the importance of conducting survey work. During the rectification period in Yan'an, the CCP Central Committee created the Central Committee Guidelines Regarding Social Survey Research.[70] After the establishment of New China, Mao Zedong twice demanded a "work-style defined by seeking guidance from the masses and wide-ranging survey work":[71] the first time in 1956,[72] and the second time at the beginning of the 1960s.[73]

When it comes to individually carrying out social survey work, Xi Jinping, the head of the new leadership cohort selected at the Eighteenth Party Congress, is himself an exemplary model. He has diligently carried out survey work over the course of his career, from serving as Party branch secretary of the Liangjia River brigade in the Wenanyi commune in Yanchuan country in Shaanxi Province and on the Party committee of Zhengding County in Hebei Province to his time on the Party committees of Xiamen, the Party prefectural committee of Ningde, the Party committee of Fujian Province, Zhejiang Province, and the city of Shanghai and serving on the Standing Committee of the CCP Politburo. In October 2002, when he took up his post in Zhejiang, he conducted intensive social investigation. In his first two months, his social investigation work outside of his office made up approximately half of his overall work; in his first nine months, he had visited sixty-nine of the region's ninety counties, cities, and districts.[74] In 2005, Xi spent 177 days outside of his office conducting investigations, which came to more than thirty in all.[75] Within five years, he had visited Zhejiang's mountains and waterways.[76] On March 27, 2007, he was transferred to the Party committee of Shanghai; three days later, on March 31, he began a special investigation of Pudong; within half a year, he had conducted investigations of all of Shanghai's nineteen districts and counties.[77] In Xi Jinping's own words, "When you serve as county Party secretary, you must certainly scour every single village; when you serve as prefectural (or municipal) Party secretary, you must scour every single village and township; when you serve as provincial Party secretary, you must scour every county, city, and district."[78] After becoming general secretary of the CCP Central Committee, he continued to hold firm to conducting grassroots social survey work.[79] It was not just Xi Jinping who did this, but all previous members of the Standing Committee of the Politburo of the CCP Central Committee have built their careers in this fashion.[80]

In comparison with the surveys conducted by scholars or think tanks, the "survey and research" work referred to here, which is meant to shape policy, has eight characteristics. First, evaluations through survey and research are a necessary procedure for policy making. For Mao Zedong, when deciding policy, "only a fool would, alone or in a group of people, not conduct social survey work, but simply wrack one's brain to 'think of a method' or 'come up with ideas.'" "This will certainly not produce any good methods or come up with any ideas. Put another way, he will certainly produce the wrong methods and bad ideas."[81] Even for those so-called elected representatives, if they do not conduct survey and research work, then their policies will have no value. As such, Mao Zedong advised that all policy making "has to uphold the mass line and all questions have to be discussed with the masses and only afterward collectively decided upon and thoroughly implemented. Cadres at every level are not permitted to forego survey and research work. It is thoroughly forbidden for the small number of people on the Party committees to forego survey and research work, to not discuss matters with the masses, to lock themselves up in their rooms and produce so-called policy that is tainted with pernicious subjectivism."[82] Mao Zedong admonished that "if there was no survey work, one had no right to speak."[83] Chen Yun [1905–1995] spoke of the demand to conduct social survey work as an antecedent to policy in a more vivid manner: "Leading organs decide policy, and one must use over 90 percent of one's time conducting survey and research work, while the time spent on discussion and policy decision making should account for not even 10 percent of one's time."[84] Xi Jinping completely identifies with this understanding of social survey work, believing that "survey work must thoroughly permeate the entire process of policy making, truly becoming *the* essential procedure."[85]

Second, those who carry out social survey work should not be support staff, like secretaries and consultants, but rather those who directly make policy. For example, though Mao Zedong entrusted the personnel around him with carrying out survey work (for example, his secretary, Tian Jiaying [1922–1966]),[86] he nonetheless emphasized that leading cadres "must themselves mount the horse," "that all those tasked with the responsibility for leading [Party] work, from the chairman of village governments to the chairman of the central government at the national level, from brigade leaders to major generals, from section secretaries to general secretaries, all of them must personally carry out concrete social and economic investigations; they cannot simply rely on written reports, for these two things are not at all the same"[87] because "those who do not directly carry out investigation work will not be able to understand."[88] Mao himself, along with Liu Shaoqi [1898–1969], Zhou Enlai [1898–1976], Zhu De [1886–1976], Deng Xiaoping, Chen Yun, and Peng Zhen [1902–1997], went to various regions to conduct survey work.[89] Today, grassroots investigation and research are a mandatory course and basic skill for first secretaries at every level across China. Xi Jinping's own personal experience is that, "in terms of knowledge and feeling, the effect on leading cadres who engage directly with masses at the grassroots level, who discuss conditions and think over problems with them, is different than indirectly listening to summary reports or simply reading [printed] materials." He therefore admonishes: "Though today's means of transportation and communication are increasingly developed, and the channels we have for receiving information more numerous, for leading cadres, none of these can replace social survey work done directly and diligently by themselves."[90]

Xi Jinping strongly emphasizes that those in charge of leading organs at every level must themselves conduct survey work, directly taking charge of surveys regarding important questions. "Policy making regarding various questions, in particular questions of major significance, must in the end be decided by leading collectives after those in charge have assembled opinions from various quarters, and if those in charge conduct survey work themselves, if they have a collective sense of empathy and experience that is shared with everyone, then it is easier to produce a unified understanding and unified opinion within leading collectives and easier to make decisions."[91] Therefore, the General Office of the CCP Central Committee in 2010 published the document "Suggestions on Promoting the Construction of Learning-Oriented Party Organizations," which clearly demanded: "In order to construct a comprehensive system of social investigation and study, leading cadres at the provincial level must every year spend no less than thirty days conducting grassroots survey work; leading cadres at the city and county level must conduct no less than sixty days of grassroots survey work; and leading cadres must every year write one or two social survey reports."[92]

Third, though the topics of social survey work can change, they should be focused primarily on comprehensive questions of strategic importance for policy makers as well as on new situations, contradictions, problems, and challenges. In relation to the present, what this entails concretely is that one must

> research deeply prominent questions that influence and constrain scientific development, research deeply the pressing and difficult questions that generate strong reactions among the masses of people, research deeply the theoretical and practical questions that are facing Party construction, research deeply the important questions concerning stable development and reform, research deeply important questions facing the world in the economic and social fields, comprehensively understand various new circumstances, diligently summarize the new experiences created by the masses, and put great efforts into exploring those things within various fields and professions that carry with them certain inherent laws, actively offering up appropriate policies. . . . Especially as concerns questions that generate the greatest amount of hope, concern, anxiety, and complaint among the masses, these must be researched with even greater enthusiasm, so that they can be understood thoroughly.[93]

Fourth, the objects of social investigation work are those people who are connected to policy formulation and "who can enter into and deeply understand social and economic circumstances."[94] Such people include "midlevel and lower-level cadres who have genuine experience as well as common people."[95] More specifically,

> we must investigate [administrative] organs, we must also investigate the grassroots; we must investigate cadres, we must also investigate the masses; we must analyze model examples [of a given problem], we must also investigate

the entire context [in which a problem appears]; we must go to those advanced places where work is proceeding well to review and summarize experiences there, we must also go to those places where there are a relatively large number of challenges, where the situation is complex, where the contradictions are sharp, in order to research the problems there. The grassroots, the masses, important model examples, and challenge areas all must become focal points for investigations, and more time must be spent researching and understanding them.[96]

What needs to be pointed out is that the objects of these investigations are not totally passive but instead active participants in these investigations. Policy makers should conduct investigations among and with the masses, carrying out research together.

Fifth, the attitude that one takes when conducting investigations is "humble yourself and be willing to be like an elementary school student," for "the masses are the true heroes, and we are often immature and laughable," and "if you only look up at heaven and utter high-sounding words," "if you do not have the courage to look at what is in front of you, you will your entire life have no ability to truly understand the affairs of China." Even more pertinently, "if you are not humble and diligent with an attitude of comradeship," the masses will "not tell you what they know, or they will speak without going into detail."[97] Only "by becoming friends with the masses, rather than acting as a spy sleuthing behind their backs . . . can one's investigation reveal the true nature of the situation."[98] According to Xi Jinping's own practical experience, his advice is:

> When leading cadres engage in investigative work, they must abandon their pride and devote themselves wholeheartedly to the work, immersing themselves completely in the finest details, discussing matters together with the masses, listening to their voices, experiencing their emotions firsthand, feeling their pain, summarizing their experience, and absorbing their wisdom. You must listen to the words of the masses when it is easy, you must listen to the words of the masses when it is hard; you must allow the masses to report on the situation, you must also allow the masses to present their own views. . . . Only in this way can you truly hear genuine speech, to investigate real situations, to gain real knowledge, to achieve real results.[99]

Sixth, the goal of social investigation is to understand the circumstances of the people and to absorb the wisdom of the people. As Mao Zedong said, "We must ask to be educated by the masses," and "we must seek truth from the masses."[100] For policy makers, the point of understanding the circumstances of the people is to understand what to do, and the point of absorbing the wisdom of the people is to understand how to do it. To actively absorb the wisdom of the people is to manifest a belief in, a reliance upon, and a respect for the pioneering spirit of the masses.

Seventh, there are various methods of social investigation, yet there are two major types: "going out" (that is, going to interview people, conducting grassroots investigations) and "welcoming in" (that is, holding discussion fora and symposia). "Going out" means "striding on two feet to go to every corner of the region encompassed within the scope of your work"; "welcoming in" means "holding a seminar as a means of assembling those people who understand a given situation, with the purpose of finding the sources of all the difficult problems you are currently grappling with to render the 'current situation' clear."[101] Regardless of whether [the method used] is "going out" or "welcoming in," what is crucial is that one must engage with grassroots cadres and masses. Only in this way "can one grasp those new situations that are difficult to hear, see, and imagine if one simply stays at one's desk, and one can find a new perspective from which to solve problems, a new mode of thought and new policies."[102] An important means of "going out" is to selectively conduct front-line [lit., "squat on a spot"] investigations, what we call "dissecting sparrows" [i.e., making detailed investigations of small test cases].[103] In conducting front-line investigations, one "must pay attention to grassroots units such as villages, communities, enterprises that not only are intimately related to one's own set of duties but also in which there are many problems, great challenges, and a host of contradictions. [One must] conduct front-line investigations, listen to the voices of the masses, and find the crux of problems."[104] Of course, methods of social investigations must advance with the times. While we maintain traditional methods, we must also "open up further channels of investigation, enrich our means of investigation, and create new methods of investigation, learning, understanding, and utilizing investigatory methods that are rooted in modern technology and science—for example, questionnaires, statistical investigations, sample surveys, specialized surveys, online surveys, and the like. We must also steadily integrate modern information technology into the investigatory field, improving the effectiveness and scientific level of our investigations."[105]

Eighth, investigation and research must be done in tandem. The purpose of investigation is to better understand a particular phenomenon or question and to grasp firsthand experience and materials related to it; the purpose of research is "to sift through large numbers of disparate materials in order to expel what is false and grasp what is true and to think, analyze, and synthesize in a comparative manner that moves between surface and depth, to systematize and organize these materials so as to penetrate complex and multifaceted phenomena in order to grasp the genuine essence of matters, finding their internal laws, transcending emotional understanding in order to reach rational understanding, and upon this foundation making correct policy."[106] To conduct research and investigative work in tandem is to "seek truth from facts." In Chen

Yun's words, "seeking truth from facts is first to clarify what exactly is 'truth.' If you do not clarify this question, then you will not be able to do anything well."[107] "'Truth' means clarifying the concrete situation; 'to seek' demands that one uses the results of one's research as a basis for making correct policy."[108] If you do not conduct detailed investigations, research "becomes water without a source, a tree without roots, becoming subjective and unreliable."[109] If one does not conduct diligent research, then investigation becomes a reckless waste, equivalent to striving through great obstacles to collect materials that will be simply discarded in the end. "The basic goal of investigation and research is to solve problems, and after investigations have been completed, you must conduct meticulous and thorough reflection as well as do the work of exchanging views, comparing [ideas], and [working through points] repeatedly; you must take one's disparate understanding and systematize it, take one's coarse understanding and deepen it until one has found the basic laws that define matters, the correct method for solving problems."[110]

From the eight characteristics just described, one can see that carrying out investigation and research is in fact the very essence of the mass line: "Everything for the masses, everything relying on the masses, coming from the masses, returning to the masses." From within the process that moves from investigation and research to the formulation of policy, we can answer the four questions regarding representation: Who is represented? By whom? What is represented? How is it represented?

In recent years, my colleagues and I have conducted two different research projects into China's model of government. One concerns the process by which China formulated policy regarding health-care reform, and the other examines the process by which China's Fifteenth Five-Year Plan was formulated. Both clearly show that examination and research are the most important characteristics of China's policy-making model.[111] Put differently, though many questions remain, China's political process absolutely practices representational democracy.

Conclusion

This article has examined the theory of representational democracy and its implementation in China, doing so by placing it in comparative perspective with representative democracy. There will be perhaps many inside and outside of China who will object to calling China's political system "democratic." For them, history has already ended, and democracy can take only one form, which is the representative democracy recognized by mainstream Western ideology. As such, because the operational forms of the Chinese political system are different from those of representative democracy, it cannot be democratic. This

Table 11.4 Different Peoples Across Asia on the Nature of Their Local Political System

	Total	Mainland China (2008)	Chinese Taiwan (2006)	Singapore (2006)	Mongolia (2006)	Philippines (2005)	Thailand (2006)	Indonesia (2006)	Vietnam (2005)	Cambodia (2008)
Completely democratic	18.2%	26.9%	5.8%	15.5%	7.9%	6.9%	17.6%	12.2%	40.7%	15.6%
Democratic but with minor problems	51.7%	50.4%	47.4%	75.5%	51.1%	40.9%	64.1%	36.2%	49.2%	60.1%
Democratic but with large problems	26.5%	21.1%	39.5%	5.2%	39.2%	42.5%	15.9%	46.8%	9.5%	20.9%
Not democratic	3.6%	1.7%	7.3%	3.8%	1.7%	9.7%	2.4%	4.8%	0.5%	3.4%
Sample size	13,431	3,796	1,499	959	1,195	1,139	1,481	1,368	1,097	897
	(100%)	(100%)	(100%)	(100%)	(100%)	(100%)	(100%)	(100%)	(100%)	(100%)

Source: Asian Barometer Study, 2103, http://www.eastasiabarometer.org/chinese/news.html.

kind of arbitrary and arrogant attitude is a classic example of "a single leaf before the eyes can blind you to Mount Tai; two beans in your ears can deafen you to thunder."[112] If China still has people who maintain this kind of perspective, then this stance can only be described as "when vision is hazy, you confuse white with black; when the mind is closed, you take the superficial for the deep."[113]

Yet the vast majority of everyday people in China believe that what China is implementing is precisely a kind of democracy. For example, table 11.4 shows that in mainland China 27 percent of the people believe their country's political system is completely democratic; another 50.4 percent believe the system is democratic, despite the existence of minor problems. Taking these two groups together, you reach 77.3 percent. Those who believe China is not democratic are extraordinarily few, making up only 1.7 percent of the population. When these figures are compared with those of other regions of Asia, only in Viet Nam does a larger proportion of people believe that their country is completely democratic.[114] Those who will object, saying that people in China do not know what democracy is, are simply displaying their own bias, which has clouded their vision. Democracy means that people are the masters of their own affairs, and to discuss democracy one must first trust the judgment of the masses and not see them as idiots who cannot stand on their own two feet. Those self-appointed Enlightenment saviors are in fact roadblocks on the path to democracy.

Why do Chinese people consider their own government to be democratic? Because their measure of whether a government is democratic is the degree to which it responds to the basic needs of common people, and the Chinese government has in fact a fairly vigorous responsiveness to those needs. Table 11.5 shows that in comparison to other regions in Asia, mainland China has the highest proportion of people who believe that the level of their government's responsiveness to the people's demands is "extremely strong," reaching 28.2 percent, which is 4.7 percent higher than in Viet Nam and 25.8 percent higher than in Taiwan. If you add the people who believe that their level of responsiveness is "relatively strong," then mainland China is still first, reaching 88.1 percent, 2.9 percent higher than Viet Nam, which comes in second at 85.2 percent, and 63.1 percent higher than Mongolia, which comes in last place.

If we respect the understanding that common people in China have regarding democracy, if we respect the judgment that common people in China have regarding their own country's political system, then the "paradox" that this article began with can in fact be solved: the Chinese people prefer substantive democracy. Because the government responds to the demands of the people, the people naturally look upon their government as democratic; this is the kind of democracy that has been discussed at length in this article: representational democracy. The people have no reason not to trust a government that represents their interests.

Table 11.5 Different Peoples Across Asia Regarding the Level of Their Local Government's Responsiveness

Level of responsiveness government exhibits in relation to the people's demands	Total	Mainland China (2008)	Chinese Taiwan (2006)	Singapore (2006)	Mongolia (2006)	Philippines (2005)	Thailand (2006)	Indonesia (2006)	Viet Nam (2005)	Cambodia (2008)
Very strong	14.2%	28.2%	2.4%	8.5%	2.8%	5.1%	10.3%	4.3%	23.5%	10.9%
Strong	46.7%	59.9%	35.4%	60.5%	22.2%	27.8%	42.6%	42.0%	61.7%	38.7%
Not too strong	33.8%	10.1%	51.4%	29.5%	65.0%	49.7%	43.3%	50.0%	14.3%	44.0%
No response	5.3%	1.8%	10.8%	1.4%	9.9%	17.4%	3.8%	3.8%	0.4%	6.4%
Sample size	14,326	4,437	1,512	978	1,191	1,176	1,369	1,561	1,122	980
	(100%)	(100%)	(100%)	(100%)	(100%)	(100%)	(100%)	(100%)	(100%)	(100%)

Source: Asian Barometer Study, 2103, http://www.eastasiabarometer.org/chinese/news.html.

Recent research by three American scholars provides support for this conclusion. They have discovered that "if one wants to understand why the Chinese people have such a high level of trust in their government, the most important reason is the government's responsiveness 'to the needs of the masses.'"[115] The research of the director of the Asian Barometer, the Taiwanese scholar of politics Chu Yun-han, is in complete accordance with the conclusion stated earlier: "This political regime displays the resolve and the ability to protect the poor and to ensure that they have the basic necessities for life; it is steadily carrying out political reform and strengthening the rule of law; the people can feel its sense of responsiveness to their own needs. These are the major reasons why the people continue to have faith in government organs." He also asserts, "Because of China's particular cultural tradition and revolutionary legacy, as well as because of the particular position it occupies in the world, it is currently constructing an alternative system of public discourse regarding political legitimacy, charting its own course of political modernization."[116]

This is of course not to say that China's political system is perfect. China's political system, like any other political system, has many problems, and, indeed, some of them are quite severe, which will require great efforts to improve. There is absolutely no reason to be content with the status quo and remain complacent. But the fact that China's political system still has flaws does not mean that we should undeservedly belittle ourselves and take our strengths as weaknesses and carelessly abandon them. It is foolish to blindly follow in others' footsteps without deep and careful reflection. If you listen only to others and denigrate your own accomplishments, you will reach a point of no return. The political systems of the world exemplify the notion that "heaven has its shortcomings and earth its strengths."[117] As such, the proper attitude is one that "weighs [various things] and then understands what is heavy or light; that measures [various things] and then understands what is long and short."[118] Only then can one "maintain calm and make the world as peaceful as the great Mount Tai."[119]

Notes

1. Wang Shaoguang, "Daiyixing minzhu he daibiaoxing minzhu" (Representative democracy and representational democracy), *Kaifang Shidai* (February 2014): 152–74.
2. Francis Fukuyama, "The End of History?" *The National Interest* 16 (Summer 1989): 3–18, n.p. cited.
3. Paul Kingsnorth, *One No, Many Yeses: A Journey to the Heart of the Global Resistance Movement* (New York: Free Press, 2004).
4. David McNally, *Another World Is Possible: Globalization and Anti-Capitalism* (Winnipeg: Arbeiter Ring, 2006).
5. *Sortition* is a term that denotes the selection of political officials at random by drawing lots from a larger pool of qualified people. It was a characteristic of Athenian

democracy based on the notion that allotting qualified people at random to governing bodies would prevent elections from being corrupted by oligarchic networks of
power that could buy and sell votes. For a more detailed discussion, see Mogen Her-
mans Hansen, "Direct Democracy, Ancient and Modern," in *The Ashgate Research
Companion to the Politics of Democratization in Europe: Concepts and Histories*, ed.
Kari Palonen, Tuija Pulkinnen, and José María Rosales (Abingdon: Routledge, 2008),
37–54.

6. *Translators' note*: Here Wang uses a phrase—*jinsi niaolong shi de minzhu*, "gilded-cage
democracy"—that denotes a structure that while shiny and seemingly resplendent is
nonetheless entrapping.

7. Mainland Chinese scholars often like to translate the English term *legitimacy* as *hefaxing*, though legitimacy and *hefaxing* have no necessary relationship. As such, the
translation used in Hong Kong—*zhengdangxing*—is more appropriate.

8. The Edelman Trust Barometer surveys more than 31,000 people from twenty-six different countries. In China, it surveys 1,500 people, including 1,000 people it deems as
coming from the "general population" and 500 from the "informed public." The latter
designation denotes people between the ages of twenty-five and sixty-four who have
university degrees, have annual household incomes in the top quarter of their age
group for their country, are accustomed to reading the news or watching it on television, and consistently pay attention to public-policy issues.

9. Edelman Trust Barometer, 2013, http://www.edelman.com/insights/intellectual-pro
perty/trust-2013/.

10. Considerable academic work has been written on the basis of such survey work. Owing
to limitations of space, I will not list them all individually.

11. John James Kennedy, "Maintaining Popular Support for the Chinese Communist
Party: The Influence of Education and the State-Controlled Media," *Political Studies*
57 (2009): 517.

12. Heike Holbig and Bruce Gilley, "In Search of Legitimacy in Post-revolutionary China:
Bringing Ideology and Governance Back In," *GIGA Working Papers* 127 (March
2010): 6.

13. For a work that uses statistical samples from across the nation taken in 2008, see
Michael S. Lewis-Beck, Wenfang Tang, and Nicholas F. Martini, "A Chinese Popularity Function: Sources of Government Support," *Political Research Quarterly*, April 30,
2013, doi:10.1177/1065912913486196. For a work that uses statistical samples from five
different cities taken in 2011, see Yang Zhong and Yongguo Chen, "Regime Support in
Urban China," *Asian Survey* 53, no. 2 (2013): 369–92. For a work that uses statistical
samples from across the nation taken in 2012 and 2013, see Wenfang Tang, Michael S.
Lewis-Beck, and Nicholas F. Martini, "Government for the People in China?" *The Dip-
lomat*, June 17, 2013, http://thediplomat.com/2013/06/17/government-for-the-people
-in-china/.

14. This view is very popular in the West. For example, in an op-ed piece Paul Krugman
wrote the following: "Where does this government's legitimacy come from? Primarily it comes from economic success" (Paul Krugman, "China's Ponzi Bicycle Is
Running Into a Brick Wall," *New York Times*, July 19, 2013, http://cn.nytimes.com
/opinion/20130725/c25krugman-blog/en-us/). In recent years, there have also been
some who have highlighted the "responsiveness" and "adaptability" of the Chinese system as a means of explaining its "legitimacy." It is true that the Chinese system is
responsive and adaptable, yet if one persists in maintaining the framework of "authoritarianism," then one will have no ability to explain why the system has these qualities, to say nothing of explaining its "legitimacy."

15. Chu Yun-han, "Sources of Regime Legitimacy and the Debate Over the Chinese Model," *ABS Working Paper Series*, no. 52 (2011): 23, http://www.asianbarometer.org /newenglish/publications/workingpapers/no.52.pdf.
16. Tang, Lewis-Beck, and Martini, "Government for the People in China?"
17. Chu Yun-han, Larry Diamond, Andrew J. Nathan, and Doh Chull Shin, eds., *How East Asians View Democracy* (New York: Columbia University Press, 2008).
18. Zhengxu Wang, *Democratization in Confucian East Asia: Citizen Politics in China, Japan, Singapore, South Korea, Taiwan, and Vietnam* (Amherst, MA: Cambria Press, 2007); Doh Chull Shin, *Confucianism and Democratization in East Asia* (New York: Cambridge University Press, 2011).
19. Zhang Mingshu, *Zhongguoren xiangyao shenmeyang minzhu: Zhongguo "zhengzhiren"* (What kind of democracy do Chinese people want? China's "political man") (Beijing: Shehui Kexue Wenxian, 2013).
20. *Translators' note*: In the Chinese version of this essay, Wang refers to Taiwan by the compound "Zhongguo Taiwan" (Chinese Taiwan), used to demonstrate to his Chinese audience that he considers Taiwan to be part of China in line with the People's Republic of China's "One-China Policy." We have included the original neologism in our English translation to preserve for English readers the political positioning of Wang's original wording.
21. In this survey, respondents were asked four different times how they understood democracy, with possible answers to the questions being presented in different orders each time. Respondents could choose one answer from four different choices: "Good Governance," "Social Equality," "Democratic Process," or "Freedom." The different arrangement of the answers was done to avoid a particular answer being favored solely on the basis of the position in which it appeared in the original questions.
22. Yun-han Chu and Min-hua Huang, "East Asian Youth's Understanding of Democracy," paper presented at the conference "Democratic Citizenship and Voices of Asia's Youth" organized by the Institute of Political Science and Academia Sinica and cosponsored by Asian Barometer Survey, National Taiwan University, September 20–21, 2012, 6.
23. Zhang Mingshu, *Zhongguoren xiangyao*.
24. Chinese communities who live in Malaysia (along with other overseas Chinese communities) are still accustomed to using the term *daiyishi*.
25. Ying Qi and Liu Xunlian, eds., *Daibiao lilun yu daiyi zhengzhi* (Representational theory and representative politics) (Changchun: Jilin Chuban Jituan Youxian Zeren Gongsi, 2008).
26. Liu Junning, "Daibiao, haishi yiyuan?" (Representative, or parliamentarian?), *Chahu*, 2013, http://business. sohu.com/20130813/n384072126.shtml.
27. Liu Junning, "Daibiao, haishi yiyuan?"
28. For a classic formulation of this position, see Joseph Schumpeter, *Zibenzhuyi, shehuizhuyi yu minzhu* (Capitalism, socialism, and democracy), trans. Wu Liangjian (Beijing: Shangwu Yinshuguan, 1999), esp. chap. 21, "The Classical Doctrine of Democracy," and chap. 22, "Another Theory of Democracy."
29. In recent years, a number of scholars and politicians have critiqued electoral politics, for even if elections are carried out in a free and competitive manner, they are stunningly easy to manipulate. Such critics have turned their attention to sortition as an alternative or supplement to electoral democracy.
30. For a relatively recent iteration of this point, see Bryan Caplan, *The Myth of the Rational Voter: Why Democracies Choose Bad Policies* (Princeton, NJ: Princeton University Press, 2007).

31. For example, when it comes to election time in America, there are always American officials who explain to the Chinese government that they should not take American candidates' rash "election talk" seriously. As early as 1981, Deng Xiaoping had this to say about his meetings with George H. W. Bush and other American politicians: "In Reagan's electoral platform, there were indeed some words that made us uncomfortable. When Mr. Bush came to see us, we told him: we understand that things said during elections will not necessarily be implemented after one comes to power. What we care about is what Mr. Reagan will do after he comes to power" (Deng Xiaoping, "Fazhan Zhong-Mei guanxi de yuanze lichang [1981-nian 1-yue 4-ri]" [Principles for the development of Sino-American relations (January 4, 1981)], Xinhua Wang, March 4, 2002, http://news.xin-huanet.com/ziliao/2002-03/04/content_2546615.htm).

32. Since 1998, 338 former members of the U.S. Congress have already become lobbyists. See Jonathan D. Salant, "Congress Members Sprint for Money to Lobby after Election," *Bloomberg*, May 8, 2013, http://www.bloomberg.com/news/2013-05-08/congress-mem bers-sprint-for-money-to-lobby-after-election.html.

33. According to a report in the *New York Times* in July 2013, since Bill Clinton left the White House in 2001, he and Hillary have spun their fame and prestige into a family business based around speaking engagements, one whose profits have already reached more than $100 million. See Amy Chozick, "Hillary Clinton Taps Speechmaking Gold Mine," *New York Times*, July 11, 2013, http://www.nytimes.com/2013/07/12/us/politics /hillary-clinton-hits-the-lucrative-speechmaking-trail.html?pagewanted=all&_r=0.

34. Bernard Manin, Adam Przeworski, and Susan C. Stokes, introduction to *Democracy, Accountability, and Representation*, ed. Adam Przeworski, Susan C. Stokes, and Bernard Manin (Cambridge: Cambridge University Press, 1999), 3.

35. Hanna F. Pitkin, *The Concept of Representation* (Berkeley: University of California Press, 1967).

36. Robert A. Dahl, *Polyarchy: Participation and Opposition* (New Haven, CT: Yale University Press, 1971), 1.

37. Mao Zedong, "Guanyu muqian dang de zhengce zhong de jige zhongyao wenti (1984-nian 1-yue 18-ri)" (Regarding some important questions of Party policy in our current moment [January 18, 1948]), in *Mao Zedong xuanji* (Selected works of Mao Zedong) (Beijing: Renmin, 1991), 4:1215.

38. Mao Zedong, "Lun lianhe zhengfu" (On coalition government), in *Mao Zedong xuanji*, 3:1031.

39. Mao Zedong, "Nongcun diaocha de xuyan he ba" (Introduction and postscript to rural surveys), in *Mao Zedong nongcun diaocha wenji* (Collection of Mao Zedong's rural surveys) (Beijing: People's Press, 1982), 17.

40. Mao Zedong, "Duoyu laodongli zhaodao le chulu, yiwen de anyu" (Commentary on "Surplus Labor Has Found an Outlet"), in *Zhongguo nongcun de shehuizhuyi gaochao* (The socialist high tide in the Chinese countryside), ed. General Office of the CCP Central Committee (Beijing: People's Press, 1956), 2:578.

41. Mao Zedong, "Zai Yan'an wenyi zuotanhui shang de jianghua" (Talks at the Yan'an Forum on Literature and Art), in *Mao Zedong xuanji*, 3:864.

42. Mao Zedong, "Dang weihui de gongzuo fangfa" (The work methods of the Party committee), in *Mao Zedong xuanji*, 4:1441.

43. Brantly Womack, "In Search of Democracy: Public Authority and Public Power in China," in *Contemporary Chinese Politics in Historical Perspective*, ed. Brantly Womack (New York: Cambridge University Press, 1991), 53–89.

44. Brantly Womack, "The Party and the People: Revolutionary and Post-revolutionary Politics in China and Vietnam," *World Politics* 39, no. 4 (1987): 479–507.

45. Mao Zedong, "Guanyu lingdao fangfa de ruogan wenti" (Some questions concerning methods of leadership), in *Mao Zedong xuanji*, 3:899.

46. Mao Zedong, "Lun lianhe zhengfu," 3:1095.

47. Mao Zedong, "Zuzhi qilai" (Organize), in *Mao Zedong xuanji*, 3:933.

48. Mao Zedong, "Guanyu muqian dang de zhengce," 4:1215.

49. A relatively early work that championed participatory democracy was Carole Pateman, *Participation and Democratic Theory* (Cambridge: Cambridge University Press, 1970). In the past twenty years, works that have critiqued representative democracy and have advocated for participatory democracy have become more numerous. For example, see William R. Nylen, *Participatory Democracy Versus Elitist Democracy: Lessons from Brazil* (New York: Palgrave Macmillan, 2003), and Thomas Zittel and Dieter Fuchs, eds., *Participatory Democracy and Political Participation: Can Participatory Engineering Bring Citizens Back In?* (New York: Routledge, 2007).

50. Wang Shaoguang, "Buying danwang de gonggong juece canyu moshi: Qunzhong luxian" (A participatory model for public-policy decision making that should not be forgotten: The mass line), in *Qunzhong luxian dajia tan* (Everyone discuss the mass line), ed. Li Zhu (Beijing: Huawen, 2013), 331–37.

51. Regarding the inequality that defines participation in American politics, see Kay Lehman Schlozman, "What Accent the Heavenly Chorus? Political Equality and the American Pressure System," *Journal of Politics* 46 (1984): 1014; Frank R. Baumgartner and Beth L. Leech, "Interest Niches and Policy Bandwagons: Patterns of Interest Group Involvement in National Politics," *Journal of Politics* 63, no. 4 (2001): 1191–213; Kay Lehman Schlozman, Sidney Verba, and Henry E. Brady, *The Unheavenly Chorus: Unequal Political Voice and the Broken Promise of American Democracy* (Princeton, NJ: Princeton University, 2012).

52. Deng Xiaoping, "Wanzheng de zhengque de lijie Mao Zedong sixiang" (Thoroughly and correctly understanding Mao Zedong Thought), in *Deng Xiaoping wenxuan* (Selected works of Deng Xiaoping) (Beijing: People's Press, 1994), 43.

53. Deng Xiaoping, "Wanzheng de zhengque de lijie Mao Zedong sixiang," 45.

54. Li Yuanchao, "Dao qunzhong zhong qu, bai renmin wei shi" (Go to the masses, salute the people as teachers), *Xuexi Shibao*, September 12, 2011.

55. Peng Mei, "Quanguo tuiguang qunzhong gongzuobu yu Xinfangju heshu bangong" (Expand across the nation the cooperative work between mass work units and the State Bureau for Letters and Calls), *Nanfang Dushi Bao*, March 13, 2001, http://news.sina.com .cn/c/2011-03-13/051122104145.shtml, posted on Sina Net at http:// news.sina.com.cn/c /2011-03-13/051122104145.shtml.

56. "Hainan shuaixian tigao Xinfangju xingzheng jibie, chengli shengwei qungongbu" (Hainan leads the way in raising the administrative rank of the Bureau of Letters and Calls, establishes provincial committee mass work unit), *Xin Jingbao*, July 13, 2011, http://politics.people.com.cn/GB/14562/15150598.html.

57. Huang Shaohe and Zhuang Yan, "Ningde 20-duo nian jianchi 'sixia jiceng' de zhizheng shijian he jingyan qishi" (Twenty-plus years of upholding the "four mechanisms of going to the grass roots" in Ningde administrative practice and experiential knowledge), *Fujian Ribao*, May 2, 2012, http://www.gog.com.cn/zonghe/system/ 2012/05/02/011433612.shtml.

58. Xu Jingyue, et al., "Xi Jinping zai shengbuji lingdao ganbu zhuanti yantaoban jieyeshi shang jianghua" (Xi Jinping's remarks at the concluding ceremony of the special-topic seminar for leading provincial-level cadres), *Zhongguo Zhengfu Wang*, February 24, 2011, http://www.gov.cn/ldhd/2011-02/24/content_1809442.htm.

59. "Xi Jinping zuo shengbuji lingdao yantaoban zongjie jianghua" (Xi Jinping makes summary remarks at the special-topic seminar for provincial-level leaders),

Guowuyuan Canshi shi Wangzhan, 2012. *Translators' note*: Xi's speech is currently available at http://news.ifeng.com/mainland/special/hujintaojianghua2012/content-3/detail_2012_07/24/16265511_0.shtml.

60. Zhou Hanmin, "Renmin, gaige, minzhu shi shiba da baogao de zhu xuanlü" (People, reform, and democracy are the main themes of the Eighteenth Party Congress report), Shanghai shi Shehuizhuyi Xueyuan Wangzhan, 2012, http://www.shsy.org.cn/node933/shsy/jczt/node1839/userobject1ai1760559.html.

61. "Zhonggong zhongyang zhengzhiju zhaokai huiyi, Xi Jinping zhuchi" (The Politburo convenes, Xi Jinping serves as chair), Xinhua Wang, December 4, 2012, http://news.xinhuanet.com/politics/2012-12/04/c_1139069 13.htm.

62. "Zhonggong zhongyang zhengzhiju zhaokai huiyi, Xi Jinping zhuchi."

63. Google Analytics offers a similar service.

64. *Translators' note*: The final suggested work method in this sentence—"strategies that start with one work unit but can be scaled up to an entire region"—is a translation of the Chinese phrase *yi dian dai mian*, more directly translated as "fanning out from a single point to an entire area." The phrase refers to using the successful techniques developed by a single work unit in a single area and scaling them up across multiple units and areas.

65. Such as the regulation issued by the General Political Department of the People's Liberation Army in April 2013 and approved by the chairman of the Central Military Commission, Xi Jinping, which demanded that leaders and cadres higher than the regiment level in the People's Liberation Army as well as the People's Armed Police go to the field to link up with soldiers, serving, working, and living among them so as to conduct on-the-ground investigation of front-line challenges. See "Jing Xi Jinping zhuxi pizhun Jiefangjun zong zhengzhibu xia fa 'guilü'" (Regulations issued by the People's Liberation Army's General Political Department and approved by Chairman Xi Jinping), Zhongguo Zhengfu Wang, April 21, 2013, http://www.gov.cn/jrzg/2013-04/21/content_2384523.htm.

66. Zheng Keyang, "Yi zhengfeng jingshen kaizhan piping he ziwo piping" (Use the spirit of rectification to carry out criticism and self-criticism), *Qiushi* 16 (2013), http://www.qstheory.cn/zxdk/2013/201316/201308/t20130813_25918 3.htm.

67. What must be pointed out is that many people speak of the mass line and mass movements in the same breath. Although mass mobilization has been used in the past in the implementation of the mass line, the mass line does not necessarily need to employ mass mobilization to be carried out.

68. Wei Liqun and Zheng Xinli, eds., *Xin shiqi diaocha yanjiu gongzuo quanshu* (Encyclopedia of survey and research work carried out in the new period) (Beijing: People's Press, 2006).

69. Mao Zedong, "Nongcun diaocha de xuyan he ba," 14.

70. "Zhongyang guanyu diaocha yanjiu jueding" (Central Committee decision regarding survey research), October 1, 1941, Zhongguo Gongchandang Xinwen Wang, n.d., http://cpc.people.com.cn/GB/64184/64186/66644/4490536.html.

71. Mao Zedong, "Daxing diaocha yanjiu zhi feng" (Energetically encourage investigation and research work) (January 13, 1961), in *Mao Zedong wenji* (Works of Mao Zedong) (Beijing: Renmin, 1996), 8:233–34.

72. The three-volume work *Zhongguo nongcun de shehuizhuyi gaochao* (The socialist high tide in the Chinese countryside), published in 1956, includes materials regarding survey work performed during the collectivization movement. The volume's introduction was written by Mao Zedong. For the survey and investigation work that was carried

out to prepare Mao Zedong's report "On the Ten Great Relationships," see *Mao Zedong zhuan (1949–1976)* (Biography of Mao Zedong, 1949–1976), ed. Pang Xianzhi and Jin Chongji (Beijing: Zhongyang Wenjian, 2003), 468–506.

73. Wen Yanshi, "Ershi shiji liushi niandai chu zhongyang lingdao tongzhi de diaocha yanjiu" (Survey and investigation work of the leading cadres of the Central Committee during the early 1960s), *Dang de wenxian* 13 (2013), Zhongyang Wenxian Yanjiushi Wangzhan, http://www.wxyjs.org.cn/ddwxzzs/wzjx/2013n3/201 305/t20130516_139304.htm.

74. Xi Jinping, "Wo shi ge nenggou tixing ziji, yueshu ziji de ren" (I am a person who is able to remind himself, a person able to control himself), *Renmin wenxian* 3 (2004), Renmin Wang, http://www. people.com.cn/GB/paper2086/11500/1037377.html.

75. Zhang Feng'an, "Xi Jinping, cong Shaanxi de shan'gou yilu zou qilai" (Xi Jinping, starting out from the mountain valleys of Shaanxi), *21 Shiji Jingji Baodao*, March 1, 2008, Fenghuang Wang, http://news.ifeng.com/special/2008lianghui/huanjie/ziliao/200803 /0310_2978_433841.shtml.

76. Chen Fang, "Xi Jinping zhuzheng Zhejiang, jiuge yue paobian liushijiuge xian" (When Xi Jinping governed Zhejiang, in nine months he visited sixty-nine counties), Fenghuang Wang, November 2012, http://news.ifeng.com/mainland/special/zhonggong18da /dujia/detail_2012_11/15/19187238_0.shtml.

77. Zhang Feng'an, "Xi Jinping, cong Shaanxi."

78. Xi Jinping, "Wo shi ge nenggou tixing ziji."

79. Kan Feng, "Zhongyang xin lingdaoceng miji 'zou jiceng,' zuji bianji ba shengfen" (The new cohort of central Party leadership intensively "goes to the grass roots," leaving tracks across eight provinces), Xinhua Wang, February 2013, http://news.xinhuanet .com/politics/2013-02/ 05/c_124322246.htm.

80. Hu Angang, "Jiti diaocha jizhi" (Mechanism for collective surveys and research), in *Zhongguo jiti lingdao tizhi* (China's system of collective leadership) (Beijing: Renmin Daxue, 2013), 103–26.

81. Mao Zedong, "Fandui benbenzhuyi" (Oppose book worship), in *Mao Zedong nongcun diaocha wenji*, 2.

82. Mao Zedong, "Zhi Zhang Pinghua" (To Zhang Pinghua), in *Mao Zedong shuxin xuanji* (Selection of Mao Zedong's letters) (Beijing: People's Press, 1983), 582.

83. Mao Zedong, "Nongcun diaocha de xuyan he ba," in *Mao Zedong nongcun diaocha wenji*, 17.

84. Chen Yun, "Zuo hao shangye gongzuo" (Conduct commercial work in a good way), in *Chen Yun wenxuan* (Selected writings of Chen Yun) (Beijing: Renmin, 1995), 3:34.

85. Xi Jinping, "Tantan diaocha yanjiu" (Discussing survey and research work), *Xuexi Shibao*, November 16, 2011, Zhongguo Gongchandang Xinwen Wang, http://cpc.people .com.cn/GB/64093/64094/16349466.html, emphasis in the original. Xi gave this speech at a ceremony for an incoming cohort of students marking the beginning of the autumn semester at the Central Party School.

86. Lü Chuanbin, "1956 nian Mao Zedong mishu Tian Jiaying hui jiaxiang diaocha shimo" (The story of how Mao Zedong's secretary Tian Jiaying in 1956 went to his hometown to conduct survey work), Xinhua Wang, January 2012, http://news.xinhuanet.com /politics/2012-01/ 19/c_122605061.htm; Yin Fuying, "Yijiuliuyi nian Tian Jiaying Zhejiang nongcun diaoyan" (Tian Jiaying's rural survey of Zhejiang in 1961), *Bainian Chao* 12 (2002): n.p.

87. Mao Zedong, "Fandui benbenzhuyi," 10.

88. Mao Zedong, "Guanyu renzhen diaocha gongshe neibu liangge pingjun wenti de yifeng xin" (Letter on diligently investigating the two different questions regarding

egalitarianism within communes), in *Jianguo yilai Mao Zedong wengao* (Mao Zedong's manuscripts after the founding of the PRC) (Beijing: Zhongyang Wenxian, 1996), 9:440.

89. Ma Shexiang, "Jianguo chuqi 'Mao Zedong shi' de diaocha" (Survey and investigation work in "the style of Mao Zedong" conducted early in the period after the founding of the PRC), *Zhongguo Zhengdang Ganbu Luntan* 4 (2012), Makesizhuyi Zhongguo-hua Luntan, http://marxism.org.cn/detail.asp?id=3083&Channel= 12&ClassID=12; Song Binquan, "Liushi niandai chu daxing diaocha yanjiu zhi feng jishu" (Account of the energetic encouragement of survey and investigation work in the early 1960s), *Dangshi Yanjiu yu Jiaoxue* 4 (1994): 43–48.

90. Xi Jinping, "Tantan diaocha yanjiu."

91. Xi Jinping, "Tantan diaocha yanjiu."

92. Zhonggong Zhongyang Bangongting (General Office of the CCP), "Guanyu tuijin xuexi xing dang zuzhi jianshe de yijian" (Suggestions on promoting the construction of learning-oriented Party organizations), Zhongguo Zhengfu Wang, February 2010, http://www.gov.cn/jrzg/2010-02/08/con- tent_1531011.htm. As early as 1958, in the document *Work Methods: 60 Guidelines*, which Mao Zedong took a leading role in drafting, the twenty-fifth guideline clearly stipulated that leading cadres should conduct survey work: "Members of the Party committees of the central government, provinces, municipalities under direct central government authority, and autonomous regions at both primary and secondary administrative levels must, except in cases of illness or old age, each year spend four months outside of their office, going to the grass roots to conduct survey and research work, hold meetings, and go to a wide cross-section of areas [in their jurisdiction]. They should adopt two kinds of [work] methods: ride the horse to see flowers and get off the horse to see flowers. Even if one must spend three or four hours discussing something in a single place, that is acceptable. One must interact with peasants and workers, increasing one's understanding. Some meetings of the central government can be conducted outside of Beijing, and some meetings of the provincial Party committees can be conducted outside of the provincial capital" (Mao Zedong, "Gongzuo fangfa liushi tiao [cao an]" [Work methods: 60 guidelines (working draft)], Xinhua Wang, January 1958, http://news.xinhuanet.com/ziliao/2005 -01/06/ content_2423605.htm.

93. Xi Jinping, "Tantan diaocha yanjiu."

94. Mao Zedong, "Fandui benbenzhuyi," 9.

95. Mao Zedong, "Nongcun diaocha de xuyan he ba," 16.

96. Xi Jinping, "Tantan diaocha yanjiu."

97. Mao Zedong, "Nongcun diaocha de xuyan he ba," 15–17.

98. Mao Zedong, "Guanyu nongcun diaocha" (Regarding rural surveys), in *Mao Zedong nongcun diaocha wenji*, 27.

99. Xi Jinping, "Tantan diaocha yanjiu."

100. Mao Zedong, "Zhi Deng Xiaoping" (To Deng Xiaoping), April 25, 1961, in *Mao Zedong shuxin xuanji*, 578.

101. Mao Zedong, "Fandui benbenzhuyi," 2–3.

102. Xi Jinping, "Tantan diaocha yanjiu." Xi Jinping has noted that "presently some cadres are adept at gauging their leader's every word and expression, making a few preparations, milling about with the plans provided by superiors, and offering up a few materials in response. Clearly, this kind of survey work will not allow one to see the true nature of a situation, gain genuine knowledge about it, and make the correct conclusions regarding it." He thus warns that one must avoid "doing surveys perfunctorily, focusing on potted plants and miniature trees, happily listening and looking around

a bit, like a dragon fly skimming over the surface of a body of water, being satisfied with gaining just a small smattering of knowledge." He suggests, therefore, that "within survey and investigation work one can operate according to a 'fixed line,' yet one should also 'make individual choices regarding one's movements,' going to see some places that you did not prepare to see, conducting some random investigations that you did not plan in advance or provide forewarning for. One must strenuously seek to correctly, comprehensively, and deeply understand a given situation, avoiding the phenomenon that one has 'been investigating,' defending against perfunctory investigations." According to Xi, "recently some leading cadres, including cadres at the provincial level, have gone deeply down among the grass roots and the masses to conduct investigation work in a straightforward manner, investigations that are not forewarned in advance, in which they are not accompanied by others." According to reports, the provincial Party secretary of Zhejiang Luo Zhijun's recent rural investigations, which have involved him living in the countryside, have been conducted particularly thoroughly. He has not been accompanied by cadres from a variety of administrative levels, who would provide reports across stratified channels, but rather has brought with him two or three assistants and directly entered village homes, with village cadres providing directions on how to get there. He has not allowed cadres from the township level to get near, and it is only at the discussion forum held after he has finished living in the village that he has engaged with municipal and provincial Party committee secretaries. For more, see Guo Bensheng, "Shengeng qunzhong, shengwei shuji xiaxiang ji" (Going deeply to the masses: The provincial Party secretary's jottings regarding going to the countryside), Xinhua Wang, March 2013, http://www.js .xinhuanet.com/2013-04/22/c_115480589.htm.

103. *Translators' note*: Wang is referring to the idiom "though sparrows are small, their five internal organs are complete," which comes originally from Qian Zhongshu's (1910–1998) famed satirical novel *Weicheng* (Fortress besieged, 1947). Here, the idiom is used to suggest the need to make detailed investigations of small test cases, which will aid investigators in grasping the problems of an entire region or larger social situation.

104. Xi Jinping, "Tantan diaocha yanjiu."

105. Xi Jinping, "Tantan diaocha yanjiu."

106. Xi Jinping, "Tantan diaocha yanjiu."

107. Chen Yun, "Jianchi anbili yuanze tiaozheng guomin jingji" (Uphold the principle of proportionality in regulating the national economy), in *Chen Yun wenxuan*, 3:250.

108. Chen Yun, "Zenyang shi women de renshi geng zhengque xie?" (How can we make our understanding more correct?), in *Chen Yun wenxuan*, 3:188.

109. Mao Zedong, "Shijian lun" (On practice), in *Mao Zedong xuanji*, 1:290.

110. Xi Jinping, "Tantan diaocha yanjiu."

111. See Wang Shaoguang and Fan Peng, *Zhongguo shi gongshi xing juece: "Kaimen" yu "mohe"* (The China model of consensus decision making: A case study of health-care reform) (Beijing: Renmin Daxue, 2013); Wang Shaoguang and Yan Yilong, *Zhongguo minzhu juece moshi: Yi wunian guihua zhiding wei li* (A democratic way of decision making: Five-year plan process in China) (Beijing: Renmin Daxue, 2015).

112. *Translators' note*: These sayings come from the "Tianze" (Heaven's Model) section of the *Heguanzi*. For more on the *Heguangzi*, see R. P. Peerenboom, "*Heguanzi* and Huang-Lao Thought," *Early China* 16 (1991): 169–86.

113. *Translators' note*: From Su Dongpo's (Su Shi, 1037–1101) poem "Mingjun ke yu wei zhongxin fu" (The enlightened man can receive sincere advice), in *Su Shi wenji* (The writings of Su Shi), annotated by Kong Fanli (Beijing: Zhonghua Shuju, 1986), 24–25.

114. When these questions are asked in China, the proportion of people who select that "they do not know how to respond" or who select "no response" is relatively high. Providing each region's respondents with these two additional choices is done in order not to force them to respond if they do not wish to. However, even taking into account those who select one of these two responses, the percentage of people in mainland China who believe that their political system is completely democratic is still a relatively high 20 percent, surpassing every other region except Viet Nam; if you add those people who believe their country's system is democratic, though it possesses some small flaws, the proportion surpasses the proportion in the Philippines, Indonesia, and Chinese Taiwan, while it is essentially on par with the proportion in Mongolia.

115. Tang, Lewis-Beck, and Martini, "Government for the People in China?"

116. Yun-han Chu, "Sources of Regime Legitimacy and the Debate Over the Chinese Model," *China Review* 13, no. 1 (2013): 24.

117. *Translators' note*: A quotation from the "Heaven's Gifts" chapter of the *Liezi*. Here the passage refers to the idea that every political system has its strong and weak points.

118. *Translators' note*: A quotation from the "King Hui of Liang" chapter of *The Mencius*.

119. *Translators' note*: A quotation from Song essayist and statesman Ouyang Xiu's essay "Xiangzhou Zhoujin tang ji" (Jottings regarding the Zhoujin Hall in Xiangzhou), an essay about the Northern Song official Han Qi's return to his hometown to govern it. Ouyang praises Han's moral rectitude as the basis of his ability to provide the people good governance. For a full version of the essay, see Ouyang Xiu, "Xiangzhou Zhoujin tang ji" (Jottings regarding the Zhoujin Hall in Xiangzhou), in *Jieti huiping "guwen guanzhi"* (The best of classical prose, annotated with accompanying commentary), ed. Wu Chucai and Wu Diaohou, annotated by Hong Benjian et al. (Shanghai: East China Normal University, 2002), 2:617–21.

CHAPTER 12

THE SIGNIFICANCE OF BORDERS[1]

SUN GE

TRANSLATED BY JOSHUA A. FOGEL

Translator's Introduction

S un Ge (b. 1955) is one of three female intellectuals included in this volume. As noted in the introduction, this small representation accurately reflects the intellectual world we are translating, in which men make up the overwhelming majority. Sun also stands in the minority as a dedicated postmodernist in the style of the postcolonial cultural theories of *Inter-Asia Cultural Studies*, the English-language journal of the pan-Asian academic group based in Taiwan of which Sun is an active member.

Sun Ge is a researcher at the Institute of Literature in the Chinese Academy of Social Sciences and an important figure in the fields of critical Asian studies and comparative history of ideas. She received her doctoral degree in political science in the Faculty of Law at Tokyo Metropolitan University. She is concerned with the concept of "Asia" in the context of modernity and globalization, and her essays address issues such as Japanese right-wing history textbooks, the Nanjing Massacre, and official visits to Yasukuni Shrine. Unlike many Chinese scholars, she addresses audiences in China, Japan, Taiwan, and Korea in the hope of transcending national borders in scholarship and politics.

Sun's essay translated here appeared in *Tianya* (Frontiers) in 2017 and draws from the introduction to her book *Chongsheng: Zai linjie zhuangtai zhong shenghuo* (Okinawa: Life on the critical border).[2] She makes a case for the self-critical value of "borders" through a disjunctive presentation of her own experience in Japan after the Fukushima nuclear disaster, the bitter history of

Okinawa, and the artistic expression of avant-garde artists. Although the language she uses is difficult to follow at times, her point is clear in the end. This essay is ultimately the pacifist appeal of a leftist activist who finds the postmodern deconstruction of language a valuable antidote to the fatal arrogance of nationalism. She makes her argument about the value of a "border sensibility" as such an antidote through concrete, embodied experiences. It employs rather than claims a notable form of feminist analysis that emphasizes embodied experience.

Although Sun Ge does not directly engage the other voices in China's intellectual public sphere—Liberal, New Left, or New Confucian—she is a frequent speaker at major Chinese universities. Her work also reflects some of the preoccupations of leftist intellectuals such as Qian Liqun (b. 1939). Like Qian, Sun repeatedly invokes China's great cultural critic Lu Xun (1881–1936) and takes pains to declare that she is just an ordinary person, suggesting a certain discomfort with her elite status as an intellectual. In a fashion similar to Qian's focus on nonelites or the grass roots (*minjian*), Sun focuses on the dispossessed of Okinawa and Korea. She is clearly speaking in the tradition of subaltern studies.

The Significance of Borders

I go to Japan and Korea for my research just about every year. After the Japanese earthquake of March 11, 2011, and the consequent leakage from the Fukushima Nuclear Power Plant, I was able to get a sense at close range of the initial reactions to the disaster within Japanese society.

These disasters are an incomparably fearful event for mankind. While they impose an enormous human cost, at the same time they afford mankind a harsh opportunity to reflect on the environment in which we live. The real circumstances that have intentionally or unintentionally been hidden to us in peaceful times suddenly, when disaster falls, reveal their reality then. No one wishes for disaster, and those of us who study the history of thought are the same. However, when disaster strikes, students of the history of thought have a responsibility to observe and analyze the real mechanisms with which "normal society" must rid itself of its covering blinders.

I unexpectedly learned this lesson in 2011. Drawing on the aftereffects of the Fukushima Nuclear Power Plant leak, I observed various aspects at work in Japanese social life and also the actual operating mechanisms of Japan's state structures. Of course, the most direct result appears on the specialized shelves of publications on the nuclear issue that have grown like mushrooms after a spring rain in bookstores, large and small. I found several convincing specialized works and gained a rudimentary understanding of the impact of nuclear power plants and nuclear accidents on daily human life. I also came to understand one basic fact: the serious imbalance between investment in developing nuclear power and investment in handling nuclear waste means that nuclear power plants in times of ordinary operations are like high-level apartment houses without toilets. Therefore, handling nuclear waste always uses a method of "dilution" to stealthily recycle radioactive matter back into the living environment upon which we rely. However, after the nuclear accident erupted, the electrical power company could not afford the enormous expense of the cleanup. In addition, because of fears that the follow-up investigation of nuclear contamination might harm the company's interests, data on the most serious contamination in 2011, how much contamination of food and water the Japanese may receive, scarcely register on the radiometer at all.

Given such a grave imbalance in the news, I concentrated my attention those days on the social-psychological aspect of people's response to the disaster: how people long for a return to normal life, even if that means avoiding the big issue and focusing on the trivial, even to the point of self-delusion, supporting the impetus to survival. Like the Japanese, I checked online for the contamination news issued daily by the Ministry of Agriculture, Forestry, and Fisheries and went out to buy certain favorite foods for safety's sake. I have come to truly understand during those days the genuinely helpless, as Lu Xun [1881–1936] depicted it in his "I Want to Deceive People."[3] After all, what choice do you have?

Times change; five years have passed rapidly. Five years of radiated material with a half-life of several hundred to one thousand years is effectively meaningless, although Japanese society had in fact already survived a crisis period and returned to tranquility. I visited Tokyo in the summer of 2016. And when I was returning home, I lined up at the airport to go through the boarding process, and I very carefully inquired of the Chinese person behind me who had lived in Japan for several decades: "What's the current status of the contamination?" She angrily glared at me and said: "What contamination is there in Tokyo? Tokyo's very safe!"

I know that I violated a taboo. Although, according to the results of monitoring in 2011, Tokyo's contamination at the time was not at a negligible level, after five years it was diluted but had not dissipated; there are no longer media reports on the contamination situation and possibly no longer scientists or circumstances to push the investigation further. Thus, it would appear that this problem no longer exists. Although we are still in the midst of the issue of how to extract the nuclear fuel from the ruined Fukushima Nuclear Power Plant, and from time to time the administration has been quite good at issuing reports on radioactive sewage flowing into the sea, the hot points of social concern have already shifted. I oughtn't rudely raise such an offensive problem to people leading a serene life. This issue has points of similarity with a story described by Lu Xun: a household gives birth to a child, and when the baby reaches one month, it receives propitious words of congratulation for the future. Although these propitious words are not certain to materialize, all those offering them receive thanks. Only one person, however, speaks the truth: this child will die in the future—and he [that person] is thereupon driven away by everyone.[4]

As for people who live in the foggy disaster area, I of course understand this compatriot's feelings. People can't live for protracted periods of time under emergency conditions, which would require superhuman willpower. In fact, I am no different from this fellow Chinese, for although I wrote the essay "'Normal Prejudice' and the Contemporary World,"[5] I, too, in reality am often prejudiced in favor of normalcy.

Under tranquil circumstances, however, Japanese have by no means forgotten the dangers of nuclear power. The mass demonstrations opposing the reconstitution of the nuclear power plant that Tokyo and many other areas continue to push forward have ultimately successfully hindered nuclear power plant operations at sites around Japan, meaning that such operations are at a standstill. The opinion in favor of abolishing nuclear power plants remains consistent, and an opposition has formed that stands face-to-face with those who want to promote the nuclear power industry. One might say that this is an example of the will of a small number of postwar Japanese curtailing the power of capital. As for follow-up effects from the ruins of the Fukushima Nuclear Power Plant, at present we cannot locate reliable sources of information. We can occasionally learn from the media's de-emphasizing that sewage still from time to time spills over and is discharged into the sea. Scientists say that the low concentration of draining sewage poses no hindrance to human life, and it is too extreme to say that they are lying: after humans accumulate a certain amount of radioactive material in their bodies, life then may face certain threats; according to scientific logic, if the level of contamination does not exceed the critical line, then we can say that people are safe.

The people in East Asia most susceptible to this critical line are Okinawans. Compared to radiation contamination, the much more severe threat they face is all manner of bullying humiliation by the American military base on Okinawan society. From the sexual assault and murder of Okinawan women to American soldiers' getting away with criminal offenses, from the destruction of the local fishing and maritime cultivation industry by the economy of the military base to environmental pollution by the base itself, the circumstances facing Okinawans may be thought of as Japan's and, indeed, all of East Asia's bitterest problem. Furthermore, the Japanese government's submissive attitude toward the United States has enabled the cabinet to take a basically laissez-faire attitude on the issue of Okinawa. Okinawan society has consistently borne the consequences of Japan's compromising with the United States and remaining isolated. Taking the opportunity following the accident at the Fukushima Nuclear Power Plant, the Japanese Marine Corps and the American military moved forward with their buildup and began to distract attention from Okinawa. Okinawan society's long resistance to the American military base and its struggle against Japan's pro-American policy are increasingly becoming normalized. Opposition to moving the Futenma Marine Corps Air Station to Henoko, opposition to the incessant incidents of sexual violence committed by U.S. servicemen—real life seems eternally unwilling to allow Okinawans peace and calm, with demonstrations and protests turning into mass events.

As for Okinawans themselves, they certainly don't want this sort of life. In fact, they have virtually no choice but to live at this critical borderline on a perpetual basis: on the one hand, there is the unceasing daily diet of gathering together in the face of crises; on the other, there are the catastrophes when the crises erupt. Life along the borderline means maintaining perpetual tension and confirming the unfamiliar in practice. The significance of all this is that the people of Okinawa are forging their own distinctive sense of the world and their own ideals for life.

In the region of Northeast Asia, Okinawa is located at what may be considered a peripheral area. Of course, in no significant way can it be thought of as a center. Strangely, though, I find it very difficult to sense on this island chain the unhappiness and injustice that one can easily feel in other so-called peripheral areas. At the same time, the ever isolated and determined Okinawans have not abandoned their struggle because of the size of the Japanese and American forces arrayed against them but instead have cultivated their own gardens with an attitude of warmth and clear-sightedness, overcoming with a spirit of perseverance the internal divisions that incessantly arise. Moreover, they do it in a way that is extremely imaginative, making a valuable contribution to the intellectual resources of humanity. I once wrote an article that focused on the writings of Arasaki Moriteru [b. 1936], Kawamitsu Shin'ichi [b. 1932], Okamoto Keitoku [b. 1934], and other intellectuals; from their perspective, Okinawa is the international political symbol of Northeast Asia, a microcosm of human society; it has compressed the densest portion of historical time and redefined spatial feelings of human society.[6]

I recall that several years ago when I paid a short visit to Okinawa, I used some free time to visit the defensive fortification built by the Japanese military during wartime in Okinawa, which is now a tourist attraction, and the war remains of the Himeyuri Memorial Tower. While we were on the tour bus, the local tour guide chatted about the present situation in Okinawa. I asked this fifty-year-old woman if Okinawans wanted independence. She replied that they had missed their chance. When the Americans first occupied Okinawa, there was a chance, but now it was behind them. At present, there was no point in discussing issues that have no chance of coming to be.

This ordinary Okinawan woman, who was neither a scholar nor a social activist, inspired in me a deep feeling of respect. In the complex resistance of the past half-century, Okinawan society has had to confront the injustice of the Japanese state; it has had to face the U.S. military occupation, which has violated and trampled on Okinawan human rights; it has had to face the power of Japanese capital, which has greedily plundered Okinawan resources; and it has had to confront incessant fracturing and contradictions amid the material temptations offered to Okinawan society. However, Okinawans have never resorted to violence in the face of humiliation and anger; literally, they have never allowed their humiliation and anger to turn into violence. In the Okinawans' resistance, there have been practically no instances of violence. All protest meetings have proceeded peacefully, increasingly becoming a moment for the creation of consensus and common emotions among the protesters. Perhaps this middle-aged tour guide offers us a clue to understanding Okinawans' behavior—that is, forging a mass political consciousness out of the feelings of living daily life on the border.

Over the past few years, Okinawan social activists have increasingly taken the initiative in establishing contact with areas outside Okinawa. I frequently hear news that they have gone to Tokyo and elsewhere to participate in various academic activities and meetings. In addition, I have heard that in the summer of 2015 a group of protesters in front of the Diet building in Tokyo opposing [Prime Minister Shinzō] Abe's [b. 1954] efforts to reform the Constitution at the same time issued a call to support expelling the U.S. military from Okinawa. Okinawans and knowledgeable people in Japan proper have thus created a close bond of solidarity.

Yi Chŏng-hwa [b. 1935], a Korean poet living in Japan, ran a project over the years 2006–2008 that primarily featured Okinawan and mainland Japanese artists; it was called "Toward the Future of 'Asia, Politics, Art.'" In the three years of this project, avant-garde artists, performance artists, and musicians from Okinawa and Japan proper—altogether eight of them—contributed their works and recorded a DVD; twelve literary and art critics engaged in a discussion and explanation of these works. As a product of their collective work on this fine-tuned project, in 2009 the Iwanami Publishing House brought out a volume entitled *The Sound of Lingering Pain: Toward a Future of "Asia, Politics, Art."* The book is divided into two parts: (1) written discussions by the critics and (2) the DVD attached at the end of the book, which includes the artists' recorded performances and a video of their work.

This is a very particular book, its particularity residing in its powerful internal tension. All of the performances, photography, painting, and music were completely new in form, going well beyond the scope of "avant-garde art." It was a dialogue between life and death, life experience being sustained under extreme conditions, going beyond the form of artistic expression. The history of suffering or the bitter history that Okinawa has experienced over more than a half century is brilliantly rendered in the mode of expression employed by these artists—grief without wound, resentment without anger. And Okinawa, as the condensation of Asia's history, has blossomed as a result.

Yi Chŏng-hwa wrote a wonderful preface to the book and engaged in a highly readable exchange with the composer Takahashi Yūji [b. 1938]. They called their dialogue "Don't Let Death Die," and they use "sound" as the medium to explore this heavy subject. Yi Chŏng-hwa started with the following proposition to Takahashi Yūji: "On seeing you today, I want to reflect with you on the meaning of sound." Takahashi agreed, and he went on to explain: "In other words, this is a question of 'manufacturing.' The act of manufacturing has to do with the realm of death, which seems not to exist but which in fact we feel exists everywhere. What I say does not exist, but which must exist, is death. This is the question of death. Linked to this is the notion of 'creation,' a behavior associated with being, or life, or breathing. . . . I constantly go back and forth between these two worlds. But these days, I don't know why, I can always hear the sound of death."[7]

The "sound" that Yi Chŏng-hwa's is talking about is not the sound of language but is rather a kind of rhythm, a tempo, the length of a musical beat; it rejects the content of language, and directly bears the weight of a body's aches and pains. Yi Chŏng-hwa uses a "needle" that appears in the works of the artist who participated in shaping the project to express this acute suffering. This is a kind of inchoate needle that wanders about the body; it and the female body form a unity. Yi Chŏng-hwa states that the instant that this needle sharply stings the human body, the point of penetration cries out, which is the origin of the "sound."

Born on Cheju Island in South Korea, Yi Chŏng-hwa, like the Okinawans, experienced great difficulty in finding a voice. She rarely speaks of her own past, and all her remembrances of trauma she blends into her search for the linkages between art and politics. This extraordinarily gifted poet has ingeniously upturned human everyday awareness, transforming "sound" into space. As for herself, casting off the sound of the spoken word also casts off its meaning, which took form only in the instance of its disappearance, in the instant that it quietly departed human society. At this point in time, the realm of "sound" differed from memory—it was dying far away, far from home.

Dying far from home is Yi Chŏng-hwa's ultimate explanation of life on the border. She argues that Asians are infrequently able to die in their own space, and the majority pass away in a place they don't know. In the past, people feared the consequences facing the corpse of one who had died away from home or just "of dying away from home," and they used all sorts of religious rituals to prevent their souls from returning home. Takahashi adds a note to this, saying that this means that an incident occurring at a given time and place cannot be locked into the culture and tradition of that place; it may actually evolve. This note is extremely interesting because it deepens Yi Chŏng-hwa's theme of "dying far from home" and intensifies the significance, beyond itself, of the sufferings of Okinawans. Drawing further on Yi Chŏng-hwa's viewpoint, perhaps we might say that we early on have lost our own "space" and are moving along a path to "dying far from home." This is precisely the route of "living far from home"—Could it be that we do not also live in an environment that cannot be cordoned off?

Yi Chŏng-hwa clings to this depiction of "dying far from home" to reveal her understanding of life. She argues that "dying far from home" is a rejection of the regularization of death; it does not allow death itself to die. In its unceasing diffusion, "dying far from home" thus transcends the individual body. It is no longer the specific death of any old Tom, Dick, and Harry as it has formed a vehicle for the fusion and convergence of all culture. Precisely for this reason, life is a process awaiting "dedicating the body."

> How should one maintain the form of not letting death die? At the very moment of thinking about this question, it has nothing and everything to do with people. We have to live. We have to go on living. At this point, if we say that we are talking in moral terms, then I feel we need an answer to the question of how to relate to no one and everyone. Maybe this answer lies in creation, or maybe it is a ritual. I feel that I need it. Maybe we should call it Asia. The moment I think about how to sustain this in a way that does not let death die, I think of something that involves people to the smallest extent. The smallest extent and also the greatest extent. Those who must live or have to go on living. If we are to speak of this in terms of some kind of ethics, then we must acknowledge our need at this very moment in history to find a way that allows us, with the least effort and greatest potential, to make connections. We create art that is a *response*, and in that sense we might call it a ritual. That's what I'm feeling. And perhaps, that is what I would call "Asia."[8]

Yi Chŏng-hwa's discussion of "dying far from home" is admittedly difficult to understand, but if we coordinate it with the contents of the entire book, especially the images in the DVD attached at the end of the book to help, her explanation is most certainly not deliberately mystifying. The book records that from the bitter sacrifices of the Battle of Okinawa to the [current] ravages, Okinawan society still has no option but to endure. Her theme, then, is "forgotten death." However, in the eyes of artists and commentators, death is not merely an unavoidable disaster; it is simultaneously a kind of religious rite in the world of humankind. This is precisely where Yi Chŏng-hwa is distinguished from Western romantic poets—she suggests that it is an issue that belongs not to God but to humanity. From a different perspective, *The Sound of Lingering Pain* looks at the living world that we bring in and, with Okinawa as its base point, links it to Cheju Island,[9] links it to Kwangju,[10] links it to humanity's violence and disaster. Yi Chŏng-hwa rejects the stance of sound turning into memory, and she rejects viewing memory simply as the recollection of past incidents because all images expressed in a book live in the present moment, and the human body is the vehicle for these images. Yi Chŏng-hwa rejects the idea of freeing oneself from sufferings and sins that go by the name of memory, and she calls on people in a way that will not allow death itself to die but will make the issue of "dying far from home" continue on.

This is indeed the picture of life at the borderline. People can escape from memory, and when they face their memories with a scrutinizing attitude, the border solidifies as a category, an assigned subject. Corresponding to this, history has become an object of retrieval unrelated to oneself. In Okinawan society today, although no longer like Okinawa in wartime when there was such large-scale mass slaughter, when there was collective suicide forced on people by the Japanese military, with the stench of blood felt to the bone, the situation has now quietly changed. At that time, the violence caused by American military mercilessly bombing Shuri Castle[11] with extraordinary brutality was hidden from everyday life. The condition of life at the border, speaking with respect to Okinawan thinkers and artists, in particular the people of Okinawa, means endlessly uncovering self-delusion and false facades; it means endlessly creating new ideas and forms of expression, endlessly breaking through perceptual inertia, and preserving a sharp power of observation of the situation at hand.

The Okinawan poet Kawamitsu Shin'ichi calls to people's attention not only the need to focus on conspicuous oppression and control but also the need to remain vigilant "spontaneously following along in the name of liberty." In Okinawan society's protests against the Japanese cabinet's repeated offers to sell Okinawa and protests against the many crimes committed by the American military in Okinawa, Kawamitsu at the same time is investigating the "structure of the imperial system" within Okinawan society. As he sees it, the greatest threat to freedom is not political pressure from without but pressure from within a person. His masterpiece, *The Latent Power of a Constitution in the Republican Society of the Ryūkyū Islands: Ideas about Archipelago, Asia, and Borders*,[12] discusses how on the basis of the freedom of the human mind we can establish a genuinely free society. This famous Okinawan poet does not engage in an abstract discussion of some general significance of freedom and equality, and when Okinawan society demands independence and autonomy, he does not stand on the opposite side of such appeals—he only stubbornly calls people's attention to the following: when the weak use the means of the strong to fight for their own power, they are in reality co-conspirators with the powerful. Because of this, the unrealistic appeal of Okinawan independence significantly is an ideal that is difficult to see as a true subjectivity established by Okinawan society. In Kawamitsu's chapter "Constitution," he opens with discussing how humanity's arrogance may bring about the ruin of civilization, how it constructs the foundations for war, and Okinawa, which is always regarded as a victim, receives a stark investigation by Kawamitsu on this question of arrogance:

> Those who boasted of Urasoe [Castle in Okinawa] were ruined by Urasoe, and those who boasted of Shuri [Castle in Okinawa] were ruined by Shuri. Those who bragged about the pyramids were ruined by the pyramids, and those who bragged about the Great Wall were ruined by the Great Wall. Those who boasted of military armaments were destroyed by them, and those who boasted of laws were destroyed by them. Those who revered deities were destroyed by them, those who relied on human beings were destroyed by them, and those who banked on love were destroyed by love."[13]

Of course, for either the strong or the weak to opt for "freedom" is very difficult. Freedom does not mean one can extract oneself from the existing power structure, though it does mean not to rely on any fixed value. Now, when Yi Chŏng-hwa stresses the perpetuity of the issue of "dying far from home" and Kawamitsu Shin'ichi interrogates the relationship between arrogance and war, both penetrate value judgments of the surface of things and invert the ossified normal state of things. This is their understanding of freedom as it is rooted in the intellectual persistence of conditions at the border. Contemporary societal formation of "spontaneously following," upon which Kawamitsu's "Constitution" focuses, suggests an ideal social structure. It organically structures a form of human existence and does not look closely at the existential form of the state.

Perhaps in Asia and even the world, however subjectivities are formed wherever they exist, however free will is formed, and however historical issues are understood, they resemble the case of Okinawan thinkers; they examine closely the concrete concept of values in a border state and thereby always work diligently to eliminate lazy thinking, something rarely observed. In the cooperation between Yi Chŏng-hwa and the Okinawan artists, we come to appreciate their vigilance against the treasonous nature of language and concepts: when Yi Chŏng-hwa stresses the significance of not relying on language and relies on the meter of "sound," when she emphasizes connecting with people at the lowest level, she hopes to convey how to avoid the ossification of received definitions of language and the interference of currently fashionable humanism. Again, we have here her repeated emphasis on the significance of the fact that "sound" is unlike the human voice. Kawamitsu in the same way distrusts language; concerning the basic concept of his "Constitution," he elaborates: "Commandments about benevolence are revealed spiritually, and one's breaking of commandments must be judged by oneself. Courts of law are established in each person's heart." To break through concretized imagination, Kawamitsu transcends the border consciousness of reality as concerns the inclusiveness of the rules of Ryukyu republican society: "Those who agree with the fundamental principles of this constitution and are of a mind to preserve it will have met requirements in their place irrespective of race, ethnicity, gender, or citizenship."[14]

Because of this, Okinawa is an open arena that characterizes borders. In this arena, anyone can subjectively contemplate the most basic issue of humankind. Amid the interactions among Kawamitsu, Yi, and their friends, I have continually learned how to preserve this border sensibility and to use it in studying intellectual history.

Today, I am running into more and more Chinese who are sympathetic to Okinawans, and intellectuals living in different areas of Northeast Asia are attempting to see Okinawa as an intermediary in assessing the history of East Asia. The border sensibility of Okinawan thinkers is truly useful for society in Northeast Asia, which is in an extremely weak position, and is continually producing the most innovative ideas. Perhaps life on the border is not only an unavoidable act but also a refusal to engage in self-deception and the courage to face human life squarely.

Translator's Notes

1. Sun Ge, "Linjie de yiyi" (The significance of borders), *Tianya*, January 2017, 25–30.
2. Sun Ge, "Daoyan" (Introductory remarks), in *Chongsheng: Zai linjie zhuangtai zhong shenghuo* (Okinawa: Life on the critical border) (Guilin: Guangxi Shifan Daxue Chubanshe, 2017), n.p.
3. Lu Xun initially wrote "Wo yao pian ren" in Japanese and published it in *Kaizō* (April 1936); it appeared in his own Chinese translation in the Shanghai journal *Wenxue congbao* in June of that year.
4. This story is taken from Lu Xun, "Li lun" (Expressing an opinion), in *Yecao* (Wild grass), in *Lu Xun quanji* (Collected works of Lu Xun) (Beijing: Renmin wenxue chubanshe, 1981), 2:207; translated in *Lu Xun: Selected Works* (Beijing: Foreign Languages Press, 1985), 1:348. With thanks to both Ted Huters and Jon Kowallis.
5. Sun Ge, " 'Changtai pianzhi' yu dangjin shijie" ("Normal prejudice" and the contemporary world), *Tianya* 1 (2013): n.p.
6. See, for example, Sun Ge, "Chongsheng: Zai linjie zhuangtai zhong shenghuo" (Okinawa: Life on the critical border), *Wenhua zongheng* 4 (2011): n.p.; Sun Ge, "Neizai yu Chongsheng de Dongya zhanhou shi" (Inherent in Okinawa's postwar East Asian history), *Dushu* 2 (2010): n.p.
7. Yi Chŏng-hwa, preface to *Zanshō no oto: "Ajia, seiji, aato" no mirai e* (The sound of lingering pain: Toward a future of "Asia, politics, art") (Tokyo: Iwanami Publishing House, 2009), n.p.
8. Yi Chŏng-hwa, preface to *Zanshō no oto*, n.p.
9. Cheju Island is the site of a major rebellion in 1948, led by leftist guerillas opposed to the first elections to be held in South Korea. The rebellion was cruelly suppressed over the course of several years.

10. Reference to the Kwangju uprising against martial law in 1980 and its subsequent suppression.
11. A palace of the Ryukyu kingdom between the fifteenth and nineteenth centuries, Shuri Castle was almost completely destroyed during the Battle of Okinawa in 1945.
12. Kawamitsu Shin'ichi, *Ryūkyū kyōwa shakai kenpō no senseiryoku: Guntō, Ajia, ekkyō no shisō* (The latent power of a constitution in the republican society of the Ryūkyū Islands: Ideas about archipelago, Asia, and borders) (Tokyo: Miraisha, 2014).
13. Kawamitsu, *Ryūkyū kyōwa shakai kenpō no senseiryoku*, n.p.
14. Kawamitsu, *Ryūkyū kyōwa shakai kenpō no senseiryoku*, n.p.

PART IV

NEW CONFUCIAN VOICES

CHAPTER 13

KANG YOUWEI AND
INSTITUTIONAL CONFUCIANISM[1]

CHEN MING, GAN YANG, TANG WENMING,
YAO ZHONGQIU, AND ZHANG XIANG

TRANSLATED BY DAVID OWNBY

Translator's Introduction

This excerpted transcript of a scholarly debate held in late June 2014 reflects an important trend in the thought world of contemporary China: the revival of interest in Kang Youwei (1858–1927), particularly among mainland New Confucians. Participants included Gan Yang (b. 1952), dean of the Boya Institute at Zhongshan University in Guangzhou (see the translations of his essays in chapters 1 and 10); Tang Wenming (b. 1970), professor of philosophy at Tsinghua University; Zhang Xiang (b. 1974), professor at the Institute for Cultural Studies, Capital Normal University, Beijing; Yao Zhongqiu (b. 1966, also known as Qiu Feng), professor at the Advanced Institute of Confucian Studies at Shandong University; and Chen Ming (b. 1962), professor of philosophy at the College of Political Science and Law, Capital Normal University, Beijing. This conference seems to have been linked with two others: "From Kang Youwei to Deng Xiaoping"[2] and "Transcend Left and Right, Unite the Three Traditions, Renew the Party-State."[3]

Kang Youwei was a towering figure in the late Qing period who, despite his controversial loyalty to the Qing court, remained important in the Republican period as the leader of a campaign to establish Confucianism as China's national religion. For mainland New Confucians, Kang Youwei is above all important as a conservative figure, one who understood the importance and potential of Confucianism in a modern context, and they propose taking up his reform agenda once again, arguing for the revival of Confucian culture through educational or perhaps religious initiatives.

In the 1890s, particularly after China's loss to Japan in the Sino-Japanese War (1894–1895), Kang and his disciple Liang Qichao (1873–1929) were important and controversial figures in reform circles among China's mandarin elite in terms of both setting an intellectual agenda and implementing reform ideas on the ground (Liang was particularly active in Hunan). Building on his status as a Confucian wunderkind, Kang fashioned a multifaceted response to the challenges of the day that broke with the conservatism characterizing most of China's reform movement to this point. In writings that shocked many of his peers, he argued that Confucius had been misunderstood throughout much of Chinese history; instead of the "ancestor worshipper" depicted in traditional portraits of the sage ("I transmit but do not create"), Confucius was instead a dynamic institutional reformer (like Peter the Great or the Meiji emperor) who might have become king had the political cards been dealt differently. Such arguments allowed Kang to agitate for important reforms while at the same time claiming allegiance to the Confucian tradition.

The concrete aim of many of these reforms was rapid modernization; Kang was impressed by Meiji Japan and other late developers. But what interests today's admirers of Kang were his efforts to reform China in such a way as to avoid a destructive political revolution or a painful rupture with China's Confucian roots. To achieve these goals, Kang proposed a thorough-going restructuring of several of the basic elements of Chinese society. He argued that the property of the temples of Chinese popular religions be confiscated to provide funding and housing for the modern schools that would be established. He further argued that Confucianism should become a religion—indeed, China's national religion—on the model of Western and other examples he had studied (the Church of England, Shintō), with a clergy, a body of texts, and weekend services. The notion was both to provide China with an educated citizenry in scientific and technical terms and to create a renewed Confucian culture by eliminating most of the practices of popular religion (now seen as "superstition") and welcoming the people into a newly popularized Confucian church. Kang's defense of the idea of a constitutional monarchy should be understood from this angle as well; the emperor would be another symbol linking past, present, and future. And the entire project was linked to utopian imaginings of a unified world of great harmony.

It is not difficult to understand the appeal of Kang Youwei's ideas to today's mainland New Confucians, who claim to be looking for a sensible conservatism that will put an end to a century of revolution and consolidate China's economic progress of the past few decades. They see most of China's twentieth-century experience as a failure: neither the Enlightenment project championed by China's liberal tradition nor the Communist project (in either its internationalist guise or its Maoist guise) made good on its promises. Under Mao, communism provided faith and common purpose, but the flame of communism was extinguished by the Cultural Revolution. If China is flourishing now, it is because Deng Xiaoping returned to Kang Youwei's reformist tradition,[4] but this success may well be fleeting because China lacks both the moral core and the social cohesion necessary to make the good life possible on a lasting basis. Xi Jinping's (b. 1953) "China Dream" calls for a revival of the Chinese nation, so why not revive Confucianism?

The absence of Jiang Qing (b. 1953) in a discussion of institutional Confucianism is surprising because his proposals to remake China's political institutions (discussed in the introduction to chapter 15 of this volume) are well known. My impression is that Jiang's proposals came at an earlier period, predating the wave of enthusiasm for mainland New Confucianism that gave rise to the discussion translated here, and the authorities perhaps saw his ideas as too outlandish to be taken seriously. By contrast, all five speakers at this event are mainstream professors of philosophy at major universities in China, addressing questions of culture, values, and education that are widely raised across the political spectrum in China.

Of course, at some level this discussion is as abstract and utopian as the writings of Kang Youwei and Jiang Qing. After all, China has a well-developed educational system, fueled by Communist ideology and a new iteration of the examination system, and the possibility of setting up a Confucian religion seems highly unlikely. Because the New Confucians' project is at present largely an abstraction, disputes turn on intellectual understandings of the meaning of "culture," "religion," and "education." Here and there the speakers wander into the deep weeds regarding details of Kang Youwei's thought and their application. There are translation difficulties as well precisely because the mainland New Confucians are hoping to re-create a world in which education and morality are not divided, as they are in most secular societies. One of the most commonly discussed terms is *jiaohua*, which under the dynasties meant "moral transformation through teaching" and included music and rites as well as formal learning. In a modern context, it is difficult not to translate *jiaohua* as "education," but it means "education" in much the way the pre-Reformation Catholic Church would have used the term. In any event, this exchange and others like it present some of contemporary China's best New Confucian thinkers discussing issues they found important at a moment such exchanges were permitted.

Kang Youwei and Institutional Confucianism

Chinese Editor's Introduction

In the 120 years since the first Sino-Japanese War, our nation's fate has gone through many changes. With the waves of Westernization and the fading of Chinese tradition, today's China is no longer the China of a century ago. But the question "What is China?" remains as pressing as ever. Kang Youwei was born in the late Qing period at a time of intense exchanges between China and the outside world. Faced with the irresistible current transforming China from an ancient empire to a modern nation-state and confronted with the powerful "other" that is Western civilization, Kang devoted himself to the institutionalization of Confucianism (or the Confucian religion), hoping to create a new cultural form from within the tradition.

Confucianism practices the way of the inner sage and the outer king.[5] But for a reasonably long historical period in the recent past, Confucianism has basically expressed itself as the study of the inner sage. A Confucianism that merely practices personal cultivation without attention to world affairs and popular livelihood is not the true Confucianism, and the idea of "institutional Confucianism" is to focus on revealing the characteristics of the "outer king" that Confucianism should have. Kang Youwei's thoughts and actions over the course of his life have much to teach us now.

The contents of this special issue reflect parts of discussions held at the conference entitled "Kang Youwei and Institutional Confucianism," held June 26–27, 2014, in Kang Youwei's home town of Nanhai, Guangdong, and jointly organized by the Philosophy Department and the Lingnan Cultural Institute of Zhongshan University. Transcriptions of the oral presentations were approved by the speakers. Editors added this brief introduction as well as subheadings.

Gan Yang: Constructing a Healthy Conservatism on the Basis of a Stable and Steady Attitude

I have been asked to say a few words, but I'm really not the person who should give the main address. I read these essays only on the way here, and what I'll offer today are just a few preliminary thoughts of my own.

Scholarly interest in Kang Youwei has clearly grown over recent years, a number of monographs have come out, and I have read even more manuscripts that are on their way to publication. I believe that today's proceedings will certainly push this trend forward.

Everyone knows that views of Kang Youwei in China, in Hong Kong and Taiwan, and even abroad are basically consistent. In general, views of Kang's earlier thought and activities in the Hundred Days Reform period[6] are viewed positively or even praised lavishly, while at the same time there is almost universal criticism of Kang's later thought and activities aiming to protect the emperor. My feeling is that this may change in important ways in the near future, and if my reading is correct, the best research on Kang Youwei will reverse these trends, with which more people are coming to sympathize and even affirm Kang's conservatism after the Hundred Days period, while there will be more criticism of Kang's earlier period. Most of what I have read over the past few years has focused on an empathetic understanding of Kang's later period.

I suspect that all of this is probably part of a reevaluation of the pro-emperor faction and the question of revolution in the context of contemporary China. We can also see this as a rethinking of conservatism. Kang Youwei was probably the only person, before or after him, to consistently oppose revolution. The reason that he wanted to protect the emperor and the monarchy was basically that he hoped China could avoid taking the road of the French Revolution and instead choose the nonrevolutionary path of reform, as England and Japan had done. To repeat, he seems to have been the only one in the late-Qing period to have been consistent on this point. Everyone else, including Liang Qichao,[7] went back and forth. But Kang was clearer than anyone else on the negative consequences that could ensue if China followed the path of the French Revolution. Reading his early discussions of world politics in his petition to the Guangxu Emperor [r. 1875–1908] as well as his comparative political thought as reflected in the travel diaries of his later period, we can see that his knowledge of world political history as well as his understanding of political reform surpassed that of many people even today.

Of course, in the period leading up to the Revolution of 1911, the debate between the "protect the emperor" party and the revolutionary party played out politically, and China after Sun Yat-sen [1866–1925], twentieth-century China, is basically a revolutionary China. And this is why Kang's political conservatism has had to be comprehensively condemned. But now we are rethinking this period of history on the basis of a century of revolutionary experience. Let me remind everyone that we should not slip into paradoxes or vicious circles. I myself believe that if today we merely condemn China's twentieth-century revolutions based on Kang's conservatism, then this is a bit faddish and not an expression of political maturity. Indeed, we might well fall into a strange pattern where we would in fact be continuing to oppose revolution on the basis of a [rigidly] revolutionary attitude [i.e., going from extreme to extreme without due reflection]. What interests me more is how a postrevolutionary society can once again cultivate a healthy conservative stance, a conservative, gradual, and progressive attitude toward current social problems and modes of reform. Of course, this is just my individual point of view. What I want to avoid is a position that seems to sympathize with the conservatism of Kang's later period but that in fact is still perpetuating a radical revolutionary attitude that has been with us for more than a century already. In my view, what has happened has happened, and what is important, in the wake of all that has happened after a century of revolution, is how to construct a healthy conservatism based on a firm and steady posture.

Beginning from this conservative standpoint, the next important question to address may well relate once again to the evaluation of Kang's early period and especially *Kongzi gaizhi kao* (Confucius as a reformer).[8] To my mind, in the two-thousand- to three-thousand-year history of Chinese political thought, there has never been a work as destructive as Kang's *Confucius as a Reformer*. It is not too much of an exaggeration to say that *Confucius as a Reformer* symbolically overturned and brought an end to Chinese traditional thought and culture in an act of extreme destruction. For example, Gu Jiegang [1893–1980], the founder of China's new historiography, wrote in his autobiography that he read *Confucius as a Reformer* when he was young and thereafter felt that nothing about China's ancient past was believable. The impact of *Confucius as a Reformer* on the creation of this completely negative view of Chinese classical history and civilization was unthinkably immense. We have a hard time imagining it now, but for many literati at the time *Confucius as a Reformer* was a catastrophe. This is very important to those of us now engaged in rethinking the Confucian tradition.

One problem I have with Kang Youwei was that although he worshipped Confucius, under the cover of that worship he emptied out all the concrete elements of the Confucian tradition of *wenjiao*;[9] his attitude appears to have been one of "abstract approval and concrete rejection." In later years, he championed Confucianism as the state religion, but a glimmer of his thoughts on these issues can be found already in *Confucius as a Reformer* because the notion of an "uncrowned king" (*suwang*) must necessarily lead to this.[10] I personally feel that we should be more critical of Kang's reading of Confucius and Confucianism in his early period, as represented by *Confucius as a Reformer*, as well as of his basic Gongyang stance in the late Qing period and should not continue, as we have in the past, to praise his role in the Hundred Days Reform, his Gongyang arguments in the late Qing, and even his development of "apocalyptic Confucianism."[11] For example, his Gongyang "three-ages theory" from the late Qing was extremely capricious because the ages could evolve at any time, so it came to mean a stance in which you could undertake any reform whenever you wanted to. I am hoping that there will be deeper criticisms of this kind of "apocalyptic Confucianism."

Simply put, my basic viewpoint is that although Kang Youwei was politically conservative, in terms of thought and culture he was an extreme radical. And this intellectual radicalism seems to have permeated his entire life, from the early period through his later years. For this reason, from my position as a conservative, all of late Qing Gongyang studies, including Kang's "apocalyptic Confucianism," are extremely suspect and should be seen as a departure from or even a betrayal of the Confucian tradition, and whether it can provide intellectual resources for the construction of a healthy conservativism is worthy of careful thought.

And I feel that behind all this lurks another big question, which is that late Qing Gongyang thinkers—and Kang Youwei's *Confucius as a Reformer* represents this thought to a certain degree—illustrate a tendency toward overpoliticization because they always insist that scholarship and thought be subservient to concrete political needs. In other words, they did not protect the relative independence of thought and scholarship so that they could remain outside currents of concrete politics but instead decided the goals of thought and scholarship based on the great political changes they envisioned. This is a very big problem and can still serve as a lesson for us today. I still believe that the true Confucian spirit gradually rectifies people's hearts and brings order to popular customs through the patient work of education and does not expect concrete results from expedient political reforms. This is the distinction between "great politics" and "small politics." And this is probably the justification behind my devotion to education over the years. That sums up what I had to say. I look forward to your comments and criticism. Thank you very much.

Tang Wenming: The Reforms of *Jiaohua* Institutions Proposed by Modern Confucians

I wrote a book about Kang Youwei's "theory of Confucian religion,"[12] and in the months that I was writing it, I was always imagining the feeling that Kang must have had while cultivating in the Baiyun cave on Mount Xiqiao. Because of time constraints, I could not write an entire paper for this conference, so I will just talk about the major points I would have made. My main point is to describe the context in which modern Confucians have proposed reforms to the *jiaohua* system. I will focus on two key people, one being Kang Youwei and the other being the Republican-period Confucian Ma Yifu [1883–1967] [Tang's discussion of Ma Yifu is not translated here], one from before the establishment of the Republic, the other from after May Fourth.

A minute ago Professor Gan noted that in the past studies of Kang Youwei tended to focus on the Hundred Days Reform period, while more recently they have examined Kang's later life. In my case, I focus on the question of Kang and Confucian religion and have emphasized the early period when Kang was basically in his twenties. I paid special attention to his book *Jiaoxue tongyi* (The comprehensive meaning of education), which has been more or less ignored by scholars. My feeling is that, from the point of view of reforming the *jiaohua* system, *The Comprehensive Meaning of Education* is perhaps Kang's most important work and that his *jiaohua* reform work in the reform period, during his period of exile and after the establishment of the Republic, was closely linked to this.

First, through *The Comprehensive Meaning of Education* we can understand how he positioned Confucianism [within the *jiaohua* project]. There is a chapter in my book called "Venerating Zhu Xi."[13] Kang had a high opinion of Neo-Confucianism, even if he also understood its inadequacies and emphasized the importance of the New Text classics.[14] We might say that his basic stance within Confucianism was that of Gongyang studies plus Neo-Confucianism. In poems and songs written in his youth, Kang compared Zhu Xi to Martin Luther [1483–1546] and Hui Neng [638–713][15] and clearly took Zhu Xi's life ambitions as his own. Of course, we would need to delve more deeply into the notion of "Gongyang studies plus Neo-Confucianism" to truly understand it, and there's no time for that today, but I would like to point out that this style of thinking was closely linked to that of Kang's teacher Zhu Ciqi [1807–1881] and was a style of thinking that developed within the context of Confucian thought of the late Qing period. In the Qing, there appeared a thought trend called "drawing on both the Han and the Song" because at the time divisions between those who preferred Han Confucianism and those who preferred Song Neo-Confucianism were quite marked. Zhu Ciqi was part of this trend, and Kang Youwei developed his own thought on this basis.

The second point I'd like to make is that the main argument of *The Comprehensive Meaning of Education* has to do with the reform of the *jiaohua* system—which I won't go into detail about here. Instead I'll just point out some connections with Kang's theory of Confucian religion (Kongjiao). In his view, ancient texts such as the *Shangshu* (or *Shujing*, Book of documents) and the *Zhouli* (Rites of Zhou) made clear that in ancient times there was a difference between the *jiaohua* system for the elite and the system for the common people. However, Kang argued, beginning with Dong Zhongshu [179–104 BCE][16] in the Han period and continuing through the elaboration of the examination system from Song times onward, the *jiaohua* system focused only on the elite element, the literati, leaving serious failings at the level of popular education. He had little to say about the village covenant system[17] of the post-Song era but had strong criticisms of the examination system. In summary, Kang felt that the past Confucian *jiaohua* system basically overlooked the education of the commoners and that now we should promote the texts to restore commoner education (*shumin zhi jiao*). This was one of Kang's important proposals concerning the reform of the *jiaohua* system. The basic method of restoring commoner education was the establishment of Confucian "churches" (*jiaotang*) and the compilation of texts on the basis of which the Confucian religion would be built. Most people say that such proposals were the result of Christian influence, but I think it is more accurate to say that it was Kang's deep understanding of modern politics that led him to his theory of the Confucian religion. His overall system of thought in fact has nothing to do with Christianity. At this time, Christianity was developing very quickly in Guangdong, and this surely prompted him to reflect on the question of a Confucian religion, but never in his life did he engage in deep research on Christianity. He instead simply felt that the Confucian *jiaohua* institutions based on the examination system were inadequate. This is especially because he felt that modern society is a society where the common people are the central figures, which meant that the education of the common people became extremely important. The emphasis on Confucian religion in *The Comprehensive Meaning of Education* is important to our understanding of Kang's later thoughts on Confucian religion, whether it be during the Hundred Days Reform, during his period of exile, or after the founding of the Republic. Of course, there were minor changes in his thinking, but his basic ideas cannot be properly understood without taking *The Comprehensive Meaning of Education* into account, which means, in other words, that what we find in this work is a basis for his later development. For example, during the Hundred Days Reform period, Kang's proposal to establish a Confucian religion was part of his ideas for the reform of the examination system and drew on his thought as expressed in *The Comprehensive Meaning of Education*. As another example, in his memorials to the emperor during the Hundred Days Reform he clearly stated that the functions of the Confucian church and [non-Confucian] schools (*xuexiao*) were not the same, meaning that schools could not replace the function of the Confucian religion. The Confucian religion was focused on society at large and was not a school for the training of the elite. And in yet another example, there used to be a popular theory that both Kang's *Xinxue weijing kao* (A study of the New Text forgeries) and his *Confucius as a Reformer* were part of the Hundred Days Reform, but this theory is very problematic. This is clear from the fact that at the time of the reforms, elites who were more conservative than Kang agreed with his concrete reform proposals, but they did not agree with his scholarship. A person of Kang's intelligence understood completely that his scholarship could produce enormous controversy, and he could have simply concentrated on the concrete details of reform, leaving scholarship aside, following a path like that of Zhang Zhidong [1837–1909].[18] But he did not do this because he considered [classical] scholarship extremely important. We might say that Kang's *jiaohua* institutional reform plans at the time were quite radical, but his overall political reform plan was more reformist. In addition,. . . according to the research of Mao Haijian [b. 1954],[19] *Confucius as a Reformer* was not submitted at the time [i.e., as part of his memorial to the Guangxu Emperor]. If this was indeed the case, then the reason for it was probably to facilitate the passage of his political reform measures. Although some might say that Kang's two works discussed here [*Confucius as a Reformer* and *Study of New Text Forgeries*] were written chiefly for the benefit of Kang's fellow Confucians and were not the same as the materials submitted in memorials to the emperor, this still only offers a partial explanation because ultimately the importance of the links between the political meaning of classical scholarship and the monarchy are no less important than the links between scholarship and elite bureaucratic institutions. We cannot see his two studies simply as strategic instruments employed in the Hundred Days Reform. Kang had thought deeply about the transformation of Confucian *jiaohua* institutions, and of course these thoughts were developed in the larger framework of the reform of political institutions. This much is clear.

Kang's thoughts on Confucian religion during his period of exile and during the Republican period focused mainly on the question of the relationship between Confucian religion and China. I won't go into detail, but his basic thinking was not to build the nation directly on the basis of classical studies but rather to build the Confucian religion on that basis and thus use the religion to build the nation. . . . For Kang, nation and religion were linked through the concept of a national religion. Religion transcends national boundaries, but from a historical perspective China and the Confucian religion had a particular relationship, the Confucian religion having been the national religion since the Han dynasty, a situation that, in Kang's view, could and should be continued at present. The key here is that Kang understood that thinking about nation building uniquely in political terms was not enough, and in fact his promotion of a Confucian religion meant that it could and should become a guiding strength holding China together. Thus, to sum up Kang Youwei's basic thoughts on modern China, there are three elements that we must fully understand.

One is of course the Republic, which is related to Kang's understanding of modern politics, whether in terms of time or in terms of space. The second is the meaning of the monarchy, and the third is the meaning of Confucianism as the national religion. At a recent conference in Shanghai, I proposed an idea: that Kang Youwei be seen as China's "legislator," in Rousseau's terms.[20] Not Sun Yat-sen, not Mao Zedong [1893–1976], and not Zhang Taiyan [1869–1936],[21] but Kang Youwei. The significance of a legislator often cannot be appreciated until several generations after his time, which means that he might have failed during his life. A legislator may not be armed and may well be an unarmed prophet. If we examine modern China in this light, we will discover that Kang Youwei's thought towers over that of Zhang Taiyan, Sun Yat-sen, and Mao Zedong. For this reason, it is my opinion that the most important thing that contemporary China's thought world should do is to affirm Kang's position as modern China's legislator, only after which can we begin to profitably discuss other questions from the proper perspective.

Zhang Xiang: The Political Meaning of Confucius as a Reformer

I would like to add something in relation to Tang Wenming's presentation. What is the political meaning of *Confucius as a Reformer*? There's a source that could help us figure this out. In *Wuxu bianfa shi yanjiu* (Study of the history of the Hundred Days Reform), Huang Zhangjian [1919–2009] used a letter that Kang wrote to Zhao Bizhen [1873–1956][22] from about 1901. In my reading, Kang reflects on his mistakes in the reform process in a way rarely seen elsewhere.

Kang points out that he himself was different before and after his meeting with the Guangxu Emperor. Before meeting the emperor, in writing *Chunqiu Dong-shixue* (On Dong Zhongshu's teaching of the *Spring and Autumn Annals*) and *Confucius as a Reformer*, his feeling was that there was no hope for the Qing, meaning that "with nothing to gain at the top, we must fight for the bottom," which led him to greatly promote popular sovereignty and similar themes. But once he met the emperor, he thought there might be hope, which meant that he by all means had to keep the confidence of the emperor. The document that we have now is incomplete, but it contains the chief points of debate between Kang and Liang Qichao and other disciples in 1903. He did not feel that the reason for the failure was that reform had proceeded too hastily but rather felt that the conditions had been in place to move quickly. He felt that the failure was because at the time people didn't know whether they could rely on the Guangxu Emperor, so they placed their hopes on the reforms under way in Hunan, where "the Chinese people would be reborn."[23] Why was the conservative reaction to the reforms in Hunan so strong? This was the result of Liang Qichao's having established schools and newspapers in Hunan. In the spring of 1898, people in Hunan were already broadcasting the revolutionary notion of "independence and renewing the race" (*zili yizhong*). Looking back from the perspective of this letter, *Confucius as a Reformer* surely contained political content.

Gan Yang: The Question Is How Kang Intended to Carry Out *Jiaohua*

Let me also mention a doubt I have about Tang Wenming's presentation. My feeling is that Kang's discussion of commoner education was nothing more than what Liang Qichao talked about in "renewing the people."[24] The idea that Kang felt that Confucianism had historically neglected commoner education is a very strange theory. How could Confucians not educate the people? The point was that Kang was not pleased with how Confucians had traditionally educated the commoners, and so he hoped for a "new teaching" (*xinjiao*) which to my mind, again, is the same as Liang's "renewing the people."[25] Confucianism traditionally of course took measures to carry out commoner education, and its entire success relied on its outreach to the people, which early on penetrated their hearts. Of course, this commoner education can be reduced to two characters, those of "filial piety" and "fraternal love" (*xiaoti*). The problem was that Kang thought this was insufficient, that there was no real educational content in the commoner education. So he turned Confucian commoner education on its head, but this does not mean that there had been no commoner education prior to this point. I think Tang Wenming's point is doubtful and needs discussion. As for Kang's differences before and after meeting the emperor, this is a problem, and here it means precisely that he can be suspected of completely turning his back on Confucianism. I feel that this still needs a lot of research, including his later discussions of national religion, which also relate to this. The whole question is: What will be taught? What transformation is he looking for? How will the teaching be carried out? If Kang meant to leave the traditional commoner education of "filial piety and fraternal love" behind and to offer a new kind of commoner education, then this would raise too many questions, such as that of the difference between this and Liang Qichao's "renewing the people." My feeling is that this was precisely his most radical point, not his most conservative. So I invite Wenming to mull this over. Thank you!

Tang Wenming: It Is Best to Reform the *Jiaohua* System Through Narrowly Focused Political Reform

I'll give a quick answer. First, as for Zhang Xiang's comment, I'm actually not intending to challenge the old theory but only want to make clear that whereas in the past we saw *Confucius as a Reformer* as a tool employed in service of reform, we now see this is inaccurate. My feeling is that Kang Youwei had reflected deeply on the reform of the *jiaohua* system; otherwise he would not have sacrificed his political reforms to it. Of course, in Kang's eyes the reform of the *jiaohua* system also had political implications. His understanding was that the goal was a narrowly focused political reform that would be in line with the reform of the *jiaohua* system. For example, this is very clear when we compare it with Zhang Zhidong's proposals. For Zhang, all that was needed was political reform; *jiaohua* could be left alone. Here, the difference is that Kang, faced with the changing times, understood that the *jiaohua* system had to be reformed as well.

As for Professor Gan's question, this relates to the two separate issues of Kang's opinions and how we evaluate Kang's opinions. Kang's views were what I pointed out earlier—that, in part, developments in Song-Ming Neo-Confucianism meant that Confucianism had already taken the road of populism, especially via community compacts. He is of course right about this. Mizoguchi Yūzō [1932–2010] has a theory that roughly conveys this idea: he argues that the rise of Neo-Confucianism in the Song and Ming periods meant a change in the focus of *jiaohua*.[26] The Song saw a move away from the original monarchy toward gentry rule, and the Ming saw a change from the gentry to the commoners. There are problems with this argument, but it probably helps us to understand social transformations in the Song to Ming periods and the relationship of Neo-Confucianism to these transformations. From another angle, Kang Youwei was also sharply critical of the methods employed in

Song-Ming Neo-Confucian *jiaohua*. He felt that community compacts had outlived their usefulness and that what was required was a move toward religion. Yet this idea was not solely a response to the challenge of Christianity but was instead based on his understanding and experience of Confucianism. . . . Kang had a profound religious experience while meditating on Mount Xiqiao, which means that he didn't invent his theories of Confucian religion out of thin air but instead fashioned them from his experiences of meditation. So while he naturally felt that Song-Ming Neo-Confucianism was superior to Han-Tang Confucianism in terms of broadening popular knowledge and consolidating popular morality, the consolidation of popular morality among the common people now required progressing to the level of religion, even if the core concepts remained the seemingly simple moral notions of filial piety, fraternal love, benevolence, and righteousness. I have a hard time seeing this as upending anything at all, unless we want to see Neo-Confucianism as a reversal of Confucianism. But these conceptual questions do not completely match up with institutional questions. I think that what Gan Yang meant was that China's traditional political institutions, in particular the monarchy and the examination system, at an institutional level guaranteed Confucian *jiaohua* for commoners. There was nothing particularly wrong with these institutions, but my feeling is that Kang Youwei understood that in a new era Confucian *jiaohua* could no longer be accomplished in the same way. In this sense, Kang's views upended the methods employed in traditional Confucian *jiaohua*. As I said a few minutes ago, when Kang Youwei was young, he saw Zhu Xi as the Confucian equivalent of Martin Luther or Hui Neng and later saw himself as the Martin Luther of the Confucian religion. Here we get a sense of Kang's self-investment in the matter of *jiaohua* reform. In terms of significance, the change from Han-Tang Confucianism to Song-Ming Neo-Confucianism can be compared to the change from Catholicism to Protestantism, in particular the change from a system based on ritual and music to a system grounded in mental or spiritual cultivation, which is extremely important in the history of Confucianism. In addition, there was a fundamentalist character to what the Neo-Confucians were searching for. They believed that they were expounding on what Confucius said, while the Han-Tang Confucians had instead revered the Duke of Zhou.[27]

As for the question of how we evaluate Kang Youwei's opinions, I basically agree with Professor Gan in the sense that Kang is not conservative enough. At the same time, in my view Kang's reflections at one level are a response to Rousseau. Once Rousseau's theories of popular sovereignty took hold, notions of political legitimacy were upended, and you could no longer seek legitimacy in traditional ideas like the divine right of kings or China's Gongyang school. To put it simply, the initial goal of Kang Youwei's Gongyang arguments was not to discuss political legitimacy but instead to consolidate the basis of *jiaohua*. In other words, it is clear that Kang was trying to solve difficult problems related to republican rule and popular sovereignty. In a republican age, in an age of popular sovereignty, in a situation where a democratic republic is the norm, how should we imagine the construction of our *jiaohua* system? Should we aim for another theocracy? Clearly this is not how Kang Youwei thought. Of course, Kang Youwei never conceived of our present Party-state system. So in Kang's thinking the sole and necessary function of the Confucian religion was as the state religion, and from the point of view of institutional change the point of having a national religion was to permit the separation of church and state. I talk about this in detail in my book. In terms of the construction of a new republican politics, national religion was an important measure to protect the republic. One of my very practical concerns is that for Confucian religion to enter society, we cannot be content with academic theories but must think of other institutions outside of the university. This means that, yes, maybe our content should be a bit more conservative, but we still need to innovate institutionally. I might call this "putting old wine in new bottles."

Yao Zhongqiu: Saving Kang Youwei from Western Educational Superstition

In my view, Kang Youwei is truly an important figure in the modern history of Chinese thought, or, as Tang Wenming put it, Kang is the legislator of modern China, and virtually all of modern Chinese thought can be traced back to Kang Youwei. I feel that Kang was more astute than others, particularly in the importance he accorded to teaching (*jiao*) because in the process of building a modern nation, he particularly emphasized this question.

Yet after reading Kang's systematic explanations, to tell the truth, I'm rather disappointed because his theories are full of contradictions. His attempt to establish his Confucian religion was doomed from the start and was destined to fail in the future as well. So from my point of view, the goal shared by people like Tang Wenming and Chen Ming [to establish a Confucian religion] is similarly doomed.

So what's the problem? On the one hand, I quite admire Kang Youwei because as an observer of China's *jiaohua* system he was able to describe it very accurately, in ways that are similar to how I view it now. For example, in a series of arguments he pointed out that the teachings of Confucius are not "sacred teachings" (*shenjiao*). Confucius was a revered teacher (*xianshi*), and people study him, which means that the teachings of Confucius are first a field of "study," something that was realized through the process of study. What most people study is *wen*, the meaning of which is very rich; at least from the time that the

Book of Documents was composed, *wen* should be understood as the most important concept for our community. I've been teaching a course on *The Book of Documents* over the past couple of years, and at the beginning I couldn't figure out what the "accomplished ancestor" (*wenzu*) in the sentence "Shun went to [the temple of] the accomplished ancestor" (*Shun ge yu wenzu*) meant.[28] In the past couple of years, I have been thinking about *wenjiao* and Confucius's explanations of *wen*, and I've come to an initial understanding of the passage. *Wen* seems to be a particularly important concept, including its meaning in compounds such as *wende* (accomplished virtue or power).

A few minutes ago Tang Wenming said that Kang Youwei believed that traditional China had no "commoner education." Gan Yang disagreed, insisting that our huge community, with its own coherence, which is still growing and expanding, must possess its own commoner education. Of course it does, but the problem is that now there are too many people using Western notions of sacred teachings to view our educational system. In fact, *jiao* is the same as *wen*, and rituals, music, and popular customs are all means by which *jiaohua* is conveyed to the masses.

I would like to add something else, which is that in fact there were two levels to China's traditional *jiaohua* system. One level did indeed produce an elite group through a program of "gentlemen studies," an elite that truly did shape its body and soul through studies of things like the Six Classics. The other level concerned the common people, who practiced rituals and music originally produced by the elites. And something else that I find extremely important is that in traditional Chinese society, the "sacred" was contained in the *wen*. In our *jiaohua* system, *wenjiao* dominated sacred teachings, and these sacred teachings were dependent on *wenjiao*. We are holding our conference on Mount Xiqiao, which is very representative in that it has all sorts of gods, but all of these gods are bearers of a common *wen*, bearers of the Chinese value system preserved by Confucians. In other words, many sacred teachings are organic elements of *wenjiao*, or, in the Confucian context, Confucius used all sorts of sacred teachings to *jiaohua* the masses. On the one hand, Confucius used his own texts to *jiaohua* the elite, so that some of them reached the stage of "those who learn and so, readily, get possession of knowledge,"[29] including those for whom "study was difficult." For those who abandoned their studies because it was too difficult, the only remaining method was to "teach using the sacred way [from *The Book of Changes*]."[30] In fact, to "teach using the sacred way" means to invest these values with religious meaning. This means that the various kinds of religion are in fact paths by which Confucian *jiaohua* has been transmitted. Among them are rituals and music, something we find in many sacred teachings. Hence, in the observable life of the common people everywhere, what we see is a religious system with many gods, and in fact an individual can believe in many gods at the same time.

There is another point we could discuss. Tang Wenming has written a book called *Fujiao zai kuan* (Spread the teachings gently) in which he argues that Confucian values not only infused low-level popular beliefs in the way described by modern academic discourse on religion but also infused mature, orthodox, mainstream Chinese religions, such as the Chinese Buddhism that everyone is familiar with. The sinicization of Buddhism was in fact, properly speaking, the Confucianization of Buddhism, which we can see very clearly in today's "Buddhism of the human realm."[31] This "humanization" of Buddhism has become ever clearer since the Song-Ming period and reflects a wide-scale adoption of Confucianism. Hence, Buddhism and Daoism can become channels for the transmission of Confucian values.

I think that this is the basic situation regarding the Chinese *jiaohua* system. In simple terms, Confucianism is a *wenjiao* that teaches and transforms the people through another set of means rather than directly through Confucian elite practice. In sum, this was the very effective *jiaohua* system in place in our China over the course of the past two millennia. Kang Youwei understood this but was not satisfied with it. He wrote a few essays on the subject, concluding that our *jiaohua* system was too primitive. So my profound feeling is that in Kang's construction of Confucian religion we see his acceptance of the Western superstition concerning the *jiaohua* system of monotheism. He saw one of these systems as primitive and the other as civilized.

The influence of Kang's thinking on this subject has been huge over the past century, to the point that the majority of Chinese intellectuals believe that the Chinese belief system and the *jiaohua* system of such a society are primitive, while that of a monotheistic society is superior. At the time, Kang's reasoning was a matter of personal feeling, while intellectuals of our generation have probably been more influenced by Weber's theories of religion, which have shaped our superstitions concerning Western *jiaohua* systems, convincing us that only monotheistic systems are sophisticated. In *The Protestant Ethic and the Spirit of Capitalism*, Max Weber proved the close relationship between Protestantism and various institutions. Hence our superstitions regarding the superiority of monotheism are perhaps stronger than Kang Youwei's, to the extent that many intellectuals have been seduced by Protestantism. I find that this is a very serious problem.

From the beginning of his exploration of the differences between Chinese and Western teachings, Kang took a heterodox path. At the outset of his comparison, he decided that we were not as good as the West. All comparisons of Chinese and Western culture seem to follow this pattern, as we get the worst of any comparison, which requires complete self-abnegation. Although Tang Wenming argues that Kang's thoughts on establishing Confucian religion were not directly influenced by Protestantism, from what I've seen they were directly stimulated by it. Even today, scholars like Jiang Qing and Chen Ming who talk about setting up a Confucian religion have been motivated by Christianity, without exception. They are most worried about the wide-scale spread of Christianity in China, which requires the establishment of another religion to block it. But the way they propose to go about it is to establish a Chinese-style Protestantism, which to me is the equivalent of a "capitulationist religion."

So here I'll come directly to my conclusion. China's complex *jiaohua* system, with *wenjiao* at its center, is both the simplest and most exalted *jiaohua* system. If mankind were searching for a universal teaching, it would be Chinese style, a *jiaohua* system with *wenjiao* at its core. I'll just mention one superior point of this kind of system, which is that it can link up with all sacred teachings and take charge of them, so that religious wars no longer need occur. This is a historical fact that we can see in China. Precisely because *wenjiao* penetrated the various sacred teachings, the extreme elements of these sacred teachings were suppressed. *Wenjiao* can also bring believers in the other religions to share a common cultural identity. And on the basis of this common cultural identity, we built a huge political community.

A core problem that China is facing now is how to bring religious believers to identify with the state. For that, we need a common *wen*, and this *wen* ultimately requires the reconstruction of a *jiaohua* system. So my conclusion is that we must rescue Kang Youwei from his superstitious belief in Western *jiaohua*.

Chen Ming: Returning to Kang Youwei

What characterizes mainland New Confucians in terms of their basic orientation is that they are concerned with the construction of the state and the nation, unlike the diaspora New Confucians, whose concerns are democracy and science, a passive reaction following the attack of Western culture. In terms of academic style, mainland New Confucians employ the discourse and perspective of religion, not philosophy or ethics, the choices of the diaspora New Confucians. Many people oppose our theory of "Confucianism" because, in the view of some of these people, it reflects the influence of Christianity. This underestimates us and overestimates Christianity as well as their own grasp of Confucian classics and history. In fact, there are clear examples attesting to a belief in God in the Confucian classics, in the *Book of Documents* and the *Classic of Poetry*, for example, where God appears as both creator and master. And it was precisely through this long tradition that Confucius pierced the primeval chaos (described in the *Ten Wings* as "the great attribute of heaven and earth is the giving and maintaining life"[32]) thus transforming a mysterious tradition, one full of the flavor of natural religion, into Confucianism, which is guided by the spirit of humanism. This was a transformation from a communication between heaven and man dominated by shamans, to a unity between heaven and man achieved through cultivation of heaven and virtue. Confucian practice plays out in the ways of the world and the hearts of men; the plaque bearing the characters "heaven-earth-lord-parent-teacher" is still found in many places.[33] If we avoid the narrow Christian definition of religion, then it is obvious that Confucianism belongs to the broad category of religion. Qiu Feng's concept of *wenjiao* is an awkward reading and is in fact an artefact of the May Fourth desire to establish a difference between Confucianism and Christianity, while at the same time describing the social function of Confucianism. If we analyze it closely, the *jiao* of *wenjiao* is a verb, meaning "to teach *wen*," as opposed to the Legalist formula of the "teaching of laws" and taking government officials as masters. The culture of Confucianism resided in the hands of the ancient Educational Ministry, which, following the logic of complementarity (*shun yinyang*), created *jiaohua*, crafting teachings out of the sacred way. The foundation of these teachings is benevolence (*ren*). Dong Zhongshu said it most clearly: "benevolence is the heart of heaven"; or in the words of Song Neo-Confucians, "[Benevolence means that] heaven and earth are the heart of living things." Or to cite Confucius himself: "[Benevolence describes] the great power of heaven and earth." This tells us that what is taught in a *wenjiao* perhaps cannot be understood as religion, but the *wen* at the core must be understood as religion. Han Wudi [r. 141–87 BCE] chose to single out Confucianism, which gave it a political function, creating the special nature of Confucianism. This was extremely important for Confucianism in the sense that it was invested with an overly worldly purpose, but this particularity does not negate Confucianism's religious nature. Obviously, there's no time here to discuss the special characteristics of religions in general. To put it simply, from a religious perspective, understanding the Confucian tradition requires attention not only to its role in building the state and the nation and not only to its concern with rebuilding a modern Confucian social basis. We must correct the error, originally committed during the May Fourth period, of "philosophizing" the Confucian classics and return to Confucianism's original nature and the values that it objectively revered.

This is also a point of departure for correctly understanding Kang Youwei. In the past few weeks, I have been talking about returning to Kang Youwei at conferences in Beijing and Shanghai and here will emphasize once again my basic points.

First, returning to Kang Youwei means returning to the problems faced by Kang Youwei, which were those of state building and nation building. The most important political narratives in modern times have been the Revolutionary Party's [i.e., the Guomindang's] plan to save the nation, the Chinese Communist Party's plan to save the nation, and the liberal theory of Enlightenment. Their respective political goals were getting rid of the Manchus, achieving communism, and gaining individual liberation. They were conceived and developed in the wake of the intensification of China's internal and external crises and the intervention of the international Communist movement. The emotional distress associated with these changes led people to blame the trauma of modern times on culture, thus leading to the Enlightenment narrative, seen as valid for all times and places. The history and philosophy of the international Communist movement are basically the same. The insights afforded by Enlightenment thought brought China's problems into clear focus, and China's path and goals became clear. But these same insights reveal the limitations of the May Fourth era and direct us toward a rediscovery and a renewed understanding of Kang Youwei. Compared to the China imagined by Kang Youwei—a China in which the frontiers of the Qing Empire, established by Manchu military force, would be maintained, a China that maintained its ethnic integration even as it navigated its transition to a modern republic—the ideas of both the Left and the Right appear pitiful.

The challenge we faced in the modern era was an existential crisis under pressure from foreign invasion, involving the protection of our territory and sovereignty and the preservation of our bodily and material safety. This crisis created a consensus around the ideas of salvation and the search for wealth and power. In this context, the effectiveness of the government's performance became the most important measure of its legitimacy and its most important goal. This is not the same thing as the social reorganization resulting from the Industrial Revolution or the understanding and pursuit of political justice arising from this reorganization. An important difference is that the rights of the individual—the central pursuit of the Enlightenment narrative, a theme explored artistically during the New Culture Movement through Ibsenism, among other doctrines—in fact exists in a certain tension and conflict with the urgent tasks of modern Chinese history. From this perspective, the sacralization of the Enlightenment project is utterly immature. Communism, with its internationalist background, also grew out of a plan to "save China." But the continuing revolution of the proletariat not only led to internal struggles in Chinese politics but also brought the national economy to the verge of collapse.

For this reason, stressing the Kang Youwei question involves not only the standpoint and wisdom of Confucian political philosophy but also the promise and challenge of Confucian political philosophy. In fact, all of those who worked on this front in the modern era—including reformers, constitutionalists, and even those who argued for "Chinese learning for fundamental principles and Western learning for practical application"—all were part of the world of Confucian thought, and in making their demands and proposals they did so from the point of view of Chinese agency. Returning to Kang Youwei means returning to the problems Kang faced, returning to this intellectual genealogy, these demands and proposals, and on this basis building a narrative structure of modern and contemporary Chinese politics. This first requires a new institutional arrangement. As a political and legal starting point for a transition away from empire, Puyi's abdication edict made the solemn promise to transfer power to the "Republic of Five Peoples."[34] As an institution, the republic, in comparison to the imperial institutions of the family-state, embodied the notions of public, common, and harmony differently. "Public" meant "the world belongs to all" (*tianxia wei gong*) and popular sovereignty; "common" signified common goals and mass participation; "harmony" evoked citizen virtues such as moderation, negotiation, public welfare. In a sense, these are in harmony with the values and principles of Confucian political philosophy. This is illustrated by the saying from the *Book of Rites* that "when the Grand course was pursued, a public and common spirit ruled all under the sky,"[35] as well as by concrete expressions of Confucian commitment to the values of "equality, wealth, peace, and harmony." If we say that the main expression of state building is an institutional arrangement, then we can also understand nation building as having social, cultural, and psychological aspects and a sense of identity with and belonging to this state. Because of its nature, function, and origin, the nation possesses a distinctive character and cannot be reduced to politics or law; it necessitates a separate discussion. This requires systematic effort from society to create a sense of identity with the state. The Confucian proposal to create a state religion should be understood in this sense.

Second, returning to Kang Youwei means returning to Kang Youwei's way of thinking. Kang's thought is rooted in the doctrine of the mean[36] and in rational analysis. This meant paying equal attention to the preservation of the state and the realization of institutional justice, balancing individual rights and national identity. This meant not forgetting the original intention (*buwang chuzhong*)[37] of self-strengthening, which was to maintain the Qing—not the Ming—borders and ethnic structures. In sum, balancing state and institutions, reality and ideals, maintaining unitary politics and law as well as plural cultural and religious relations. Kang was clear in his mind as to the nature of China's predicament: foreign powers were attacking, a minority ethnic group was in power, the territory was extensive, and the ethnic situation complex. This meant that the transition would be perilous and that the only possible course would be gradual reform and not utopian experimentation. Kang Youwei's golden mean and his rational approach meant remaining faithful to original intentions, respecting reality, valuing results, and not surrendering to perverse principles or logic.

The point of state building and nation building was to effect the modern transformation of the empire, but the resulting national institutions and social structures had to be appropriate, capable of guaranteeing their survival in the dog-eat-dog world of international competition, while also creating wealth for the citizens through management of society. In this context, the preservation of the nation and of the people's livelihood takes historical priority over individual rights, constitutional democracy, freedom of belief, and other values cherished by the Enlightenment project. For reasons of sequence, priority could not be accorded to the individual; the philosophy of struggle and utopian longings should have been refused as well. In other words, from the beginning we should not have foregrounded "modernity" in our project of state building and nation building. The original goal should have been to "protect the county, protect the race, and protect the faith." The Enlightenment project and the utopian narrative should have been chosen only if they were effective means of salvation; we should never have allowed theory to swallow up facts or means to become ends, but sadly this is precisely the source of today's biggest problems.

Kang Youwei's way of thinking can be found in this passage: "The Way of the state is first to avoid chaos and then to seek proper governance. . . . The best plan for China today is to rectify law and social order, carry out the laws and directives, restore order, and maintain the borders. The key to everything is to avoid violence and chaos so as to reassure the occupations." There is nothing brilliant about this, but the reason that the Left and the Right are called "antiquated" and "heterodox" is basically that they have forgotten this.

Third, returning to Kang Youwei means transcending Kang Youwei. First, Kang's notion that "state's rights are more important than people's rights" made sense at the time or as a means to the next objective, and today we must still accord a certain importance to the interests of the state, but the concept of popular sovereignty needs to be established. Especially in terms of Chinese domestic politics, the logical relationship of "people's rights are higher than state's rights" needs to be clear. The effectiveness of the governing power must forever be guaranteed, but the principle of popular sovereignty must never be obscured. Because today we have already made important advances on the road to industrialization and urbanization, questions of "civilization, equality, freedom, and self-reliance," which have long been given short shrift, now can and should be improved. The most pressing objective of the China Dream is to ensure a happy life for the people, which means feeling at ease as well as enjoying material fulfillment, which means that individual self-expression and political participation should also be part of the equation. As a consequence, proposals to make Confucianism the national religion must also be adjusted to admit the importance of civil religion, to better create common republican values, and to contribute to national cohesion. Kang Youwei understood the importance of cultural homogeneity in republicanism as well as the important role and function of Confucianism in this process. But whether this should be achieved through a national religion is something that should be discussed. When the republic replaced the monarchy with its constitution, this naturally meant that the status of citizens rose to the top and that in addition to politics and law the question of cultural homogeneity should be examined within the context and principles of modern politics and law. Civil religion may be a more appropriate alternative. In China's traditional society, the Chinese people arrived at a homogeneity in terms of culture and citizenship via Confucian *jiaohua* and identity, and at the same time Confucianism came to play an important role in terms of basic political values and social cohesion. Given the changes over the years, Confucianism will have difficulty achieving the same support and foundation and will need to be updated. In concrete terms, this means making use of modern political principles and structures to guide the political community, currently held together by ambiguous interest relations, toward a relationship with clearer legal and economic foundations, which will both reduce the tension among the current structure of national politics, the status of citizenship, and Confucianism as well as maintain Confucianism's positive function in terms of national identity and social cohesion. The idea of civil religion is to transform the Confucian system from its historical political character into a contemporary social character, allowing it to compete freely and achieve its own position and influence in the "cultural marketplace."

Fourth, this is truly possible. In left-wing discourse, the state is in fact the Party because it is based in class theory. Indeed, from the perspective of historical development, both the Chinese Communist Party and the Guomindang were founded with the original intention of saving the country and for this reason cannot be understood in the same way as in Western theories of political parties, and cannot be confused with political parties that aim to win political power through their organization and activities, especially against the background of elections and representation, where their goal is to represent the demands of special interests. For the Right, the "state" is in reality society (society standing in for the activities of people). In fact, the challenge the Chinese people are facing or the problem they need to resolve is how to maintain China's existing borders, sovereignty, and people (*renmin*) in the face of the pressure from Western powers and the related question of finding a government that will lead the Chinese people to wealth and power. In the search to fulfill this basic demand, questions have been raised concerning the justice of the system. From a developmental standpoint, justice follows the achievement of wealth and power. However, when questions of justice become important, they leap to the head of the line regardless of questions of logic. This often leads liberals not only to separate the two but also to think about them as antagonistic. It is in this opposition to the Right that the Party-state theory of the Left finds its basis in legitimacy. From a Confucian standpoint, seeking a balance between the two is the golden mean and the proper Way.

Replacing "individual" and "class" with "state" and "people" is the basic characteristic of the new generation's ideological discourse whose goal is the China Dream. This is a return to the central question of the modern era, a return to Confucian ideas, and a new understanding of the Party's original intent to "save China." To propose returning to Kang Youwei in this context not only has theoretical significance but also possesses an equally important practical significance.

Translator's Notes

1. Chen Ming, Gan Yang, Tang Wenming, Yao Zhongqiu, and Zhang Xiang, "Kang Youwei yu zhiduhua Ruxue" (Kang Youwei and institutional Confucianism), *Kaifang Shidai* 5 (2014), Ai Sixiang Wang, http://www.aisixiang.com/data/79543.html.
2. See Tang Wenming, Zeng Yi, Hao Zhaokuan, Chen Bisheng, Guo Xiaodong, Wu Zengding, Chen Ming, et al., "From Kang Youwei to Deng Xiaoping," roundtable discussion, November 2016, trans. Selena Orly, Zhang Hongbing, and David Ownby, Reading the China Dream, https://www.readingthechinadream.com/kang-xiaowei-to-deng-xiaoping.html.
3. See "Transcend Left and Right, Unite the Three Traditions, Renew the Party-State: A Confucian Interpretation of the China Dream," roundtable discussion, March 17, 2015, trans. David Ownby, Reading the China Dream, https://www.readingthechinadream.com/chen-ming-transcend-left-and-right.html.
4. See Tang Wenming et al., "From Kang Youwei to Deng Xiaoping."
5. The idea of "inner sage and outer king" (*neisheng waiwang*) refers to the core Confucian idea that the ultimate goal of self-cultivation is service to state and society.
6. A brief period during 1898 when the Guangxu Emperor, allegedly influenced by Kang Youwei, attempted sweeping reforms of China's basic institutions.
7. Originally Kang's disciple, Liang Qichao was a leading figure in the reform movements of the 1890s and went on to have a major influence as a journalist and public intellectual.
8. First published in 1897, Kang's work *Confucius as a Reformer* offered a radical revision of traditional views of Confucius, casting him as a dynamic, innovative reformer. Kang's goal was perhaps to mobilize as much elite support as possible by suggesting that major institutional reform could be consistent with Chinese tradition, but his arguments shocked many of his contemporaries.
9. *Wen* means "pattern," "form," "writing," "culture," and *jiao* means "teaching" or a set of "teachings." In modern Chinese, *wenjiao* means "culture and education," but in the context of the discussion translated here it refers to teachings, like those of Confucius, that ground their truth claims not in gods or sacred mysteries, but rather in human possibilities.
10. That is, the notion that as a statecraft master Confucius would have been made king were it not for unfortunate political circumstances.
11. The *Gongyang*, or *Gongyang zhuan*, is a commentary on the *Spring and Autumn Annals*, a Zhou-period work classically attributed to Confucius, in which Confucius can allegedly be seen as a visionary reformer. Over the course of China's long history, Confucians such as Kang Youwei have used the *Gongyang zhuan* as an intellectual source for the advocacy of profound political changes that will emerge organically from the Confucian tradition. The Gongyang school also argued that history moves through three great ages: the age of disorder, the age of approaching peace, and the age of universal peace. Gan Yang's mention of Kang's "apocalyptic Confucianism" surely refers to such arguments.

12. Tang Wenming, *Fujiao zai kuan: Kang Youwei Kongjiao sixiang shenlun* (Spread the teachings gently: Kang Youwei's thoughts about Confucian religion) (Beijing: Renmin Daxue, 2012).

13. Zhu Xi (1130–1200) was a major figure associated with the rise of Neo-Confucianism in the Song dynasty.

14. A major debate among Confucian scholars over the centuries opposed the "old texts" and the "new texts" as valid sources of moral and textual authority. Both were bodies of texts purporting to contain the essence of Confucian culture. Kang Youwei, a proponent of the New Text school, argued in *Xinxue weijing kao* (Study of New Text forgeries) that they were actually older and more authentic and had been denied their rightful place in history.

15. Hui Neng was a major figure in the establishment of the Chan Buddhist tradition in China.

16. Dong Zhongshu was a major figure in the adoption of Confucianism as Chinese state ideology in the Former Han period.

17. The village covenant system (*xiangyue*) was originally imagined as a source of village self-government but became over the centuries, especially in the Qing period, a more top-down exercise through which officials sought to spread Confucian ideology via periodic lectures.

18. Zhang Zhidong was an influential scholar-official in the late Qing period, active in a variety of reform efforts. In the educational context to which Tang Wenming is referring, Zhang is best known for his proposal that "Chinese learning serve as fundamental principles and Western learning as practical application" (*Zhongxue wei ti, xixue wei yong*). Tang clearly thinks that Zhang's proposal to simply add Western studies to existing Chinese practices was simplistic in comparison to Kang's more far-reaching reflections.

19. Mao Haijian is professor of history at East China Normal University in Shanghai.

20. *Legislator* is a term borrowed from Jean-Jacques Rousseau (1712–1778), who in *The Social Contract* (1762) uses it to refer to the figure who intervenes at a critical moment to give concrete institutional shape to the popular will. The speakers here seem to mean "conceptual founder," the person who lays the intellectual groundwork for something to come.

21. Zhang Taiyan was a complex if important figure in the intellectual world of late Qing China.

22. Zhao Bizhen was a prolific translator of Japanese texts in the late Qing period.

23. This phrase is taken from Kang's letter to Zhao, the source under discussion. See Yin Feizhou, *Hunan weixin yundong shiliao* (Historical materials on the reform movement in Hunan) (Changsha: Yuelu Shushe, 2013), 227.

24. Gan Yang is referring to Liang's well-known essay on "renewing the people" (*xinmin*), in which he argued that China needed a new citizenry to go along with new institutions.

25. *Xinjiao* also is the word for Protestantism; Gan Yang likely puts it in scare quotes to distinguish Kang's new teaching or Liang's ideas from Christianity.

26. Tang is likely referring to Mizoguchi Yūzō's book *Chūgoku zenkindai shisō no kussetsu to tenkai* (Refraction and development in early-modern Chinese thought) (Tokyo: Tokyo University Press, 1980). This work was translated into Chinese in 2011 by Gong Ying, entitled *Zhongguo qianjindai sixiang de quzhe yu zhankai* (Beijing: Sanlian Shudian).

27. The Duke of Zhou was one of Confucius's heroes and a towering figure in China's cultural history, credited with creating the "mandate of heaven" and many court rituals.

28. "On the first day of the first month (of the) next year, Shun went to (the temple of) the Accomplished Ancestor. He deliberated with (the president of) the Four Mountains how to throw open the doors (of communication between himself and the) four (quarters of the land), and how he could see with the eyes, and hear with the ears of all." See Chinese Text Project, n.d., https://ctext.org/pre-qin-and-han.

29. In this passage of *The Analects*, Confucius says, "Those who are born with the possession of knowledge are the highest class of men. Those who learn, and so, readily, get possession of knowledge, are the next. Those who are dull and stupid, and yet compass the learning, are another class next to these. As to those who are dull and stupid and yet do not learn—they are the lowest of the people." See *The Analects*, Chinese Text Project, n.d., https://ctext.org/pre-qin-and-han.

30. "The sages, in accordance with (this) spirit-like way, laid down their instructions, and all under heaven yield submission to them." See Chinese Text Project, n.d., https://ctext.org/pre-qin-and-han.

31. "Buddhism of the human realm" (*renjian Fojiao*) is one of the major expressions of modern Chinese Buddhism, seen particularly in large Taiwanese Buddhist institutions such as Ciji Gongdehui.

32. The *Ten Wings* is a collection of commentaries on the *Book of Changes*. The quoted phrase is James Legge's translation; see Chinese Text Project, n.d., at https://ctext.org/pre-qin-and-han.

33. These plaques were the objects of devotion for Confucians and were found in Confucian temples, among other places of worship.

34. "Republic of five peoples" refers to the multiethnic republic of China, including Han, Manchu, Tibetan, Mongol, and Hui.

35. James Legge's translation; see Chinese Text Project, n.d., https://ctext.org/pre-qin-and-han.

36. The doctrine of the mean is both a basic principle of Confucian practice, emphasizing moderation and self-control, as well as a classic in the Confucian canon, the *Zhongyong*.

37. "Not forgetting original intentions" is a phrase often evoked in efforts to suggest parallels between Confucianism and communism. A true Confucian, like a true Communist, should not lose sight of "original intention." See, for example, Jiang Shigong, "Philosophy and History: Interpreting the 'Xi Jinping Era' through Xi's Report to the Nineteenth National Congress of the CCP," January 2018, trans. David Ownby, Reading the China Dream, https://www.readingthechinadream.com/jiang-shigong-philosophy-and-history.html.

CHAPTER 14

A CENTURY OF CONFUCIANISM[1]

CHEN LAI

TRANSLATED BY CRAIG A. SMITH AND JUN DENG

Translators' Introduction

A noted professor of philosophy at Tsinghua University, Beijing, Chen Lai (b. 1952) is among China's most eminent academic Confucians, having studied at Beijing University with Zhang Dainian (1909–2004) and Feng Youlan (1895–1990). He is also an influential public intellectual in contemporary China, having lectured even before Xi Jinping (b. 1953) and the Politburo on questions of patriotism and Confucianism in December 2015.[2] Since earning his PhD from Peking University's Philosophy Department in 1985, he has written widely on Chinese thought and tradition, particularly on Zhu Xi (1130–1200) and Song dynasty Neo-Confucianism. Numerous translations of Chen's works have already appeared in many languages, and since 2009 English-language readers have access to an entire volume of his writing through Edmund Ryden's translation of *Chuantong yu xiandai* as *Tradition and Modernity: A Humanist View*.[3]

Originally published in the social sciences edition of the *Shenzhen University Journal* in May 2014, this essay, "A Century of Confucianism: Looking Back and Looking Forward," presents Chen Lai's methodical approach to the twentieth-century history of Confucianism as well as his advocacy for its future development. Dividing this history into periods of challenge and opportunity, Chen charts the various major changes to the system of thought from the late Qing dynasty to the end of the twentieth century. Through brief explanations of major historical events from the perspective of Confucianism, including the fall of the imperial system to the reform-and-opening period, as well as the responses to these events by Chinese philosophers ranging from Kang Youwei (1858–1927) to Xiong Shili (1885–1968), Chen charts the religious, educational, cultural, and philosophical developments that have led to contemporary New Confucianism. Paying little heed to Confucianism beyond China, Chen links the system of thought to China, the Chinese people, and mainland Chinese nationalism, identifying the myriad opportunities for Confucianism through the twenty-first-century rise of China. This article offers readers an example of a Confucian-centered modern history to contextualize the movement from the perspective of one of its leading proponents.

The rise in popularity of Confucianism that has accompanied the new confidence in Chinese traditions and nationalism since the 1980s has greatly benefitted Chen Lai's career, yet in some ways he remains on the margins of the New Confucianism movement, despite being widely recognized as China's leading authority on Confucianism. He does not subscribe to the religious New Confucianism of Chen Ming (b. 1962) and Kang Xiaoguang (b. 1963) or to the vulgarized Confucianism of the television personality Yu Dan (b. 1965), but his enthusiasm for *guoxue* (national studies, classical studies) and his writings on "universal values" illustrate that he has not completely ignored the siren call of politicization.[4]

Cementing the connection between China's intellectual future and past is a focus of Chen Lai's work. However, although interested primarily in the intellectual forms of Confucianism, in this article he also considers the "subconscious" aspects of Confucianism that have survived in the Chinese people's daily lives. Chen is supportive of the reform-and-opening period's acceleration in the popularity of academic, folk, and cultural Confucianism, a popular movement of which Chen is both a product and a proponent. He argues for the reestablishment of all elements of Confucianism, a reconstruction of the philosophical system, and a promotion of the cultural and intellectual elements as the rise of China proceeds hand in hand with the revival of Confucianism.

A Century of Confucianism: Looking Back and Looking Forward

In this essay, I examine the development of Confucianism in the twentieth century.[5] The term *development* might give the impression that Confucianism has progressed effortlessly throughout this period, but this examination of the past century reveals a tortuous course through various crises and challenges.

Challenges and Responses in the Modern Era

Chinese Confucianism faced four periods of challenge in the twentieth century. The first was the political and educational reforms in the late Qing and early Republican era. The Qing government announced the Edict on the Establishment of Schools in 1901 to launch the establishment of new institutions across the country. This was an extremely important initiative, leading to the gradual decline of the old form of Confucianism, a form dominated by a particular type of school that trained scholars to enter the system of imperial civil service examinations.

Officials opened these new schools in great numbers across China. This move posed a clear challenge to the civil service examination system before the Qing government decided to end the examinations entirely in 1905. The examination system was of utmost significance to the continued existence of the Confucian scholar. In total, there were three important bases for the existence of Confucian scholars' thought and culture in premodern Chinese society. The first was the state and the imperial court's propagation of Confucianism as the official ideology and the Confucian classics as official doctrine. The second basis was the educational system, in particular the civil service examination system, which stipulated that the Confucian classics be the primary subject of the exams. And the third basis for Confucianism was the prevalent social foundations of family and rural governance systems that have existed in China for several thousand years.

The strategic reforms of the late Qing period played an important role in determining the ways in which Confucianism would continue to exist. Despite the abolition of the examinations in 1905, one of the most radical of the early reforms, the Qing government was still determined to preserve the study and curriculum of the classics in all schools, and it also required schools to continue to offer sacrifices to Confucius [551–479 BCE] on his birthday. This, however, also changed with the 1911 Revolution. Once the Ministry of Education fell under the control of Cai Yuanpei [1868–1940] in 1912, the state resolved to do away with sacrifices to Confucius and to abandon the study of the classics. Therefore, in the years after the revolution, the system of "honoring Confucius and reading the classics" suffered a fundamental setback. During this process, Confucian scholars experienced the first significant period of "challenge and response"—that is, their first fundamental predicament.

From the late Qing to the early Republic, although the Confucian scholar already found himself removed from the center of politics and education, the role of Confucian thought and culture continued in the realm of ethics.[6] Not long after this, from 1915 to 1919 the New Culture Movement arose, and Confucianism encountered its second challenge. The New Culture Movement raised banners of criticism, reflection, and enlightenment. This was a cultural

enlightenment, drawing upon modern Western culture, posing Chinese traditional culture as its binary opposite, and particularly posing Confucian rites
and culture as its primary and critical opponent. This seemed reasonable to
many at the time, and they raised the slogan "Down with Confucius and sons!"
From the late Qing to the 1911 Revolution, Confucianism had maintained its
ethical influence even while it stepped away from the political stage, but in the
following years it suffered its second crucial reverse. The 1911 Revolution forced
Confucianism into a form of exile that extended through the New Culture
Movement. The New Culture Movement then expanded the mission by ban-
ishing Confucianism from the realm of ethics. The New Culture Movement
left Confucianism fragmented and drifting.

The third major predicament was from the 1949 revolution through the "Cultural Revolution." I view this period as a whole because the collectivization
movement, the organization of the people's communes, and the "Great Proletarian Cultural Revolution" all changed the system of rural governance and
made the collective the foundation of society. The people's commune system,
based on the brigade and the three levels of ownership,[7] thoroughly transformed
the old lineage-based village order.

Scholars in the modern era have argued that once the Confucian social system was severed from its base, Confucianism became a "lost soul" (youhun).[8]
This image of a lost soul suggests that the changes of modern culture cut off
Confucian thought from its ancient roots. The revolution in and of itself had
political significance, and, moreover, the transformations it wrought in the
countryside were extremely important. In addition, another important factor
was the Cultural Revolution, especially the movement to criticize Lin Biao
[1907–1971] and Confucius. Successive campaigns of absurd political criticisms
of Confucianism and Confucius wrought havoc with people's thinking. This
was an even greater attack on Confucian culture.

The fourth period of challenge for Confucianism in the twentieth century
was the first twenty years of the reform and opening from the late 1970s. The
mobilization of the reform period in the 1980s brought about a form of enlightenment thinking echoing that of the New Culture Movement in the May
Fourth period, embracing a principal theme of the twentieth century in its critique of tradition. Confucianism therefore emerged as the enemy of modernization. As the vigorous development of the market economy brought utilitarian thought into prominence in the 1990s, it also provided a powerful challenge
to the traditions of Confucianism and Chinese culture.

Dividing the attacks on Confucian thought and culture in the twentieth century into four principal periods, we find that all four had a profound influence
on the fate of Confucian culture. However, it would be inaccurate to suggest
that Confucianism only suffered attacks and never experienced progress in the

twentieth century. Sometimes challenges can present opportunities for advancement. In this historical context, there was only one significant period of development for Confucianism: the period stretching from the Mukden Incident of 1931 to the end of the War of Resistance Against Japan [1937–1945], in particular the wartime period. The Chinese people as a whole united during this period, and national defense and revival became matters of critical importance. This was the central theme of the period, and it was a rare historical opportunity for the advancement of Confucianism, as explained later in this essay.

Philosophical Responses and Development

I have roughly divided one hundred years of the history of Confucianism into four stages of challenge and one of opportunity, five stages altogether. We can see the history of Confucianism in the twentieth century as a response to these challenges, which unfolds in the following five stages.

The first stage, or rather the first person, to be discussed is Kang Youwei [1858–1927]. Although Kang had been thinking about Confucian religion long before the 1911 Revolution, he placed even more stress on it afterward. On several occasions, Kang himself, or his students, proposed that Confucian religion be the state religion. These were positive proposals. Political and educational reforms—from the Edict on the Establishment of Schools of 1901 to the abolition of the civil service examinations in 1905 and the beginning of Cai Yuanpei's leadership of the Ministry of Education in 1912—had already robbed Confucianism of the institutional bases upon which it had rested. In response, Kang Youwei looked to religion to preserve and develop Confucian thought. He saw that Christianity had a place within the framework of modern Western culture. And there were examples of it being established as the state religion in Western countries. So he thought that a new China needed new institutions and Confucianism could play a role. Kang's argument to establish Confucianism as a state religion represents the first response.[9] This was a religious response to the difficulties faced by Confucianism, and, of course, it failed. All of Kang's various projects and proposals failed, and history made clear that this was not the path to follow. Despite its failure, we can take this episode as the first active Confucian response to a century of challenges.

The second stage covers the New Culture Movement, by the end of which new developments had occurred. They were the result of cultural reflections by Western intellectuals on World War I and the emergence of socialism in the Soviet Union. These events in turn led a few outstanding intellectuals to reconsider the question of Chinese culture. The representative figure from this period was Liang Shuming [1893–1988]. In the early 1920s, Liang wrote *Dong Xi wenhua ji qi zhexue* (Eastern and Western cultures and their philosophies).

This book is representative of the second response to the predicament faced by Confucianism in the twentieth century. Rather than being a religious response, it was a cultural response. Liang believed that although Chinese society should undergo complete Westernization, Confucian culture and its values were still necessary: "In the very near future of our world, in the wake of the Western cultural period in which Europeans and Americans have conquered and exploited nature, it will be time for the revival of Chinese culture."[10] This "very near future" referred to the culture of a Confucian socialism, because in Liang's assessment Confucianism already embodied the values of socialism. He believed that Western culture's identifying characteristic was that it resolved the relationship between humanity and the natural world, the relationship between humanity and the material realm. Confucian culture, however, resolved the relationship between human beings, the relationship between the individual and society, much as socialism could resolve issues between labor and capital.

In the modern period, all of the challenges encountered by Confucianism were posed by modern Western culture to Chinese society and culture. The response by Confucianists could be directed only toward this macrolevel cultural challenge.

The philosophical response during the third stage, from the Mukden Incident of 1931 to the end of War of Resistance in 1945 was not only the product of the surging nationalism of the period but also a response to the onslaught of modern Western culture. Among the intellectuals involved were Xiong Shili [1885–1968], Ma Yifu [1883–1967], Feng Youlan [1895–1990], and He Lin [1902–1992]. Xiong Shili's system of philosophical Confucianism, *guiben dayi* (returning to the *Yijing*), may be seen as new research on the *Book of Changes*.[11] Ma Yifu focused on the Six Classics and the Six Arts. His system of Confucianism can be termed *xin jingxue*, New Classical Learning. Feng Youlan called his own philosophical system *xin lixue*, the New Philosophy of Principle. He Lin's was *xin xinxue*, the New Philosophy of Mind.[12]

Xiong Shili upheld the philosophical concept of "original mind" established by Mencius [372–289 BCE].[13] Based on the principles of the *Yijing*, he established the original mind as an absolute entity and established a cosmology concerning *xipi chengbian*, transformation through closing and opening.[14] He then named his cosmology "the inseparability of substance and function."[15] His philosophical thinking was a Confucian system that emphasized cosmological constructions.

Ma Yifu was a scholar who tenaciously defended the entirety of traditional culture. He synthesized or unified the traditional study of the classics and Neo-Confucianism. He argued: "All the techniques of the *dao* are governed by the Six Arts, and the Six Arts are actually governed by One Mind."[16] "All the techniques of the *dao*" refers to the various fields of study or "disciplines," as we refer to them today. And by the "Six Arts," Ma was actually referring to the Six

Classics. This is the terminology used by a classical Confucian. This approach emphasizes the classics for the reconstruction of New Confucianism.

Feng Youlan's philosophy was what he himself referred to as the "New Philosophy of Principle."[17] He hoped to continue the work of the Cheng-Zhu Neo-Confucians, stressing the world of *li* (principle).[18] By assimilating the new realism of the West, he created a world of principle within philosophy, establishing an important segment of the metaphysics of Confucian philosophy. Feng Youlan's philosophy was a modern Confucian philosophy that concentrated on metaphysical constructions.

He Lin openly professed himself to be a follower of the Lu-Wang School.[19] He argued that "heart/mind (*xin*) is the substance (*ti*) of the material (*wu*), while the material is the function (*yong*) of *xin*." Much of what he wrote placed this School of Mind as the foundation of Confucian philosophy. But, more importantly, we find that He Lin played an important role through his formation of a plan for the Confucian revival. His slogan was "Confucian thought as substance; Western culture as function," which could also be read as "National spirit (*minzu jingshen*) as substance; Western culture as function."[20] He constructed an elaborate design for the Confucian revival.

In addition to his early contributions to the ideas of cultural identity, Liang Shuming spent much of the 1940s to the 1970s writing *Renxin yu rensheng* (Psychology and life). From this book we can see that Liang Shuming's philosophical system emphasized a construction of modern Confucian philosophy based in psychology.

The work of these philosophers illustrates how a new and constructive form of Confucianism emerged during this period. Their response was primarily a philosophical one. This was the time that I have identified as the only period of historical opportunity in this century of Confucianism, and it is related to the surge of national cultural identity accompanying the war against Japan. This emphasis on national culture made important progress.

The fourth stage stretches from 1949 to the end of the Cultural Revolution. We cannot say that Confucian thought was absent in China during this period. If we examine the changes displayed by Xiong Shili and other intellectuals from the 1950s, 1960s, and 1970s, then we see it was a period of adaptation for modern Confucianism as well as one of integration with and absorption of socialism. In Xiong's book *Yuan Ru* (On Confucianism) from the early 1950s, he calls for the abolition of private ownership and the leveling of class differences, an approach borrowed from socialism. Liang Shuming wrote a book late in his career entitled *Zhongguo, lixing zhi guo* (China, a rational country), in which he examines the question of the transition from a class society to a classless society and of socialism to communism. All of these examples indicate that these philosophers were not passively acquiescing to the times but were instead attempting to integrate their own thought with the questions of the day. They never faltered in their belief in Confucian thought and culture.

New Confucians in Taiwan and Hong Kong were left rootless and drifting yet carried forward the legacy of the third stage of Confucian thought. In other words, in the face of the changes, adjustments, and challenges of twentieth-century society and confronted with a general spiritual anomie, they developed a new path in Confucian thought that was in accord with conditions of the time, a new Confucian philosophy that absorbed Western culture and developed national spirit as well a guiding philosophy for universal issues facing the world and the human condition from a Confucian perspective. All of this contributed to the revitalization of mainland culture from the late 1980s.

Latent and Manifest Forms of Confucianism

The existence of Confucianism cannot be regarded simply as commensurate with the existence of the philosopher, nor can we say that Confucianism exists because there is a Confucian philosopher. This would be a superficial point of view. From the 1950s to our current day, the existence of Confucianism has, as Li Zehou [b. 1930] has explained, not merely been limited to a set of commentaries on the Confucian classics, but at the same time been evident in the psychology and culture of the Chinese people.[21] Therefore, once all contact with the old system of Confucianism had been severed, it became a tradition that lived on intrinsically within the populace. Confucian values continue to exist, particularly among the common people, where they may even be more deeply engrained than they are within the intellectual realm, which has been more infected by Western culture.

The Confucian tradition within the common people exists in a "subconscious form in daily life." Even in the People's Republic of China, the Chinese concepts of morality have been profoundly influenced by traditional Confucian morality. However, as this role resides within the subconscious, it is constantly influenced by the environment of different times. Therefore, the existence of Confucianism cannot be confidently elucidated, nor can we say much about its present state. At times it is quite distorted.

Here I must emphasize the fact that in this fifth period—the period of reform and opening—or even since the fourth period the concept of Confucianism has certainly undergone a transformation. We cannot contend that only with the existence of the Confucian philosopher does Confucianism exist.

We move now to discuss the existential forms of Confucianism that have endured since the reforms that began in 1978. Over the past thirty years on the Chinese mainland, we have not seen Confucian philosophers of the likes seen in the 1930s and 1940s. There are, however, a number of aspects of this period that are worthy of our notice.

The first is academic Confucianism. The past thirty years of research into Confucianism has created a culture of academic Confucianism. This culture stems from the thorough research conducted on traditional Confucianism and grasps the contexts of its historical evolution, combs through its doctrine, explicates the various schools of thought, and includes thorough research into the thought of contemporary New Confucianism. This set of studies is what I refer to as academic Confucianism. It has undergone more than thirty years of development, offering up many new horizons. In the academic world of contemporary China, it occupies an important position and has produced considerable influence.

The second form of Confucianism in the reform era is cultural Confucianism. Over the past thirty years, there have been a great number of cultural trends and discussions that are of direct relevance to Confucianism, such as discussions of the relationship between Confucianism and democracy, human rights, globalization, modernization, [and] the clash of civilizations as well as, of course, [discussions of] the relevance of Confucianism to the construction of a harmonious society, which we are talking about today. Many scholars commend the positive significance of Confucian values from the perspective of cultural Confucianism. They discuss the ways in which Confucianism can affect contemporary society, expounding upon the valuable cultural concepts and ideas and interacting with contemporary trends in a number of ways. This has provided a noticeable effect upon the sociocultural strata of contemporary China. I believe that these discussions and activities have also created a distinctive existential form for Confucianism, which I have called cultural Confucianism.

Therefore, we cannot say that these thirty years have not seen major Confucian philosophers, nor can we say that Confucianism disappeared. Aside from the latent forms of existence, we must acknowledge that there are many more manifest forms of Confucian culture. We need to define these manifest forms of Confucian culture that have adapted to survive in the past thirty years. I therefore use "academic Confucianism" and "cultural Confucianism" to summarize this period's manifestations of Confucianism. In fact, although the philosopher is still of importance, compared with the systems of abstract metaphysics that have appeared, it is really academic and cultural Confucianism that have proven to have an even more penetrating and extensive influence on society, culture, and thought. These forms have constructed the foundations for the new developments of Confucian thought.

The third form of Confucianism that exists today is folk (*minjian*) Confucianism. It includes both latent aspects, in daily and subconscious existence of the common people—a Confucianism in the psyche of the masses—and manifest aspects seen in overt activities, much like those of academic and cultural Confucianism. The new century has seen an unceasing development of folk Confucianism and popularized Confucianism. This cultural form first appeared near the end of the previous century and continues to develop today, including all kinds of courses on national studies (*guoxue*) in schools, academies, and lecture halls; various digital magazines; readers for the common people; children's courses on the classics; and the like. The majority of events on the level of academic and cultural Confucianism are activities aimed at the intelligentsia, but those on the level of folk Confucianism receive a much more extensive and active participation of Chinese people from all levels of today's society. This is a cultural manifestation on the level of folk practice, and I therefore term it "folk Confucianism." In the past ten years, national studies have received a great amount of encouragement from folk Confucianism.

Conclusion: Opportunities for Revival and Visions for the Future

I believe that the second period of opportunity has arrived for a modern Confucian revival with the advent of the twenty-first century. The first period of opportunity was during the War of Resistance, a time marked by a surge in national consciousness and a consciousness of a national revival. Beginning in the late 1990s and accompanying the rise of China and the deepening and development of China's modernization, China entered an early phase of modernization. It is with this background, under the conditions of the people's enormous recovery of confidence in their national culture, with the arrival of the great revival of the Chinese nation and Chinese culture, that the second period of opportunity has arisen for the modern revival of Confucianism. And how can Confucianism grasp this opportunity? How can Confucian scholars take part in this revival of Confucianism? Apart from the continued efforts of academic and cultural Confucianism, there are at least a few things to be done, such as the reconstruction of the national spirit (*minzu jingshen*), the establishment of moral values, the organization of an ethical order, the formation of educational principles, the forging of a common value system, the cohesion of the nation-state, and the further promotion of our spiritual civilization, among others. All of these tasks are important for our participation in the movement for a Confucian revival. Only if Confucianism consciously participates in the great revival of the Chinese nation, integrating itself within the mission of our times and our social and cultural needs, will it be able to develop.

In addition, there is a central task that needs our attention—the reconstruction and development of the Confucian philosophical system. A new Confucian philosophy should and undoubtedly will emerge alongside the further development of the China's modernization, and this philosophy must be a cornucopia. On the foundations of traditional Confucianism and contemporary New Confucianism, alongside the revival of Chinese culture, this philosophy will make its mark throughout the entire world. We can see the cultural fever of the 1980s and the growing trend in classical studies from the 1990s as episodes recalling the cultural controversies of the May Fourth Movement, the issues of national heritage in the 1920s, and the development of national philosophy in the 1980s. We can hope that new theories of Confucian thought and new Confucian philosophy will join the revival of the Chinese people and Chinese culture.

Notes

1. Chen Lai, "Bainian lai Ruxue fazhan de huigu yu qianzhan" (A century of Confucianism: Looking back and looking forward), *Shenzhen Daxue Xuebao* (*Renwen Shehui Kexueban*) 31, no. 3 (May 2014): 42–46.

2. See "Chen Lai wei Zhongyang zhengzhiju jiangjie aiguozhuyi, lingdao ti wenti hen shenke" (Chen Lai explains patriotism before the Politburo, the leadership raises profound questions), Xinhua Wang, January 15, 2016, http://www.xinhuanet.com/politics/2016-01/15/c_128631705.htm.

3. Chen Lai, *Tradition and Modernity: A Humanist View*, trans. Edmund Ryden (Leiden: Brill, 2009).

4. See Hoyt Tillman, "China's Particular Values and the Issue of Universal Significance: Contemporary Confucians Amidst the Politics of Universal Values," *Philosophy East and West* 64, no. 4 (October 2018): 1265–91.

5. *Translators' note*: Many Chinese terms are translated into English as "Confucianism." "Ruxue" generally refers to the system of learning and study of classical texts. "Rujia" refers to the scholars or philosophers who have embraced Confucianism as a system of thought. And "Rujiao" refers to Confucianism as a religion, including rites, ceremonies, and sacrifices to Confucius, a system promoted by Kang Youwei in the modern period. With a number of exceptions, particularly when referring to scholarly thought or Kang Youwei's ideas, Chen Lai uses "Ruxue" in this article.

6. *Translators' note*: Here and later in the essay Chen Lai uses the phrase *lunli de jingshen* or *lunli jingshen*, which refers to both the ethical and the spiritual domains in an intellectual rather than a religious understanding of "spiritual." For a popular example of scholarly usage of the "ethicospiritual," see: Tu Wei-ming, "Hsiung Shih-li's Quest for Authentic Existence," in *The Limits of Change: Essays on Conservative Alternatives in Republican China*, ed. Charlotte Furth (Cambridge, MA: Harvard University Press, 1976), 242–72.

7. *Translators' note*: The "three levels of ownership" were the commune, the production brigade, and the production team.

8. *Translators' note*: John Makeham translates *youhun* as "lost soul" and has provided an analysis of this narrative in his book *Lost Soul: "Confucianism" in Contemporary Chinese Academic Discourse* (Cambridge, MA: Harvard University Asia Center, 2008).

9. *Translators' note*: See the articles by Kang Youwei in *Kang Youwei zhenglunji* (Kang Youwei's political writings) (Beijing: Zhonghua Shuju, 1998).

10. Liang Shuming, *Dong Xi wenhua ji qi zhexue* (Eastern and Western cultures and their philosophies) (Beijing: Shangwu Yinshuguan, 1999), 244.

11. *Translators' note*: See Tu Wei-ming's translation and explanation of Xiong Shili's meditations on the *Book of Changes* in "Hsiung Shih-li's Quest," 266–68.

12. *Translators' note*: Chen Lai expands on these four thinkers in extremely technical language; this paragraph has been abridged.

13. *Translators' note*: For Xiong Shili, the original mind determines understandings of reality and is in the constant flux of the great transformation. It is the humanity, or *ren*, common to humanity and all things.

14. *Translators' note*: The phrase *xipi chengbian* is utilized to explain how, through contraction, *xi*, and expansion, *pi*, an entity can be transformed into different phenomena within the mind. Contraction is the process of focusing, whereas expansion expands from phenomenon to create a semblance of order for the mind. See Tu Wei-ming, "Hsiung Shih-li's Quest," 269.

15. Jésus Solé-Farràs, *New Confucianism in Twentieth-Century China: The Construction of a Discourse* (New York: Routledge, 2014), 112. The term *xipi chengbian* is translated in "The New Idealistic Confucianism: Hsiung Shih-li," in *A Source Book in Chinese Philosophy*, comp. and trans. Wing-tsit Chan (Princeton, NJ: Princeton University Press, 1969), 769–72.

16. Ma Yifu, *Ma Yifu ji* (Ma Yifu's collected works) (Hangzhou: Zhejiang Guji, 1996), 20. "One Mind" (*yixin*) refers to a unified metaphysical mind, a concept particular to Mahayana Buddhism.

17. *Translators' note*: Wing-tsit Chan translates "New Philosophy of Principle" as the "New Rational Philosophy," in *Source Book*, 751.

18. *Translators' note*: The Cheng-Zhu School is the central branch of Neo-Confucianism typified by Zhu Xi, Cheng Yi (1033–1107), and Cheng Hao (1032–1085) in the Song dynasty. It was later adopted for the civil service examinations.

19. *Translators' note*: The Lu-Wang School is the School of Mind, or *xinxue*, represented by Lu Jiuyuan (1139–1192) and Wang Yangming (1427–1529). The School of Mind became popular in the Ming dynasty, and Chinese scholars often viewed it in opposition to the School of Principle, or *lixue*.

20. He Lin, *He Lin quanji, wenhua yu rensheng* (Complete works of He Lin, culture and life) (Shanghai: Shanghai Renmin, 2011), 13.

21. Li Zehou, *Li Zehou xueshu wenhua suibi* (Li Zehou's writings on academic culture) (Beijing: Zhongguo Qingnian, 1998).

CHAPTER 15

ONLY CONFUCIANS CAN MAKE A PLACE FOR MODERN WOMEN[1]

JIANG QING

TRANSLATED BY DAVID OWNBY

Translator's Introduction

J iang Qing (b. 1953) is China's best-known New Confucian thinker and has devoted most of his career to building a new "political Confucianism" that will respond to China's current conditions. This Confucianism is political in two ways. First, Jiang has broken with New Confucian thinkers as they have existed in the Chinese diaspora (chiefly Hong Kong, Taiwan, and the United States) for some decades. These thinkers, perhaps best represented at present by Tu Wei-ming (b. 1940), have largely accepted the universal claims of modernity, particularly in terms of political economy and governance, but have continued to insist on the relevance of Confucianism as a possible communitarian counterweight to the excessive individualism and consumerism of modern life. Jiang Qing rejects the universal claims of modernity and insists that the Confucian way is superior. Second, Jiang has invested considerable intellectual energy in the imagination of Confucian institutions that could theoretically replace those of the ruling Communist Party. Jiang imagines a tricameral government, with one body selected by the people (the Shuminyuan, or House of the Commoners), one body made up of a meritocratic, largely Confucian, elite (the Tongruyuan, or House of Confucian Tradition), and one body made up of actual descendants of Confucius (the Guotiyuan, or House of National Essence).[2] Jiang's aim is to construct a legitimacy that will go beyond what he sees as the petty, grasping utilitarianism of modern democracies and to ground authority in something sacred and traditional.

It is perhaps the audacious impracticality of Jiang's propositions that have so far kept him out of serious political trouble.

The text translated here—in fact, it is an interview—is quite different. Here, Jiang attempts to establish the superiority of Confucianism as a guide to life and happiness for Chinese (and presumably other) women who have been beguiled by the false charms of modern life. The "interviewer" is one of Jiang's assistants, a female retiree named Fan Bixuan, who serves up one softball after another, allowing Jiang to hold forth at length. Fan's role is presumably to break up the monotony and to suggest that women are part of Jiang's conversation.

In any event, most of Jiang's arguments are concerned not directly with women, but with the denunciation of Confucians as oppressors of women during China's May Fourth and New Culture Movements (roughly 1915–1930). During this period, iconoclastic radicals condemned Confucianism as the main reason for China's weakness and backwardness, claiming that Confucian insistence on family hierarchy and ritual had perverted the development of the sort of individualism necessary to survival in the modern world. The place of women in traditional Confucian society served as a glaring example, and both modernizers and revolutionaries competed to denounce footbinding, concubinage, and arranged marriage.

Jiang argues first that Confucianism had little or nothing to do with these practices and furthermore that China's record on this score is no worse than that of other countries, past and present. He is probably right to some extent that critics exaggerated somewhat the degree to which Confucianism as a body of thought or doctrine contributed to the ill treatment of women; the condemnation of Confucianism in early-twentieth-century China was based on politics, not on scholarship, even if it is true that the Confucian patriarchy indeed ignored the mistreatment of women over the centuries. However, the facts that corsets inflicted lasting harm on Western women in centuries past and that plastic surgery continues to disfigure women today hardly prove that "Confucianism has a place for modern women." That we all are sinners does not remove or excuse the sin.

When Jiang tries to describe the Confucian "Way" for modern women, he falls immediately into crude and conventional stereotypes: Premodern societies were "natural," built on families and hierarchies rather than on abstractions deduced by rationality. Men and women are by nature different. Men are extraverted, action oriented; women introverted and passive. Women have their own superiority, developed mostly in the feminine realms of domesticity and motherhood, where they can be a true helpmate to their husband and children. Of course, some women might be interested in professional careers, but if China (like South Korea) had a genuine family policy that paid husbands enough for wives to remain home, Jiang is sure that this is the path Chinese women would follow.

I confess for my part that I can't see Jiang's arguments (or his supercilious tone) appealing to many of the smart, independent Chinese women I have met over the course of my career, but perhaps he knows his audience better than I do. To me, this interview suggests that Jiang's creativity at an institutional level does not extend to the level of culture or society. The problem is larger than Jiang; the mainland New Confucians can, at moments, seem very much like an old boys' club. The casual misogyny that we find in certain New Confucian texts, in which women are blamed for divorce and other marital problems afflicting contemporary Chinese society, is shocking.[3] In this light, the New Confucians look less like principled cultural conservatives and more like alt-right groups in the West, some of whom of course also see themselves as "principled cultural conservatives." Jiang's defense of Confucianism might be more convincing if he acknowledged at least some of the gains achieved by modernity.

Only Confucians Can Make a Place for Modern Women

Confucians Did Not Encourage Concubinage; the Phenomenon of One Man Taking Several Wives Was a Custom Found Among All Traditional Peoples and Has No Direct Relationship to the Basic Principles of Confucianism

Fan Bixuan: With the acceleration of the Confucian cultural revival, the Confucian view of women has attracted more and more attention. The social conditions that face contemporary Confucians are different than in traditional times. In traditional social life, women had little position. Men set the tone for society, and most social customs discriminated against and limited women. This was expressed in well-known sayings such as *nanzun nübei*, "men are noble and women are base"; *fuwei qigang*, "the husband guides the wife"; *wei nüzi yu xiaoren nan yang*, "women and petty people are difficult to endure";[4] *nüzi wucai bian shi de*, "a woman's lack of talent is her virtue"; and in the system of concubinage, among other things. This directly influences women's affinity for Confucian culture.

With the development of productivity and the advance of human civilization, women have greatly entered social life. Yet in the process of assuming roles in society, modern women have encountered new obstacles and difficulties. Neither Buddhism nor Daoism provides a positive valuation of women as they face these problems. Confucianism emphasizes social ethics and not only argues that there are differences between men and women and that each has a role to play but in addition takes seriously the kind of moral transformation suggested by the *cancong side*, "three obediences and the four virtues."[5] In this sense,

Confucianism has a positive message that protects women. However, the exaggerated negative view of Confucianism propagated since the "May Fourth"[6] period has seriously damaged the feelings of contemporary women toward Confucianism. How can we convince contemporary women, in particular intellectual women, to identify with and embrace Confucianism as a philosophy of life? How can we bring them to construct a sense of reliance and belonging to Confucianism in the course of the Confucian cultural revival?

Jiang Qing: You provide a comprehensive overview of the question. Since the beginning of the modern period, Confucianism has faced a question that demands a positive resolution and response, and this is precisely the question of women. What is the value of women in Confucian doctrine? What place should be made for women? This kind of question did not exist in traditional society because traditional society was a natural society. This question did not exist in premodern Christian, Islamic, or Indian civilizations because they all provided an appropriate place for women based on nature and society, a place that embodied women's value. And in the specific case of Confucianism, this was not an important question either.

However, we should not completely equate Confucian ideas about women with the social existence of women in traditional societies because some aspects of the social existence of women in traditional societies were the product of social customs and had no relationship with Confucian principles. For example, we find no textual support for the practice of concubinage in Confucian teachings. In fact, according to classical customs, the nobles[7] could not remarry and, indeed, could marry only once, even if their wife died, because remarriage might lead to confusion in the inheritance of political power. But if they couldn't get married, then what happened when a wife died? A nobleman could not remain single just because his wife died, so in ancient society the custom came to be to allow the nobility to have one wife but many "companions." This was the system wherein the nobility took as companions the sisters of the wife. But this system was confined to people with national power and was not widespread in society. When we look at traditional Confucians like Confucius, Mencius [372–289 BCE], Sima Guang [1019–1086], Zhu Xi [1130–1200], Wang Yangming [1427–1529], and Liu Zongzhou [1578–1645],[8] we note that none of them had concubines. Liu Zongzhou established a "group of witnesses" (*zhengrenhui*) whose charter clearly stated that none of the members could take a concubine without a good reason. This meant that only when the wife was unable to bear children could one take a concubine to continue the family line. But Confucians did not universalize concubinage, arguing that anyone could unconditionally take a concubine, much less encourage concubinage. In fact, the custom of one man taking many wives was a widespread custom among all traditional peoples and has no direct connection to basic Confucian principles, and when "May Fourth" intellectuals blamed concubinage on Confucianism, this was unjust.

Intellectuals from the "May Fourth" Period Demonized the Traditional
Concubine System, Although If We Employ Their Critique Against
the Current Practice of Keeping Mistresses, It Is Fully Appropriate

Jiang Qing: Of course, traditional people with money and position frequently
took concubines, especially militarists from the Republican period. They were
unconstrained by the ritual system and had no taboos, so they took ten or
twenty at once. We can't call these militarists Confucians. They took concubines based on social customs, which had nothing to do with basic Confucian
principles. You can't blame Confucians for this. As for certain Confucians
who did take concubines, such as Kang Youwei [1858–1927],[9] they were exceptions, and most Confucians did not take concubines. In sum, Confucians
advocated the system of one man–one wife, and if they tacitly acknowledged
the custom of concubinage at a very limited level, they never gave it positive
encouragement.

Of course, in history we find many people who took concubines to fulfill
their personal desires and not to perpetuate the bloodline. Republican-period
intellectuals were basically criticizing this kind of person, whom Confucians
criticized as well. Zhu Xi said: "One man–one wife is a heavenly principle; three
palaces and six concubines are man's desire." Nonetheless, because of the
ancient custom of one wife and many companions, emperors often pushed this
to the extreme out of personal desires, taking concubines wherever they went
so that there were thousands in the empress's palaces, but this clearly conflicts
with the Confucian view of marriage.

Even if Confucians conditionally acknowledged concubinage, and even if in
traditional times the concubine system clearly existed to serve private selfish
desires, it was still not like in the criticisms of "May Fourth" intellectuals, who
said that this was a system that "ate people,"[10] an extreme form of suppression
of and cruelty toward women. In traditional times, even if a concubine was not
the wife, she still had a legal standing and was seen as a kind of wife. It was not
as casual as the custom of keeping mistresses in modern France or in today's
China. To take a concubine, one had to guarantee her legal independence, her
rightful claims to inheritance, and the legal status of her children. The ritual
process had to be followed, meaning that there had to be a master of ceremonies for the wedding, an exchange of gifts, and a wedding ceremony. Once the
concubine was married, her position was less than that of the wife, meaning
that household affairs and accounts were managed by the wife, as we see in the
title given to the main wife, "lord of the courtyard" (*yuanjun*). If the main wife
fell ill, or if something else happened, the position of the concubine could rise.
If the main wife died, then the concubine had the opportunity to become the
main wife.

I remember Gu Hongming [1857–1928][11] once asking, Isn't it common practice in France to have mistresses? When we compare mistresses to concubines, mistresses are too miserable; they are like *ernai* [mistresses] in today's China, having no legal status, so that if they have children, the children are only the women's children. The children of concubines had legal status and could carry forward the family line. French mistresses seem as if they have a lot of freedom. They seem to control their own lives and take up with whomever they want to, marry whomever they wish, and if they don't want to marry, then they don't. Even if they look very dashing when they're young, when they get old, it's hard to imagine how miserable they are.

Chinese concubines were not like this. They could not be abandoned without a proper, legal reason, and when they got old, they had legal protections, so that at the very least they could live a normal life, enjoying stability and respect. This is why I say that while "May Fourth" intellectuals demonized the traditional system of concubinage, their attacks are really extremely appropriate when aimed at the practice of keeping mistresses in today's China. These mistresses are really in a sad state. Things are OK when they're young, but once they're old, they are cast aside, with at best a bit of cash to compensate for their losses. There is no guarantee for the rest of their lives, to say nothing of obtaining any sort of legal status.

In traditional times, fashionable gentry also took concubines. Su Dongpo [1037–1101][12] was an example. Su had deep feelings for his concubine Wang Zhaoyun [Chaoyun, 1062–1096] and wrote many poems for her. When he was exiled to Hainan, she followed him to share this difficult period. After she died, Su built the Liuru Pavilion at her gravesite to mark her passing and wrote a couplet: "I am out of step with my times, and only Zhaoyun understands me. Alone I pluck the old songs, and in the rainy dusk my affection grows." Gu Hongming took a Japanese concubine and was very good to her, but she died young. He wrote a poem to mourn her passing: "Everyone knows grief, but how many times in a century will one experience such loss? Such pain. The water of the Yangzi flows onward, never to return." And on the title page of his English translation of the *Zhongyong* (Doctrine of the mean), he movingly wrote: "I dedicate this work to my departed concubine Yoshida Sadako." He also bought her a plot in Shanghai's best cemetery and wrote on the gravestone: "A filial Japanese woman." Clearly, Gu's beloved concubine Yoshida Sadako was from a legal standpoint his beloved wife. What is sad is that mistresses in China today do not receive such treatment.

Our current system of one man–one wife is in imitation of Christianity, and I suspect that among all world civilizations only Christianity has legally stipulated the one man–one woman system. Thus, we cannot say that systems that allow more than one wife are bad. Look at Islam, where one man can take multiple wives. There is less family corruption, and relations between man and wife are much better in Islam than in the West. In the West, there are children born out of wedlock, and there are mistresses; in China, there are mistresses as well. There's none of this in Muslim countries. It may be that in those countries only people with status and ability can have multiple wives, so we can't say that they all are corrupt. By "corrupt," I mean not observing proper ritual behavior between men and women and behaving licentiously. In the West, the legal norm is one man–one woman, yet married lives are very corrupt. For example, everyone knows about the affairs of the American president. And the private lives of many politicians and rich people have been revealed as well. I have a friend who returned to China after studying abroad. His thinking has been greatly influenced by the West, and he basically divorces and remarries every two or three years—and sometimes in as little as one year. To my mind, this is another system of one man–multiple wives; the only difference is that my friend does this serially, and he doesn't violate the marriage law. Of course, there are lots of reasons for this, but one is surely that he gets bored with the old wife and looks for a new one, justifying his actions by saying, "If we don't get along, we'll divorce, and then I'll find a new wife."

Footbinding Grew out of Popular Practices and Was Opposed by Confucians. If We Say That Footbinding Was Cruel, Then Western Practices of "Girdling" Are Even Crueler.

Jiang Qing: Other issues, such as footbinding, are even less worth discussing [Jiang is still responding to May Fourth criticisms of Confucianism]. We find no clear rules in ancient scriptures about footbinding. Scholars have proven that this custom gradually took shape from Song times forward and was created by the people themselves. Every era has its aesthetic criteria, and at that time everyone felt that women with small feet were very elegant and refined and easy to marry off. Men at that time must have felt that small feet were aesthetically prettier than big feet, or maybe they had no particular opinion, and social customs simply evolved in this manner, so men just followed along. Of course, this placed great pressure on women, so that even poor women in remote villages had to bind their feet. Nevertheless, Confucians were against this custom. For example, a local Confucian scholar-gentry in the Qing dynasty wrote to the court saying that too many women in the surrounding countryside bound their feet and that this was inhumane. He hoped that the state would pass laws forbidding the practice, and the state did issue an order forbidding footbinding, but the force of custom was too great, and the order made no difference.

In this context, Gu Hongming noted that if footbinding is cruel, the Western practice of girdling or corseting is even worse. At the time [i.e., the nineteenth century], it was fashionable in France for women to be thin waisted, so from a very young age they bound their waist, so that it remained very thin even after they grew up. Of course, this created a deformity and robbed women of their ability to reproduce. Thus, there is absolutely no relationship between Confucianism and footbinding, which was imposed instead by social trends as a traditional custom. Modern people no longer bind their feet or cinch their waists, but they redo their breasts or their noses through plastic surgery. Perfectly normal people inject silicone here, carve off the odd bit there, which has produced many disastrous outcomes. The plastic-surgery business is booming, but they are not aiming for traditional good looks. These surgeons instead show people pictures of foreigners and say, "Your nose is no good," "your cheekbones are no good," "your eyes are no good." European-style eyes and eyelids are all the rage, so with a little suction, they hollow out the eye sockets, and with a flick of the knife the eyelids open up. This kind of so-called cosmetic surgery is also cruel to the body, yet our new-style intellectuals do not oppose it. Why not? They believe that this is a question of aesthetics or fashion and that women have freedom over their bodies—thus, morality is not an issue. If that's the case, and it's all a question of aesthetics and fashion, then on what basis do they criticize footbinding? And all the more blame it on Confucians?

The Basic Aim of Confucian Ritual Teachings Is to Provide a Just and Reasonable Place for Women Based on Their Natural and Social Character.

Jiang Qing: There are also questions of social class, where once again we find the "May Fourth" intellectuals launching their most serious criticisms of Confucianism, arguing that it fashioned a society in which women were completely oppressed by the "three bonds and five constants" (*sangang wuchang*)[13] and other similar ritual practices. They argue further that such constraints weighed heavily on women, so that they lost their humanity, their freedom, their personality. In other words, in Confucian society women were not people, and women's lives were hell. In matter of fact, there are extreme cases in any period, and if you want to look for extreme cases over this very long period of time, then you will no doubt find them. Lu Xun's words magnify these extreme cases: China's two millennia of ritual teachings served to "eat people." In other words, during these two thousand years the Chinese people suffered cruelly, and women suffered the most of all.

We argue that in the long course of history in which, in extreme cases, women were oppressed, this oppression occurred in the West as well as in China, in traditional times and in the present day. This is hard to avoid. Yet the basic objective of Confucian ritual teachings is to make a proper, reasonable place for women according to their gender and social nature and hence provide them with their own life meaning and existential value. This is in the spirit of "making distinctions" as prescribed by "ritual" and is the very "way of women." This "ritual" spirit is conceived for women, not for universal application. For example, one point that "May Fourth" intellectuals criticized harshly was the idea that "the husband guides the wife." In their eyes, this meant that the husband was the master of the household, and the wife had to obey the husband in all things. She had no right to speak in the household and hence no power of decision. She had no position and was no better than a slave. In matter of fact, the meaning of "guidance," whether in abstract terms or in terms of social practice, is far from this.

In traditional times, families were very big; in some cases, it was like a small society. It was like this at the beginning of the Republican period, when one family could have dozens of people. In Han Yu's [768–824] essays,[14] we note that he frequently complains of being poor, which meant that he had no choice but to work as a secretary to an official because he had to find a way to support his family of fifty or sixty people. And he did not take concubines, so his family was probably not overly large. In this kind of big family, there had to be a central person who would take command naturally; otherwise, the family would not be manageable. Democracy works only with strangers because it is created by choices other than natural rationality.

For example, when we organize ourselves into a group, everyone raises his hand to vote for a leader, whether we call him president or premier or leader or manager—in any event, the vote is the product of unnatural [i.e., man-made] rationality. But a family is different. A family is a product of bloodlines and forms naturally; it is not the result of rational election. A family, especially a large, traditional family, requires a leader. This leader must have both authority and responsibility. What is authority? Authority means that the leader oversees the family's food, livelihood, living situation, order, disputes, and the like. So authority is not necessarily something people desire; if you have the authority, you must also exercise responsibility. Han Yu didn't want to work as a secretary, but life forced this upon him, and he had no choice. This was his responsibility, and if he didn't go, then several dozen people would have had no food to eat. For this reason, the meaning of "the husband guides the wife" means that a family needs someone who will have overall responsibility and that if there are family problems, the "guide" will take responsibility. The "guide" is thus the family leader and bearer of responsibility—the husband.

Of course, this doesn't mean that women had no purpose in traditional families, but rather that they did not bear primary responsibility for sustaining the family. For example, if the family was out of food, family members didn't seek out the wife but rather looked for the husband, and if the husband could not solve the problem, then the wife would assist him to take responsibility. In the villages, men went to work in the field, and women took care of the housework, but sometimes the women would join the men in the fields to help. But most of the heavy agricultural labor and other chores were the husband's responsibility. In traditional Confucian society, women also had another special responsibility, which was that of the basic education of the children. Taking care of and nourishing children is women's social role and gender nature. Nothing is more natural than for women to take care of children. Everyone knows that in a family paternal love and maternal love are not the same. From the time of their birth, children are nurtured and taken care of by their mother, and if they have something on their mind, it is to their mothers that they want to say it, in the same way that mothers are naturally oriented toward caring for their children.

Many sages and worthies in traditional times in China were raised by their mother after the death of their father. This was the case of Confucius, Mencius, Ouyang Xiu [1007–1072], and Gu Yanwu [1613–1668], among others.[15] Moreover, traditional family management and the handling of family affairs was the wife's responsibility. So if the husband had to bring home the bacon, family accounts were the wife's responsibility. This division of labor was not established by law but rather evolved naturally. So when we say that "the husband guides the wife," we mean that the husband must assume the chief responsibilities for the family and not that he is the sole authority in the family who must oppress his wife. In fact, in traditional families, the wife was the general manager of the family and had considerable power and authority, especially in financial matters. Moreover, women's power in the family increased with age, and an old grandmother possessed considerable power and status, to the point that her son would not dare oppose her. One example is Grandmother Jia in *Hongloumeng* (Dream of the red chamber).[16] For this reason, what we observe in traditional families is not like the distorted version presented to us by "May Fourth" intellectuals. In traditional marriages and families, we do not find the phenomenon of universal cruelty toward and oppression of women.

In Traditional Marriages, the Source of Women's Feelings of Happiness Was Not the Lack of Control Over Her Fate Because Men Had No Such Control Either.

Fan Bixuan: In traditional marriages, most of which were accomplished "on order of the parents and with the help of a matchmaker," women had little choice over whom they married. Might this have influenced the women's happiness once married?

Jiang Qing: On the question of the happiness of women in traditional marriages, "May Fourth" intellectuals criticized these marriages because they were arranged, which meant that there was no happiness for the women. Actually, if the marriage were really conducted in proper ritual terms, both the man and the woman would have to go through a lengthy procedure, and the woman's opinion was not completely ignored. Every step of the process was carried out with care, and if a step went wrong, then the marriage did not happen. There were only a few very poor families who married off their daughters even before they were born, after which they would be brought up in their future husband's family. In traditional married families, the happiness of the woman was not a product of her degree of control over her fate because the man had no such control either.

Many sources tell us that the happiness of women in olden times was not worse than that in modern free marriages. There is a new term now—*shanhunzu*, "the marriage-dodging elite"—that describes my friend who gets divorced every year. Are the women in these marriages happy? What if a woman is married to a university professor, and suddenly a female doctoral candidate takes a liking to him, and the professor is no longer satisfied with his wife? Well, if you're not satisfied, then you get divorced, right? It's simple. But at the beginning the woman had decided to marry the professor. So is the power of decision a guarantee of happiness? Obviously not. Now there are some women who, even though they succeeded in finding a capable husband, are always uneasy because they know that a third party may intervene at any time and that once the husband has a change of heart, the marriage is over. By way of contrast, traditional marriages were much more stable. Divorce could not be had on demand, unlike now, when divorce requires no reason, when you give up as soon as you don't get along. Everyone knows the traditional "seven justifications for divorce,"[17] and if these conditions weren't met, then there was no divorce. (Fan adds: "There were also the "three conditions precluding divorce,"[18] which protected the women). Right! Not getting along was not a reason.

I have a friend—I know his wife, too; she's an outstanding high school teacher. One day he called me out of the blue to tell me he'd just remarried. I thought this was strange and imagined that there must have been some kind of problem. Later when we met, he said, "Only now have I understood what marriage means," which meant that his current wife was better than his past wife. I thought, well, sure, the former wife is twenty years older. She worked hard to raise your children, and now she's old. Now the new wife is young and pretty, so what else are you going to say? Unbelievable, this is a so-called high-level intellectual saying, "Only now do I understand what marriage is."

Traditional Marriages Were Happier [Than Modern Marriages]
Because in Addition to Legal Protection, There Was Also
the Protection of Social Customs.

Jiang Qing: The conditions demanded for granting a divorce in traditional ritual laws constituted a high barrier and thus served as a kind of protection for women. Now people decide on their own marriages, and divorce is free. There are no conditions restricting all of this, and the result is a tragedy for the weaker member of the couple. For example, the fact that women age easily is a weak spot and can result in the breakup of the family because they are without legal protection. Currently there are two ways to break up a family: one is divorce, and the other is taking a mistress. The man doesn't bring the mistress home, but if his family finds out, he doesn't care even if the law is on the side of the wife and not the mistress. For this reason, when we compare women's happiness in traditional and modern families, we need to reduce by quite a bit the happiness identified by the "May Fourth" crowd as being associated with arranging one's own marriage.

Many things that occurred in the early Republican period, which was a period of transition between two types of marriage systems, were often quite strange. There were very few cases like Lu Xun's wife, Zhu An [1878–1947]. Zhu An was someone who suffered from the new style of marriage, not from the traditional style of marriage.[19] Had there not been new-style intellectuals who refused traditional marriage, then she would have been happy. Zhu An took good care of Lu Xun's parents and produced heirs to perpetuate the family line and thus should have been very happy. Thus, we cannot say that Zhu An's tragedy was the tragedy of traditional marriage. For example, Hu Shi [1891–1962][20] also had a traditional marriage, but his wife was very happy. He was very respectful of his wife and even took her with him to the United States when serving as ambassador. You can see how happy she was.

Thus, I feel that there was more happiness in traditional marriages than in modern marriages because, in addition to the legal protection, traditional society also added the protection of customs. Moreover, traditional women had many types of happiness; their happiness was not built uniquely on the husband, and because the husband had the husband's propriety and the wife the wife's propriety, much of the traditional wife's happiness was built upon this ritual life. For example, filially serving her in-laws, raising the children with her husband, managing the family, protecting the family name were all part of the woman's role, and she could feel great happiness in accomplishing these various tasks. If a woman could raise an outstanding child who gained the broad praise of society, then how happy she must have been! In supporting her husband, if the woman did her utmost morally in daily life to support her husband professionally, thus nurturing his sense of accomplishment, then she would feel much happiness as well. In olden times, many women did this very well; we find many representative examples in the *Lienüzhuan* (Biographies of virtuous women): women who understood principle, who helped their husbands with ideas concerning politics or society, who encouraged their husband to maintain high standards of performance and personality.

All of the previous [points] illustrate that Confucians provide a reasonable place for women according to their gender nature and their social nature, allowing them to obtain their own life meaning and existential value according to the "way of women" (*fudao*) and to "women's rites" (*fuli*).

Marriage Is Not Sustained by Man's Natural Character, but Rather Through Religion, Morality, Duty, and Responsibility.

Jiang Qing: Of course, that was traditional society. Things have changed with modern society. Are Confucian views of women obsolete? I don't think so. Because of the West's influence, marriages throughout the world, with the exception of Islam, are facing a huge crisis. At present, the divorce rate in China is the highest in the world. Things such as mistresses, one-night stands, wife swapping, trial marriages, and [de facto] gay marriage are constantly challenging the normal marriage system. The family is the basic building block of social life, and if there are no cultural values to sustain the family, meaning that family may one day fall apart, then society will fall apart, too. In this situation, I feel that the Confucian views of women and of marriage should be strengthened.

At present, the Chinese family still preserves the faint outlines of a few traditional elements. For example, in the education of children we note that the majority of those taking their children to extra classes are women. Women's nature makes them even more concerned with children's education, and this is their family responsibility as mothers as well as their authority in managing the family. Moreover, women run the finances of most households, and very few women say they don't handle the money, that they turn it over to their husband. In addition, Confucius noted that "the husband is just, and the wife is loyal" (*fuyi fuzhen*). By "loyal," he meant "upright," so "the husband is just, and the wife is loyal" means that the husband has his role and the wife has her role. For example, the husband should be "loyal" to the household, as should the wife. I think that no wife gets married hoping that the family will be unstable; she hopes to be loyal to the family. Of course, the man has the same demands and also demands that the wife be "loyal" to the family.

But if we hope to convince people of these ideas, there is still work to do. Due to the excessively negative propaganda of the "May Fourth" intellectuals, people have greatly misunderstood the Confucian view of women and marriage. Once modern people hear someone talking about responsibility in the context of married life, they get annoyed; all they care about are rights and freedom. If you bring up responsibility and duty, they are unhappy and feel that they have been oppressed. But there is no doubt that marriage is sustained by responsibility and duty. In fact, looking at it based on common sense and experience, once a couple is married and especially after they have children, marriage is sustained precisely by responsibility and duty. Of course, in China feelings are important, so that if marriage is based on freedom, rights, and the sexual love that the Marxists emphasize, then once children are born, the marriage is in crisis.

Marriage is not sustained by man's nature (or natural instincts), but rather by religion, morality, duty, and responsibility. Only by accepting these conditions will both parties to the marriage feel constrained. For example, is it not right to use morality, propriety, and public opinion to keep men from taking mistresses and destroying families? In the West, Catholic countries still consider the stability of marriage the major priority in their church work. And Protestant countries, such as the United States, with the rise of evangelical churches have also felt the crisis of the decline of the family and emphasize a return to a traditional view of marriage. As a result, after George W. Bush was elected, he turned his back on the American principle of division between church and state and for the first time allocated money for church organizations to use to maintain traditional family values. In China, we clearly cannot rely on Christianity but instead should rely on Confucianism to maintain traditional family values.

Confucians View the Relationship Between Husband and Wife as a Concrete and Special Form of Social Relations, and for This Reason Husband and Wife Have Different Rights and Responsibilities.

Fan Bixuan: What you say is true and answers many questions that I have been thinking about over the years. Thank you. But are the rights and responsibilities of husbands and wives abstractions? When we look at women, as their social nature becomes fully developed, what sort of value system should we construct to raise their rational self-image?

Jiang Qing: I know what you mean. Many people ask me this question, and it is clearly something that women have to resolve for themselves. They need to fight for their own sense of consciousness, meaning, happiness, achievement, and belonging.

In an ideal Confucian society, there are differences between men and women, between husband and wife. Although Confucians talk about universal "benevolence" (*ren*) and "conscience" (*liangzhi*), this is not like Western rationalism and does not produce abstract values that transcend concrete social relationships. For instance, men and women have distinct sexual natures, and husbands and wives have distinct family natures, but Western rationalism removes these natural and social attributes and, taking an abstracted notion of universal equality as a theoretical base, talks about the rights of universal, abstract people. They ignore the Confucian observation that there are differences between men and women, husbands and wives, arguing that in their natural and social attributes men and women and husbands and wives are equal, possessing the same rights and freedoms.

But Confucians are not like this. Confucians start from concrete natural and social attributes and view husbands and wives as concrete and particular instances of social relations and for this reason believe that husbands and wives have different rights and responsibilities. This means that in the Confucian discourse on men and women, husbands and wives, men have men's principle, and women have women's principle; husbands have husbands' principle, and wives have wives' principle. This "principle" is not abstract or universal but instead refers to concrete and distinct status. The view of marriage in the eyes of Western reason is that men and women should respect the same principle, meaning that men and women have legal rights and duties, while the Confucian view of marriage argues that men follow the men's principle and women the women's principle. Men, women, husbands, and wives—all should live according to their different status, in accord with their own social relations.

In actual social life, we do not see abstract people. All we see are men and women, who after marriage are husbands and wives. Among husbands and wives, some are younger, and some are older; some have children, and some don't. These are not the same concrete people, nor are they the same abstract universalized people. As a consequence, in the context of the feelings of accomplishment and belonging that you mentioned, Confucians do not confer universal standards and abstract values that all men, women, husbands, and wives can follow but rather confer concrete standards and individualized values appropriate to particular men and women, husbands and wives. For example, husbands should be just, and women loyal. Men follow the code for men, women the code for women.

Thus, in family and social life and in political life, the functions of men and women, husbands and wives, as well as their feelings of accomplishment and belonging are not the same. For this reason, Confucians do not put forth universal, abstract standards demanding that men and women be seen as equal or receive equal treatment. In today's Western society and in the Chinese society influenced by the West, there is only one standard for men and women. In politics, men can be president, and so can women, which is the greatest career accomplishment. In the economy, a man can be CEO, and a woman can be CEO, and careers and social customs are all like this, demanding that men and women be viewed as equal. In this way, men and women receive the same sense of accomplishment and belonging. Yet I feel that this is wrong. It goes against the Confucian principle that "there are differences between men and women" (*nannü youbie*) because although men and women do share some common values, such as "benevolence" and "filial piety" (*xiao*), nonetheless in terms of men and women's natural gender and social affinities their senses of accomplishment and belonging are definitely not the same.

Being a Good Daughter, a Good Mother, and a Good Wife Is
the Natural Gender Character of Women and a Necessary
Demand of Family Life, and It Is the Basic Value Support
for Judging the Meaning of Chinese Women's Lives.

Fan Bixuan: What I meant by the question I just asked is: How are today's
women, in particular today's intellectual women, meant to find a sense of
belonging and support for their own values within Confucian teachings? In
other words, how can they find a meaning and purpose in life within the values expressed by Confucian teachings? I'm not talking now about looking for
inspiration within Confucianism, but rather support. Today's women are facing just such a question, and in the search for life beliefs feel a bit lost.

Jiang Qing: Current society is based on careers, so we have intellectual
women and women with careers. In the past, women basically did not participate in public life. Of course, some did, like when empress dowagers and
empresses interfered in court life as well as women who ruled as emperor, but
they were exceptions and do not represent the social mainstream. Today's intellectual women's sense of belonging and attachment should be multifaceted,
just as the design of Confucian "rituals" is multifaceted. As Gu Hongming said,
If you are to be a daughter, then be a good daughter; if you are to be a mother,
then be a good mother; if you are to be a wife, then be a good wife. Society has
changed, and women can obtain all sorts of knowledge and engage in all sorts
of careers and thus can participate in social life. Consequently, we should add
a sentence [to Gu Hongming's formula]: If women are to be professionals, then
they should be good professionals.

The traditional Confucian view of "female literati" (*nüshi*) was "a women
who nonetheless participated in public life." Thus, when modern women
participate in public life, this is a modern expression of "participation" that
does not betray the basic spirit of Confucianism. Concretely speaking, if a
woman is filial to her parents and in-laws, so that her praise extends to
future generations, then this is being a good daughter. If a woman brings up
her children well so that they become healthy adults with good character and
education, then she has been a good mother. If she ably performs the role
assigned to her and sustains a good home life, avoiding shame throughout her
life, then she is a good wife. These are three roles that women assume and that
characterize traditional as well as modern society or, to put it in your terms,
three expressions of value carried over from traditional society and still
existing today. If these three are done correctly, then she can fulfill herself
without shame and thus obtain the woman's sense of accomplishment and
belonging of which you spoke. Then and only then can she think about seeking accomplishments in modern social life or becoming a successful career
woman.

Nonetheless, being a good daughter, being a good mother, and being a good wife are the necessary demands of her gender nature and her family nature and constitute the basic sense of value in the life of a Chinese woman. Hence, this is also where Chinese women find their basic sense of accomplishment and belonging. As for her participation in public life or her role as a successful career woman, these naturally are not where she will find her basic sense of accomplishment and belonging. Having a successful career is at most a secondary demand of a woman who participates in public life. A woman's life meaning and existential value cannot reside in an exterior career, to say nothing of locating her sense of accomplishment and belonging in career success, which is always hit or miss. In other words, an intellectual or career woman's professional success has meaning only to the degree that it does not come at the expense of the three womanly roles mentioned earlier. Of course, if you are a full-time wife and don't work outside the home, then being a good daughter, a good mother, and a good wife is enough. Such women can completely fulfill their purpose in life and their existential value and achieve a sufficient sense of accomplishment and belonging in that way, which means achieving the valuation that women have always had.

But this is hard to do in today's society, and stay-at-home wives are fewer and fewer. And given the influence of Western egalitarianism on Chinese women, many women unconsciously have come to view their professional accomplishments in public life as constituting the basis of their sense of values, accomplishment, and belonging, to the point of seeing these as the very basis of their life meaning and existential value. In so doing, they turn their back on women's gender and family affinities, and women are no longer women, being no longer any different from men. For this reason, Western gender egalitarianism in fact asks that women define themselves and act according to men's standards and no longer allows women to act in accordance with women's standards because in today's world career and professional accomplishments are defined according to the men's standards. For example, to be a great politician is defined in terms of men's standards.

Although modern Confucians do not deny women's sense of career and professional accomplishment, they do not agree that career and professional accomplishments are the sole goal or the basic value of a woman's life. Even less do they agree that other roles and positions for women constructed on their gender or family affinities are worthless. At present, some intellectual women emphasize career and professional achievements, ignoring or downplaying the rest. Confucians do not approve of this. But if today we ask women to cling to traditional roles constructed on the basis of gender and family affinities and ignore the fact that career and professional success adds to women's sense of accomplishment and value, then we're perhaps being too resistant to change because at present we cannot ask all women to return to the family and make the family the center of their lives.

If in the future Chinese society develops in a more balanced manner, as in South Korea, where men's wages are sufficiently high to maintain family life with little problem, so that women can choose not to work and can devote themselves wholeheartedly to the management of the family, then the value of women can completely express itself through the three roles mentioned earlier. But we are not to that point yet because in China the system of distribution is not rational, which forces women to work to meet the expenses of family life. Even in the case of a small family and a young couple, if the woman doesn't work, the man's wages are insufficient to support the family. You say that women really want to work outside the home? I think that according to their basic nature they don't want to; it's just that they don't have a choice. If we designed a more reasonable system where men earned higher wages and thus could support the entire family, and if at the same time we designed a system that could protect women so that, for example, according to law half of the men's wages were allocated to women through the state distribution system, then men would have no reason to feel that it was completely up to them to support the family, and they would not look down on women.

If we had this sort of systemic arrangement that could guarantee women's ability to fulfill their own natural gender and family affinities, allowing women to receive the respect and the sense of accomplishment that they deserve in family life, what would be wrong with that? Now in the cities, almost all preschool-age children are looked after by their grandparents because the parents have no time to take care of them outside of Saturday and Sunday. If the grandparents are not available, then they have to hire a nanny, but nannies don't take care of education, to say nothing of encouraging the development of family feelings. Now many mothers would prefer to take care of their own children, but given the obstacle posed by family finances, they drop the idea. Thus, our current wage-allocation system is not reasonable and should be reformed.

That Chinese Women Seem to Feel Less Affinity for Confucianism Than for Buddhism Is a Question That Confucians Must Take Seriously and Resolve in the Course of the Current Confucian Renaissance.

Fan Bixuan: I have another question: How do we increase the attractiveness of Confucianism for women? For example, Buddhism claims to provide a feeling of safety and intimacy to women who become Buddhists. This kind of intimacy seems to be largely missing in Confucianism, and there seems to exist a certain exclusion of or discrimination against women in Confucianism. I think that Confucianism should look for a solution to this problem in its original teachings and devise a set of theories appropriate to modern women who wish to cultivate themselves and manage their families. This would allow women to find self-confidence in Confucianism. In Buddhist scriptures, we can locate here and there passages that express a concern for women. Of course, some of these are no more than a kind of psychological comfort, but they still express a Buddhist concern and empathy for women.

Jiang Qing: I know. What you are talking about is a question of life or death of the soul. It's not like the various questions concerning society and the family that we've just been talking about. We've been talking about the family, society, and politics, but what you're worried about here is an otherworldly matter. To put it in Buddhist technical terms, Confucianism deals with worldly matters, which is what we've been talking about to this point. Buddhism transcends worldly affairs as well as people's natural gender and social affinities to look squarely at the meaning of life and views all forms of life as equal, which of course includes men and women as well. In fact, the question you raised exists for men as well. Once they believe in Buddhism, then distinctions between men and women no longer exist; there are no more family roles or social mobility. The five ethical relationships no longer exist, nor do this-worldly ethical or value standards. Everything becomes selflessness and co-arising, as if you're floating in a dream. Everything is empty. Both the Buddhist Heart Sutra and the Diamond Sutra explain this.

Nonetheless, even if Confucianism concentrates on this-worldly affairs, it still has its transcendent dimension. On questions concerning the existence of God, the eternal nature of the soul, and the meaning of life, Confucianism has its own points of view, and from a religious standpoint Confucianism can be the Confucian faith. But Confucianism's original point of departure is not like Buddhism and did not set out to solve the problem of man's release from the cycle of life and death but instead focused on solving problems of the meaning of life that went beyond questions of belief. Because the Buddha's original goal was to break through the cycle of life and death, the vast numbers of Buddhist writings that followed in his wake continued to devote a great deal of time to this question. By contrast, Confucius created his teachings so as to foster a sincere faith that heaven would realize man's heavenly dictated nature as well as the transcendent meaning and sacred value of this nature. As for the question of whether the soul is immortal, when we read the *Book of Poetry* or the *Book of Rites*, we find an answer. Confucians also believed that the soul is immortal, just as the Buddhists did, but Confucians had no notion of reincarnation. The idea that the soul is eternal is the basic characteristic of all religions, and Confucianism is no exception. But different religions have different teachings about this. Buddhism has its elaborate theory of reincarnation, and Christianity has its theories about the final judgment. Confucianism rejects both reincarnation and the final judgment and believes that the soul of a good man ascends to heaven "to be close to God" and enjoy heavenly blessings. The soul of an evil man becomes an evil spirit and cannot ascend to heaven, but rather stays on earth to harm people. In addition, Confucianism accords much importance to ritual, especially funeral rituals. The precondition of offering sacrifices to the gods is that the soul must be eternal, as is life. If the soul perishes, then ritual offerings have no meaning because the point of ritual offerings is to facilitate the movement of the soul from the heavens to the human world, where it can partake of the ritual offerings.

In traditional Chinese Confucianism, both men and women took ritual occasions very seriously. These occasions enabled them to communicate with the spirit world, thus evidencing the eternal nature of life. In the *Book of Poetry*, especially the "Ernan" section, there are many women who participated in ritual. Indeed, women were entrusted with the preparation of many rituals, which they treated with reverence and engaged in actively. Collecting ritual plants, purification, and arrangement of ritual instruments were all tasks that were allocated to women.

You ask about women's ultimate resting place.[21] My answer is that: while living, they use rituals to rejoin the souls of their ancestors, and after they die, their eternal soul ascends to heaven to be with the gods. As long as you do not engage in evil affairs, your soul can receive eternal blessings in heaven. This doesn't mean that once the soul is in heaven, there's nothing more to do. The soul of a good person must take care of his or her sons and grandsons. This is true for both men and women; there is no difference. That said, we must admit that Confucian scholars after the Han period did not accord enough importance to belief in the eternal soul, which leads many people to feel that Confucianism is lacking on this question when compared to Buddhism and thus fails to provide the necessary comfort to those concerned with questions of life and death. This is why you feel that Confucianism is less attractive than Buddhism. This is precisely a question that the contemporary Confucian revival in China must address and resolve.

Why is it that the things you feel in Buddhism, you feel less in Confucianism? In part, this is a lack in Confucianism because Confucianism is the learning of an elite, concerned mainly with questions of good governance, so that it focused less attention to such questions. Even if we do find materials in Confucianism to address such questions, it is not where the focus has been, and this is the fault of Confucianism, which must be elevated and improved. From another perspective, women are less interested than men when it comes to involving themselves in social or political life, and for those who are interested in this side of life, Buddhism offers relatively little because it does not address questions of politics or ritual.

Song-Ming Confucians talked about the nature of the heart-mind (*xinxing*), which they drew from Buddhism and gave their writings a little Buddhist feeling, but Han Confucianism does not feel at all like Buddhism because Han Confucians talked about good government. Even if life-and-death questions were a concern for Han Confucians, it was not their primary concern, which was how to govern the country. So they had no feeling for Buddhism. From another angle, women were relatively uninterested in politics, society, ritual, and the like, and even if in modern times there are some women who are interested in society and politics, they remain a minority, and most women are by nature creatures of feeling, introverted, while men by nature are rational and extraverted. For this reason, Buddhism can readily move women: it is unconcerned with society and politics and is focused on questions of life or death. Life-and-death questions are closest to questions of one's own life and can incite feelings of empathy, which is why they affect women and their feelings, leading them to believe that Buddhism is attractive.

The questions you ask about the end of life or about release from life are perhaps important for introspective, sensitive women, but less so for men. For example, Liang Shuming [1893–1988][22] was a Buddhist until the end of his life, but his principle concerns were politics and government, the reconstruction of China and of China's villages. He achieved liberation in these political and social activities, which gave him a sense of belonging and accomplishment, thus fulfilling his life's meaning and his existential value. Because women are by nature sensitive and introverted, most of them will not be oriented toward exterior social and political activities and will not search for life's liberation of meaning therein.

Buddhism is a relatively closed, self-referential belief system and provides an answer to the life questions that concern women. Hence, you feel that Buddhism is attractive because you yourself are one of those sensitive, introspective women looking for answers to concerns about release from your own life, about finding a place, about belonging. If you weren't worried about these questions and instead were worried about the reconstruction of the Chinese political system, then you wouldn't find a home in Buddhism; you wouldn't find it attractive because Buddhism has no resources to address such questions. You would instead find your home in Confucianism, which would seem attractive because Confucianism is a belief system that deals with affairs of government.

It Is Urgent That We Transform Women Through Education Based on Model Women and Through the Molding of Women's Character.

Fan Bixuan: I have also been thinking about the question of women's education. I feel that of many contemporary questions in society, many bad phenomena, some come from women, and some from men. Take, for example, the question of mistresses. Women who are willing to be mistresses have a problem with their values. There are also women who have forgotten that they are women, have forgotten their own natural affinities. They devote themselves entirely to their careers and work until they are in their thirties before they realize that they should have a family, that they should get married and have children. Then either they don't get married, or by the time they are married, they are too old to have children, and when they realize this, they are devastated. What I am thinking about now is how Confucianism should teach modern women so that they maintain traditional moral standards and also meet the challenges of modern social life.

Jiang Qing: This has nothing to do with Buddhism, but rather with Confucianism. Confucianism dominated education in ancient times, and from the time of their birth women were naturally educated in the culture of the larger society. Women didn't necessarily go to school because they had no need to be like the boys who read the classics and took the exams. But when they were young, they would learn from their mothers and grandmothers how to be a good girl, which means how to be a good woman. This education was carried out through daily life. This is no longer the case. Now our daily life is completely Westernized, and family education has declined. The idea is that this would be replaced by education in the schools, but what is taught in the schools is Western values and Western views of women—in other words, it teaches girls how to grow up independent and free.

Faced with this situation, what we need to do is to have the family carry out Confucian preschool education before the girls go to school. Of course, we also need for educational groups outside the family to take up this educational work, so that there are classes and lectures on the topic. (Fan: Zhu Xi in his *Xiaoxue* [Elementary learning] also said that fourteen-year-old girls should learn to do something.) Right, because at present Confucianism is weak, not like the Catholics, who have believers organized into women's leagues that devote themselves to the education of girls in Catholic families. If Confucians had this sort of women's leagues, then we could devote ourselves to the work of educating women and could use the examples of modern women to mold the female personality.

China currently has the Women's Association, but this is basically a political organization, and they don't engage in this kind of thing. Of course, things are a little better now, and we're starting to propagate Confucian values—for example, promoting filial piety and respect for the elderly. This return of Confucian values will proceed slowly because at present the Confucian revival is just beginning and remains fragile. There's a great resistance to carrying out [Confucian] education. I have observed that Catholicism currently pays attention to two questions: education and marriage. The Catholic Church pours its energy into education and builds elementary schools and middle schools all over the place. Even in Protestant countries such as the United States, most schools are Catholic. This is because Catholicism believes that education is extremely important, so that if they have primary and secondary schools, they can promote Catholic values in these schools and use these Catholic values to transform young men and women.

Consequently, as we today revive Confucian values, books like *Biographies of Virtuous Women* and Confucian teachings designed for women remain important teaching materials that can resolve the problem of educating women in modern society. Of course, to do this will require that we make progress in correcting the May Fourth period's extreme demonization of Confucian thought.

Translator's Notes

1. Jiang Qing, "Zhiyou Rujia neng andun xiandai nüxing" (Only Confucians can make a place for modern women), interview, August 12, 2015, http://cul.qq.com/a/20150813/010233.htm.
2. For a concise introduction to Jiang's ideas, see Jiang Qing and Daniel A. Bell, "A Confucian Constitution for China," *New York Times*, July 11, 2012, https://www.nytimes.com/2012/07/11/opinion/a-confucian-constitution-in-china.html. For a more detailed study, see Jiang Qing, *A Confucian Constitutional Order: How China's Ancient Past Can Shape Its Political Future*, ed. Daniel A. Bell and Ruiping Fan (Princeton, NJ: Princeton University Press, 2012).
3. See, for example, Zeng Yi and Guo Xiaodong, eds., *He wei pushi? Shei de jiazhi* (What is universal? Whose values?) (Shanghai: Huadong Shifan Daxue, 2013), a transcript of the oral proceedings of a conference organized by mainland New Confucians in Shanghai in November 2011. Jiang Qing was not in attendance.
4. This is a deformation of a quote from the Confucian *Analects* based on a confusion between two similar characters: *ru*, an archaic character meaning "you," and *nü*, the character meaning "women." Thus, while Confucius meant "you and petty people are hard to take," directing his remark at a particular disciple, over time the object of his remark was taken to be women. See "Wei nüzi yu xiaoren shei yang ye" (Women and petty people are difficult to endure), n.d., http://baike.baidu.com/view/1408365.htm.
5. The "three obediences" were as a daughter to the father, as a wife to the husband, and as a widow to the sons. The "four virtues" included proper womanly morality, speech, appearance, and work ethic.
6. The May Fourth period, roughly from 1915 to 1930, is often identified as "China's Enlightenment," an iconoclastic moment when many intellectuals and young people broke definitively with Confucianism, which they blamed for Chinese weakness and backwardness. Throughout this interview, quotation marks are added to the expression "May Fourth," signaling Confucian skepticism as to the validity of the criticisms of Confucianism advanced at the time.
7. Jiang uses the term *zhuhou*, which refers to the elite of the predynastic period.
8. Mencius or Mengzi was the best-known Confucian after Confucius himself; Sima Guang was a famous Song dynasty Confucian scholar; Zhu Xi was a Song dynasty scholar famed for his role in launching Neo-Confucianism; Wang Yangming was a famous Ming Confucian who reacted against certain currents in Neo-Confucian

thought of the Song; Liu Zongzhou was a famous Ming Confucian who criticized Wang Yangming's attacks on Zhu Xi's Neo-Confucianism.

9. Kang Youwei was a Qing-era Confucian scholar and modernizing reformer most often identified with the Hundred Days Reform of 1898.

10. "A system that 'ate people'" is a reference to Lu Xun's (1881–1936) famous story "Diary of a Madman," first published in 1918, in which Lu, modern China's most famous writer, compared the conformism of traditional Confucian society to cannibalism.

11. Gu Hongming was from Penang, now part of Malaysia, and educated in Scotland. In the latter part of the nineteenth century, he moved to China, where he served in various posts and came to be strongly identified with the imperial regime.

12. Su Dongpo (Su Shi) was a famous Song dynasty poet.

13. The "three bonds" refer to the service that a minister owes to his lord, a son to his father, and a wife to her husband. The "five constants" refer to the five basic ethical principles regulating human life through proper hierarchy. For women, the important one is that "there is a difference between husband and wife."

14. Han Yu was a well-known Tang dynasty Confucian.

15. Ouyang Xiu was a famous Song-era Confucian scholar; Gu Yanwu was a famous Confucian scholar who lived through the Ming–Qing transition and was greatly influenced by the change.

16. *The Dream of the Red Chamber*, written by Cao Xueqin (1617–1763), is perhaps traditional China's finest novel.

17. The seven justifications for divorce included (1) the wife's failure to obey the husband's parents; (2) the wife's failure to produce a son; (3) adultery; (4) excessive jealousy on the wife's part; (5) serious illness (preventing, for example, performance of necessary rituals); (6) excessive talkativeness; and (7) theft.

18. The three conditions precluding divorce were (1) when the wife did not have a parental home to return to; (2) when the wife had mourned the death of her in-laws for three years; and (3) when the wife married a poor man who subsequently became rich.

19. Zhu An was married to Lu Xun in a traditional, arranged marriage. There is no evidence of Jiang's claim that she produced heirs for Lu Xun.

20. Hu Shi was a major intellectual during the May Fourth period and later and is regarded as a major figure in Chinese liberalism.

21. Jiang Qing uses the term *guisu* here, which can also mean "destiny" or "final destination"; he seems to be using it in a way related to identity.

22. Liang Shuming was an important philosopher and rural reformer in Republican-period China. He variously identified as Confucian or Buddhist or both.

GLOSSARY OF NAMES AND TERMS

(Most toponyms have not been included in this list; they are easily accessible.)

"1956 nian Mao Zedong mishu Tian Jiaying hui jiaxiang diaocha shimo" 一九五
    六年毛泽东秘书田家英回家乡调查始末

Abe Shinzō 安倍晋三

Ai Siqi 艾思奇

Aisixiang Wang 爱思想网

Ai Weiwei 艾未未

Anbang zhi dao: Guojia zhuanxing de mubiao yu tujing 安邦之道:国家转型的目标
    与途径

Arasaki Moriteru 新崎盛暉

Bainian chao 百年潮

Bai Tongdong 白彤东

bentuhua 本土化

bianfuxing renwu 蝙蝠性人物

Bianlun "Zhongguo moshi" 辩论「中国模式」

biexing 鳖星

Bo Xilai 薄熙来

buwang chuxin 不忘初心

buwang chuzhong 不忘初衷

"Buying danwang de gonggong juece canyu moshi: qunzhong luxian" 不应淡忘
    的公共决策参与模式：群众路线

Caijing 财经

Caijing niankan, shijie 财经年刊，世界

Cai Yuanpei 蔡元培

Cai Xia 蔡霞

cancong side 三从四德

Cao Jinqing 曹锦清

Cao Xueqin 曹雪芹

Chahu 搜狐

"'Changtai pianzhi' yu dangjin shijie" 「常态偏执」与当今世界

Chen Boda 陈伯达

Chen Duxiu 陈独秀

Chen Fang 陈芳

Chen Kuan-hsing 陈光兴

Chen Lai wei Zhongyang zhengzhiju jiangjie aiguozhuyi, lingdao ti wenti hen shenke 陈来为中央政治局讲解爱国主义：领导提问题很深刻

Cheng Hao 程颢

Cheng Yi 程颐

Cheng-Zhu 程朱

Chen Lai 陈来

Chen Ming 陈明

Chen Yinke (Yinque) 陈寅恪

Chen Yun 陈云

Chen Yun wenxuan 陈云文选

Chen Zuwei 陈祖为

Chiang Kai-shek 蒋介石

Chongsheng, zai linjie zhuangtai zhong shenghuo 冲绳,在临界状态中生活

Chuantong yu xiandai 传统与现代

Chūgoku zenkindai shisō no kussetsu to tenkai 中国前近代思想の屈折と展開

Chunqiu Dongshixue 春秋董氏学

Chu Yun-han 朱云汉

Ciji Gongdehui 慈济功德会

daibiao 代表

"Daibiao, haishi yiyuan?" 代表，还是议员

Daibiao lilun yu daiyi zhengzhi 代表理论与代议政治

daiyishi 代议士

da minzhu 大民主

dang de sixiang 党的思想

Dangshi biji, cong Zunyi huiyi dao Yan'an zhengfeng 當史筆記,從遵義會議到延安整風

Dangshi yanjiu yu jiaoxue 党史研究与教学

"Dang weihui de gongzuo fangfa" 党委会的工作方法

danwei 单位

dao 道

"Dao qunzhong zhong qu, bai renmin wei shi" 到群众中去，拜人民为师

"Daoyan" 导言

datong 大同

datong shijie 大同世界

"Daxing diaocha yanjiu zhi feng" 大兴调查研究之风

dawo 大我

dazhongzhuyi 大众主义

Dazhai 大寨

Deng Xiaoping 邓小平

Deng Xiaoping wenji 邓小平文集

Deng Xiaoping wenxuan 邓小平文选

Deng Yuwen 邓聿文

Deng Zhenglai 邓正来

diduan renkou 低端人口

"Ding Ling bujiandan: Mao tizhi xia zhishifenzi zai huayu shengchan zhong de fuza juese" 丁玲不简单：毛体制下知识分子在话语生产中的复杂角色

Ding Xueliang 丁学良

Dongfang Zaobao 东方早报

Dong Xi wenhua ji qi zhexue 东西文化及其哲学

Dong Zhongshu 董仲舒

"Duoyu laodongli zhaodao le chulu, yiwen de anyu" 多余劳动力找到了出路，一文的按语

Dushu 读书

Du Yaquan 杜亚泉

"Dui 'wusi' de sikao" 对「五四」的思考

Du Yaquan yu Dong-Xi wenhua wenti lunzhan 杜亚泉与东西文化论战

Eguo zhengdang shi 俄国政党史

ernai 二奶

Ernan 二南

"Ershi shiji liushi niandai chu zhongyang lingdao tongzhi de diaocha yanjiu" 二十世纪六十年代初中央领导同志的调查研究

Ershiyi Shiji 二十一世纪

Ershiyi Shiji Jingji Baodao 二十一世纪经济报道

"Eryi ji, xiao zagan" 而已集，小杂感

Fan Bixuan 范必萱

"Fandui benbenzhuyi" 反对本本主义

Fan Peng 樊鹏

fanshipai 凡是派

"Fazhan Zhong-Mei guanxi de yuanze lichang (1981-nian 1-yue 4-ri)" 发展中美关系的原则立场（1981年1月4日）

fei Maohua 非毛化

Fengfu de tongku, Tang Jihede yu Hamuleite de dongyi 豐富的痛苦,堂吉訶德與哈姆雷特的東移

Fenghuang wang 凤凰网

fengjian 封建

Feng Xingyuan 冯兴元

Fengwanggang 鳳凰綱

Feng Youlan 冯友兰

fudao 妇道

Fujian ribao 福建日报

Fujiao zai kuan: Kang Youwei Kongjiao sixiang shenlun 敷教在宽：康有为孔教思
    想申论

fuli 妇礼

Futenma 普天間

fuwei qigang 夫为妻纲

fuyi fuzhen 夫义妇贞

Gan Yang 甘阳

Gao Hua 高華

"Gei Jiang Qing de xin" 給江青的信

Ge Zhaoguang 葛兆光

gongchanzhuyi wenming 共产主义文明

Gongshi Wang 共识网

Gong tianxia 公天下

Gongyang / Gongyang zhuan 公羊/公羊傳

Gong Ying 龚颖

Gong Zizhen 龚自珍

"Gongzuo fangfa liushi tiao (cao an)" 工作方法六十条（草案）

Guan Yu 關羽

"Guanyu lingdao fangfa de ruogan wenti" 关于领导方法的若干问题

"Guanyu muqian dang de zhengce zhong de jige zhongyao wenti (1984-nian
    1-yue 18-ri)" 关于目前党的政策中的几个重要问题（1984年1月18日）

"Guanyu nongcun diaocha" 关于农村调查

"Guanyu renzhen diaocha gongshe neibu liangge pingjun wenti de yifeng xin"
    关于认真调查公社内部两个平均问题的一封信

"Guanyu tuijin xuexi xing dang zuzhi jianshe de yijian" 关于推进学习型党组织建
    设的意见

"Guanyu 'Zhongguo yu dangjin qianxinianzhuyi' de jijuhua" 关于「中国与当今
    千禧年主义」的几句话

Gu Hongming 辜鸿铭

guiben dayi 归本大易

guisu 归宿

Gu Jiegang 顾颉刚

Guo Bensheng 郭奔胜

Guo Yuhua 郭于华

"Guojia zhongli xing yuanze de daode weidu" 国家中立性原则的道德维度

"Guoji zhishi baogao" 國際指示報告

Guo Moruo 郭沫若

Guotiyuan 国体院

Guowuyuan canshi shi wangzhan 国务院参事室网站

Guo Xiaodong 郭晓东

guoxue 国学

Gu Yanwu 顾炎武

Gu Zhun 顾准

"Hainan shuaixian tigao Xinfangju xingzheng jibie, chengli shengwei
　　qungongbu" 海南率先提高信访局行政级别，成立省委群工部

hanjian 汉奸

Han Li 韩莉

Han Qi 韩倚

Han Wudi 漢武帝

Han Yu 韩愈

He Fang 何方

hefaxing 合法性

Heguanzi 鶡冠子

heipi 黑皮

He Lin 贺麟

He Lin quanji, wenhua yu rensheng 贺麟全集，文化与人生

Henoko 边野古

He wei pushi? Shei de jiazhi? 何谓普世？谁的价值？

hezuohua 合作化

Himeyuri 姫百合

Hong Benjian 洪本健

Hongloumeng 红楼梦

*Hong taiyang shi zenyang shengqi de: Yan'an zhengfeng yundong de lailong
　　qumai* 紅太陽是怎樣升起的:延安整風運動的來龍去脈

Hong Xiuquan 洪秀全

hou 后

houqi 猴氣

Huadong shifan daxue xuebao (Zhexue shehui kexue) 华东师范大学学报(哲学社
　　会科学)

"Huagaiji, tongxun" 華蓋集,通訊

Hua Guofeng 华国锋

Hu An'gang 胡鞍钢

Huang Shaohe 黄少鹤

Huang Yanpei 黄炎培

Huang Zhangjian 黄彰健

Hu Feng 胡風

Hui Neng 惠能

Hu Jintao 胡锦涛

hukou 户口

Hunan weixin yundong shiliao 湖南维新运动史料

hunzhongzi 混种子

Huozhe de liyou 活著的理由

huqi 虎氣

Hu Qiaomu 胡乔木

Hu Shi 胡适

Jia 贾

"Jianchi anbili yuanze tiaozheng guomin jingji" 坚持按比例原则调整国民经济

"Jianguo chuqi 'Mao Zedong shi' de diaocha" 建国初期「毛泽东式」的调查

Jianguo yilai Mao Zedong wengao 建國以來毛澤東文稿

Jiang Qing 蒋庆

Jiang Zemin 江泽民

jiao 教

jiaodai 交代

jiaohua 教化

jiaotang 教堂

Jiaqing 嘉庆

Jia Yi 賈誼

Jieti huiping "guwen guanzhi" 解题汇评「古文观止」

Jin Chongji 金冲及

Jiefang ribao 解放日报

jingu 金箍

Jin Guantao 金冠涛

"Jing Xi Jinping zhuxi pizhun Jiefangjun zong zhengzhibu xia fa 'guilü'" 经习近
  平主席批准解放军总政治部下发「规律」

jinshi 进士

jinsi niaolong shi de minzhu 金絲鳥籠式的民主

Jintian 今天

"Jiti diaocha jizhi" 集体调查机制

"Jitihua yu bei jitihua" 集体化与被集体化

Jiushi niandai fansilu 九十年代反思录

Jiushi niandai riji 九十年代日记

Ji village 骥村

"Ji wo de sanci fansi licheng" 记我的三次反思历程

Ji Xianlin 季羡林

Kaifang Shidai 开放时代

Kaizō 改造

Kan Feng 阚枫

Kang Sheng 康生

Kang Xiaoguang 康晓光

Kang Youwei 康有为

Kang Youwei zhenglunji 康有为政论集

Kawamitsu Shin'ichi 川満信一

"Kesi de zhonggao, sixiang shichang shi Zhongguo zhuanxing chenggong de guanjian" 科斯的忠告：思想市场是中国转型成功的关键

Kongjiao 孔教

lahua 拉话

Lei Yi 雷颐

li (principle) 理

li 里

Liangjia River 梁家河

Liang Qichao 梁启超

Liang Shiqiu 梁實秋

Liang Shuming 梁漱溟

liangzhi 良知

Li Dingming 李鼎铭

Liening quanji 列宁全集

Lienüzhuan 烈女传

Liezi 列子

Li Hongzhang 李鴻章

"Li lun" 理论

Lin Biao 林彪

Lin Rongyuan 林荣远

Lin Tongqi 林同奇

Lin Yusheng 林毓生

Li Rui 李锐

Li Shenzhi 李慎之

Li Shitao 李世涛

Li Tuo 李陀

Liu Bei 劉備

Liu Fenglu 刘逢禄

Liu Junning 刘军宁

Liuping 柳平

Liu Qing 刘擎

Liuru 六如

Liu Shaoqi 刘少奇

Liushi jieyu 六十劫語

"Liushi niandai chu daxing diaocha yanjiu zhi feng jishu" 六十年代初大兴调查研究之风记述

Liu Xiaobo 刘晓波

Liu Xiaofeng 刘小风

Liu Xunlian 刘训练

Liu Zongzhou 刘宗周

lixue 理学

Li Yongquan 李永全

Li Yuanchao 李源潮

Li Zehou 李泽厚

Li Zehou xueshu wenhua suibi 李泽厚学术文化随笔

Li Zhu 李朱

Li Ziyun 李子云

Lu Jiuyuan 陆九渊

Lun guojia de zuoyong 论国家的作用

"Lun lianhe zhengfu" 论联合政府

lunli de jingshen 伦理的精神

lunli jingshen 伦理精神

"Lun Zhongguo 'fengjianzhuyi' wenti, dui Zhongguo qianxiandai shehui
    xingzhi he fazhan de chongxin renshi yu pingjia" 论中国「封建主义」问题，
    对中国前现代社会性质和发展的重新认识与评价

Luo Hongguang 罗红光

Luo Zhijun 罗志军

Lu-Wang 陆王

Lu Xueyi 陆学艺

Lu Xun 鲁迅

Lu Xun quanji 鲁迅全集

Lü Chuanbin 吕传彬

Makesi, Engesi, Liening, Mao Zedong, Deng Xiaoping, Jiang Zemin lun minzhu
    马克思，恩格斯，列宁，毛泽东，邓小平，江泽民论民主

Makesi Engesi xuanji 马克思恩格斯选集

"Makesi 'Heige'er fazhexue pipan'" 马克思「黑格尔法哲学批判」

Makesizhuyi Zhongguohua luntan 马克思主义中国化论坛

Mao Haijian 茅海建

Mao wenti 毛文体

Mao Yushi 茅于轼

Mao Zedong 毛泽东

Mao Zedong nongcun diaocha wenji 毛泽东农村调查文集

Mao Zedong shuxin xuanji 毛泽东书信选集

Mao Zedong xuanji 毛泽东选集

Mao Zedong yu Mosike de enen yuanyuan 毛澤東與莫斯科的恩恩怨怨

Mao Zedong zhuan (1949–1976) 毛泽东传（1949–1976）

Ma Shexiang 马社香

Ma Yifu 马一浮

Ma Yifu ji 马一浮集

Ma Yong 马勇

Meigui ba 玫瑰坝

"Mingjun ke yu wei zhongxin fu" 明君可與為忠言賦

minjian 民间

minsheng 民生

Minzhu sijiang 民主四讲

Mincuizhuyi 民粹主义

minzu jingshen 民族精神

Mizoguchi Yūzō 溝口雄三

Nanfang dushi bao 南方都市报

Nanfang zhoubao 南方周报

Nanfang Zhoumo 南方周末

nannü youbie 男女有别

nanzun nübei 男尊女卑

neisheng waiwang 内圣外王

"Neizai yu Chongsheng de Dongya zhanhou shi" 内在与冲绳的东亚战后史

"Ningde 20-duo nian jianchi 'sixia jiceng' de zhizheng shijian he jingyan qishi"
    宁德 20 多年坚持「四下基层」的执政实践和经验启示

"Nongcun diaocha de xuyan he ba" 农村调查的序言和跋

nü 女

nüzhi 女士

nüzi wucai bian shi de 女子无才便是德

Okamoto Keitoku 冈本惠德

Ouyang Xiu 欧阳修

Pang Xianzhi 逄先知

Peng Mei 彭美

pi 辟

"Pushi jiazhi ben shi changshi" 普世价值本是常识

puxue 朴学

Qian Daxin 钱大昕

qianggu 强箍

Qian Liqun 錢理群

Qianlong 乾隆

Qian Tianhe 钱天鹤

Qian Tianhe wenji 钱天鹤文集

"Qian Tianhe zhuanlüe" 钱天鹤传略

Qian Zhilan 钱治澜

Qian Zhongshu 钱钟书

qingli 清理

Qingyuan jinzuoji 清园近作集

Qingyuan shujian 清园书简

Qin Hui 秦晖

Qin Shihuang 秦始皇

Qiu Feng 秋风

Qiushi 求是

"Quanguo tuiguang qunzhong gongzuobu yu Xinfangju heshu bangong" 全国推
广群众工作部与信访局合署办公

Quanqiuhua shidai de wenhua rentong: Xifang pubianzhuyi huayu de lishi pipan
全球化时代的文化认同:西方普遍主义话语的历史批判

Quanqiuhua yu Gongchandangren jiazhiguan 全球化与共产党人价值观

Qunzhong luxian dajia tan 群众路线大家谈

qunzhong zhuanzheng 群众专政

ren 仁

"Rengran you hen chang de lu yaozou" 仍然有很长的路要走

renjian Fojiao 人间佛教

renmin 人民

"Renmin, gaige, minzhu shi shiba da baogao de zhu xuanlü" 人民，改革，民主是
十八大报告的主旋律

Renmin wang 人民网

Renmin wenxian 人民文献

"Renwen jingshen yu ershiyi shiji de duihua" 人文精神与二十一世纪的对话

Renxin yu rensheng 人心与人生

renyi 仁义

Rong Jian 荣剑

ru 汝

"Ruhe huigu naduan geming lishi?" 如何回顾那段革命歷史

Ruhe yanjiu Zhongguo 如何研究中国

Rujia 儒家

Rujiao 儒教

Rujia yu ziyouzhuyi 儒家与自由主义

Ruxue 儒学

Ruzhe zhi wei 儒者之维

Ryūkyū kyōwa shakai kenpō no senseiryoku: guntō, Ajia, ekkyō no shisō 琉球共和
社会憲法の潜勢力：群島、アジア、越境の思想

sangang wuchang 三纲五常

san-san zhi 三三制

Shanghai shi shehuizhuyi xueyuan wangzhan 上海市社会主义学院网站

Shangshu 尚书

shanhunzu 闪婚族

"Shehui shisuhua tiaojian xia dangdai Zhongguo ren de jingshen shenghuo" 社会
世俗化条件下当代中国人的精神生活

Sheng Hong 盛洪

shenjiao 神教

Shen Yuan 沈原

Shi Anshu 石岸书

"Shijian lun" 实践论

Shiwan 石湾

Shiyi da shangde zhengzhi baogao 十一大上的政治报告

shudao 恕道

Shujing 书经

Shuminyuan 庶民院

shumin zhi jiao 庶民之教

Shun ge yu wenzu 舜格于文组

shun yinyang 顺阴阳

Shuri 首里

sichao 思潮

Sima Guang 司马光

siqing 四清

siwei 思维

sixiang 思想

sixiang gongzuo 思想工作

sixiang jiben yuanze 四项基本原则

Sixiang yu wenhua 思想与文化

Song Binquan 宋斌全

Song Jiaoren 宋教仁

"Song yilai xiangcun zuzhi chongjian, lishi shijiaoxia de xin nongcun jianshe"
宋以来乡村组织重建，历史视角下的新农村建设

Su Dongpo 苏东坡

Sun Ge 孫歌

Sun Liping 孙立平

Sun Yat-sen 孙逸仙

Sun Yefang 孙冶方

Su Shi 苏轼

Su Shi wenji 苏轼文集

Takahashi Yūji 高橋悠治

Tang Wenming 唐文明

"Tang-Wu geming" 汤武革命

"Tantan diaocha yanjiu" 谈谈调查研究

ti 体

Tian Jiaying 田家英

tianxia 天下

"Tianxia sixiang yu xiandaixing de Zhongguo zhi lu" 天下思想与现代性的中国
之路

tianxia wei gong 天下为公

tianxiazhuyi 天下主义

Tianya 天涯

Tianze 天则

tifa 提法

Tongruyuan 通儒院

tong san tong 通三统

Tong Shijun 童世骏

tuo gu gai zhi 托古改制

Tu Wei-ming 杜维明

Urasoe 浦添

Wang Guowei 王国维

Wang Hui 汪晖

Wang Huning 王沪宁

Wang Jiaxiang 王稼祥

Wang Ming 王明

Wang Ruoshui 王若水

Wang Shaoguang 王绍光

Wang Xiaoshi 王小石

Wang Yangming 王阳明

Wang Yuanhua 王元化

"Wang Yuanhua zhi Lin Yusheng" 王元化致林毓生

"Wang Yuanhua zhi Wu Qixin" 王元化致吴琦辛

Wang Zhaoyun (Chaoyun) 王朝云

"Wanzheng de zhunque de lijie Mao Zedong sixiang" 完整地准确地理解毛泽东思想

Weicheng 围城

Wei Jingsheng 魏京生

Wei Liqun 魏礼群

wei nüzi yu xiaoren nan yang 唯女子与小人难养

"Wei nüzi yu xiaoren shei yang ye" 唯女子与小人难养也

Wei wanshi kai taiping: Yige jingji xuejia dui wenming wenti de sikao 为万世开太
平:一个经济学家对文明问题的思考

Wei Yuan 魏源

wen 文

Wenanyi 文安驿

wende 文德

Wenhua de jieshi 文化的解释

wenhua re 文化热

Wenhua zongheng 文化纵横

Wenjian he yanjiu 文獻和研究

wenjiao 文教

Wen shi zhe 文史哲

Wenxue congbao 文學叢報

Wen Yanshi 闻言实

wenti yishi 问题意识

wenzu 文组

Wo de jingshen zizhuan 我的精神自傳

"Wo shi ge nenggou tixing ziji, yueshu ziji de ren" 我是个能够提醒自己，约束自己的人

"Wo suo renshi de Wang Yuanhua" 我所认识的王元化

"Wo yao pian ren" 我要骗人

wu 物

Wu Chucai 吴楚材

Wu Diaohou 吴调侯

Wu Jiaxiang 吴稼祥

Wu Liangjian 吴良健

Wu Qixin 吴琦辛

Wuxu bianfa shi yanjiu 戊戌变法史研究

xi 翕

xiahai 下海

xiangyue 乡约

"Xiangzhou Zhoujin tang ji" 相州昼锦堂记

xianshi 先师

"Xianzheng yu renmin minzhu zhidu zhi bijiao yanjiu" 宪政与人民民主制度之比较研究

xiao 孝

Xiao Gongqin 萧功秦

xiaoti 孝悌

xiaowo 小我

Xiaoxue 小学

Xiao Yi 萧易

Xia Yan 夏衍

Xi Jinping 习近平

"Xi Jinping, cong Shaanxi de shangou yilu zou qilai" 习近平，从陕西的山沟一路走起来

"Xi Jinping zai shengbuji lingdao ganbu zhuanti yantaoban jieyeshi shang jianghua" 习近平在省部级领导干部专题研讨班结业式上讲话

"Xi Jinping zhuzheng Zhejiang, jiuge yue paobian liushijiuge xian" 习近平主政浙江，九个月跑遍六十九个县

"Xi Jingpping zuo shengbuji lingdao yantaoban zongjie jianghua" 习近平作省部级领导研讨班总结讲话

xin 心

xin (new) 新

Xinhua ribao 新华日报

xing 性

Xinhua wang 新华网

Xinhua wenti 新华文体

xinjiao 新教

Xin jingbao 新京报

xin jingxue 新经学

Xinling de tanxun 心靈的探尋

xin lixue 新理学

xinmin 新民

"Xin quanweizhuyi zai Zhongguo shifou kexing?" 新权威主义在中国是否可行

xin san tong 新三通

Xin shiqi diaocha yanjiu gongzuo quanshu 新时期调查研究工作全书

xinu 西奴

xinxing 心性

xin xinxue 新心学

xinxue 心学

Xinxue weijing kao 新学伪经考

xipi chengbian 翕辟成变

Xiqiao (Mount) 西樵

Xi village 西村

Xiong Shili 熊十力

xuexiao 学校

Xuexi shibao 学习时报

Xu Jilin 许纪霖

Xu Jingyue 徐京跃

Yan Fu 严复

Yang Jialing 楊家嶺

Yang Kuisong 杨奎松

Yangming (Mount) 阳明山

Yang Xiaoqing 杨晓青

Yanhuang Chunqiu 炎黄春秋

Yan Xishan 阎锡山

Yan Yilong 焉一龙

Yao Wenyuan 姚文元

Yaozhe de shangdi—zongjiao, zhengzhi yu xiandai Xifang 夭折的上帝—宗教,政治
与现代西方

Yao Zhongqiu 姚中秋

"Yecao, Tuibaixian de chandong" 野草,頽敗線的顫動

"Yecao, Ying de gaobie" 野草,影的告別

yegui 野鬼

Yi Chŏng-hwa 李静和

yi dian dai mian 以点带面

Yijing 易经

"Yijiuliuyi nian Tian Jiaying Zhejiang nongcun diaoyan" 一九六一年田家英浙江
农村调研

Yin Feizhou 尹飞舟

Yin Fuying 尹福瑛

Ying Qi 应奇

Ying Xing 应星

yishi 意识

"'Yiwang' beihou de lishiguan yu lunliguan" 「遺忘」背後的歷史觀與倫理觀

yixin 一心

yiyi guanzhi 一以貫之

"Yi zhengfeng jingshen kaizhan piping he ziwo piping" 以整风精神开展批评和自我批评

yong 用

Yoshida Sadako 吉田貞子

youhuan yishi 忧患意识

youhun 游魂

yuanjun 院君

"Yuan Ru" 原儒

Yuan Shikai 袁世凯

Yuan Xunhui 袁训会

Yu Dan 于丹

Yu Jianrong 于建嵘

yuxing 鱼星

Yu Ying-shih 余英时

"Zai Yan'an wenyi zuotanhui shang de jianghua" 在延安文艺座谈会上的讲话

Zanshō no oto: "Ajia, seiji, aato" no mirai e 残照の音：「アジア、政治、アート」の未来へ

zazhong 杂种

Zeng Yi 曾亦

"Zenyang shi women de renshi geng zhengque xie" 怎样使我们的认识更正确些

Zhang Chunqiao 张春桥

Zhang Dainian 张岱年

Zhang Feng'an 张风安

Zhang Mingshu 张明澍

Zhang Shuguang 张曙光

Zhang Taiyan 章太炎

Zhang Wentian 張聞天

Zhang Xiang 张翔

Zhang Xudong 张旭东

Zhang Zhidong 张之洞

"Zhanzheng he zhanlüe wenti" 戰爭和戰略問題

Zhao Bizhen 赵必振

zhengdangxing 正当性

"Zhengdangxing, quanti yizhi yu zhishan lun" 正当性、全体一致与至善论

Zheng Keyang 郑科扬

zhengquan xingshuai zhouqi lü 政权兴衰周期率

zhengrenhui 证人会

Zheng Xinli 郑新立

Zhengzhi Ruxue, dangdai Ruxue de zhuanxiang, tezhi yu fazhan 政治儒学: 当代儒学的转向、特质与发展

zhibing jiuren 治病救人

zhidao sixiang 指导思想

"Zhi Deng Xiaoping" 致邓小平

Zhishifenzi lichang 知识分子立场

Zhishifenzi lichang, ziyouzhuyi zhi zheng yu Zhongguo sixiang jie de fenhua 知识分子立场，自由主义之争与中国思想界的分化

"Zhi Zhang Pinghua" 致张平化

zhizheng siwei 执政思维

Zhonggong zhongyang bangongting 中共中央办公厅

"Zhonggong zhongyang zhengzhiju zhaokai huiyi, Xi Jinping zhuchi" 中共中央政治局召开会议，习近平主持

Zhongguo dangzheng ganbu luntan 中国党政干部论坛

Zhongguo Gongchandang xinwen wang 中国共产党新闻网

Zhongguo jiti lingdao tizhi 中国集体领导体制

Zhongguo, lixing zhi guo 中国理性之国

Zhongguo minzhu juece moshi, yi wunian guihua zhiding wei li 中国民主决策模式五年规划的制定为例

Zhongguo nongcun de shehuizhuyi gaochao 中国农村的社会主义高潮

Zhongguo qianjindai sixiang de quzhe yu zhankai 中国前近代思想的屈折与展开

"Zhongguoren daodi you duo teshu" 中国人到底有多特殊

Zhongguoren xiangyao shenmeyang minzhu: Zhongguo "zhengzhiren" 中国人想要什么样民主：中国「政治人」

Zhongguo shi gongshi xing juece, "kaimen" yu "mohe" 中国式共识型决策：「开门」与「磨合」

Zhongguo sixiang 中国思想

Zhongguo Taiwan 中国台湾

"Zhongguo xuyao liweitan?—Jinshinian lai Zhongguo guojiazhuyi sichao zhi pipan" 中国需要利维坦?—近十年来中国国家主义思潮之批判

Zhongguo zhengdao 中国政道

Zhongguo zhengfu wang 中国政府网

"Zhongguo ziyouzhuyi ershinian de tuishi" 中国自由主义二十年的颓势

Zhonghua minzu 中华民族

zhongjian didai 中间地带

"Zhongjian didai" de geming, guoji da beijing xia kan Zhonggong chenggong zhi dao 「中間地帶」的革命: 國際大背景下看中共成功之道

Zhongnanhai 中南海

Zhong-Xi duihua zhong de xiandaixing wenti 中西对话中的现代性问题

Zhongxue wei ti, Xixue wei yong 中學為體,西學為用

"Zhongyang guanyu diaocha yanjiu jueding" 中央关于调查研究决定

Zhongyang wenxian yanjiushi wangzhan 中央文献研究室网站

"Zhongyang xin lingdaoceng miji 'zou jiceng,' zuji bianji ba shengfen" 中央新领导层密集「走基层」足迹遍及八省份

Zhongyong 中庸

Zhou Baosong 周保松

Zhou Enlai 周恩來

Zhou Hanmin 周汉民

Zhouli 周礼

Zhou Xiaoping 周小平

Zhou Yang 周扬

Zhu An 朱安

Zhuang Cunyu 庄存与

Zhuang Yan 庄严

Zhu Ciqi 朱次琦

Zhuge Liang 諸葛亮

zhuhou 诸侯

Zhu Xi 朱熹

Zibenzhuyi, shehuizhuyi yu minzhu 资本主义,社会主义与民主

zili yizhong 自立易种

Ziyouren de pingdeng zhengzhi 自由人的平等政治

Ziyouzhuyi zhonglixing ji qi pipingzhe 自由主义中立性及其批评者

Zoujin dangdai de Lu Xun 走進當代的魯迅

Zunyi 遵義

"Zuo hao shangye gongzuo" 做好商业工作

"Zuowei xueshu shijiao de shehuizhuyi xin chuantong" 作为学术视角的社会主义新传统

"Zuzhi qilai" 组织起来

ESSAYS TRANSLATED IN THIS VOLUME, WITH ORIGINAL TITLES

Gan Yang 甘阳. "Xin shidai de 'tong san tong': Zhongguo sanzhong chuantong de ronghui" 新时代的"通三统"：中国三种传统的融汇. In Gan Yang, *Tong san tong* 通三统.

Liu Qing 刘擎. "Zhongguo yu jingxia de ziyouzhuyi: Qianli yu kunjing" 中国语境下的自由主义：潜力与困境. *Kaifang shidai* 开放时代.

Rong Jian 荣剑. "Meiyou sixiang de Zhongguo" 没有思想的中国. Gongshiwang 共识网.

Guo Yuhua 郭于华. "Chuxin suozai yiren weiben" 初心所在以人为本.

Guo Yuhua 郭于华. "'Gongchanzhuyi wenming' de yinying—Gongshiwang zhuanfang Guo Yuhua" "共产主义文明"的阴影——共识网专访郭于华.

Cai Xia 蔡霞. "Tuijin xianzheng minzhu yinggai shi Zhongguo Gongchandang de zhizheng shiming" 推进宪政民主应该是中国共产党的执政使命. *Aisixiang* 爱思想.

Xu Jilin 许纪霖. "'Wo shi shijiu shiji zhi zi'—Wang Yuanhua de zuihou ershinian" "我是十九世纪之子"—王元化的最后二十年. *Dushu* 读书; *Aisixiang* 爱思想.

Qian Liqun 錢理群. "Mao Zedong shidai he hou-Mao Zedong shidai, 1949–2009, ling yizhong lishi shuxie" 毛澤東時代和後毛澤東時代：1949–2009，另一種歷史書寫.

Xiao Gongqin 萧功秦. "Cong weiquan zhengzhi dao xianzheng minzhu de wubu luoji, da lishiguan shijiao xia de Deng Xiaoping gaige" 从威权政治到宪政民主的五步逻辑：大历史观视角下的邓小平改革. in Xiao Gongqin, *Chaoyue zuoyou jijinzhuyi, zouchu Zhongguo zhuanxing de kunjing* 超越左右激进主义：走出中国转型的困境. Orig. pub. in *Dongfang Zaobao* 东方早报.

Gan Yang 甘阳. "Ziyouzhuyi, guizude haishi pingminde?" 自由主义：贵族的还是平民的？ *Dushu* 读书.

Wang Shaoguang 王绍光. "Daiyixing minzhu he daibiaoxing minzhu" 代表性民主与代议性民主. *Kaifang Shidai* 开放时代.

Sun Ge 孙歌. "Linjie de yiyi" 临界的意义. *Tianya* 天涯.

Chen Ming 陈明, Gan Yang 甘样, Tang Wenming 唐文明, Yao Zhongqiu 姚中秋, and Zhang Xiang 张翔, "Kang Youwei yu zhiduhua Ruxue" 康有为与制度化儒学. *Kaifang shidai* 开放时代.

Chen Lai 陈来. "Bainian lai Ruxue fazhan de huigu yu qianzhan" 百年来儒学发展的回顾与前瞻. *Shenzhen daxue xuebao (Renwen shehui kexueban)* 深圳大学学报（人文社会科学版）.

Jiang Qing 蒋庆. "Zhiyou Rujia neng andun xiandai nüxing" 只有儒家能安顿现代女性.

CONTRIBUTORS

Editors/Translators

Timothy Cheek is director of the Institute of Asian Research and professor and Louis Cha Chair in Chinese Research at the School of Public Policy and Global Affairs and Department of History at the University of British Columbia, Vancouver. His research, teaching, and translating focus on the recent history of China, especially the Chinese Communist Party and intellectual debate in China. His books include *The Intellectual in Modern Chinese History* (2015), *The Cambridge Critical Introduction to Mao* (2010), and *Propaganda and Culture in Mao's China* (1997), as well as the coedited volume *Mao's Road to Power: Revolutionary Writings, 1912–1949*, vol. 8 (2015, with Stuart R. Schram). t.cheek@ubc.ca.

Joshua A. Fogel is Canada Research chair and professor of history at York University in Toronto. His work primarily concerns the political and cultural interactions between China and Japan over the past few centuries, and he maintains a lively interest in the practice of translation. His most recent publications are: *A Friend in Deed: Lu Xun, Uchiyama Kanzō, and the Intellectual World of Shanghai on the Eve of War* (2019); *Japanese for Sinologists: A Reading Primer with Glossaries and Translations* (2017); and *Maiden Voyage: The* Senzaimaru *and the Creation of Modern Sino-Japanese Relations* (2014). He has also published twenty-eight volumes of translation. fogel @yorku.ca.

David Ownby is professor of Chinese history at the University of Montréal. He has worked on the history of secret societies (*Brotherhoods and Secret Societies in Early and Mid-Qing China*, 1996) and popular religion (*Falun Gong and the Future of China: Making*

Saints in Modern China, 2010), as well as on contemporary Chinese intellectuals, including translating and editing Xu Jilin's book *Rethinking China's Rise: A Liberal Critique* (2018), among other works. ownbydavid@gmail.com.

Translators

Gloria Davies is professor of Chinese in the School of Languages, Literatures, Cultures, and Linguistics at Monash University, Australia. She is a literary scholar and historian of China who conducts research, supervises, and teaches in several areas: Chinese intellectual and literary history from the 1890s to the present; contemporary Chinese thought; comparative literature and critical theory; and studies of cultural flows in the digital age. Her publications include *Lu Xun's Revolution: Writing in a Time of Violence* (2013), *Worrying About China: The Language of Chinese Critical Inquiry* (2007), and *Voicing Concerns: Contemporary Chinese Critical Inquiry* (2001). gloria .davies@monash.edu.

Matthew Galway is a Hansen Trust Lecturer at the University of Melbourne. He is an intellectual historian of modern China, with interest in the transmission of Maoism globally through transnational organizations and friendship associations. His current book project is *Global Maoism: China's Red Evangelism and the Communist Movement in Cambodia*. He recently published a chapter in *Afterlives of Chinese Communism* (2019) and has forthcoming works in *Translating the Japanese Occupation of China* and the journal *Cross-Currents*. mgalwo59@gmail.com.

Jun Deng (邓军), associate professor in the School of Marxism at Shanghai Jiaotong University, is interested in the modern Chinese revolution and the Chinese Esperanto movement. His publications include *The Passion of Sacrifice: A Study on the Religiosity of Chen Duxiu* (2014) and *Making Hope: Esperanto's Imagination in Secondary Students in 1920s* (2018). ellaecnu@163.com.

Dayton Lekner is a doctoral candidate in history and Chinese studies at the University of Melbourne. His dissertation explores the Hundred Flowers and Anti-Rightist campaigns through the lens of literary exchange. His work focuses on the impact of literary circulation and practice on the intellectual and political fields of the Mao and post-Mao era. His first article is "A Chill in Spring: Literary Exchange and Political Struggle in the Hundred Flowers and Anti-Rightist Campaigns of 1956–1958" (2019) but foresees that another may be published in the future, referees be willing. daytonlekner@gmail.com.

Lu Hua (卢华) is a doctoral candidate at the Si-Mian Institute for Advanced Studies in Humanities, East China Normal University, Shanghai. His main research interest is modern Chinese history and thought, in particular the revolutionary history of the late Qing and early Republican periods. His doctoral thesis focuses on the formation process of Sun Yat-sen's and the Kuomintang's "Soviet Russian Turn" (1919–1925) from a world history perspective. 380169547@qq.com.

Mark McConaghy is an Assistant Professor in the Department of Chinese Literature at National Sun Yat-sen University in Kaohsiung, Taiwan. His research focuses on Modern Chinese and Taiwanese literary and cultural history. He is particularly interested in how practices of language, writing, and narrative have changed. His writings and translations have appeared (or are forthcoming) in journals such as *China Information*, *Modern Chinese Literature and Culture*, *The International Journal of Taiwan Studies*, and *Asian Studies Review*, among others. markmcconaghy6@gmail.com.

Shi Anshu (石岸书) is a PhD candidate in the School of Humanities at Tsinghua University, Beijing. His main research areas are modern and contemporary Chinese literature and contemporary Chinese intellectual history. He has published several articles, including "The Recasting of Chinese Socialism: The Chinese New Left since 2000" (2018). anshi1017@126.com.

William Sima is a PhD candidate at the Australian National University. His research focuses on historical memory of the Republican period (1912–1949) in contemporary China and the history of Australia–China diplomatic relations. In 2012 he co-edited with Christopher Rea a special issue of the online journal *China Heritage Quarterly* focusing on *The China Critic*, a Shanghai intellectual magazine of the 1920s and 1930s. His first book, *China and ANU: Diplomats, Adventurers, Scholars* (2015), recounts the experiences of Australia's first ambassadors to China in the 1940s and their role in establishing Sinology at Australian National University. will.sima@anu.edu.au.

Craig A. Smith is lecturer in translation studies in the Asia Institute at the University of Melbourne. His research focuses on twentieth-century intellectual history and contemporary Chinese intellectual. His articles on the history of translation and regionalism have appeared in journals such as *Modern Chinese Literature and Culture*, *Twentieth-Century China*, *China Information*, and *Cross-Currents*. He is an active translator and has translated works by numerous Chinese intellectuals and historians. shijun1@gmail.com.

Song Hong (宋宏) is associate professor in the Department of Social Sciences at East China Normal University, Shanghai. He works on the intellectual history of modern China. His essays include "*Ineluctable Predicament: Debates About Radicalism and Conservatism*," in the collected volume *Self-Destruction of Enlightenment: Studies on Debates About Some Important Issues Since the 1990s in China* (in Chinese, 2007). He has edited (with Xu Jilin) the volume *Benjamin Schwartz on China* (in Chinese, 2006) and *Core Concepts of Modern Chinese Thought* (in Chinese, 2011). hsong8@163.com.

Tang Xiaobing (唐小兵) is associate professor in the History Department at East China Normal University. Tang's research covers modern Chinese history, in particular change and continuity in Chinese intellectuals' thought and culture and the development of Chinese journalism in the first half of the twentieth century. His books (in Chinese) include *Public Opinion in Modern China* (2012), *Intellectuals at a Crossroads* (2013), and *Encounters with Intellectuals in the Republican Period* (2017). fengshiyan nfc@163.com.

INDEX

213; decline of, 155; economic, 57; and
egalitarianism, 52, 55–56; elitist and
mass, 210; equal respect in, 55–56,
67–68; features and principles of, 55–56,
68; as foreign paradigm, 13, 47, 48, 51,
99; French, 214–15; Gan Yang's critique
of, 7, 29, 209–10, 210–20; indigenization
of, 52, 53, 57, 69n9; and individualism,
53, 55, 61; introduction to China, 51, 79;
key words for, 79; left-wing, 56, 61; Liu
Qing's defense of, 4–5, 7, 18, 45, 47–68;
Mao Zedong's ignorance of, 87; myth
of, 176; in the 1980s, 94; neutrality
principle of, 56, 61; and pluralism, 46,
54–56, 66–67; and premodern spiritual
remnants, 58–59, 61, 63, 64; principle of
equal freedom, 55, 56, 66, 67, 211, 218;
secular, 58, 68; and the state, 17, 61–63;
suppression of, during early PRC, 51–52;
and traditional values, 60–61, 63–64.
See also Liberals; neoliberalism
Liberals: debates with New Left, 13, 17, 45;
narrative of, 12; nomenclature, 22n3;
engagement with the West, 10, 13–14;
range of, 4. *See also* Cai Xia; Guo
Yuhua; liberalism; Liu Qing; Rong Jian;
Xu Jilin
Liberation Daily (Yan'an), 86
Libya, 205
Lienüzhuan (Biographies of virtuous
women), 329, 340
Liezi, 266n117
Lilla, Mark, 62
Lin Biao, 186, 309
Lin Tongqi, 159
Lin Yusheng, 164, 166
Liu Bei, 189, 197n36
Liu Dong, 21
Liu Fenglu, 78
Liu Qing: academic career of, 45; and
Chinese liberalism, 13, 46; compared
with Xu Jilin, 155, 156; defense of
liberalism, 4–5, 7, 18, 45, 46; as Left
Liberal, 9; "Liberalism in the Chinese
Context," 47–68; philosophical
citations, 3
Liu Shaoqi, 186, 239, 249; May Fourth
directive, 119, 120, 132n9; rehabilitation
of, 200, 208n3

Liu Xiaobo, 4, 9
Liu Zhongzhou, 321, 341n8
Liuping village (Sichuan), 111
Liuru Pavilion, 323
lobbyists, 235, 260n32
Long March as metaphor, 206, 208n9
Longxi (Gansu), 199
"low-level population" (*diduan renkou*),
104, 105, 107
Lu Jiuyuan, 317n19
Lu-Wang School (School of Mind), 312,
317n19
Lu Xueyi, 128, 133n15
Lu Xun, 169n9; compared with Mao, 183;
"Diary of a Madman," 341n10; focus of
Qian Liqun, 175, 177; on government and
people, 185, 196n26; "I Want to Deceive
People," 269, 277n3; invoked by Sun Ge,
268, 269–70; as the "last intellectual
of traditional China," 182; "Li lun"
(Expressing an opinion), 269–70, 277n4;
Nahan, 152n3; on reformers, 187–88;
rejection of Confucian civilization, 15;
"The Shadow's Farewell," 182; on system
that "eats people," 322, 325, 341n10;
translations from, 24n28; translations of
East European revolutionary poetry by,
169n10; "Tremors of Degradation," 182;
The True Story of Ah Q, 181; and the
twentieth-century Chinese experience,
178; and twenty-first-century China, 16;
Wang Yuanhua and, 158, 161. *See also*
Zhu An
Lufrano, Richard, *Sources of Chinese
Tradition*, 20
Luo Hongguang, 114
Luther, Martin, 288, 293

Ma Licheng, 20; *Dangdai Zhongguo*,
26n44
Ma Yifu, 287, 311–12
Ma Yong, 79
Mafiaization, 205
Maistre, Joseph de, 213
Makeham, John, *Lost Soul*, 316n8
Malaysia, 259n24
Mao culture, 175–76, 182, 184–87, 188–91
"Mao genre" (Li Tuo), 176
Mao Haijian, 289